THE Sandwich Fair
SINCE 1888

THE Sandwich Fair
SINCE 1888

DeKalb County, Illinois

Vivian C. Wright, Ed. D.
Editor

Forewords by
J. Dennis Hastert, Congressman
Orion Samuelson, WGN Farm Show

The Sandwich Fair Association, Inc.
Sandwich, Illinois

Copyright © 2001 by The Sandwich Fair Association, Inc.
Publisher: The Sandwich Fair Association, Inc., Sandwich, IL
Designer: Olga Lindsay, Lindsay Design Group, Batavia and Marseilles, IL
Printer: Timeline Graphics Corporation, Lake Zurich, IL
Editor: Vivian C. Wright, Ed. D.
Project Coordination: Karen Breunig
Photo Coordination: Jacquelin Dannewitz
Research Verification: Joan Hardekopf
Research Support: Donald Stahl, Douglas R. Stahl

Library of Congress Catalog Card Number: 2001091338

ISBN: 0-9711529-0-X

Printed and Bound in U.S.A.

Grateful acknowledgment is made to LaSalle Bank of Chicago for permission to use the watercolor by Francis Chase on the book jacket.

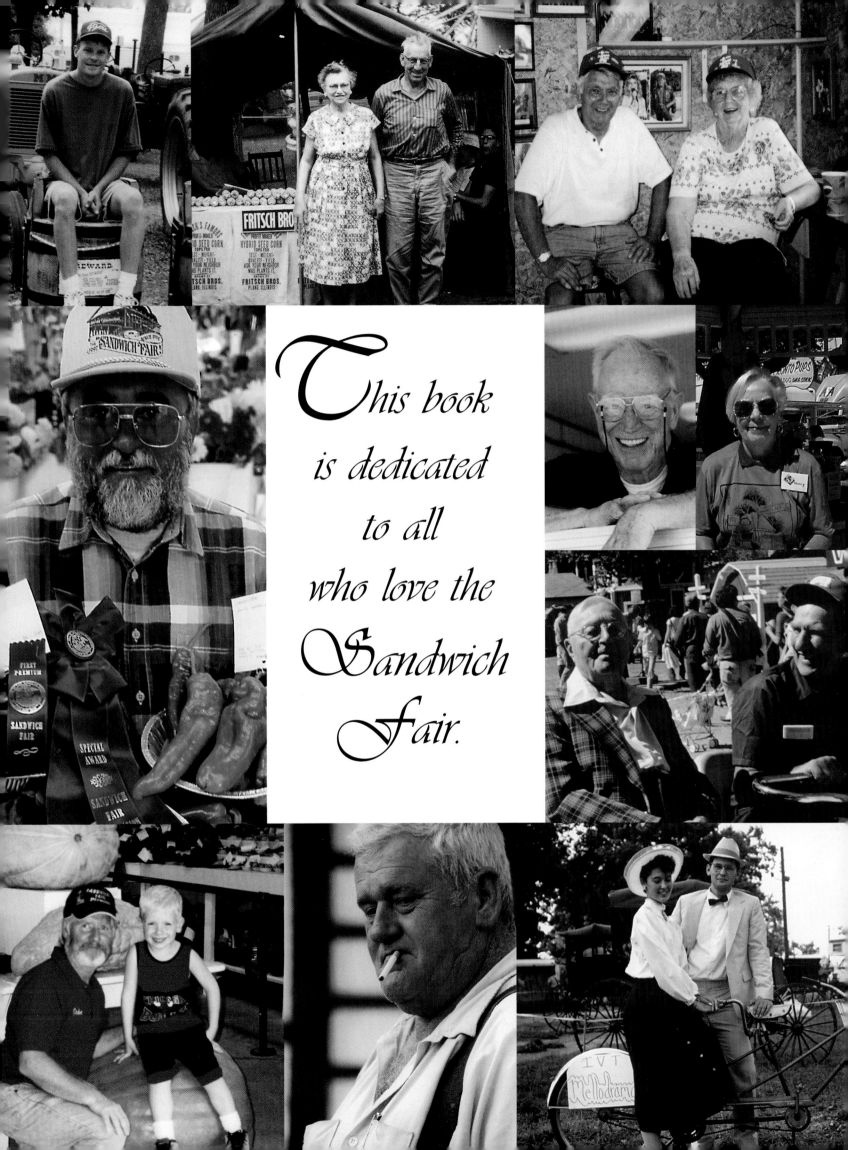

This book
is dedicated
to all
who love the
Sandwich
Fair.

Forewords

Illinois is fortunate to be home to one of the most historical county fairs in America, the Sandwich Fair.

Back when I first started attending the Fair, there were livestock, of course, as well as farmers' wives bringing pickles and pies. They still do this today.

The Sandwich Fair was always after the State Fair, so you saved up all the good stuff for the Sandwich Fair. To win a prize or a blue ribbon, or a grand champion at the Sandwich Fair—you really did something!

It is the same now as it was then, only now it is so much larger. People come from all over Northern Illinois to see the best cross section of the Midwest. It has been and remains the social event of the year.

The Sandwich Fair is people coming together and sharing memories, sharing values and competing with each other in a wholesome American way. It is the best of what makes the best of this great country.

I have grown up with the Sandwich Fair. From the days I came here with my dad's feed business to the booth I have held here as a service to my constituency for the past 20 years, the Sandwich Fair has been an important part my life and a staple of the DeKalb County community.

The Sandwich Fair is truly a local legacy. It is important that we celebrate this heritage and remember the people and history that are contained within this book and add to its history and value for generations to come. I have been privileged to be a part of this event for most of my life and am honored to welcome you to *The Sandwich Fair Since 1888*. I hope you enjoy it!

J. Dennis Hastert
Representative in Congress, 14th District of Illinois
Speaker of the House

For many of us the annual visit to the Sandwich Fair is a stroll down memory lane. For me, it takes me back to my 4-H days at the Vernon County Fair in western Wisconsin showing my Guernsey heifer calf, riding a Ferris wheel for the first time and taking my first airplane ride in a Piper Cub. The Sandwich Fair brings together the best of every county fair I have ever attended and presents it in a beautiful way. Stroll with me through the fairgrounds that always remind me of a Currier & Ives print on a beautiful September "blue sky" day.

Enjoy the shade trees showing the first signs of autumn; hear the sounds of the one-cylinder engines and appreciate the hours of work that make decades-old tractors look better than new; ride the train (I did it first with my two children; now I do it with my two grandchildren); view the stunning display of fruits, vegetables and flowers in what I call the round building; enjoy the delicious taste of the best barbecued pork chops in the world; watch the drama in the livestock judging ring as 4-H and FFA members show off a year of hard work and hope the judge will select their animal for the blue ribbon and then, there are the people, the smiling faces and friendly handshakes, stopping every few feet to say hello to old friends or to meet new ones.

September days don't come any better than a day at the Sandwich Fair. To the hundreds of volunteers who make it all happen: Keep doing what you do because a fair like this is an important part of Americana that brings farm and city folks together. At the same time, it creates life-long memories for young and old. See you at the Sandwich Fair!

Orion Samuelson
WGN Radio 720AM

From the Editor

Why are history books written? To record events and to honor the past are the obvious reasons, but there is more to some history books than the obvious. For example, a local history book like *The Sandwich Fair Since 1888* is more than a list of events. It is a compilation of memories and information from neighbors, friends, and kin about a topic they have grown up with—the Fair. The memories and facts in this book are the same ones shared on front porches, at the dinner table, at church socials, in beauty and barbershops, and in taverns.

Because the content of this book is both personal and of actual past events, the tone is both nostalgic and factual. The factual information shows the growth of the Fair while the memories reveal the heart of the Fair. Memories are powerful yet fragile. They establish traditions and turn events into legends, yet they slip away with time because memories seldom become words on a page.

Memories are either too private to describe, or they are feelings that sound "fluffy" when written down. It's difficult to find words for fresh, poignant smells in the livestock barns, sugary cotton candy matted in hair, hearty hugs and handshakes of old friends, and the brittle evening air in the grandstand that sends shivers to the bone.

Aware of the fragile nature of memories, in March 1998 before any more memories were lost, the Sandwich Fair Association proposed that a book be published about the Fair. A committee of volunteers was formed, and I was asked to be the editor.

At times, the task was overwhelming, consuming evenings and weekends of the committee. Members of the Fair board reassured us, however, that since there was no prior publication, anything we produced would be the best reference available. In one sense that was encouraging; on the other hand, we realized the high expectations of generations of people who had been waiting a long time for a book about their favorite fair—the Sandwich Fair. What did they want? Their suggestions were candid: Don't skimp on the pictures. Make it entertaining and fun to read. Include all the information you have. Don't limit the number of pages.

A target distribution date for the book was set for the 113th Fair in 2000. Information was solicited via radio, television, newspapers, and a Reminisce Tent during the Fair. The response was tremendous. The secretary's office received e-mails, faxes, letters, telephone calls, and personal visits from people eager to share their memories. Citizens in DeKalb County and surrounding

counties began reading old diaries, searching old photo albums, sorting unlabeled slides, and digging through trunks stored in attics and barns, looking for information about the Sandwich Fair.

As data surfaced, it became clear that we were working on more than a "little booklet." We were documenting an American tradition in DeKalb County, Illinois, that involved family gatherings, customs, accomplishments, and local commerce. One well-wisher, realizing the challenge of including all the information that had been collected, assured us that "if everybody put everything in the book they wanted to, it would take a wheelbarrow to move it around." With that knowledge we pumped up the tire on our wheelbarrow and continued our work.

By December 1999 we realized that a 2000 copyright was not a reality. New topics and leads continued to develop. More and more people were aware that a book was being written. We resigned ourselves to a 2001 copyright and were consoled by the fact that all good things take time, and this book was no exception. It would be more complete and better than anyone imagined possible.

One of the most challenging and time-consuming aspects of writing a history book is verifying the information. Sometimes the memories of veteran fairgoers and the stories that have been passed down from parents and grandparents do not agree with newspaper accounts and Fair Board minutes. At other times the information is so ambiguous that interpretation is difficult. This was especially true concerning the location of some of the early buildings on the grounds. *The Somonauk Reveille*, *The Sandwich Argus*, *The Sandwich Free Press*, and *The Sandwich Fair Times* were invaluable resources.

Despite the painstaking efforts of the researchers, there is bound to be an occasional reader who believes an important story or event has been left out or that it occurred another way. This is to be expected of a book that chronicles the multiple facets of a fair with the longevity of the Sandwich Fair. There are many stories and sometimes many versions of the same story.

After twenty-eight months of researching, confirming, writing, and rewriting, the first draft of the manuscript was finally finished. With mixed emotions—excitement, trepidation, and jubilation—we presented copies of the draft to copyreaders with an invitation to mark on the pages. This first step of the final stage was a difficult one for us. One member of the committee voiced the anxiety of everyone: "It's like showing someone your baby [and fearing they will say] the baby isn't very cute."

Weeks later when all the "babies" were returned, we reviewed the suggestions one by one. It was goose-bump time—all the drafts received good reviews. We were ready to begin the final steps of preparing the manuscript for the book designer who would prepare it for the printer.

From start to finish, preparation of the manuscript took more than three years and required the help of more than 300 volunteers who wrote, researched, and contributed information and pictures for a total of more hours than it is possible to calculate. The History Book Committee alone logged more than 400 meeting hours and immeasurable personal-work hours.

Just like the Fair, there is something for everyone in the book. There are facts, maps, and pictures as well as human-interest stories. The Timeline and Chapter 1 give an overview of the Fair and shows the components of a fair that has withstood the test of time.

We determined the topics of the remaining chapters by answering the question "What makes a fair successful?" Nine factors stood out.

Chapter 2: Expert leaders who show tireless dedication.

Chapter 3: A setting with beautiful trees and distinctive architecture.

Chapter 4: Exhibitors who are proud of their accomplishments and enjoy friendly competition.

Chapter 5: Entertainment for all interest and age groups.

Chapter 6: Food so irresistible that it steals the glamour of picnics.

Chapter 7: Commercial vendors who offer a sundry of products that draw people from miles around.

Chapter 8: Fairgoers who laugh and talk and have fun whether it rains or shines.

Chapter 9: Souvenirs and keepsakes that are symbols of good times and exhibitors' pride.

Chapter 10: Celebrations and recognition of a job well done.

The last chapter, for the convenience of the reader, is an appendix with lists of people and events too lengthy to be included in the text of the chapters.

When I accepted the position as editor of this book, I had no idea what I was getting myself into. I expected it to be an experience of a lifetime; but I didn't realize how many hours of my life it would consume, nor did I realize how much I would enjoy the time I spent working on it. Rarely does one have an opportunity to work with a committee that shares the same vision and spirit of volunteerism, as did my coworkers on this project. Each one's dedication kept the project moving: Jackie's systemic cataloging of pictures and artifacts, her eye for design, and her diplomacy in working with the copyright lawyer on the legal details of publication; Joan's memory

The Daily Times

Clockwise from l.: Jackie Dannewitz, Vivian C. Wright, Douglas R. Stahl, Donald R. Stahl, Karen Breunig, Joan Hardekopf

for details, her love of research, her tenacity in acquiring permission to use the watercolor of the Home Arts building on the cover of the book, and her delicious recipes; Karen's organizational skills in assigning writing topics, her thoroughness, her dream of reading a book about the Fair, her tactfulness when making endless follow-up telephone calls, and her investigative spirit when tracking down the cartoon copyrights; Don's longevity, his first-hand knowledge and experience, and his stack of newspaper articles that were the impetus for our research; Doug's positive attitude and his belief that we could write a book.

So, here it is—*The Sandwich Fair Since 1888*. If you enjoy reading this book even a fraction as much as we enjoyed producing it, we have accomplished our goal.

Vivian C. Wright

Vivian C. Wright, Ed. D.
Editor

Introduction

Sandwich Fair Times

From Wiley Updike,
President of the Sandwich Fair Association, Inc.

This book has been written to help preserve the rich history of the Sandwich Fair Association, as well as the history of the dedicated men and women who were and are committed to making this an outstanding fair. The history contained in this book is a result of many hours of searching for facts and compiling them in an orderly fashion by many volunteers. As this project has unfolded, a thread of community pride, enthusiasm, and vision running through the entire history of the fair has been evident. We hope that all who read this will appreciate the hard work and dedication of all the people who have worked so hard to make the Sandwich Fair what it is today.

From the Board of Directors,
Sandwich Fair Association, Inc.

We wish to thank everyone who gave so generously of their time and energy toward the completion of this book. Whether it was a picture, clipping, words, or remembrance, it has all been important to the contents. We thank Karen Breunig, Jackie Dannewitz, Joan Hardekopf, and Vivian Wright without whose diligence and dedication, this book would not have been possible.

opposite page: Courtesy of L.M.
(l. to r.) Five-year-old Dorothy (Klotz)
Olson and three-year-old Loretta (Klotz)
Martin at the Fair in 1921

Contents

Forewords . . . . *viii*

J. Dennis Hastert (R) 14th District and Orion Samuelson

From the Editor . . . . *x*

Introduction . . . . *xiii*

Contents . . . . *xiv*

Sandwich Fair Timeline . . . . *xvi*

CHAPTER 1 1

Decade by Decade: 1888 to 2000

A look at the Fair from a historical perspective provides a context and an appreciation of changes that have occurred since the inception of the Fair.

CHAPTER 2 20

Dedicated Leaders: Past and Present

Operating Structure, Stockholders, Current Board of Directors, Secretary's Office, Department Leadership, Past Leaders, Behind the Scenes

CHAPTER 3 52

Buildings and Grounds: Built to Last

Land Purchases, History of the Buildings, Maps, Maintenance and Improvements

CHAPTER 4 98

Departments and Exhibitors: Friendly Competition

History of the Departments: Livestock, Horticulture, Home Arts, and Collections; Exhibitors

CHAPTER 5 134

Grandstand and Grounds Entertainment: Music, Thrills, Crafts, and Comedy

Harness Racing, Draft Horse Pull Contest, Variety Shows, Melodramas, Thrill Shows, Tractor and Truck Pulls, Sky Shows, Music, Ag Land Stage, Miniature Steam Train, Horseshoe Pitching, Antique Farm Machinery, Antique Cars, Crafts and Demonstrations, Horse Shows, Micro-Mini Truck-Tractor Pull, Baseball, Fair Queens, Sheep Dog Trails, Midway

CHAPTER 6 192

Food: A Taste of the Fair

Church and Organization Stands, Recipes, Food Vendors, What's in a Name?

CHAPTER 7 214

Commercial Vendors: Something for Everyone

Early Vendors, Long-time Vendors, Today's Vendors

CHAPTER 8 230

Fairgoers: Meet Me at the Fair

Special Memories, Meeting the Needs of the Fairgoers, Education Committee

CHAPTER 9 274

Souvenirs: Keepsakes and Treasures

Collectibles and Souvenirs, Ruby-Stained Glass, Premium Books, Cancellation Stamps

CHAPTER 10 288

Recognition and Celebrations: A Blue Ribbon Fair

100th Fair, Sandwich Photographic Society, Illinois State Historical Society, Illinois State Board of Education Exemplary Partnership, Library of Congress Local Legacy, Illinois Humanities Council

CHAPTER 11 298

Appendix: It Takes Many People to Operate a Fair

Contributors; Photographers, Permissions, Courtesies; Names of Participants from 1888 to the Present

Sandwich Fair Timeline

1858 - 1887 CHRONOLOGY OF EARLIER LOCAL FAIR

1858 and 1859 First fairs held on east edge of Sandwich on the Weeks farm called Union Agriculture Institute; one-day events in October; two tables of corn exhibited for farmers to compare

1859 Purchased present fairgrounds

1860 First fair at present site, reorganized and renamed Sandwich Agricultural Institute

1867 - 1880 (approx.) Union Agriculture Institute held—a local agriculture society organized to found a library and offer winter courses and lectures on agriculture; later, members of this society started the Sandwich Fair

1877 Ten men bought 20 shares of fair stock for $2,000 in a reorganization; many new buildings

1884 Fair Association disbanded; grounds sold to Lewis Dieterich tile factory; most buildings were moved

1883 – 1887 Fairgrounds renamed Sandwich Driving Park Association; county fair held at Sycamore

1888 - 1899 CHRONOLOGY OF SANDWICH FAIR

1888 Leadership: local livestock group repurchased 20 acres from Dieterich for $2,500 (same amount for which it was sold), 100 shares of stock sold at $50 each, by June decision was made to hold fair on September 18-21, Fair Association incorporated;

Improvements: amphitheatre built; Grounds: 3 1/2 more acres purchased; Entertainment: horse races were popular; Finance: adult admission $0.35, children $0.15, season ticket $1; first year $722.17 deficit

1889 Improvements: large dining hall built, new ticket office at the east end; Grounds: racetrack located near Suydam Road in back of Secretary's Office; Entertainment: horse races, balloon ascension held; Attendance: 11,000 for 3-day fair; Finance: gate receipts $2,085, adult admission $0.35, children $0.15; $1,541.70 paid in premiums, $278.92 profit; stables and track rented for $1 per horse per month

1890 Entertainment: horse races, several bands played— Somonauk Military Band, The Plowboys Band of Freeland Corners, Crescent Band and Union Band (both of Sandwich); Exhibits: exhibitors entries doubled from 1889; Attendance: estimated 7,000 people on grounds each day

1891 Improvements: new regulation track, horse barns, cattle sheds and grandstand; Grounds: 19.6 acres purchased from Lewis Dieterich; Entertainment: area fire companies put on program, steam merry-go-round; Events: ladies horse and cart driving contest held Wednesday on Children's and Firemen's Days; Attendance: estimated 20,000; Finance: $409.72 profit

1892 Improvements: two-story 100' x 150' Floral Hall built for $5,000 by W. D. Dean, Secretary's Office, 200 new chairs placed in dining hall (old Floral Hall); Grounds: 40 acres, 12 buildings and 400 stables for

livestock; Entertainment: snake charmers; Exhibits: ostriches on display

1893 Exhibits: winner of best loaf of bread received 196 pounds of flour in barrel from local merchant; Weather: threatening on the closing days of the five-day fair

1894 Entertainment: 100 horses entered in races; Publicity: "Come to the Fair and Meet Everybody You Have Ever Seen"; Weather: fickle but did not deter interest in the five-day Fair

1895 Improvements: open display building erected for Betz John Deere; Entertainment: Millington Band played one day, hot-air balloon ascension and parachute drop from balloon every day of Fair, balloonist injured in parachute drop, "Punch and Judy," many fakirs [a loose term that referred to carnival vendors] on grounds; Attendance: shuttle bus from Somonauk

1896 Improvements: porch added to north side of Floral Hall, poultry house enlarged; Events: Tuesday and Wednesday were political days, lady speaker on equal suffrage; Exhibits: Floral Hall [Home Arts building] used for business exhibits by local merchants; Attendance: Fair held Monday-Friday

1897 Improvements: California Windmill Co. hired to supply water [located north of Floral Hall]; Entertainment: balloon ascension and woman parachutist from balloon, Aurora Military and Sandwich Union bands; Exhibits: cocoa and cream of wheat samples given away by commercial vendors; Sandwich Fair stock sold at local sale for $38 per share

1898 Leadership: residents of Sandwich encouraged to have city "looking nice" to give a good opinion of city; Improvements: water pipes laid to fairgrounds from Castle and Third Streets for $1,000; Entertainment: advertised balloonist did not appear; Exhibits: acetylene gas light exhibit by California Windmill Co. of Somonauk drew much attention; Weather: heavy rains; Finance: $884.48 balance in November

1899 Improvements: purchased Gage grandstand from private party, graveled drives and walks, water pipes laid to grounds, poultry house doubled; Entertainment: balloon ascension and parachute drops from balloon daily

1900 - 1909 CHRONOLOGY OF SANDWICH FAIR

1900 Improvements: two open-display buildings erected for Sandwich Mfg. Co. and Enterprise Company, Round Office and sheep barn built; Entertainment: jubilee singers and dancers daily; Attendance: estimated 15,000 people at Thursday's Fair; Finance: season tickets $1; full-course dinner $0.25

1901 Entertainment: Gualano Brothers orchestra, Aurora band played on Aurora Day (Friday); Weather: rained every day except Friday, fair extended through Saturday; Finance: bad financial year, $61.39 balance in November

1902 Improvements: drainage tile installed; Entertainment: National Sewing Machine Band of Belvidere; Attendance: Thursday was Aurora Day, Friday was Sycamore Day, 500 came on train from Sycamore; Finance: paid out $1,621 in premiums and $438.50 for entertainment

1903 Entertainment: large

number of fakirs on grounds; Exhibits: 147 entries; Weather: poor, Fair extended to Saturday; Attendance: malicious rumor of diphtheria epidemic in Sandwich hurt Fair attendance, estimated 8,000-10,000 people, special train brought about 1,100 people from Sycamore area; Finance: $5,199 taken in for ticket, gate, and amphitheatre sales

1904 Improvements: 56-pen swine barn, fence put around inside of track; Entertainment: balloon ascensions; Attendance: Thursday was Sycamore Day, special 10-car train from Sycamore via Aurora brought about 600 people for $1.50 round trip, Earlville train brought about 400 people, 4-day Fair; Finance: $427.91 balance in November

1905 Improvements: replaced Floral Hall that was struck by lightning and burned in May ($7,000 loss and no insurance) with new 40' x 100' colonial-design building called Industrial Hall built by Ahrens and Humiston for $5,000, octagon-shaped Horticultural Hall 48 feet across built for $2,000, both buildings painted yellow with red trim, amphitheatre remodeled and 500 new chairs purchased for it, dining hall thoroughly remodeled and managed by Congregational Church; Grounds: windmill and tank also burned in May fire; Finance: $1,924 profit, $52.52 balance in November

1906 Grounds: Industrial Hall now called Floral Hall, first Chautauqua held July 20-29 at fairgrounds, Ku Klux Klan was refused use of fairgrounds; Finance: net profit of Fair $2,200, $16.26 balance in November

1907 Grounds: dining hall run by Plano Methodist Church ladies; Entertainment: world-famous Gleason, king of horse tamers; automobile races

1908 Improvements: 127' x 40' cement-block horse barn with 24 box stalls, heavy coating of

manure plowed into racetrack; Grounds: dining hall run by Plano Methodist Church ladies; Entertainment: airship exhibition flights, exhibition drill by Sandwich Fire Dept., Round's Ladies orchestra; Attendance: largest Thursday crowd to date

1909 Improvements: picket and wire fence added in front of grandstand, 24" tile catch basin installed, woven wire fence replaced board fence on south side of grounds, topped with barbed wire; Entertainment: Sandwich Union Band played throughout the week, baseball games each day; Attendance: estimated at 22,600; Finance: total receipts were $9,630

1910 - 1919 CHRONOLOGY OF SANDWICH FAIR

1910 Leadership: rigid rules resulted in fewer fakirs and fewer refreshment and lunch stands; Improvements: ladies restroom, rest pavilion, and timers stand built; Grounds: Industrial Hall is too small to meet display requests; Entertainment: automobile races one day, also motorcycle races, Degen and Bradley's electric theater company

1911 Entertainment: Baldwin's Flying Machine (biplane) disappointed a large group when it failed to appear; Exhibits: new automobiles on display

1912 Improvements: old horse barn torn down; Entertainment: flying machines featured, Max Lillie flew plane non-stop from Chicago to Sandwich in record 65 minutes; Exhibits: large exhibit of machinery between Floral Hall and dining hall; hog cholera went through the area resulting in fewer hog exhibits; Attendance: several special trains brought people to Fair; estimated 1,500 cars parked on grounds behind Floral Hall and around the Secretary's Office

1913 Improvements: new

amphitheatre (grandstand) built at a cost of $5,250 to replace old one, seating doubled; Entertainment: "games of chance" at Fair were subject of much controversy concerning gambling and immorality; Events: E. A. Danielson lined up 80 Ford cars and drove around the racetrack, other cars were on display; Finance: $3,242 balance in November

1914 Improvements: 135' x 40' barn for show horses built by Gates with 20-foot alleyway and 19 single and 4 double stalls on each side, timers stand built at track, collapsible steel poultry coops added; Entertainment: aerialists and gymnasts each day

1915 Improvements: large addition put on horticulture building, sidewalks laid from city limits to first gate (2,100 feet), building erected east of the grandstand for ballplayers' dressing room; Entertainment: "human frogs" and high-wire acts; Events: large Motor Drome was in operation; Publicity: advertising expedition was held before the Fair, visiting all towns in the area; Weather: heavy rains, some races were canceled, Saturday's Fair was canceled

1916 Entertainment: Selleck-Sinclair airship accident badly wrecked the airship and seriously injured the aviator, mule races held, large circus featured at grandstand; Exhibits: manure spreader displayed by Sandwich Mfg. Co. was a popular item; Attendance: rumor spread that children age 12 and under were to be barred from the grounds because of infantile paralysis in LaSalle County

1917 Entertainment: noted aviator "Dare Devil" Mills performed each day, Ferris wheel and merry-go-round, mule races, fewer side shows on midway; Exhibits: small showing of draft horses as automobiles were taking the place of horses, conditions of war resulted in fewer exhibits; Weather: heavy rains closed the Fair the last afternoon

1918 Entertainment: Hill's Society Circus, also aerialists; there was not enough help to move the merry-go-round to the Fair because of war effort, children rode ponies around a circle, midway banned by State Board of Agriculture, airships not available because of war; Events: Wednesday was Red Cross Day; Weather: poor; Finance: large deficit, net proceeds went to Red Cross ($682.50) as a patriotic gesture

1919 Entertainment: midway was back, games of chance and gambling devices were absent; Exhibits: war exhibit from Camp Grant at Rockford; large doll house on display in Horticulture building; Publicity: directors were paid $6 per day for advertising the Fair on their autos; Finance: ticket sales were $10,614, most profitable Fair to date, 1918 deficit was paid, war taxes added

1920 - 1929 CHRONOLOGY OF SANDWICH FAIR

1920 Entertainment: Auto Polo show, acrobatics, vaudeville shows, and aeroplane stunts; Attendance: horse-drawn livery service brought people from town to the fairgrounds; Weather: rain; Finance: financially a good year

1921 Improvements: 14' x 20' kitchen built on Congregational Church food stand; Grounds: five acres purchased from M. Fanning for $6,500; Entertainment: air daredevils, western show "Sports of the Plains"

1922 Improvements: big addition to swine barn, Striegel and Stolp erected 40' x 60' dance pavilion; Entertainment: high-wire performers, Flying LePearls, Musical Palmer Trio, no side shows; Exhibits: new ruling by State Dept. of Agriculture required cattle have certificates to show them

free of TB, special exhibit by Boys Pig Club; Weather: very hot and dry throughout four-day Fair; Finance: $500 purse for ball games

1923 Grounds: first year that Fair hours continued into the night because fairground was wired at a cost of $2,250; Entertainment: fireworks, double midway, six big vaudeville acts; Exhibits: State of Illinois had two tents of displays about agriculture, hard roads, and state institutions; Dept. of Public Health had exhibits from all the insane hospitals in the state, parade of prize-winning animals on Friday morning; Finance: adult admission $0.50, children $0.25, autos $0.25, autos free at night

1924 Grounds: Red Cross had tent for medical emergencies; Entertainment: fireworks every night, Ferris Wheel girls performed, Arabian tumblers, pantomime comedian Kiljoy, baseball games Wednesday through Friday

1925 Improvements: 40' x 60' bleachers put in west of the grandstand; Grounds: three barns, racetrack and some land leased out from1925-1927; Entertainment: monkey orchestra, European hand balancers, dancing every afternoon and evening with Falletti's orchestra; Finance: $18,000 paid in premiums and for entertainment

1926 Entertainment: musical comedy Circus Solly, vaudeville acts, historical "Spirit of 1776" fireworks show; Events: prizes for oldest car on grounds and oldest married couple, Wednesday was Sandwich Chamber of Commerce Day with big parade before races; Exhibits: State Dept. of Agriculture livestock judging contest for boys 19 years old and under, large number of Holstein cattle entered

1927 Entertainment: saxophone group, boomerang throwers, ball games each morning, harness races and stage program each afternoon; Exhibits: pig and calf

shows for DeKalb County boys and girls, calf show in former draft horse building, school exhibits

1928 Entertainment: skaters, gymnasts, singers and dancers, three nights of fireworks; Events: horseshoe tournaments for two days in place of ball games; Attendance: Wednesday was American Legion Booster Day, all Legion men were admitted to the grounds free, Fair held Tuesday through Friday

1929 Exhibits: newspapers reported unusually good exhibits; Entertainment: horseshoe pitching, ball games, horse races, free grandstand attractions; Attendance: smaller crowds; Weather: rain

1930 - 1939 CHRONOLOGY OF SANDWICH FAIR

1930 Entertainment: Chenette's Band of DeKalb, fireworks every evening, wheels of chance available; Exhibits: commercial spaces now to be paid for by exhibitors, extra space in Industrial Hall used for county school exhibits; Fair held August 27-29

1931 Grounds: Horticulture building destroyed by fire in April, rebuilt same year, dance area also damaged; Entertainment: horse races, three ball games; Exhibits: no displays in Industrial Hall by local merchants, building now filled with school exhibits, state education exhibit on display; Attendance: smaller crowds; Finance: admission charges reduced last day, tough times financially as Great Depression intensified

1932 Entertainment: high school bands and singers, horse races on Thursday and Friday, mule race on Wednesday; Exhibits: fancy work entries limited to four area counties;

Attendance: three-day Fair; Finance: admission reduced to $0.25, no night fair because of the Depression, premium monies very limited, some premiums not paid until January 1933

1933 Entertainment: first horse-pulling contest held; Attendance: two-day fair, smaller crowds expected as the Century of Progress fair underway in Chicago; Finance: $3,548 in debt

1934 Leadership: Fair board borrowed money to pay expenses and premiums; Entertainment: WLS radio artists appeared each evening, softball tournament; Events: Thursday was Democratic Day, Friday was Republican Day, horse pulling contests were popular; Attendance: three-day and night Fair returned

1935 Improvements: two barns, 4-H Club calf barn and hog barn with 60 pens built; Entertainment: draft horse show returned, local VFW band, 19-year-old Pat Buttram and others of WLS; Events: softball tournament; Exhibits: school educational exhibits for grades 1 through 8; Attendance: big crowds; Finance: admission $0.25

1936 Entertainment: ball games in mornings, horse-pulling contest afternoons, three days of softball; Events: grandstand filled for political speeches; Exhibits: 4-H clubs had large number of exhibits; Attendance: three-day total about 25,000 including 15,000 on Thursday

1937 (50th Anniversary) Leadership: Wm. Fraser has been poultry superintendent for 50 years; Improvements: buildings painted white and grounds put in first-class shape, rebuilt front fence and gate and trimmed the trees for $3,645; Grounds: valued at $40,000; Entertainment: WLS stars; Finance: admission $0.40; three-day Fair

1938 Grounds: custodian hired;

Entertainment: Tattersall Diner's schooled horses performed, penalties added if ball games didn't start on time, tractor race, Eakle family drum and bugle corps of Waterman entertained all three days, WLS star Georgie Goebel and others featured, Sandwich VFW band, KoKo the clown; Finance: $2,348 balance in November

1939 Improvements: well drilled, city wanted to put in water meter, new lighting system including parking lot lights, Floral Hall was shingled for $750; Entertainment: Faletti's band; swing-show revue with Charlie Agnew's orchestra; large draft, saddle and harness horse show; Exhibits: Boy Scouts had tent and display; Weather: three ideal days

1940 - 1949 CHRONOLOGY OF SANDWICH FAIR

1940 Leadership: C. R. Brady replaced C. L. Stinson as secretary, Tom Mercer resigned as Speed Superintendent after 40 years; Entertainment: magic show, motor maniacs, aerialists, trained dogs, acrobats and a revue; Events: prize-winning livestock parade on Friday, baseball with teams from Sheridan, Kaneville, Sandwich, Plano, Lee, and Yorkville; Weather: ideal

1941 Entertainment: three-ring circus one evening, midget-car races, 12 vaudeville acts, Whitey Ford (The Duke of Paducah), Little Wonder Horse, hurdy-gurdy man with monkey; Exhibits: record 2,692 total entries; Weather: wind and rain resulted in an "equitable and amicable adjustment for damage" caused to patron's car when a tree fell on it; Finance: $5,125 in gate receipts

1942 Leadership: stockholders given tickets to grandstand night shows, Fair board voted to buy two defense bonds each for $740 and to donate $50 to Army

and Navy Relief Fund; Improvements: grandstand entrances changed by adding east-end exit and larger west-end gate; Entertainment: Gay Nineties parade and revue, three-ring circus; Events: DeKalb County 4-H show and auction; Weather: "frowned" upon the three-day Fair; Fair was one of nine held in Illinois in spite of WW II

1943 Improvements: flag and flag pole donated; Grounds: five acres purchased from Annie Grover Estate, including brick caretaker's house for $3,200; Entertainment: WLS barn dance, rodeo stars, annual revue, dance group, girls and boys pony race; Events: Farm and Home Day on Friday; Exhibits: Victory Garden displays; wildlife, fire prevention, and agriculture exhibits by the state; also cooking, canning, and food dehydrating school by utility company; no car exhibits; Finance: livestock premiums increased, adult admission $0.40, children $0.25, under 6 free; war bonds sold at some booths during the four-day Fair

1944 Leadership: Fair board voted for no special political days, no political speeches or posters on grounds; Improvements: concrete floor put in 4-H hog barn, water piped to some buildings, new drainage in barn area; Entertainment: summer follies, vaudeville and circus; Attendance: one day's attendance at 57th fair was a record 21,000, men and women in military uniform admitted free; Weather: rained first day in morning, then ideal

1945 Improvements: new gate and track crossing east of grandstand, ticket office built near grandstand, new entrance on east end, more parking space leased; Grounds: Nurses Club had first-aid station, local churches had rest tent, 3.2 acres purchased from Gilbert Gletty; Entertainment: rodeo held two days, summertime follies, vaudeville; Events: first twilight church service held;

Exhibits: State Welfare Department had exhibit, planes could be ordered at an aeroplane exhibit during the five-day Fair which included the weekend to attract city dwellers

1946 Improvements: lights and new front section added to grandstand, large stage built across from grandstand, 1,200 reserved seats added, poured concrete floor below west end of grandstand and leased space to vendors; Entertainment: WLS National Barn Dance, Rock Falls Municipal Band daily, Ward Beam's thrill show, circus; Exhibits: poultry shows for entire U. S. suspended by Department of Agriculture; Finance: five-day season ticket $1.50 plus tax; Weather: weekend ball games rained out, thrill show in mud

1947 Improvements: new well, cattle barn, lights on grandstand doubled, 100 trees planted at east end, old brick house on Grover property and barn on caretaker's place torn down; brick machine shed and garage built with materials salvaged; Grounds: four acres purchased from Eber Merrick. Entertainment: Siamese twins, follies revue; Exhibit: camera club display and contest, Department of Welfare exhibit; Events: white horse show, Saturday was Veterans' Day; Finance: receipts $58,944

1948 Improvements: picket fence put around racetrack; Entertainment: Lynch "Death Dodgers" thrill show, parachute jumps, Western Ranch round-up; Events: final 4-H show; Exhibits: kitchen, pantry, and dairy departments moved from the Horticulture building to the Home Arts building (formerly called Industrial Hall); cooking entries for girls 18 and younger, first seed-corn entries, no commercial or school displays in the Home Arts building, poultry show returned, final year for draft-horse judging, society horse show added with 12 classes; Attendance: 40,000 people the last 4 days, veterans of all wars admitted free on Saturday;

Finance: $7,000 purse for harness races

1949 Leadership: reincorporated as a not-for-profit corporation; Improvements: electrical lines and transformers, 38' x 100' cattle barn built to hold about 66 head of cattle; Grounds: acreage totaled 56.5; Entertainment: Joie Chitwood's auto and motorcycle daredevils, original amateur hour, Roy Acuff star of Grand Ole Opry; Events: Friday—Aurora Day, Saturday—Veterans' Day, first Junior Fair on Saturday and Sunday; Exhibits: 4,333 entries, Sandwich Hospital auxiliary's booth sold raffle tickets for two bicycles, Bendix washing machine and a TV; Attendance: estimated 40,000; Finance: increase in premiums to over $25,000 including $3,500 and seven Elgin watches for Junior Fair prizes

1950 - 1959 CHRONOLOGY OF SANDWICH FAIR

1950 Entertainment: illusion show, hippodrome acts, thrill show, style show, four days of ballgames, bands from Burlington Kiwanis Civic, Big Rock, Hinckley; Exhibits: poultry show discontinued, open-steer show; Publicity: movies of Fair taken and shown at local theatre; Finance: $26,000 in premiums and purses offered

1951 Improvements: large tent added for vendors, 500 bleacher seats bought for $2 each; Entertainment: rides $0.09 on Children's Day, circus, Roxyettes, diving champion, Aut Swenson's Thrillcade; Exhibits: Curtiss Candy Co. exhibited six-pony hitch; Finance: gate admission $0.60, reserved grandstand $0.60, season tickets $2, grandstand circus tickets $0.30

1952 Improvements: permanent stage added in front of grandstand; Entertainment: concert by Dee Palmer Band of DeKalb,

White Horse Troupe, WLS stars Lulu Belle and Scotty and barn dance show, Ward Beam's daredevils, Roxyettes; Events: horse show discontinued; Weather: rain one day; Attendance: large crowds

1953 improvements: new midway with new lighting, improved women's restrooms, better lighting along roads and parking areas; Entertainment: first time Augie Otto operated his Iron Pony a miniature steam train, Ranch Rodeo, a South of the Border Fiesta, WLS entertainers, daredevils, bands from Somonauk, Big Rock, Sandwich, Hinckley, and DeKalb; Exhibits: Sandwich Stamp Club in Home Arts building; Finance: $30,000 paid in premiums and purses

1954 Improvements: north end of grounds fenced, 40' x 80' dance floor added to south side of Home Arts building; Grounds: tractor purchased for maintenance, 3.27 more acres purchased from G. Gletty; Entertainment: WLS Captain Stubby and the Buccaneers, ostrich and camel races, some Fair board members rode an elephant; Events: livestock parade held on Thursday evening, dances held three nights of the Fair and every Thursday night during the summer for the next 16 years

1955 Improvements: grandstand painted, dining hall remodeled, new Sandwich Moose Lodge building; Entertainment: International daredevils, Bub and His Boys played for dances, Stars on Parade show, fireworks, trapeze and high-wire act, circus, organist Ken Griffin and dancers; Events: first queen contest

1956 Improvements: stone building over the old well was removed, new 48' x 180' hog building; Entertainment: musical comedy ice show, WLS barn dance, gala stage revue, Trans-World daredevils; Exhibits: 1,105 swine and 736 sheep entries; Publicity: expanded advertising to Chicago suburbs

1957 Improvements: converted

scale house into livestock office, addition to Horticulture building; Entertainment: Minnie Pearl of Grand Ole Opry, *Oklahoma* musical-comedy sketch, Rock 'n' Roll revue; Attendance: 12,000 autos parked, 228 season tickets, 32,000 adults' and 5,000 children's tickets sold; Exhibits: $5,000 cash and seven watches for Junior Fair winners

1958 Improvements: Secretary's Office remodeled, chain link fence installed, asphalt applied to midway, livestock loading chutes added; Grounds: tornado-like storm in August did much damage, first year for St. Paul's Catholic Church food stand, map hung in horticulture building to pinpoint visitors' home cities; Entertainment: roller skating on a card table 60 feet above ground, minstrel show, Leo "Pancho" Carrillo featured, dancers, Freedom chorus; Exhibits: Nike-Hercules guided missile on display; Weather: two days of rain; Attendance: 37,256; Finance: $30,000 in premiums and purses

1959 Improvements: train has new tracks and crossing signal; Entertainment: locally-owned colt Fairside Pal broke track records, children's Kiddyland started near Otto's train, grandstand clown returned, local mayors and aldermen raced ostriches and camels, polka band, follies ice show, girls as auto daredevils, Rhapsody in Blue show, puppets; Finance: Wednesday's grandstand show 1/2 price— $0.25

1960 - 1969 CHRONOLOGY OF SANDWICH FAIR

1960 Improvements: stage remodeled, judges stand improved; Entertainment: free grandstand on Wednesday evening, Monte Carlo revue, Golden Horse thrill show, Drum Dancers of Tahiti; Exhibits: Atoms at Work display

1961 Improvements: sheep barn changed to a cattle barn, chain link fence installed on east and north sides; Entertainment: barber shop quartet, fair queen contest, motor derby, The Harmonicats, clown Emmett Kelly, Jr., 50 people auditioned in August for talent show; Weather: hot; Attendance: smaller crowds

1962 Improvements: water lines were run across Wilkening's farm for $6,000, 56' x 170' cattle barn built for $8,000; Grounds: first time for Fay's Chicken and Pork Chop BBQ, grounds were rented to the Sandwich Sportsmen's Club for a wrestling match; Entertainment: Radio City Music Hall dancers, diving mules, Roy Rogers Liberty horses, auto daredevils, pony races; Exhibits: Civil War history mobile

1963 Entertainment: Myron Floren of the Lawrence Welk Show, barnyard burlesque, helicopter rides; Events: swine carcass show and auction; Exhibits: state history mobile on display; Attendance: hundreds came on Burlington steam train excursion from Chicago Saturday and Sunday for $4.65 round trip; Finance: Fair nearly a $100,000 per-year operation

1964 Improvements: first commercial building with 38 booths erected for $11,650; Grounds: 14 acres purchased; Entertainment: *The Music Man* presented by New York road show, thrill circus; Events: queen crowned, two livestock parades; Fair postcards available

1965 Improvements: new gate on the east end; Grounds: seven more acres purchased from the Gletty family; Entertainment: first tractor pull, Poncie Ponce of Hawaiian Eye, John Dears a women's garden tractor drill team from Sheridan; Weather: rained Wednesday, Thursday, and Friday during Fair; Grounds: no parking on grounds, mud warning signs posted;

Attendance: fairgoers traveled by Burlington steam train for third year

1966 Improvements: Home Arts building updated, buildings painted different colors, midway expanded south and east of Home Arts building, eight-inch water main installed; Grounds: 6.7 more acres purchased from G. Gletty, 22.8 acres from Charlotte Rud, 7.4 acres from Clarence Wilkening, portions were voted to annex to the city, total grounds now 100 acres; Entertainment: The Harmonicats; stunt men, Magical Moments show; Exhibits: largest livestock exhibits in history of Fair; Attendance: 800 people filled steam excursion train from Chicago to Gletty Road railroad crossing and were led to fairgrounds by Sandwich High School Band

1967 Grounds: first year for FFA farm zoo and the antique farm machinery display in the center of train track; Entertainment: Homer and Jethro show, auto thrill show; Events: 75 cars participated in first antique car parade; Exhibits: total entries 8,723, poultry show returned; Attendance: 800 people filled excursion train from Chicago, 2,000 people participated in poll about Vietnam; Finance: gate receipts $40,400

1968 Improvements: shower house and office built for livestock area, Treasurer's Office built, water fountains installed, new front gate, large sign; Grounds: total acreage about 140; Entertainment: harness racing Wednesday and Thursday afternoons, most midway rides $0.15 on Wednesday, final performance of Illinois sesquicentennial play; Events: Saturday was National Teacher of the Year Day for David Graf; Publicity: Fair's 80th birthday, February news article asked for an advertising design; Attendance: those arriving in horse-drawn vehicles admitted free

1969 Grounds: parking at the fairgrounds in July for the Bob Hope Charity performance at the airport; Attendance: all children admitted to Fair free on Wednesday, children were given chances to win one of 100 prizes; Entertainment: Chitwood thrill shows, country and western show with Jim "Ed" Brown and Red Blanchard, three-ring circus, sky wheel rides $0.35 on Wednesday, other rides $0.15

1970 - 1979 CHRONOLOGY OF SANDWICH FAIR

1970 Improvements: added east exit to Lisbon Street, commercial building #2, 1920 windmill erected; Events: honored couples married 50 years, Wednesday was Family Day, Thursday was Homecoming, Friday was Armed Forces, Saturday was Youth, Sunday was Neighbors; Exhibits: Sandwich Art League had exhibit of creative art media, antique auto display east of midway on Saturday; Finance: adult admission $0.75, children $0.25, autos $0.50, $32,235 paid in premiums and purses

1971 Improvements: first aid station, flag pole memorial at main entrance; Entertainment: free general admission to grandstand, two big midways; Events: Friday was Armed Forces Day; Exhibits: 10,787 entries, first junior livestock sale, Secretary of State trailer for fairgoers; Entertainment: Henneberry Family Troupe, country and western variety shows, hell drivers; Weather: good; Attendance: record crowds; Finance: $34,263 paid out in premiums and purses

1972 Improvements: 50' x 85' Arts and Crafts exhibit building, snow fences put up at tractor pull for crowd control; Entertainment: Indian group from Canadian Northwest, racing ostriches returned,

gospel singers, talking birds, Diana Trask show; Exhibits: records broken for most entries and most exhibitors, bonsai show and demonstration; Attendance: record-breaking attendance on Saturday, Gov. Richard Oglivie attended; helicopter rides available

1973 Improvements: shower house on west end, new road on west end; Entertainment: garden tractor pull, old-fashioned tent-theater shows called Toby Shows, country singer Roy Acuff, Jr.; Exhibits: Augie Otto's new train engine on display; Events: Arts and Crafts demonstrations started in back of Home Arts building; Weather: sunny and fine; Attendance: record 117,000 paid; Finance: admission $1, season tickets $4 for adults, parking $1.75; churches provided "cup of water" booth

1974 Leadership: directors presented with blazers and insignia; Improvements: Sandwich Band and "The Spot #1" food stands rebuilt after storm damage, new east-end main-gate ticket office and three additional gates, tent placed over open pavilion; Entertainment: larger, miniature steam train and nearly 1/2 mile track by A. C. Otto, double Ferris wheel and giant slide, Donald "Red" Blanchard, Clay Hart of Lawrence Welk Show, tractor pull Saturday evening, puppet show; Events: older adults held senior citizen king and queen contest, Secretary of Agriculture Earl Butz spoke, livestock auction grossed over $41,000; Publicity: WSPY started broadcasting from Fair; Weather: "fabulous"; Attendance: estimated 65,000, Boulder Hill couple won attendance contest award and trip to Disney World

1975 Improvements: multi-purpose display and exhibition building called the Pavilion near the windmill, sheriff's building and Sandwich Lion's Club building added; Entertainment: Bub and His

Boys, lion and tiger exhibits, performing bears, marionette show, Bob Atcher family singers, Bill Bailey banjo group, tight-wire artists; Exhibits: 55th year for Betz and Grandgeorge farm implement company at Fair, Bonsai Club show

1976 Improvements: sanitary sewer lines installed, Fair litter collector "Bi-Cen" placed on grounds; Grounds: after purchase from Gletty farm, grounds total 160 acres; Entertainment: Gail Farrell of Lawrence Welk Show, two tractor pulls, Tennessee Walkers, WGN noon show, demolition derby, first year for Buttons the Clown; Attendance: Gov. James Thompson visited

1977 Improvements: new east restrooms, portable show ring provided by 4-H Foundation; Entertainment: Grand Ole Opry and Lawrence Welk stars, Mackinaw Music Show, marionettes; Events: bicentennial group buried time capsule to be dug up in 2026, first cancellation stamp and postal sub-station, scarecrows "married" at sweet corn tent by Fair Secretary L. P. Brady; Grounds: ESDA helped with traffic; Weather: perfect; Finance: $3 per carload on Friday until 3 p.m.

1978 Improvements: old gates and ticket office moved to west end, handicapped parking added; Entertainment: Joie Chitwood, Jr. auto daredevil shows, four-wheel-drive truck pull, dancers Bobby and Cissy from Welk show, Mariah singers, Kahlua dancers; Weather: 90 degrees or more on most days; Attendance: estimated 136,000

1979 Improvements: memorial flag pole erected at west gate, 180' x 82' shelter and show ring for sheep; Grounds: Farm Bureau took charge of rest pavilion in west end; Entertainment: Danny Davis and Nashville Brass, Conlee Country and Western show with Bob Atcher family, clowns

Buttons and Korky; Exhibits: about 1,500 exhibitors and 15,000 entries; Finance: adult admission $2, children $0.50, under 6 free

1980 - 1989 CHRONOLOGY OF SANDWICH FAIR

1980 Improvements: 54' x 84' poultry building with workshop added, more parking lot lighting; Entertainment: first micro-mini tractor pull, four-wheel drive truck pull, Danny Davis and Nashville Brass returns, tractor pull, 81st Army Band, Frankie Masters orchestra; Events: 10,000 meter road race; Exhibits: first dairy goat show, decorated pumpkins added for junior exhibitors; Attendance: 140,600; old-fashioned portraits available

1981 Improvements: arena built for Western Horse Show, addition built on to livestock office, infield track lighting, more roads blacktopped; Entertainment: micro-mini tractor pull in livestock area, bagpipe band, Hit Paraders, country singer Donna Fargo; Events: first Western Horse Show; Finance: adult admission $2.50, children $0.50, autos $0.50

1982 Improvements: addition put on Arts and Crafts building, middle restroom; Entertainment: Dr. Barth's Medicine Show, clowns Buttons and Korky, Bub and His Boys, hot air balloon rides, Porter Wagoner Country and Western Show, Northern Illinois University show band, Clay and Sally Hart Show; Exhibits: over 17,000 entries, first year for photography entries in Arts and Crafts building

1983 Leadership: Fair board President Carlton "Dutch" Hough received Outstanding County Fair Award and State Fair Person of the Year Award from Gov. James Thompson; Improvements: rest pavilion

added, 54.5' x 54.5' food stand replaced old Log Cabin south of grandstand, exit-gate building; Entertainment: melodrama theater started, singer Brenda Lee

1984 Improvements: copper water lines installed in all buildings, blacktopping by front and west gates; Entertainment: Grandpa Cratchet's General Store puppet show, demolition derby, country star Dottie West, McBarker Boys; Events: sheep dog trials, horseshoe pitching contest returns; Exhibits: bowling lane trailer; Finance: Thursday was $5 wrist-band rides on Midway, weekend trip for two given away

1985 Improvements: Home Arts building newly sided, painted and preened for its 80th year, covered show ring in the livestock area, memorial rock garden and monument; Entertainment: singing star Reba McEntire; Events: craft demonstrations under tent on south side of Home Arts building

1986 Leadership: Carlton "Dutch" Hough elected President Emeritus after 30 years as president; Entertainment: singer Shelly West, The Arbors; Events: first miniature horse show, 10K road run; Exhibits: log cabin replica near Farm Zoo; Finance: adult admission $3, children $1, autos $1; Sandwich City Council voted no parking on streets near fairgrounds

1987 (100th Fair) Improvements: picnic tables with umbrellas placed on old dance floor, Arts and Crafts demonstration building added, anniversary monument placed by Round Office; Grounds: 43 permanent buildings; Entertainment: singer Marie Osmond, Bear Foot monster truck crusher demonstration, Britt Small, Bub and His Boys, melodramas; Events: sheep dog trials, 10 K road race; Exhibits: over 400 commercial exhibitors, first llama show; Finance: Friday admission same as 1888—adults $0.35, children $0.15 and $0.25

1988 Improvements: goat barn; Entertainment: singer Louise Mandrell, 37th year for Bub and His Boys, Bear Foot monster truck crusher demonstration, harness racing, truck and tractor pulls, miniature horse show, New Odyssey group; Events: first monthly summer antique shows; Attendance: 300,000 estimated fairgoers; 30 years for St. Paul's food stand

1989 Entertainment: first year for Sugar Squares dance club, country stars Cissie Lynn and Ricky Skaggs, giant gondola ride; Exhibits: mobile homes, State Lottery show van

1990 - 2000 CHRONOLOGY OF SANDWICH FAIR

1990 Grounds: land purchased for north exit to Pratt Road; Entertainment: country singer Mickey Gilley, first night harness racing, magician Magic Mike strolled the grounds; Events: horseshoe pitching; Exhibits: heirloom vegetables in Horticulture building; Attendance: first bus transportation from town by Fox Valley Older Adult Services; Finance: senior citizens admitted for $2 until 5 p.m. on Thursday

1991 Entertainment: additional carnival midway east of grandstand, country singer Tammy Wynette, Grandpa Cratchet, Buttons the Clown, Bear Foot monster truck crusher demonstration, two demolition derbies, truck and tractor pulls; Exhibits: sheep lead classes; Finance: adult admission $4, children $1, autos free

1992 Improvements: Home Arts building painted, additions to dairy and goat barns, 20 trees planted each year, new livestock building; Grounds: 11 tanker trucks of rainwater removed from grounds after heavy rains; Entertainment: bungee jumping from 175' platform for $65 and $85 per jump, singer Lee Greenwood; Events: sheep dog trials

1993 Leadership: Education Committee formed to help with school trips to Fair; Improvements: gazebo information and souvenir booth; Entertainment: first Ag Land entertainment, Sturgis marionette shows, truck and tractor pulls continue to draw large crowds, singer Eddie Rabbit, Dr. Barth's Medicine Show returns; Events: draft horse show returns, $5,000 in Western Horse Show premiums, WGN noon show

1994 Improvements: Gletty barn remodeled, grandstand painted, restrooms improved, exit to north opened, new animal wash racks; Entertainment: monster truck demonstration, singer Patty Loveless, Cowan puppets, The Festival show; Exhibits: 75th year for King and Sons Monuments Company to exhibit at Fair, 152.5 pound pumpkin entered

1995 Leadership: Dr. Craig Stevenson became Fair veterinarian; Improvements: Sportsman Club food stand and Gletty corn crib removed, road added near Arts and Crafts building, fencing and landscaping, blacktopping in the horse arena area; Entertainment: 20th year for Buttons the Clown, first Old Time Fiddle contest, Pearson's Bell Wagon, bands at Ag Land were Cumberland Mountain, American Legion and others, draft horse pull, singer Kathy Mattea; Events: sheep dog trials; Exhibits: rabbit show returned, agriculture information building started by FFA members

1996 Improvements: grandstand remodeled and aluminum seats added, some roads blacktopped, dance floor at Ag Land stage; Entertainment: Country Reminisce six-draft horse hitch, country group Shenandoah, JP and the Cats; Events: Soup and Sandwich promotion with parade and prizes; Finance: adult admission $5, children $2; Automatic Teller Machine (ATM) at Fair dispensed over $22,000; shortage of public pay phones

1997 Leadership: recognized by State Board of Education for work with vocational school; Improvements: laid clay track inside racetrack for truck and tractor pulls, 50' x 80' beige and green building for collection exhibits, judges stand relocated to track infield, Burlington-Northern caboose for office space near Home Arts building, commercial building west of Otto's train, grandstand stage removed, new pay phones; Entertainment: 15th year for melodramas, country singer Neal McCoy performed for over 7,000 people in two sold-out shows, Bear Foot monster truck crusher demonstration, exotic petting zoo, Coast-to-Coast Draft Horse hitch, singer Patty Jo Timmons; Events: pig races

1998 Improvements: a year of paint and repair, one new road near track, a second new road near the Collections building; Entertainment: singer Tracy Byrd, Dan Barth's Old Time Medicine Show, Magician-Comedian Dick Stoner, Pearson's Bell Wagon, Ag Land stage bands; Events: two worship services on Sunday; Exhibits: Reminisce Tent to collect information for Fair history book to be published in 2001, WGN's Max Armstrong displayed his Farmall tractors, 670 pound pumpkin entered; Weather: great

1999 Leadership: Louis Brady recognized as Secretary-Emeritus; Improvements: reserved seating in grandstand remodeled, new roof and area for wheelchairs; Entertainment: WGN noon shows, country singers Sammy Kershaw and David Lee Murphy and the Ricochet Band, Bear Foot monster truck crusher demonstration, Patty Jo Timmons back; Publicity: bookmarks given away to promote Fair's history book; Weather: cool; Attendance: 197,000; Events: 5th year for fiddle contest

2000 (113th Fair) Improvements: replaced pumps in sewer system, new fence on north side of racetrack; Entertainment: country singer Pam Tillis, Charlie Daniels' Band, Dan Barth's Medicine Show, Pearson's Bell Wagon, Amazing Arthur; tractor and truck pulls sanctioned by National Tractor Pullers; Publicity: pencils given away to promote Fair's history book; Weather: cool mornings, hot afternoons; Events: two shows by WGN △

Decade by Decade: 1888 to 2000

Distinctive buildings, an ever-evolving array of exhibits and commercial displays, harness races, carnival rides, food stands, and a variety of other attractions constitute the material presence of the DeKalb County Fair better known as the Sandwich Fair. However, it is people who give life to an activity, and the Sandwich Fair is full of life. The Fair is a place where families meet for breakfast, friends reminisce, and teens thrill to midway rides. They talk, laugh, and shed tears—some even scream. In other words, the Sandwich Fair is a place where people enjoy each other's company and have fun. The Sandwich Fair is a people place.

A decade by decade glance at local, national, and world events that affected the lives of fair patrons will help put the development of the Sandwich Fair into historical perspective. Using the magic of imagination, the reader can mingle with the crowds and sample the news that made headlines in days past. The effort will provide context and an appreciation of changes that have occurred since the inception of the Fair.

1888-1889

By 1888 the long reign of England's Queen Victoria was nearing its end, and the early years of the Sandwich Fair definitely qualify as part of the Victorian era. Ready-to-wear clothing was available, but the seamstress and the tailor still ruled the sartorial world. The Sandwich Fair was a dress-up occasion and fairgoers came in

In 1899 fairgoers came in their Sunday best.

their Sunday best. Beards were popular with the men; large flowered hats adorned fashion-conscious women. They arrived at the fairgrounds in buggies, surreys, and buckboards. Some rode in on horseback, and those living nearby came on foot.

People were hungry for news, and print was the choice of the day. During the 1880's, daily newspapers in the United States increased in number from fewer than a thousand to over sixteen hundred. The total circulation of those papers rose to 8.4 million. Fairgoers gleaned local papers for news that would improve their lives as well as entertain them. The Sycamore *True Republican* reported that "the Sycamore fair last week was not a success financially. The association was . . . left in debt about $100. . . ." Sandwich *Argus* encouraged citizens to come to the Sandwich Fair: "Don't be afraid of dust. Ample arraingments [sic] are made for sprinkling."

Like today, scams were a reality in 1888. The *Somonauk Reveille* reported that "Persons who responded to an advertisement that promises 'twenty-five useful household articles for 25 cents' are receiving by mail a literally pointed response–25 needles." The *Reveille* also reported that "At Sycamore recently three cows were sold at ten, seven, and three dollars. . . . Feed is scarce, and there is no market for them."

The Ottawa *Republican* printed, "The powder explosion at Streator was not altogether a disaster. The lightning which fired the powder was accompanied by a heavy rainfall, which was worth thousands of dollars. . . . Streator and vicinity has suffered more from the drouth than any other portion of the country, and the rain was a veritable blessing."

There were no wonder drugs to treat the intractable illnesses prevalent in the countryside, so folk remedies and patent medicines were often the last hope. No documentation exists to verify whether or not quack doctors barked their cure-alls at the Sandwich Fair, but fairgoers who were ailing likely tried concoctions such as

A 1873 poster from the Union Agricultural Institute's 13th Fair

opposite page: Courtesy of SFA

Fairgoers arrived in buggies, surreys, buckboards, on horseback, and on foot.

Courtesy of SFA

top: On the midway looking north towards the Grandstand circa 1890's

top right: These postcards were used to advertise the 1895 Fair during the bicycle craze.

The Warner's Cash Store display inside Floral Hall was a popular place for ladies. Area merchants displayed their wares in the two floors of this building.

Kickapoo Indian Salve or Lydia Pinkham's Vegetable Compound.

Many in attendance at the Sandwich Fair were sports enthusiasts. In 1889 baseball was played at the fairgrounds between teams from Monmouth and Aurora, "two of the best nines in the state."

People were on the move. Migration to undeveloped land in the Western plains was heavy. Undoubtedly, some of the fairgoers in 1889 must have known a few of the 100,000 men and women who massed on the border of the Oklahoma Territory on April 22, 1889, when it opened to settlement.

1890-1899

During the "Gay Nineties" many inhibitions were shed. In 1893 the World's Columbian Exposition was held on the Chicago lakefront. Attendees at the Sandwich Fair probably discussed an exciting excursion to see the exposition in the state's most populous (and reputedly scandalous) city. For people who through choice or necessity stayed closer to

Courtesy of SFA

home, the Sandwich Fair provided a diversion from mundane rural life.

Visitors to the Sandwich Fair saw a prize-winning herd of cattle displayed by Mr. Benjamin of Sugar Grove. The herd included the winner of first premium at the World's Fair. A Southwick hay press also attracted much attention; it produced a 16" x 20" bale of hay weighing a remarkable 160 pounds. Other exhibits included Warner's clothing, Burkhart's furniture, Kleinsmid's hardware, and Castle &

Courtesy of SFA

Latham's hardware.

Some fair patrons pedaled their "wheels" to the grounds. A bicycle craze swept America in the 1890's. By 1896 four million Americans were active riders. There were bigger and more powerful "wheels." Henry Ford built his first motor car in 1896. The folly (or the promise) of the horseless carriage was cussed and discussed.

Gold was the topic of conversation for many fairgoers when the Klondike gold rush attracted sixty thousand prospectors to a remote tributary of the Yukon River. The Gold Standard rather than gold mining was on the political agenda. Populist William Jennings Bryan touched a chord with Midwestern farmers when he attacked that arbitrary standard in his "Cross of Gold" speech at the 1896 Democratic Convention in Chicago. The Sandwich Fair designated Tuesday as Republican Day and Wednesday as Democratic Day.

Education was on people's minds. To provide teacher and vocational training, the Northern Illinois State Normal School was opened in DeKalb. On the international front, Commodore Dewey's warships destroyed the Spanish navy in Manila Bay and Teddy Roosevelt and the Rough Riders charged up San Juan Hill in Cuba. The United States was becoming a power to be reckoned with.

1900-1909

By 1900 the official U.S. population totaled 76,295,220, and there were forty-five states in the Union. Eastman Kodak had a new Brownie camera on the market for one dollar. Undoubtedly more pictures were taken at the Fair than ever before. Friends and neighbors could document their day at the Sandwich Fair.

Interest in baseball continued to grow. In 1901 baseball's American League was launched. The Fair game that year, Sycamore versus DeKalb, advertised a larger than usual purse

Around 1900 many tents were used for commercial displays on the grounds.

of $150.

Attire for the fair was a bit more relaxed. The Gibson girl look was popular in fashion at the Fair as well as on the posters advertising the Fair. The news of the day indicated that women had expanded their interests beyond homemaking. Anna Edson Taylor went over Niagara Falls in a barrel and lived to tell about it. Her advice to others: "Don't try it!"

In 1902 in Naperville, Mayor Thomas Betz attempted to rid his city of all slot machines. He reportedly smashed them with an axe that he kept in the woodpile behind his house. It seems that the businesses had failed to follow his edict concerning the gambling devices. The Fair Association agreed with Betz's attitude. It took pride in the general feeling reported in the *Sandwich Free Press* in 1909: "The fair is a good, clean, live show from start to finish. Gambling fakes are cut out, booze is tabooed and the fair grounds are properly the place for family reunions."

Trains were a popular and convenient mode of travel in the 1900's. Special excursion trains ran on the Chicago and Northwestern and Burlington Routes bringing young and old to the Sandwich Fair. To ensure the good reputation of the Fair, a Chicago detective met the trains in Sandwich. It was his job to "spot the hoodlums and tell them to get back on the train." The train that came from Sycamore in 1903 also carried the Belvidere Band.

The Fair closed at dusk, but patrons who wanted to continue socializing were encouraged to stop at J. M. Hummel's Amusement Parlors

and Hall in Sandwich. His advertisement in 1903 in the *Sandwich Argus* promised "First-class entertainment and instructions in bowling, billiards and pool, as well as 'how to dance properly.' " The establishment welcomed ladies; it was a place where profane or obscene language was not permitted.

The world had a preview of incredible "heavier than air" flight in 1903 by the Wright brothers. Sky shows were already popular at the Fair. Balloon ascensions had been a major attraction since 1889. It would be only a few more years before Dare Devil Mills and his death-

Baseball was an important sport at the earlier Fairs. Games were held inside the racetrack. Rivalries between towns created great interest in the games.

Courtesy of SFA

defying air stunts would thrill Sandwich audiences. In 1904 the ice cream cone debuted at the World's Fair in St. Louis, and it didn't take it long to catch on at the Sandwich Fair. Fairgoers could now enjoy this tasty treat while walking around the grounds.

Courtesy of B.H.

right: Looking west from the present-day Home Arts building about 1906, one could see the Round Office and the Adolph Betz pavilion filled with carriages for sale.

previous pages: Courtesy of B.H.
pages 4-5: A postcard, circa 1915, shows a picket fence on the south edge of the racetrack.

bottom: Fairgoers entered the Main Gate in the early 1900's; some arrived in horse and buggy, others in automobiles.

Courtesy of J.W.

More important to them were the noises and fumes of a smattering of automobiles that frightened horses and enraged the men and women holding the reins. More than 10,000 Model T Roadsters rolled off production lines in 1908 at an affordable price of $825. Any fairgoer could have one in his favorite color—as long as it was black. In New Jersey, members of the Automobile Club of America were arrested for breaking an eight-mile per hour speed limit. They paid a ten-dollar fine and sped away probably on a gravel or dirt road because there were only ten miles of paved roads in America.

Like today, food was a major topic at the Fair. Many brought picnic lunches and ate in the beautiful oak grove. For others it may have

been the only time during the year that they ate in a "for pay" establishment. The beef sandwiches made by the ladies at the Congregational Church dining hall were a favorite. These sandwiches were made with two large slices of homemade bread mounded with roast beef accompanied with mashed potatoes and gravy. This entrèe could be purchased for twenty-five cents and a slice of pie could be had for a few cents more. Those prices don't seem so low when they are compared to the prevailing wages of the day; the average worker made $12.98 per week for 59 hours of labor.

1910-1919

Sandwich Fair patrons could hardly escape politics, government, and war during these years. Theodore Roosevelt made it a three-way race for the U.S. Presidency when the Bull Moose Party nominated him, and the Federal Reserve System was founded.

Fairgoers loved competition, so it is a strong probability that they discussed auto racing and baseball scores because the Indianapolis 500 auto race was run for the first time, and Ty Cobb batted .420. Both auto and motorcycle races were part of the grandstand entertainment during this decade. Rivalries between towns created even greater interest in the baseball games. In 1910 three games were played at the Fair: Sandwich vs. Plano, Aurora vs. Rangers, and Hinckley vs. Paw Paw. Also in 1910, Fair

Courtesy of B.H.

left: In the 1890's many fairgoers brought their picnic lunches and ate in the beautiful oak grove.

center: Auto racing was featured at the Fair about the same time the Indianapolis 500 auto race was run for the first time.

bottom: Peanuts and popcorn were sold at this early vendor's wagon.

Secretary C. Stinson was asked by the Fair board to publicize that ball games would be prohibited on the grounds on Sunday.

Other news that may have mixed with talk about prize-winning livestock, fancy needlework, and the new manure spreader displayed by Sandwich Manufacturing Company was the opening of the Panama Canal in 1913.

Courtesy of B.H.

After the 1913 Fair, "games of chance" were a controversial topic covering many column inches in local papers. Rev. Clancy carried the topic into the pulpit. In his sermon he denounced gambling and immorality at the Sandwich Fair. Letters to the editor questioned whether or not "paddle games" or "throwing rings at worthless canes" was really gambling.

In 1915 G. F. Wilder set up the first automatic corn popper in Sandwich. There is no record that it appeared at the Fair, but it was the main attraction on Railroad Street on Saturday nights as shoppers watched kernels of popped corn being individually buttered.

Fair attendance increased as special trains from Sycamore via Aurora and from Earlville brought almost a thousand sightseers to the Fair. More local residents walked to the Fair because a new 2,100 feet long sidewalk extended from the Sandwich city limits to the east gate. William Kell was awarded the contract for "the longest single stretch of cement walk ever constructed in this vicinity." By 1913 assembly-line production allowed Ford to reduce the price of a Model T to as little as $500; as a result, more and more automobiles crowded onto the fair-grounds.

World War I weighed heavily upon everyone, including the Sandwich Fair. In 1918 the proceeds of $682.50 were given to the Red Cross. With the war effort in full effect, there was no midway because there wasn't enough manpower to move the merry-go-round to the fairgrounds. The result of all this was a large deficit, which was made up the next year by dint of advertising, the return of the midway, and a war exhibit from Camp Grant.

The DeKalb County Soil Improvement Association was organized. Professor William Eckhardt was enticed from the University of Illinois to undertake the acquisition of

Courtesy of R.P.

Courtesy of R.W.

right: In 1913 E.A. Danielson lined up 80 Ford cars that drove around the racetrack.

center: Model T trucks were popular by the 1920's. This one is shown at a 1980's antique car show.

top-quality seeds for area farms and to demonstrate the use of lime, rock phosphate, and other fertilizers to increase soil productivity. Three widely known organizations evolved from the Soil Improvement Association: the Cooperative Extension Service, Farm Bureau, and DeKalb Ag Research (now part of Monsanto Corporation).

The Chautauqua Circuit brought high-quality entertainment and outstanding speakers to tent meetings across small-town America. Some years they rented the grounds; other years the Fair Association donated the use of the grounds to them.

Photo by N.U.

1920-1929

Times were changing. The 1920 census revealed that the urban population of the U.S. exceeded the rural for the first time. A long and bitter struggle culminated with the adoption of a constitutional amendment granting women the right to vote.

Americans were mobile. By 1920 nearly 4,000,000 Model T's were on the roads in America. Parking space for cars was an increasingly important consideration at the Sandwich Fairgrounds. In 1920 the *Sandwich Free Press* reported that "the greatest number of automobiles ever parked on the grounds was on Thursday. . . ." The reporter predicted that if the weather had permitted better attendance, the grounds would have lacked adequate parking space.

America was experiencing a "Better Health Movement." The crusade to banish the evils of alcohol won a huge victory on January 16, 1920, when Prohibition took effect. Although this law affected many Americans, the Sandwich Fair continued as usual. Alcohol had never been permitted on the grounds. In 1923 thousands of people at the Sandwich Fair took advantage of a free health test sponsored by the state of Illinois.

The post-war boom was accompanied by high prices, short skirts, and a lean, lithe look for women; the "flapper era" was born. In 1921 the first Miss America pageant was held in Atlantic City. Excitement was in the air figuratively and literally. At the Sandwich Fair dance pavilion, dancers could have a whole evening of fun for a dollar dancing the Charleston, the latest dance fad. At the 1923 Fair, an elaborate fireworks demonstration enticed patrons to stay on the grounds for the Fair's first nighttime hours, the grounds having been wired for electric lights at a cost of $2,250.

In 1927 Babe Ruth hit sixty home runs. Baseball was both big-time and small-time entertainment. Small towns and villages proudly sponsored teams, and during Fair week, the Sandwich Fair Association continued to schedule spirited intercommunity competition in "America's pastime." On October 24, 1929, the stock market crashed, ushering in the Great Depression and lean times for the nation and the Sandwich Fair.

1930-1939

The thirties were a decade of depression

SANDWICH FAIR
SANDWICH, ILL.
SEPTEMBER 6-7-8-9
1921

Courtesy of SFA

Courtesy of J.A.D.

and dictators. The Sandwich Fair was staggered by the impact of national economic collapse. While the 1930 Fair was deemed a financial success, lack of attendance resulted in a deficit the following year. In 1931, 4.8 million people were out of work in the United States, and by 1932 that number grew to eleven million. The Fair Association cut admission prices to twenty-five cents and scaled back to a three-day fair in 1932 and to two days in 1933. The 1933 Fair closed with a $3,548 deficit. Defying the lean years, the "Century of Progress" exposition opened a two-year run in Chicago that same year.

Not to be daunted, the Fair board borrowed money to keep the action going. Their efforts paid off. There were ball games every morning. Chicago radio station WLS sent one of its popular performers to boost the entertainment. Big bands dominated the music world and influenced attendance at the dance pavilion. The Fair offered a few days diversion from the bleak circumstances of the decade.

Dust storms decimated 135 million acres of agricultural land in the plains states, adding to the misery of financially strapped farm families. Dirt from these storms sifted down in Northern Illinois. To relieve the suffering of victims of the economic crisis, Social Security was enacted along with numerous other federal programs. Farming was important to the nation's gradual recovery from the Great Depression. Benefiting from its agricultural bias, by 1934 the Fair was on the rebound. The local press declared 1935 the best Sandwich Fair ever.

The Depression was not the only bad news for Fair patrons. War clouds were once again darkening the skies in Europe. War was familiar to this generation of Fair visitors. World War I still burned in their memory. From newspaper accounts and newsreels at the local movie theaters, they knew the League of Nations had done nothing to stop Mussolini when he invaded

top center: A poster from the 1921 "flapper era"

left: Mrs. Ed Legner and son Fred and Mrs. Forrest Hough in a 1913 hot air balloon picture backdrop

bottom: Dancers could have a whole evening of fun for a dime a dance at the Striegel & Stolp pavilion.

56   SANDWICH FAIR PREMIUM LIST

DANCING

Every Afternoon and
Evening

At the Dance Pavilion
on Fair Grounds

Faletti's Orchestra

STRIEGEL & STOLP

Courtesy of SFA

Sandwich Free Press

top: An advertisement for the 50th Fair that appeared in the 1937 newspaper

center: At the 50th Fair, in 1937, ribbons were given to fairgoers who had attended each Fair since 1888.

Courtesy of SFA

I Have Attended The Sandwich Fair For

50 YEARS

Courtesy of SFA

and conquered Ethiopia. Stalin had arrested and executed millions of dissidents, and it was becoming clear that Hitler was amassing military power in Germany.

In 1937 isolated from the threat of war abroad, the Fair celebrated its 50th anniversary. It promised good baseball games, the best draft horses in the area, band concerts each day, and other entertainment day and night. All this and more for forty cents admission at the gate. Fairgoers competed, laughed, and relaxed; and in general, they had a good time at the three-day fair. They were temporarily able to ignore the signs of war. Although in reality, parents and grandparents must have wondered if this might

be the last Fair they would attend with their children and grandchildren.

The decade ended prosperously for the Fair. In return, the Fair Association made improvements to the grounds for the benefit of the fairgoers. New electric wiring was installed that included parking lot lighting, and a new well was drilled.

1940-1949

The decade opened in DeKalb County with plans for the 53rd Sandwich Fair. Audiences could expect a fine stock and grain show, harness races, and grandstand entertainment for the entire family. Baseball was a topic of the day nationally and locally. Joe DiMaggio was making baseball history and the accomplishments of baseball players Fritsch, Smiley, and Thompkins were creating interest in games scheduled to be played at the Fair.

With the Japanese air strike at Pearl Harbor on December 7, 1941, the United States went to war. The economy slowly emerged from the

Depression as factories geared up to produce military goods. Within a year, civilian auto production had given way to military needs. Tires in any condition were in scarce supply, and gasoline was rationed. There were no car dealers at the Sandwich Fair in 1942.

The International Livestock Exposition in Chicago and many county fairs were canceled, but the Sandwich Fair soldiered on. Despite, or perhaps because of, wartime restrictions on civilian consumption, people came to the Fair. Booths at the fairgrounds sold war bonds and contributions were accepted for "Smokes for Yanks Overseas." Special cash awards were offered for a new Victory Garden exhibit. The Fair Association was in excellent financial condition and showed its patriotism by investing surplus funds in government bonds.

When World War II came to a dramatic close, America's men and women returned home. They were ready to pick up where they left off, ready to buy new homes and new cars. From 1947 to 1949, the Fair board recognized its mili-

tary men and women by declaring Saturday as Veterans' Day during Fair week. Veterans in uniform or those presenting their cards or buttons were admitted to the grounds free.

An automobile passing through the fairground's familiar iron gates might have been a Packard, Studebaker, DeSoto, Nash, or Willys. Whitewall tires were in fashion, and cars were sold in a variety of colors. In the postwar half of the decade, there were other milestones in American history. Dr. Spock published *Baby and Child Care* in response to the baby boom that was sweeping the country. The birthrate skyrocketed, reaching a high of 26.6 newborns per 1,000 Americans in 1947. It would take only a few years before the increased population would impact the Fair.

1950-1959

No sooner had the decade begun and the

top left: During World War II many county fairs were canceled, but the Sandwich Fair soldiered on.

top right: View from the top of the Ferris wheel

left: A 1940's photo showing automobiles passing through the familiar iron gates

top: (l. to r.) Jack Duvick, Sherelyn "Winky" Kell, and Beverly Faber at the Fair during World War II. Veterans in uniform were admitted free to the grounds.

bottom: Eating cotton candy at the Fair

U.S. was casting an eye on yet another war. North Korea sent its armies into the South of that divided country; the United Nations responded, and the American military headed overseas again.

At home serious topics dominated radio and television stations. Senator McCarthy was creating a national scare with his Communist witch-hunts. In Alabama, Rosa Parks refused to give up her seat in the black section of a bus to a white passenger. Over 38,000 children contracted polio in 1954 before Salk's vaccine reduced the number to fewer than 6,000 in 1957.

There was also fun and excitement in the fifties. The Sandwich Fair board provided grandstand entertainment that fit the times. The first Fair queen was crowned. Aut Swenson's Thrillcade included death-defying stunt drivers who crashed through blazing barriers and played leapfrog on motorcycles. To complement his show, he had an array of circus acts and a famous ragtime pianist.

The directors themselves, along with local businessmen, joined in the fun when they agreed to race ostriches and camels in competitions that fairgoers would never forget. Some directors volunteered to sit atop an elephant for a memorable photograph.

In 1951 New York Yankee Joe DiMaggio retired. Interest in the major leagues continued, but baseball games at the Fair were drawing smaller crowds. As the decade progressed, interest continued to wane. Although the 1956 schedule slated four contests, only one was a traditional baseball game. The others were two Little League matches and one Pony League game. That was the last year baseball competition was scheduled at the Sandwich Fair.

Young women fairgoers with their bobby socks and poodle skirts were swooning over Elvis. Young men in James Dean shirts were as eager as the girls to attend the dances held three nights of the Fair on the south side of the Home Arts building—even if they only watched

the others rock 'n' roll. In 1954 the Fair board recognized the popularity of the dances when they voted to sponsor them most of the summer and to add concrete walks around the dance floor.

The fifties were a decade for children. Disneyland opened. Barbie and Matchbox toys went on sale. Lassie, Captain Kangaroo, and Howdy Doody were favorite television stars. At the Fair, clowns, trick mules, circuses, and wild west shows entertained children. Continuing a tradition that began in 1948, the Fair board provided reduced-price rates for children on Wednesday, opening day of the Fair.

Other Americans, regardless of age, enjoyed one of the country's 2,200 drive-in theaters and their first 15-cent hamburger and 20-cent shake at McDonald's. Automobiles were more popular and affordable than ever. Most families owned at least one car, but the term *carpooling* had not yet become a household word; this fact could not have been more evident than at the Sandwich Fair in 1954. Local papers reported the parking area was completely filled and many motorists had to park outside the grounds.

Automobiles also made it easier for families to go beyond their own city limits and even county limits to find entertainment. People were willing to drive greater distances to attend a fair that patrons were calling "the best county fair in Illinois." Driving to the Fair on a sweltering September day was even more enjoyable now because automobile air conditioning was available, and many of the cars even had power steering.

1960-1969

With the advent of the 1960's, Brazil had a

Courtesy of SFA

top: Sandwich Fair Board members rode a huge elephant at the 1954 Fair. (l. to r.) Carlton "Dutch" Hough, Carl Scent, C.R. Brady, LaVerne "Dutch" Johnson, Donald Stahl, L.P. Brady, Henry White, and owner of the show Gene Holter

new capital and if the Sandwich Fair's farm visitors were uninterested, they hadn't yet grasped the significance of that fact. Brasilia symbolized the economic development of the interior of the South American continent. With the opening of those fertile hinterlands, United States agriculture would never be quite the same. Grain belt farmers were about to face serious competition.

Other issues dominated fairgoers' conversations. The weather during the 1961 Fair was so hot that large silo blowers were installed at both ends of the sheep barns. Otherwise, it was feared the animals might die from the extreme heat. Away from home John Glenn's orbit of the Earth put America back in the space race and expanded children's career aspirations. Now they wanted to be astronauts as well as firemen and nurses.

This decade has been dubbed the Turbulent Sixties for good reason. Human rights issues and an unpopular war in Southeast Asia were the focus of protests and civil disobedience. Martin Luther King, Jr. delivered his "I Have a Dream" speech in 1963. Many young men and women were missing in attendance at the Fair in

the sixties because close to half a million Americans were fighting in Vietnam.

Other tragic news included President Kennedy's assassination in Dallas in 1963. In 1964 the U.S. Surgeon General spoke to America warning them of the dangers of smoking cigarettes. One-half of the U.S. men and nearly one-third of the U.S. women were smokers.

On the lighter side, the Beatles were introduced to America on the Ed Sullivan Show. Area teens danced to their music and the music of various other rock groups on Thursday nights at the fairgrounds from mid-June through the week of the Fair. There were skateboards and miniskirts, and the microwave oven was introduced. SpaghettiOs and Diet Pepsi were new on the market. At least one of these—the microwave—impacted the entries at the Fair; the Home Arts Department added several new food items to the exhibitors list.

1970-1979

If terms had to be chosen to describe the

bottom: In cooperation with various seed corn companies, a seed corn show was started in the Horticulture building in 1948.

Courtesy of SFA

13

The Sandwich Fair Association
requests the honour of your presence
at the
"Golden Wedding Day"
of the
83rd Annual DeKalb County Fair
on Thursday, the tenth day of September
nineteen hundred and seventy
Sandwich Fairgrounds
Sandwich, Illinois

Courtesy of SFA

Sandwich Fair Ass'n., Inc.

GUEST LUNCHEON TICKET

Golden Wedding Day

Thursday, September 10, 1970

Good for $1.75 at any food stand on date shown

top: In 1970 the Fair saluted the institution of marriage. Golden Wedding couples were admitted to the fairgrounds free.

right: Since 1967 all ages have enjoyed the farm machinery from years past.

previous pages: Courtesy of SFA
pages 14-15: At one time the addition to the Horticulture building contained school exhibits with the flower show. Many of the walk areas in the early 1970's were still unpaved.

bottom: Area teens danced to music of Bub and His Boys and other bands Thursday nights during the summer. The dance floor behind the Home Arts building is shown in the far left area of the photo.

mood of the nation during the 1970's, for some the logical choices would be *irreverence* and *cynicism*. On network television, *All in the Family* and *M*A*S*H* examined assumptions about prejudice and patriotism. However, while traditional values were being questioned on many fronts, the Sandwich Fair was recognizing the importance of stability provided by family and friends.

In 1970 the Fair saluted the institution of marriage. Golden Wedding couples were admitted to the fairgrounds free. They were given luncheon tickets, and each couple was photographed beside an antique automobile or surrey. Each day of the Fair was dedicated to those who were in the mainstream of America's values: Wednesday was Family or Kids Day, Thursday was Senior Citizens or Homecoming Day, Friday was Armed Services Day, Saturday was Youth Day, and Sunday was Neighbors Day. The *Sandwich Free Press* encouraged "Bring a picnic and eat lunch or supper on picnic tables under the trees. . . . Entertainment is available for every member of the family." The Sandwich Fair is a place to "examine the roots of America."

In the seventies, also known as the polyester decade, the Sandwich Fair may have seemed a little corny for the tradition-breakers, but it was solace for those who weren't comfortable with the phoniness of the times. The Sandwich Fair was a place where all ages still enjoyed farm and home exhibits, harness racing and antique farm machinery, the smells of barbe-

cuing pork chops and chicken, and the pleasant sight of the young and the young at heart.

In this decade the Fair board began providing free grandstand entertainment. In the afternoons families and friends rested in the shade of the grandstand canopy and enjoyed harness racing and at the same time caught up on events of the past year. The tractor and truck pulling contests and the Joie Chitwood Thrill Show weren't especially conducive to conversation, yet the

Courtesy of SFA

grandstand remained a good place to reunite with family and friends.

Dress was becoming more casual. Even those who dressed up were in leisure suits or other permanent-press garments. Blue jeans and "grubbies" were the typical uniform of the day. The felt fedoras and derbies that men wore to the Fair at the turn of the century had long ago been replaced with caps. Now, advertising on the caps (and T-shirts) enabled corporations to transform fairgoers into walking billboards.

Courtesy of SFA

National and world headlines that dominated conversations centered on farm economics, war, Watergate, and gasoline prices. A tractorcade to Washington D.C. dramatized deteriorating conditions in the farm belt. A truce ended the Vietnam conflict in 1973. Intruders were caught burglarizing the Democratic Party's offices in the Watergate Complex, setting in play a sequence of events that would result in President Nixon's resignation. Bob Woodward, who had ancestral roots in Sandwich, and Carl Bernstein made Watergate a household word with their investigative reporting for the *Washington Post*. In this same year, a drive to the Sandwich Fair became considerably more costly when the Arab oil embargo sent petroleum prices soaring and brought in a financial gusher for oil producers.

The Fair grew bigger and better every year, yet fairgoers could depend on the Fair to be the same, old-fashioned county fair it had always been. It was a place where family and friends were revered.

1980-1989

The eighties literally opened with an explosion. On May 5, 1980, the world was reminded once again of the awesome power of nature when a volcanic eruption blew off the top of Mount Saint Helens in Washington.

Politically, President Reagan predicted that America was on the rebound. The economy improved but deficit spending soared. Fortunately the Sandwich Fair board directors continued their practice of sound financial planning to ensure that the Fair would continue to be a tradition in DeKalb County.

Young people continued to meet their friends at the Fair in spite of outside diversions offered by Pac Man and Music Television (MTV). One of their favorite hangouts was the midway. For the fifth year, Blomsness All Star Amusement Company supplied thrills and excitement with such rides as the Giant Gondola, Cobra, and Zipper. A youthful group, the Sandwich Striders Track Club, sponsored the Sandwich Fair 10,000 Meter Road Race. It attracted 150 runners from neighboring communities. The race was run on Sunday morning beginning and ending inside the fairgrounds.

Serious issues were on the minds of fairgoers. Doctors announced the discovery of a deadly disease that had no cure called Acquired Immune Deficiency Syndrome (AIDS). Chinese troops swarmed Beijing's Tiananmen Square killing hundreds of people and crushing a democratic movement. In 1986 Americans listened with horror to the news that the space shuttle *Challenger* had exploded 73 seconds after liftoff.

Lighter issues, but still important to some fairgoers, involved baseball, dancing, and technology. Boston Red Sox first baseman Bill Buckner's error was blamed for Boston losing the World Series to the New York Mets. Dancing returned to the Fair in 1989. Members of the Sugar Squares Dance Club were swinging their partners at the pavilion behind the Home Arts building.

It was a changing decade for technology and communication. Personal computers hit the market. Superconductors were in the news. Fairgoers began listening to music recorded on compact discs rather than records and tapes. The courts ordered the split up of communications giant AT&T.

Most of the nation was oblivious to the fact that the Sandwich Fair was celebrating its 100th year. Nevertheless, the celebration was a grand success. For this special event, the Board of Directors issued a gold, oversized premium book. It included heritage pictures and a longer list of exhibitor classes. A variety of music, livestock shows, a petting zoo, harness racing, powerful and noisy trucks and tractors, clowns, and craft demonstrations were just a few of the events that entertained fairgoers. Even though the Fair was much larger in 1987 than it was in

Blue Max at the 1987 tractor pull

Photo by D.S.

its youth, the main focus had not changed. The centennial activities emphasized that the Sandwich Fair was an agricultural fair with entertainment for the whole family.

During this decade the family farm experienced its worst times in fifty years. Land prices plunged. Drought in the Great Plains, the South, and the Midwest exacerbated the situation. Old-timers at the Fair talked about 1988 as the driest Fair they had ever seen. Horticulture and floriculture exhibits were reduced, but the drought did not dry up the spirit of the exhibitors.

The decade ended on a quieter and more optimistic note than it had begun. East and West Germans tore down the Berlin Wall and celebrated the end of the Cold War. Although the stock market experienced another crash, it recovered quickly. The Sandwich Fair continued to grow.

1990-1999

This decade was replete with contradictory circumstances. There was encouraging and discouraging news, rises and declines, and conveniences and inconveniences. The particulars reached far beyond the farm families exhibiting at the Sandwich Fair, but they were certainly affected. Farmers and agribusiness first basked in some of the best economic times, and then watched the bottom fall out of livestock and commodity prices. Machinery and equipment displayed at the Fair got bigger and bigger as the number of farmers declined and each handled more acres. As the century closed, the promise of unprecedented advances in crop production techniques soured when consumers opposed genetically modified crops. On a more positive note, a unique market developed for food raised without pesticides and manufactured fertilizers. To older citizens, this seemed like a shift back to earlier organic farming methods.

Attendance at the Fair increased each year. The negative side of the large crowds was the time spent waiting in line; yet, there was a positive side: The time spent waiting forced fairgoers to slow down and enjoy the company of others who were also in the long lines. For the first time, their conversations were products of the news they received via the Internet as well as traditional media. Startling accounts of bombings, shootings, and domestic violence were linked with names such as Hussein, McVeigh,

and O. J. Simpson.

There was also good news during this decade: the stock market skyrocketed, Communism waned, and East and West Germany reunited. The good news for fairgoers who dared to try bungee jumping for the first time at the Fair in 1992: A spokesperson for the North American Bungee Association assured those who were willing to free-fall from a platform 175 feet in the air that the company had logged over nine thousand jumps with no injuries.

Continuing the theme of contradictions in the decade, for some it was easier than usual to arrive at the Fair—for others it was harder. For those who opted for shuttle service provided through the cooperation of The Sandwich Fair Association, the Voluntary Action Center of DeKalb County and the Fox Valley Older Adult Services, arriving at the Fair was relatively simple. The van dropped off passengers and picked them up at a scheduled time within a few feet of the entrance. There was no car to park and no car to find when it was time to go home. On the other hand, those who waited in long lines and walked long distances to and from their cars alerted Fair directors to a problem that needed to be addressed. As a result, the Fair Association purchased land for a new exit and developed a better entry plan.

The last Sandwich Fair of the 1900's closed on Sunday, September 12, 1999. It was a time of desperation and celebration. Desperation because the 112th Fair was closing before some fairgoers had time to consume one more cinnamon roll, strawberry milkshake, pork chop, ear of corn, elephant ear, pronto pup, tempura, cotton candy, pizza log, bratwurst, or lemon shake-up. Desperation because there wasn't time to have one more ride on Augie Otto's train or time to collect one more yardstick from King and Sons Monuments. However, it was also a time of celebration—for the record-breaking crowds, exemplary exhibits, and good weather. A time to celebrate the strong leadership and dedication that had made the DeKalb County Fair at Sandwich, Illinois, successful for one hundred and twelve years. ▲

Photo by V.B.

top: Apples waiting to be judged in the Horticulture building

opposite page: Courtesy of SFA
Even though the midway was much larger in 1987 than it was in its youth, the main focus has not changed.

bottom: A young fairgoer enjoys a fresh roasted ear of sweet corn.

Photo by L.H.

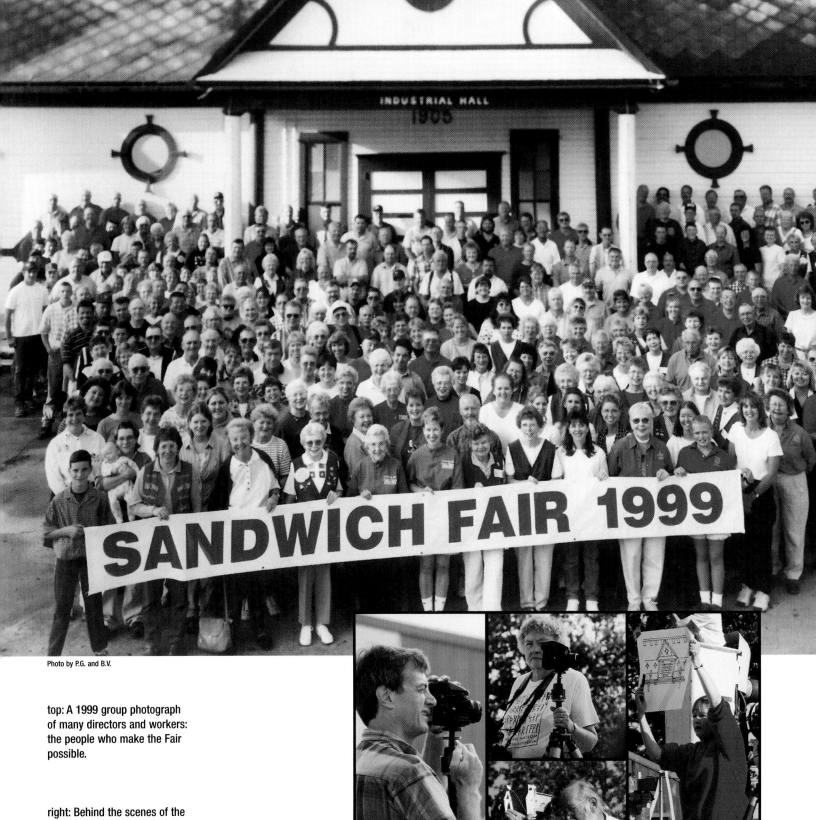

Photo by P.G. and B.V.

top: A 1999 group photograph of many directors and workers: the people who make the Fair possible.

right: Behind the scenes of the picture above: Photographers Bruce VanPelt (left) and Paul Gleason (bottom center). Assisted by Virginia Grimes (top center) and Jackie Dannewitz (right).

Photos by V.C.W.

Dedicated Leaders: Past and Present

In the September 24, 1891, issue of *The Free Press,* a local reporter applauded the leaders of the Sandwich Fair: ". . . we feel like borrowing our neighbor's hat and throwing it up and giving three good big cheers for the Sandwich Fair of 1891 and its management." While the year was 1891, the praise is still appropriate today.

More accolades were published in the August 16, 1917, issue of the *Free Press* when the Fair celebrated its thirtieth anniversary.

Thirty years is a long time for an organization such as the Sandwich fair association to hold together, especially when there are no dividends coming each year to those who have made the fair possible by investing their money and giving without pay a whole lot of time. It is local pride that is responsible for the continued success of the local agricultural association. It grows better with each succeeding year. . . . Not every year has there been sufficient money taken in at the gate to pay expenses. Rain and adverse weather conditions have reduced the profits and oftentimes money has been borrowed to meet the expenses. Yet with all this the Sandwich Fair Association has always met all of its obligations and no one has had to wait for money coming to them. It is this promptness that has earned for the local institution a reputation of dealing fair with those who enter the competitive classes.

The Sandwich Fair has a long history of strong leadership. The individual personalities have changed, but dedication to the Fair has remained the same. The directors, superintendents, and department heads know how to keep a good thing going.

Courtesy of A.K.

Board of Directors in 1964:
Front row: C.R. Brady, Carlton Hough, Louis Wagner, Carl Scent
Back row: Kenneth Klotz, Spencer Gord, Donald Breunig, Henry White, Edward Duvick, Armand Legner, Russell Stahl, Louis P. Brady, Lewis Rex

Courtesy of SFA

Board of Directors in 1979:
Front row: John Wagner, Louis Wagner, Carlton Hough, Louis P. Brady, Jack Norling, Donald Bark
Back row: Armand Legner, Fredrick Lindner, Russell Stahl, Donald Stahl, Robert Guehler, Wm. Mason, Wiley Updike, Donald Breunig

Courtesy of SFA

Board of Directors in 1987:
Front row: Donald Stahl, Donald Breunig, Jack Norling, Louis P. Brady, Carlton Hough
Back row: John Wagner, Russell Stahl, Robert Guehler, Scott Breunig, Donald Augustine, Wiley Updike, Donald Bark

The Operating Structure

STOCKHOLDERS

BOARD OF DIRECTORS

SUPERINTENDENTS

EMPLOYEES AND VOLUNTEERS

CONCESSIONAIRES

EXHIBITORS AND FAIRGOERS

Since 1888 the structure of the Sandwich Fair Association, Inc. has remained essentially the same. Stockholders elect a Board of Directors who in turn elect the officers. The directors appoint superintendents; most directors also serve as superintendents. Directors and superintendents hire employees. Concessionaires and organizations that have rented space hire their own employees or arrange for volunteers. Beginning several weeks before the Fair, exhibitors purchase exhibitor tickets and submit lists of entries to be judged at the Fair.

On the first Wednesday after Labor Day, stockholders, directors, superintendents, employees, volunteers, concessionaires, and exhibitors are joined by fairgoers who pay general admission to attend the Fair.

A principal reason for the continued success of the Sandwich Fair is the important part it plays in the lives of those involved. The directors and superintendents are given a great deal of autonomy because of the experience and expertise they have in their departments. They are trusted to make decisions that will produce a good fair each year and perpetuate the Sandwich Fair for generations.

The Board of Directors of The Sandwich Fair Association, Inc. is committed to maintaining strong ties to its agricultural beginnings and to continually improving the beautiful grounds. At the same time they endeavor to keep up with what is new in the fair industry and with what current fairgoers expect in the way of entertainment. Their hope is that this mix of good old county fair and exciting up-to-date concessions and entertainment will keep fairgoers coming to the Sandwich Fair forever.

Courtesy of SFA

Courtesy of SFA

top: Most shares of stock are a cherished family possession, being passed from generation to generation.

bottom: There are no dividends, but stockholders receive passes to the Fair.

Stockholders

In 1888 one hundred shares of stock were issued forming the Sandwich Fair Association. People engaged in business and agriculture in the surrounding area purchased these shares for fifty dollars each. Sale of the stock provided capital for operating and maintaining the Fair. Over the years these shares have changed hands for one hundred to one hundred and fifty dollars each and in more recent years for as much as three hundred dollars.

No additional stock has ever been issued and no dividends have ever been paid. All proceeds have been returned to the Fair Association for maintenance and growth. In the early years whenever there was a share of stock for sale for whatever reason, the seller usually sold it back to the Fair Association; an interested party could then purchase the share from the Association.

Today, there is seldom any stock for sale. Most of the stock is a cherished family possession, being passed from generation to generation. There are very few multiple stockholders; most families own only one share. Shareholders are now scattered all over the United States.

Owning a share of stock is a way of connecting with home and roots. Shareholders take pride in being part of an organization that has been successful for over a century. Although there are no dividends, stockholders do receive two five-day passes to the Fair as well as two tickets for each of the grandstand shows.

The Current Board of Directors

In 2000 the Board of Directors consisted of thirteen members: Wiley Updike, President; Donald Stahl, Vice President; Nancy Lou Rex, Secretary; Louis P. Brady, Secretary Emeritus; Donald Augustine, Treasurer; Donald Bark, Scott Breunig, Harold Dannewitz, Larry Dannewitz, William Haag, Kenneth Tyrrell, John Wagner, and Matt Wilson.

All directors are required to own at least one share of stock in the Fair association, must be willing to attend monthly board meetings and numerous committee meetings, and must have a history of dedication to the Fair. Directors receive a small stipend as a token for their time, but as one director said, "If you're in it for the money, you're in it for the wrong reasons."

The real compensation comes from the

enjoyment of working with a group of people who take pride in what they do. Each fall the association hosts a large banquet of appreciation for its directors, superintendents, and dedicated workers. The board members have made the Sandwich Fair a part of their lives, or perhaps it is more accurate to say, the Sandwich Fair has made the board members a part of its life.

The Sandwich Fair belongs to the Illinois Association of Agricultural Fairs (IAAF). At the annual convention in January in Springfield, Illinois, directors have an opportunity to meet with vendors who are hoping to sell their entertainment or products. Training sessions called roundtables are also a part of the convention. At these sessions directors discuss a variety of topics and listen to people from county fairs from all over the state.

The Sandwich Fair Association, Inc. is also a member of the International Association of Fairs and Expositions (IAFE) that meets annually in Las Vegas. The Sandwich Fair tries to have at least one representative at this convention, which is attended by people from all over the United States and several foreign countries.

The concept of a working Board of Directors is one of the key factors that has made the Sandwich Fair the success it is today. Each director is responsible for a specific part of the Fair and represents that department at board meetings. This gives the Fair balance and prevents one part from overshadowing the rest. A major goal is to uphold the tradition of the Sandwich Fair being a family event where there is something for everyone to enjoy—whether it is fruits, vegetables,

Courtesy of SFA

flowers, livestock, crafts, commercial exhibits, entertainment, good food, or the carnival.

Wiley Updike

President Wiley Updike remembers his childhood days of attending the Fair with his parents

Courtesy of SFA

and working with them at the Log Cabin. His connection with the Fair began as a gate watcher at the grandstand when he was in his twenties. He became Sheep Superintendent in 1967 when Don Stahl offered him the job. Although Wiley knew very little about sheep, he was a quick study.

While he was Sheep Superintendent, he began assisting with the tractor pulls. He later became Tractor Pull and Truck Pull Superintendent. He was also Superintendent of the Antique Car Show. He has watched the Sandwich Fair grow from a three-day mostly live-stock-oriented fair, to the phenomenally successful event it is today attracting approximately 200,000 people over its five-day duration.

Wiley was elected president of the Fair Association in 1992. He remains Superintendent of Truck Pull and Tractor Pull but has given up the car show. Two weeks before the Fair, Wiley spends a great deal of time giving radio and some television interviews. During the Fair besides his regular duties, he spends time talking to Fair workers, listening to their opinions, letting them know they are an important part of the Fair, and overseeing the Fair as a whole. Wiley makes it a practice to compliment the directors, superintendents, and workers

top: **Current Board of Directors:** Front row: Nancy Rex, Donald Augustine, Wiley Updike, Louis P. Brady, Donald Stahl, Donald Bark Back row: Scott Breunig, Matthew Wilson, Harold Dannewitz, Wm. Haag, Larry Dannewitz, Kenneth Tyrrell, John Wagner

center: The real compensation comes from the enjoyment of working with a group of people who take pride in what they do. A 1985 caricature of board members by Quen Carpenter. Back row: Wm. Mason, Jack Norling, Donald Stahl, Robert Guehler, Wiley Updike Middle row: Donald Breunig, Donald Augustine, L.P. Brady, Donald Bark, Russell Stahl Front row: Carlton Hough, caretaker Herman Carlson, Scott Breunig, Stuart Phillips, John Wagner

bottom: The Sandwich Fair Association is a member of the International Association of Fairs and Expositions.

Photo by B.V.

Education, Secretary's Office, Gazebo Information
Front row: Dorothy Carlson, Jean Swenson, Nancy Brady, Louis P. Brady, Patti Webber, Charlotte Albert, Norma Norling, Row 2: Cindy Grimmeaux, Nancy Updike, Virginia Hann, Irma Grady, Joan Hardekopf, Karen Breunig, Ginger Dannewitz, Row 3: Marcia Nagel, Van Mathre, Beryl McKanna, Linda Munson, Nancy Rex, Row 4: Jackie Dannewitz, Cheryl Augustine, Carole Van Winkle, Charlotte Tyrrell

Photo by B.V.

Open & Jr. Swine, Poultry, Rabbits, Dairy Goats, Llamas, Open & Jr. Sheep, Micro-Mini Tractor Pull
Front row: Wayne Christopher, Kyle Huss, LaVerne Mattson, Brenda Craddock, Becky Craddock, Ashley Beins, Taylor Beins, Sandra Dannenberg, Tammy Baker, Donna Ricci, Row 2: Dick Delp, Dan Hoyt, John Guehler, Clarence Schnitz, Jeff Hoyt, Mary Hoyt, Jack Smith, Clint Schnitz, Sarah Craddock, Tyler Hoyt, Mike Crayton, Mike Twait, Tim Hoyt, Krystal Pennington, Ally Ricci, Row 3: Barry Smith, Brad Temple, Ken Tyrrell, Doug Wackerlin, Mark Setchell, Dennis Craddock, Dennis Craddock, Jr., Not pictured: Al Dietz, Brenda Dietz, Steve Dietz, Dawn Dietz, Jerry Hartel, Angela Van Vooren

for their tireless efforts to make the Sandwich Fair a success.

Donald Stahl

Vice President Donald Stahl recalls that his father showed horses at the Fair and so did his grandfather back in 1890. In 1935 when he was eleven years old, he followed their lead and entered his steer in the Fair. He won Grand Champion. Some years later when World War II created a labor shortage, he helped set up tents. Little did he know at that time that he was beginning a relationship with the Sandwich Fair that would touch thousands of people.

Don became a director in 1951. He has served continuously, except from 1959 to 1966 when he resigned so his son Doug could show cattle. In 1966 the Fair board asked him to be General Livestock Superintendent, and in 1986 he was elected vice president.

Don continually looks for ways to improve the Fair. He knows the Fair has come a long way since the days he and fellow exhibitors had to share one pump and walk a long distance to water their livestock. Nevertheless, he believes the best can always be better. He is always on the lookout for new breeds or classes of livestock that can improve the livestock show. Don strongly supports the Education Committee. He says, "A lot of people don't realize that their jobs relate back to agriculture—that agriculture is one of the backbones of this country." He is pleased that several school administrators are allowing field trips to the Sandwich Fair so students can learn about the role agriculture plays in their lives. Don was the Fair representative for an award-winning partnership activity with Indian Valley Vocational Center [see Chapter 10].

Don describes his goals for the Sandwich Fair: "It's important to keep the family farm alive here. We just keep encouraging entries and diversifying classes."

Nancy Lou Rex

Secretary Nancy Lou Rex became a director of the Sandwich Fair Association in 1991. She followed her brother-in-law Jack E. Norling as Superintendent of Ticket Sales. In a sense, Nancy has grown up with the job [See Chapter 3 Main Gate].

When she was a youngster, she successfully pleaded with her father Lewis B. Rex, who was in charge of hiring ticket sellers and takers, to let her take tickets and later sell tickets at the entrance gates. If she were a ship, she was "charting new waters" because selling tickets was a job that only males did. Nancy continued to be a trendsetter when she was elected secretary in 1999, a position that only men—four through the years—had held previously. In 1993 she became Superintendent of the Education Committee.

Prior to her election as secretary, Nancy was an elementary school teacher for 26 years. She also has an insurance license and was part owner of Rex Agency, Inc. until it was sold. Nancy continues her responsibilities as Superintendent of Ticket Sales as she performs the responsibilities of the secretary's position.

Louis P. Brady

Secretary Emeritus Louis P. Brady retired from his role as secretary in 1999, a position he held for 26 years. He passed on his responsibilities of overseeing the preparation and mailing of premium books and opening stacks of letters that come in every day all year long. Now, his successor answers the numerous questions on the telephone about renting the fairgrounds, entering exhibits, procuring commercial space, and driving to the Fair from Chicago or "Timbuktu."

Even though he is "retired," he continues to oversee the Secretary's Office on the fairgrounds during the Fair, and he continues to work in the Fair office on South Main Street in Sandwich almost every day. He has been a director since 1952.

Lou's memories of the Fair go back to his grade school days. He says, "They used to pass out blue ribbons for the best pictures drawn by grade school age kids, and I remember running into the Education Tent to see if my picture was hanging on the wall." One year his picture was displayed; he won a red ribbon.

Donald Augustine

Treasurer Donald Augustine has lived nearly his entire life in Sandwich. He remembers showing hogs at the Fair when he was a youngster. He can't remember exactly when he started working at the Fair, but somewhere around 20 years ago, he began helping Donald "Did" Breunig with his duties.

Today, Don is Grandstand Entertainment Superintendent. His duties include booking popular country and western music stars and rebooking popular features such as the Demolition Derby. During his tenure the grandstand has been remodeled making it wheelchair accessible, and the track has been restructured to comply with safety regulations.

He describes the efforts that go into the Sandwich Fair as never-ending. Planning the following year's events and improvements start immediately after each year's Fair. He gives credit to everyone who helps at the Sandwich Fair for its success, including the groundskeepers, exhibitors, people in the community, volunteers and workers. "Without them, the Fair couldn't run."

Donald Bark

Director Donald Bark has been the Superintendent of Concessions since 1978. During his tenure the exhibiting space for vendors has doubled. He started out as a "go-fer" sometime around 1962, moved up to be the assistant to the assistant, and then an assistant to the superintendent before taking his present position. His advancement was gradual just like changes at the Fair. Don told a *Fair Times* reporter, "You think about it [a change] one year, you look at it the next year to see how your idea will work out, and then you do it the third year." That's what Don's job is all about—making changes to make fairgoers and vendors happier.

Like all the directors, he is concerned with making space for everyone. To alleviate congestion around the grandstand, he suggested that a second midway be developed east of the first one. It was a positive change because it gave fairgoers more room, and it boosted the business of vendors in the outer area of the grounds. Don also suggested to the Board that a decrepit, old horse barn be torn down in order to improve the sight lines to the livestock area in the hopes

of drawing more people to that area. This is now the present site of the Ag Land Stage.

A *Beacon News* reporter in the September 11, 1983, issue says of Don: "[He] is usually too busy to be interviewed. While he stops to answer one person's question, several others will form a line waiting to have a question answered or problem solved. He covers the several acre grounds many times each day. Whether he is on foot or in a motorized cart, he has a difficult time getting very far without being stopped, but he loves every minute of it."

Don says, "I have a gift for gab." With hundreds of commercial exhibits to book and manage, Don draws on his gift, his good humor, and his dedication to help make the Fair a success. He is well known in the fair industry and is currently serving as first vice president of the Illinois Association of Agricultural Fairs.

Photo by B.V.

Concessions, Electricians, Grounds Crew
Front row: Mary Keeton, Joanna Bark, Don Bark, Tyler Bark, Dorothy Scent, Beth Swanson, Row 2: Dan Bark, Karen Bark, Gene Olson, Gary Bark, Row 3: Frank Moran, Reed Johnson, Harold Dannewitz, Scott Breunig, Jim Webber, Row 4: Arnie Bark, Jim Webber Jr., Bob Whiteis, Andy Krafft, Not pictured: Fern Eade

Scott Breunig

Director Scott Breunig's earliest memories of the Fair are visiting the tractor exhibits with his parents. He remembers always trying to talk them into buying him a toy tractor. Sometimes he was successful, and sometimes he wasn't.

Scott organizes the parking, hires help, and oversees the parking on the west side of the grounds. He took over the job from Armand "Doc" Legner who wanted a job that required less walking. Scott says the worst problems he faces are traffic jams on the weekends when traffic is the heaviest. Some of the other problems include lost cars, dead batteries, and mud when it rains.

A recent project Scott is proud of is the Ag Land Stage. Since its creation people are drawn to the livestock part of the Fair in greater numbers than ever before. Scott books the bands that perform on the stage, and he coordinates the other talent that appears there. Scott is also superintendent of another popular attraction, the Draft Horse Pull. He says he got the job more by suggesting the idea than his knowledge

Photo by B.V.

Antique Car Show, Tickets, Parking, Security
Front row: Dean Farley, Vanessa Fletcher, Don Lawyer, Doug Carter, Millie Carter, John T. Walker, Randy Ellis, Row 2: Kevin Peterson, Rich Smith, Dave Johnson, Trevor Hall, John Carls, Nancy Carter, Brian Wickens, Peggy Walker, Scott Breunig, Reed Anderson, Dale Merkel, Row 3: Pat Schuerman, Bill Haag, John Hallaron, Virgil Beukelman, Norma Norling, Nancy Lou Rex, Roy Wahlgren, Pat Hallaron, Jim Stahl, Jim Webber Jr., Mike Fox, John Fox, Gary Skinner, Ed Stahl, Not pictured: Bill Guy, Joe Webber, Tracy Rogers, Dawn Rogers, Sean Rogers, Kelly Rogers, Theresa Rogers, Sarah Rogers, Merlyn Wiley, Sherm Morgan, Bonnie Morgan, Diane Angelo, Bill Angelo, Laurie Morgan

Grandstand, Tractor Pull, Harness Racing, Draft Horse Show
Front row: Wiley Updike, Jaime Hanson, Julie Wilson, Audrey Meyer, Peg Dummer, Roberta Troeger, Charlie Lackey, Scott Frieders, Row 2: Joe Crisman, Roger Grandgeorge, Gary Augustine, Dr. Mark Weinhold, Mark Weismiller, Keith Knight, Larry Dannewitz, John Smith, George Smith, Norm Troeger, Row 3: Dave Rogers, Robert Dierzen, Greg Wickens, Phil Nielsen, Don Augustine, Bill Werner, Roger Thorson, Ron Wallis, Gene Frieders, Don Kosulic, Chad Frieders, Not pictured: Rich Augustine, Jill Friestad, Matt Wickens, Dan Breunig, Darren Merkel, Bernie Frieders, Ryan Jacobs, Jim Meade

Livestock Office, Western Horse Show, Open & Jr. Beef, Open & Jr. Dairy, Draft Horse Pull
Front row: Paula Bandy, Lorna Donnelly, Amber and Cody Ansteth, Carole Hilleson, Owen Kahle, Row 2: Don Stahl, Jonie Knox, Kristen Hilleson, Sandy Plapp, Row 3: Julie Wilson, Steve Hillison, Bob Pennington, Mark Tuttle, Ron Anderson, Joe Steffen, Row 4: Douglas R. Stahl, Pat McCormick, Dr. Craig Stevenson, Larry Hoffman, Kim Hoffman, Carman Plapp, Merwin Plapp

of horses.

Scott, who has been a director about twenty years, cites the growth of the Fair as the biggest change in his department. When asked what he likes most about his duties at the Fair, he said, "The action. There's always something going on."

Harold Dannewitz

Director Harold Dannewitz says, "Everything is based on the weather." He has been in charge of electricity since 1991 and a board member since 1994. He likes everything about his job: meeting people, visiting (when he has time), and rebuilding equipment that needs attention [see Chapter 3 Electricity].

Harold's early memories of the Fair date back to his grade school days. He sold score cards for the harness races, and he also worked in the old Log Cabin. Before he retired from Commonwealth Edison in late 1999, Harold usually worked every weekend at the fairgrounds from April to the end of October as well as three or four weeks of his vacation. Now that he is retired, he will probably be spending even more time at the fairgrounds—if that is possible. The growth of the Sandwich Fair has placed large demands on Harold and his crew. One director half-jokingly says, "Harold has saved us from an electrical meltdown."

The best part of the Sandwich Fair, in his opinion, is the people—those who work so others can enjoy themselves and those who come for the food and entertainment with their families and friends.

Larry Dannewitz

Director Larry Dannewitz likes "watching

people have fun" at the Fair. He has been a director since 1993, working in the grandstand area with Don Augustine. His duties include organizing the early ticket sales on Labor Day, overseeing the setup of the main stage, laying out the track seating, and setting up the chairs.

He is also in charge of crowd control before, during, and after the shows. On Friday night at the popular country and western shows, crowd control is especially important. Because of the close timing between performances, one audience is being seated while the audience from the previous performance is exiting the grandstand.

Occasionally Larry even has to soothe the feelings of a dissatisfied customer who isn't happy with his or her seat or the weather or some other problem that is impossible to solve.

Larry thinks the Fair has been so successful for more than 100 years because of the people who plan it. They work hard because it is *their* Fair. He says the best thing about being a director is "being a part of something so successful." He adds, "The worst part is being so busy during the Fair you don't get to see everything."

William Haag

Director William Haag says parking and security fall under his job description. He began his training in parking Fair traffic in 1983 working for Stuart Phillips. When Stuart became seriously ill, he asked Bill to take over for him.

Bill has been a director for just over ten years. His job involves hiring people to park the cars, organizing the parking, and overseeing the east side of the fairgrounds. He spends a lot of time helping people find their cars and even start their cars. Traffic jams on the weekends are a problem, but he notes there have been improvements in traffic flow with many vehicles leaving now through the Pratt Road exit, which gives suburban and northbound drivers quicker access to roads that lead to interstate highways.

According to Bill, everything usually runs pretty smoothly in his department, but the rain in 1983 was a real catastrophe. He and his parking lot attendants helped push fairgoers' cars out of slippery, deep mud. He likes the "overall excitement" of the Fair that spurs on the directors who display what he calls "year-round devotion."

Kenneth Tyrrell

Director Kenneth Tyrrell has been a member of the board since 1988. He is Superintendent of Sheep. In his position he has become acquainted with three generations of exhibitors and visitors. He has seen big changes in sheep raising and exhibiting since he started working in the department long before he was selected as its superintendent. He says the quality and size of the animals have steadily improved. He believes a lamb is a good beginning project for many 4-H kids. The exhibitors who show today are often farmers who keep a few sheep. In the past many of the exhibitors were large commercial-flock owners.

Ken hasn't always been in the livestock area. His first recollections are working in the Methodist Church food stand as a small child.

In his opinion the popularity of the Sandwich Fair has continually grown because of the beautiful grounds, the variety of interesting exhibits for all ages, and the old-fashioned family atmosphere.

John Wagner

Director John Wagner believes, "The most important person to keep happy is the exhibitor." John works hard to achieve his goal because as Superintendent of Collections, Superintendent of Open Class Plants and Flowers, and Superintendent of Grains, Fruits and Vegetables, he oversees five display buildings. In other words, he is in a lot of places at the same time. When the Fair closes in early September, like most of the directors, John continues to work on Fair activities. He researches and scouts seed catalogs for new ideas.

John recently told a *Fair Times* reporter in 1999, "I like to arrange things. I've been working in vegetables for 50 years or more. It [arranging] comes natural." When he was about seven, he helped his father Director Louis Wagner hang pictures on the walls in the Home Arts building. He was familiar with the Fair long before he became a member of the Fair board in 1973.

John also supervised the Junior Horticulture Show from 1967 until 1983. He proudly says he has never missed a Fair, and the "Wagner name has been in the Fair book since 1947." He said he will "keep on working at the Fair

as long as they'll have me. I'd just as soon sit out there all day! I hate to see the Fair get over."

Matthew Wilson

Director Matthew Wilson says the Petting Zoo at the Fair is known as the best one in the state. "The state FFA officers . . . can't believe our setup." Matt has bragging rights because he works closely with the young men and women from area FFA Chapters who look after the zoo every year.

Matt has been a director on the Fair Board for six years. His participation with the petting zoo dates back to 1979 when he began teaching agriculture at Somonauk High School. Matt, along with other advisors, supervises members of local FFA Chapters who help put up the main stage, set up chairs, tear down after the shows, and pick up the grounds during and after the Fair. The FFA Chapters under Matt's and Joe Steffen's directions have done several landscaping projects at the Fair, which have helped to make the grounds beautiful and appealing to the public.

During the year he also supervises FFA members who help with activities on the grounds that are sponsored by organizations such as the Sandwich Antiques Market, Sandwich Early Days Engine Club, and Silver Springs Car Club.

Good quality family events at the Sandwich Fair have always been important to him. He feels like the fairgrounds is his "second home."

Photo by B.V.

Farm Zoo, Antique Farm Machinery, Horse Shoe Pitching
Front row: Fred Morel, Kenneth Huff, Leota Huff, Bob Miller, Mike Krafft,
Row 2: Matt Wilson, Joe Steffen, Gary Blankenship, David Krafft, Craig Fox,
Not pictured: Kathy Prestegaard

Photo by B.V.

Horticulture
Front row: Joan Curnutte, Diane Wagner Cole, John Wagner, Kristina Wagner, Theresa Wagner Rettig, Nancy Glover,
Row 2: Alma Gavin, Phyllis Benson, Cathy Meyer, Ginger Smith, Kelly Wagner, Kathy Wagner, Alice Graver, John "Bud" Abens,
Row 3: Al Whitehead, Joel File, Lisa Meyer, Becky Gavin, Byron Curnutte, Jeff Wilson, Sheryl Wilson, Not pictured: Bradley Meyer, Wade Meyer, Charles Ecklund, Jeanine Ecklund, Bill Moris, Steve Wolf

Past Presidents

Stephen D. Coleman (1888-1895)—Having spent his early years in Vermont, Coleman came to Illinois in 1856 and started farming north of Somonauk. As a leader he took an active part in the agricultural life of his community. He became a fine example in the farming community by adding many substantial and modern improvements in his fields. He was an early member of a local Mutual Insurance Company. Coleman was born in 1826 and died in 1904.

William Beveridge (1896–1902)—Before moving to Sandwich, Beveridge farmed in the United Presbyterian Church area north of Somonauk for many years. In Sandwich he was active in the grain business and in the manufacturing of carriages. He was a director before being elected president of the Fair board. Beveridge was born in 1853 and died in 1902.

Henry A. Severy (1903–1932)—Severy grew up in the Leland area and became a teacher. After teaching, he started farming and was active in the community. He was an organizer of the Farmers Trust and Savings Bank in Sandwich. Severy was born in 1851 and died in 1952.

Philip S. Lindner (1933–1935)—Lindner was a native of Sheffield, Illinois. He came to Sandwich in 1908 and started a lumberyard business. He was the first board president of the Woodward Memorial Hospital. Lindner was born in 1884 and died in 1935.

M. E. Lake (1936–1945)—Lake moved to Sandwich in 1913 after retiring from farming in the Paw Paw area. He served on the Fair board for 25 years and was in charge of the grounds. He was active in the Sandwich community serving on the cemetery and school boards and as township assessor. He was director of an insurance company. His friends knew him as "Erkie." Lake was born in 1863 and died in 1953.

Charles Howison (1946)–Howison was raised in the Somonauk United Presbyterian Church area. He was an architect and involved with the construction of the old Sandwich High School. As a Fair board member, he was Superintendent of Buildings. He served as a school board member and city alderman. Howison was born in 1872 and died in 1948.

Henry J. White (1947–1961)–White, a native of Somonauk, was a Poland China hog breeder at Maple Lawn Farm. He was a member of the Illinois State Legislature from 1937 to 1947. The governor appointed him business manager of the Illinois State Fair in 1949. He was also active with the DeKalb County Farm Bureau and with the Waterman and Somonauk banks. He was president of the Illinois Association of Agricultural Fairs 1954-1955. White was born in 1887 and died in 1974.

Carlton "Dutch" Hough (1962–1985)–Hough started his involvement with the Fair in 1942 as Assistant Speed Superintendent. He was elected to the Board of Directors three years later and served as vice president. During his tenure Dutch improved the electrical wiring at the Fair as well as designing and building many structures on the grounds. He was president of Illinois Association of Agricultural Fairs in 1960-1961 and received the "State Fair Person-of-the-Year" award from the governor in 1983. Hough was born in 1906 and died in 1988.

Jack Norling (1986–1991)–Norling came to Sandwich as a teacher and taught for 20 years before taking over the insurance business of his late father-in-law Lewis Rex. He was active in church, the Northern Illinois University Foundation Board, DeKalb County Board, Sandwich Township, Lions Club, and Illinois Association of Agricultural Fairs. His first job at the Fair was working at the main gate. Norling was born in 1929 and died in 1991.

Donald Stahl (Interim President 1991–1992)–Stahl is a native of the Sandwich area. He started showing Angus cattle at the Fair in 1935 when he was eleven years old. After high school he started working at the Fair in the livestock department. He has served on the board since 1951. Today, as General Livestock Superintendent, he has introduced new animal shows such as dairy goats, llamas, sheep dog trials, and miniature horses. He has been involved in relocating and construction projects such as the windmill, the livestock office, and drainage. Stahl builds homes in the area. He was born in 1924.

top right: Former Office and Data Manager Audrey Hoffman

bottom right: Current Office and Data Manager Ginger Dannewitz

The Office of the Sandwich Fair Secretary

One of the most significant factors contributing to the tremendous growth of the Sandwich Fair has been the consistent leadership provided by the secretaries of the association. In its 113-year history, only five secretaries have served in this office: Eugene Randall, 1888-1900; Charles Stinson, 1901-1940; C. R. Brady, 1941-1970; Louis P. Brady, 1971-1998; Nancy Lou Rex, 1999-current.

Louis P. Brady, Secretary Emeritus, indicated that as the Fair has grown, the title of "Fair Manager" has been added to the position because the duties in overseeing the year-round operations have become so extensive.

As the twenty-first century begins, the secretary is in charge of editing and distributing the premium books, processing the entries, preparing the premium checks, processing the bills and payroll, and filing reports with the state and federal government. The office also oversees advertising, and oversees the year-round events and care of the fairgrounds.

The advent of the computer has been one of the most significant factors affecting the responsibilities of the secretary especially in the processing of entries and the payment of premiums. Before the days of the computer, a crew of secretarial assistants worked long hours in the back room handwriting names on entry tags and judges' sheets. They recorded information meticulously while they enjoyed a cup of tea or coffee and the conversation of the day. Past employees and volunteers include Lorene Stinson, Doris Delano, Addie Olson, Dorene Wright, Verna Graf, Lucile Kegel, Florence Brandenberger, Gladys Brady, Dorothy Carlson, Frances McMillen, Jeanette Dillon, Doris Buttles,

The Secretary's Office in 1970 at the Fair. (l. to r.) Ellen Brady, Verna Graf, Lucile Kegel

Judy Klessendorf, Ginger Dannewitz, Susan Hough and Lorraine Little.

After the winners were determined, premium statements were filled out for reporting to the state. Lucile Harger Kegel, who worked part-time for 50 years, recalls working at the Secretary's Office at the fairgrounds one cool fall day: "We wrote fair entries with our gloves on and wore boots to keep our feet warm." Lu was 90 years old when she retired after the 1998 season.

"We were lucky if we were finished by Sunday afternoon. Sometimes we were still working on that at 7 p.m. when we were supposed to be paying off the premiums. In the early days our entry volume was considerably lower than it is now," said Secretary Emeritus L. P. Brady.

Today, although the computer streamlines much of the work, a dedicated crew is still needed a few weeks before the Fair. These helpers include Becky Kinney, Irma Grady, Jean Swenson, and Ginny Hann. Ginger Dannewitz, Office and Data Manager, coordinates the work.

Advertising for the Fair continues to be supervised by the Secretary's Office. During Secretary Stinson's term, the directors were each assigned a community where they distributed handbills and window cards to local merchants. Stinson's son William recalled accompanying his father in a horse and buggy distributing advertising to the barber shops and grocery stores of nearby towns. A neighbor of Stinson's recalled handing out advertising on Saturday night before the Fair to the local carriages in the Sandwich business district.

In 1915 Fair Directors and Commercial Club members were encouraged to meet on Thursday, August 26 at 7:30 a.m. to begin a caravan through neighboring towns to "stir up enthusiasm and attract the crowds" to the Fair. The *Free Press* printed the details: "A pathfinder and a pacemaker car" were selected and drivers of other cars drew numbers for places. Forty or fifty cars were expected to participate in the 75- to 80-mile run.

Advertising changed throughout the century as the territorial range of fairgoers was extended. Advertising in the premium books was eliminated because space was needed for the increasing number of entries. Newspaper and radio advertising replaced the counter cards, bumper stickers, farm-fence placards, and posters. The Internet has given publicity unlimited boundaries. Advertising has become so specialized that the Secretary's Office uses a qualified agency to meet today's far-reaching needs.

With scheduled events nearly every weekend May through October, year-round administration of the fairgrounds has become an additional responsibility for the secretary. As the size of the fairgrounds has increased from the original 20 acres in 1888 to the present 170 acres, management responsibilities have increased accordingly. "The grounds are maintained like a park," said L. P. Brady, and the staff has increased to two full-time custodians plus four extra personnel in the summertime. The well-maintained grounds plus the shade provided by the annual planting of trees has attracted a long list of annual events: an antique show six times a year, motorcycle rallies, ham radio festival, bluegrass festival, craft show, etc.

For the future, Secretary Nancy Rex foresees that "the duties and responsibilities of the secretary will necessitate more year-round help either through full- or part-time employees and through special services." The tremendous growth in the business operation of the Fair already requires the help of a bookkeeping service. Today the computer streamlines the process of paying bills, issuing payroll checks, and filling out W-2 forms for over 400 temporary people who are employed during Fair week.

Photo by S.B.

The Fair Office

During the year, directors' meetings and other Fair business are conducted at 121 South Main Street, Sandwich. This has been the office location since 1941 when Secretary C. R. Brady continued the practice of using the secretary's home or business location to conduct Fair business. Prior to that, Secretary Stinson had an office above Newton's Drug Store on Railroad Street, Sandwich.

The Fair office is open every weekday morning except during Fair week. During Fair week business is conducted at the Secretary's Office near Gate # 2 in the middle of the fairgrounds.

The Fair Office has been located at 121 South Main in Sandwich since 1972. From 1941-1972 it was located at 113 South Main.

Photo by V.G.

Before the days of the computer, a crew of secretarial assistants worked long hours in the backroom handwriting names on entry tags and judges sheets. From left clockwise: Jean Swenson, unknown, unknown, Addie Olson, Rachel Datschefski, Doris Delano

Courtesy of SFA

left: Advertising for the 1940 Fair

Sandwich Free Press

Past Secretaries:
Randall, Stinson, Brady, and Brady

Eugene Randall

Randall served as secretary of the Fair Association from 1888 until 1900. In 1888 he was a Sandwich attorney; but shortly thereafter, he went to work for Sandwich Manufacturing Co. In 1900 he became a branch manager for Sandwich Manufacturing Co. in Peoria. Randall passed away in 1920 in Peoria. (No photo available.)

Sandwich Free Press

Charles L. Stinson

Stinson, known as "Charley," served as secretary from 1900 until 1942. He was born in 1863 to a prominent Sandwich family. His father S. B. Stinson was the first lawyer in Sandwich and was the corresponding secretary of the Fair prior to 1888. C. L. Stinson moved to Marseilles and lived there until the death of his father S. B. Stinson. At that time he returned to Sandwich and opened an insurance business in the office his father had occupied.

He was a township clerk and a bank director. He was also an active member of the church, the Masonic Lodge, and the cemetery association. In the early days, the secretary was

paid an annual stipend that could be used to pay hired help. He employed his daughter Lorene. For many years, entries were prepared at his home on his dining room table. He died in 1942.

Courtesy of SFA

Charles R. Brady

Brady was known to many as "C. R." He became secretary in 1942 after serving for three years as Superintendent of Concessions. He moved the fair office to the backroom of 113 South Main Street where he was a partner in the Insurance and Realty office. Many changes took place during his term, including the move to a five-day fair in 1945. The attendance increased substantially and a large number of land parcels were added to the grounds. Brady was a merchant for most of his life having operated the "Brady 9-19 and Up" store from 1927 to 1942. The last years of his life were spent as Supervisor of Assessments of DeKalb County. He died in 1972.

Beacon News

Louis P. Brady

Secretary Emeritus Louis P. Brady, son of C. R. Brady, retired from his role as secretary in 1999 after 26 years. He is known as L. P., Phil, Lou, and Mr. Brady. Even though he is "retired," he continues to come to the Fair office almost every day to answer questions for the new secretary so the transition from past to present will be smooth.

Before becoming secretary, he was Superintendent of Concessions and assistant secretary. His father was his mentor in all three positions. Except for his college days and from 1943 to 1945 when he was in the U.S. Air Force, Brady has attended the Fair every year.

Department Leadership

The Sandwich Fair has a reputation of having some of the best exhibits in Illinois. This success is attributed to providence, smart planning, and dedicated leadership. Not only are the produce and livestock grown in the heart of some of the finest farmland on earth, but since the Fair is held in late summer, most gardens and crops are at their peak for exhibiting. When these two factors are combined with the forum and atmosphere developed by faithful superintendents and their assistants, exhibitors are attracted to the tough competition that has developed at the Sandwich Fair.

Superintendents and their assistants are responsible for setting up the classes and organizing their departments. They hire the workers and judges. They also ready the buildings and display areas for exhibitors. Superintendents in every department are continually updating to accommodate growth in their areas.

Sometimes they address the growth by adding an entirely new category. For example, in the early 1960's microwave cooking was added to the premium list. In 1992 a "Brides" category was added in photography. The Arts and Crafts Department has extended the categories for wearable art such as clothing and accessories.

Sometimes a department completely outgrows its space. When this happens, a new building must be constructed. This was true of horticulture, arts and crafts, photography, and collections. In 1905 a new Horticulture building was constructed to accommodate the bountiful garden exhibits. In 1973 photography, originally located in the Home Arts building, eased into the new Arts and Crafts building, which had been built in 1972. When the Collections Department expanded beyond its boundaries, another new building was constructed in 1997. This growth is also evident in all areas of livestock. Change created by growth and advancement are circumstances that all superintendents must deal with to make their departments convenient for exhibitors and comfortable for fairgoers.

Two general superintendents are in charge of all exhibits. They are Donald Stahl, who is in charge of all livestock entries, and John Wagner, who is in charge of all other entries.

> *Your fair has remained rural and country. It's fun, especially the train and the horticulture and craft buildings. This is really a fair to be proud of.*
>
> Patty Keeley Smith
> Winthrop Harbor, Illinois

LIVESTOCK DEPARTMENT

The current superintendents and their areas are Doug Stahl and Bob Pennington, Open Show Beef Cattle; Bill Coultrip and Mark Tuttle, Open Show Dairy Cattle; Phil Nielsen and Cindy Davidson, Draft Horses; Kenneth Tyrrell and Brad Temple, Open Show Sheep; LaVerne Mattson, Open and Junior Show Dairy Goats; Jeff and Mary Hoyt, Llamas; Dick Delp, Open Show Swine; Larry Hoffman, Junior Show Beef Cattle; Ronald Anderson and Pat McCormick, Junior Show Dairy Cattle; Al Dietz, Junior Show Sheep; Mick Cronin, Junior Show Swine; Brenda Craddock, Rabbits; and Mike Crayton and Jane Banka, Poultry.

Horses

There were two facets to this department for many years: horses entered individually for judging and horses entered in the Department of Speed (also known as harness racing). The Department of Speed is included in the Grounds Entertainment section of this book.

Horse superintendents in 1888 were A. G. Greenman for roadster, carriage, and general- purpose horses and R. 0. Lincoln for draft and Englishire breed. Each breed of horse seemed to have its own superintendent for a few years until Charles W. LaSuer became Horse Stall Superintendent in 1897. He served through 1905 with the exception of 1900 when J. H. Latham was superintendent. In 1906 Thomas Mercer became head of Horse Stalls. Mercer and Latham were heads of the department from 1908 through 1911. Mercer was a lifelong resident who was active in local and county politics. He was Somonauk village president and Sandwich postmaster, and he had a great interest in horses and harness racing. Mercer later became Superintendent of Speed. He retired from the Fair Board at age 82.

By 1916 S. D. Newton was Superintendent of Horse Stalls. Newton, born in the Somonauk area, was active in community affairs. He was a teacher, editor of the *Somonauk Reveille*,

(l. to r.) Douglas R. Stahl and his father Donald Stahl, Director since 1951

Photo by J.A.D.

Ben Eade
Director 1936-1952

Sandwich High School Yearbook 1960

Well-known and well-liked Ben Eade began his leadership role at the Fair in 1933 as Draft Horse Pull Superintendent; he served as a director from 1936 to 1952. In the 1930's he was also Horse and Cattle Superintendent. In the 1940's in addition to Open Show, he was 4-H Club Superintendent. Eade organized the Junior Livestock Show in 1949 with the help of Elmer Henderson.

Eade came to Sandwich High School as the agriculture teacher in 1919. Records show that the U.S. Department of Agriculture paid part of his salary the first year. His first job was to visit local farmers with high-school-age boys and convince them that their sons needed training in farm practices such as finer hogs with large, healthy litters and newer varieties of seed for more profitable grain production. In time, the training he gave produced a consciousness in the area that in turn helped to create friendly, healthy competition at the Fair.

He taught agriculture and biology and later science for over 40 years. This much-respected Fair Superintendent taught several past and present Fair directors. Eade was mentor to long-time Director Don Stahl who clearly remembers helping mix animal feed under Eade's direction in the hallway of the old Sandwich High School in 1939 and 1940. It was a trinity mixture of tankage or meat scraps, soybean meal, and alfalfa meal; it was bagged and sold to area farmers for swine feed.

Past board member Ed Duvick, who was Swine Superintendent in the late 1950's and early 1960's, credits Eade as an influence for his becoming involved with the Sandwich Fair.

Eade retired as a Fair superintendent in 1952 and retired from teaching in 1962 after 43 years of influencing many students and Fair exhibitors.

partner in the local monument business, Sandwich alderman, and mayor. C. Sherm Bark, well-known resident and longtime Fair Board director, followed him. In later years Bark was superintendent of other livestock entries.

In 1937 Horse Superintendents were A. C. Baie and Ben Eade. Together they headed this area for a few years, Baie working with draft horses until his death in 1944, and Eade assisting draft horses and heading beef cattle.

James Wiley followed Baie and Eade as department head in mid 1940's. By 1946, however, the number of horse entries had declined; therefore, they were no longer listed in the premium book. A Society Horse Show with a wide range of entry choices replaced single horse entries. Superintendents Walt Nelson and Latham Castle continued these into the early 1950's. Nelson was a local car dealer; Castle, a Sandwich native, was an attorney, Chairman of the Board of Sandwich State Bank, and later County Judge and Illinois Attorney General. By 1952 traditional horse shows were no longer held.

In 1987 miniature horses 34 inches and under appeared at the Fair in a Sunday horse show under the guidance of Joye Gommel. They continued through 1989.

Draft horses, after a 45-year absence, reappeared at the 1993 Fair with Oswego veterinarian Dr. Howard Koch as Superintendent and Cindy Davidson as assistant. In 1995 current Superintendent Phil Nielsen took over; Davidson assists him. Today, draft horses are at the Fair on Friday and have competition in halter class, hitches, and draft-pony hitches.

Cattle

In 1888 all cattle were under the supervision of W. H. Toombs. He continued as superintendent into mid 1890's although he was not the sole department head. Those listed in 1895 were each in charge of a different breed of cattle: T. H. Robinson, Charles Patten, I. M. Hay, M. Knight, Frank Seeley, Charles Dewey, and Louis Rohrer.

By 1897 John H. Latham was sole superintendent of cattle and sheep. Some years, he was active in the horse and swine departments as well. Latham was born north of Sandwich on the family homestead, and in adulthood he was a partner in a local hardware store and active in several community organizations.

In 1901 Pernett Potter joined Latham as head of Cattle/Sheep/Swine Departments and went on to become combined superintendent of those departments. A Sandwich native, Potter held this position until about 1920 when S. D. Newton joined him to head the departments.

By 1927 Henry White of Somonauk was superintendent. C. Sherm Bark joined White in 1933; Ben Eade and A. C. Baie joined him by 1936. In the late 1930's and early 1940's Bark was Cattle/Sheep Superintendent and was assisted by Eade, who became Cattle Superintendent in 1944. He also headed dairy cattle in 1946 and 1947 and continued as head of beef cattle until the early 1950's when Don Stahl became superintendent. Stahl worked in beef cattle with Don Ogilvie and LeRoy Suppes.

In 1962 Spencer Gord was head of beef cattle. Gord was a farmer, coming to the Sandwich area from Leland in 1933. He was superintendent until his death in 1972. At that time Charles Waechter took over and was assisted by Doug Stahl. Waechter and Stahl worked together with beef cattle until 1989 when Stahl became superintendent and Bob Pennington his assistant. Stahl is a self-employed contractor with his father Don.

Doug Knights supervised the Dairy Cattle Department from 1948 through 1965. Knights was a local farmer, recognized horticulturist, and hybrid rose grower who exhibited his produce at the Fair. In 1966 Franklin Mall became Dairy Superintendent. Mall is remembered for his Christmas project now sponsored by the Sandwich Lions Club and for his 39 years with a local dairy. After assisting Mall for several years, Somonauk farmer G. W. "Gus" Grandgeorge assumed the Dairy Superintendent position in 1980 and served until 1990. During that time it was common for Open Show to have over 200 head of dairy cattle entered.

The present Dairy Superintendent William Coultrip took over in 1991 after assisting Grandgeorge for a number of years. Mark Tuttle assists Coultrip.

Junior Fair Beef Cattle

In 1956 Junior Fair beef entries were given their own superintendent. Donald Ogilvie was Junior Beef Superintendent for a short time, followed by James Herrman; Warner White, Ogilvie again, this time sharing the responsibilities with Dale Rogers; Milford Clausen; and in

1963 Clarion Clausen. Clarion was head of beef until 1971 when his brother Milford again took charge. Larry Hoffman followed in 1973 and has continued to the present time as Junior Beef Superintendent.

Junior Fair Dairy Cattle

The first Junior Fair Dairy Superintendents in 1956 were James Herrman and Al Linden. In 1958 Linden became superintendent, and in 1962 Bob Anderson took over the position. The following year Ron Anderson shared the responsibilities. The Anderson brothers worked together in this department nearly three decades. In 1991 Bob retired. Ron is the current Superintendent; Pat McCormick has been his assistant since 1993.

Sheep

The Sheep Superintendent at the 1888 Fair was Philo Slater. He supervised seven classes of sheep. Premiums were given for fine, middle, and long grades of wool. Superintendents following Slater were J. P. Washburn, Charles Scoggin, and Walter Finnie. In the late 1890's, sheep was combined with cattle then swine with one superintendent.

In 1900, the year a new sheep barn was built, L. Hubbard headed the department. At that time directors had a number of responsibilities; Hubbard was also co-chairman of the Finance Committee. Following Hubbard was P. H. Potter and S. D. Newton. In 1927 Henry White was head of sheep, and by 1937 C. Sherm Bark had taken over. Bark was head of the Sheep Department until 1947.

In 1948 Elmer Henderson took over; after working with Henderson several years, Wilbur Dienst became superintendent in 1958. Leland farmer Norman Wesson was Sheep Superintendent in 1962, followed by Don Miller in 1963 and Wiley Updike in 1967. Updike was department head until 1987 when current Sheep Superintendent

Photo by J.A.D.

Kenneth Tyrrell took over. Brad Temple became Tyrrell's assistant in 1999. Sheep entries have increased consistently.

Junior Fair Sheep

Superintendents of Junior Fair Sheep since 1956 have been Elmer Henderson, Wilbur Dienst, Norman Wesson, Jack Smith and Al McCowen. In 1965 David and Nancy Birch became head of junior sheep. The Birches were the heads of the Junior Fair Sheep through 1979. Don Stahl took over for a year, and in 198 John Guehler was superintendent. Ruth Ann Guehler and later Jean Guehler Fabrizius assisted him. John and Jean were in charge until Al Dietz took over in 1991. Dietz is the current superintendent.

Swine

Edwin Fraser was Superintendent of Swine in 1888 and A. Lange by 1893 to 1896. Swine was not included in the 1897 premium book; by 1900 it was combined with cattle and sheep and L. Hubbard served as the superintendent. In 1901 P. H. Potter took over and continued in that position for several years, some years with the help of John Latham.

In 1916 S. D. Newton joined him, and by 1925 Newton had taken over as department head with cattle/sheep/swine still combined with one superintendent. Henry White was the combined superintendent in 1927 and by 1933 was assisted by C. Sherm Bark. The Swine Department was separated from cattle and sheep in 1937. White remained department head until 1962. Elmer Henderson assisted him in 1947 and LeRoy Suppes from 1948 to 1954. Suppes and LaVerne "Dutch" Johnson were in charge from 1955 to 1957. Johnson was a native of Sandwich though the Johnson family farmed and raised hogs in the DeKalb area.

White returned as superintendent in 1958 with the help of Orland McAllister and from 1959 to 1961 with Ed Duvick. Duvick took over as

I love the Sandwich Fair because it's the only fair left that still has the charm and fun and charisma of an old fashion county fair. We come every year and enjoy it more and more.

Lorraine Stewart
Streamwood, Illinois

Swine Superintendent in 1962 and held that position until Bob Guehler of Somonauk became superintendent in 1966. Guehler says he and other livestock superintendents focused their attention on keeping the traditional county fair atmosphere.

Guehler says the biggest challenge he faced was preventing the livestock exhibits from being overrun by professionals. Competition was intended for local amateur breeders. He says that while competition remained about the same while he was superintendent, the number of exhibitors steadily increased, necessitating a bit of shifting and expanding. In 1977 Richard Delp was named his assistant in the Swine department. Guehler retired after the 1994 Fair, and Delp was named head of Swine; he is the current superintendent.

Junior Fair Swine

Robert Howey and T. W. Anderson were Junior Fair Swine Superintendents in 1956. Ed Duvick joined them in 1960. In 1961 Duvick was superintendent; Andy Krafft was the assistant. Jack Suddeth, who started as department head in 1963, held that position until Kenneth Tyrrell took over in 1975. Tyrrell served until 1987 when J. M. "Mick" Cronin took over.

Poultry

Poultry entries were numerous as early as the 1888 Fair under the supervision of George Keene. William Fraser started his long span as Poultry Superintendent in 1889. About 1900 while Fraser was in charge, the poultry house was cut in half and an addition inserted between the ends. By 1937 the poultry coops were usually all occupied. Fraser retired as Poultry Superintendent in 1940 at the age of 83 after serving 50 years in the position.

At one time there were as many as 600 exhibits. Later, out-of-county entries were limited to ten varieties, reducing the number of exhibits to a more manageable size. In 1941

Frank Skinner became head of poultry. There were no poultry entries in 1946 and 1947 because of a ruling from the Department of Agriculture regarding poultry disease.

Poultry returned in 1948 headed by Skinner. James Duvick was superintendent in 1949. However, poultry was short lived. The premium book shows that it was absent from the Fair from 1950-1966. In 1967 poultry and rabbits were again departments at the Fair, headed by Lyle Troeger and assisted by Charles "Cub" Mall. This team continued until 1984 when Michael Crayton was named Troeger's assistant in the poultry department. Crayton has been Superintendent since 1985. His assistants have been Bob Carothers and Janie Allen. Presently his assistant is Jerry Hartel. Poultry exhibits may be seen in the horse barn near the livestock gate during the Fair, as the horses are removed from the barn at Fair time.

William S. Fraser
Poultry Superintendent 1889-1940

Superintendent of Poultry William S. Fraser was recognized for fifty years of service in 1937. During that time he was absent only once because of illness. He was also an active Fair Board member for 50 years until he resigned in 1937. During his time, there was enormous growth in his department. At first a small poultry house was used; then, around 1902 it was cut in half and an addition was built between the two halves. This expansion was necessary because in the days of the traveling exhibitors, as many as 600 chickens needed exhibiting space at the Fair.

Fraser was born on April 1, 1854, to William and Mary Fraser in a log house three miles north of Sandwich, one of thirteen children. As a youth he was a top-ranking athlete. Although his education was limited, he had a keen and receptive mind. He acquired knowledge that gave him much poise and dignity in his adult years. He had a good sense of humor and was well known and well liked throughout the community. He died at age 90 at the home of his daughter Mrs. Ethyl Franklin.

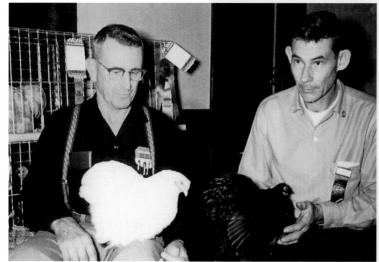

Rabbits

Rabbits were exhibited in mid 1920's and referred to as hares until mid 1930's. They were listed with the poultry department. In 1941 William Fraser was poultry and rabbit superintendent. He was followed by Frank Skinner and in 1949 by James Duvick. Rabbits continued under their leadership, but by 1951 rabbits were not listed in the premium book.

In 1967 they were again exhibited at the Fair and listed along with poultry under the supervision of Lyle Troeger and Charles "Cub" Mall. However, again in 1980, they disappeared from the entry lists. Rabbits returned in 1995 with both fancy and commercial classes. This department continues to flourish with Superintendent Brenda Craddock's leadership.

Goats

The Open Dairy Goat show began in 1980 with LaVerne Mattson as superintendent. The Junior Show Dairy Goats also started in 1980 with Steve Miller as superintendent through 1984. Since 1985 Mattson has been both Open and Junior Show Dairy Goats Superintendent.

Llamas

Llamas are the "new kids on the block" to be entered for competition at the Fair. Open Show llamas were added in 1987 with Donna Ricci as superintendent. Her assistant was Leslie Friedrich. They were in charge until 1997.

center: (l. to r.) Lyle Troeger and Charles "Cub" Mall

Courtesy of SFA

Louis Wagner
Fruits, Vegetables, and Grain Superintendent
1947-1984

Louis Wagner, described by an area journalist as the "genial superintendent of the horticultural display," was a hard-working dairy farmer. He was not a very big man, but he made a big difference in the Horticulture Department.

Wagner accepted the superintendent's position in 1947. He was in charge of the Horticulture and Home Arts buildings and before his retirement, the Arts and Crafts building. In 1948 he started the first hybrid corn show with eight hybrid companies participating. Three of the original exhibitors still had entries in the 1998 Fair: DeKalb, Pioneer, and Pfister. In 1958 herbs and bundle grains were added. That same year, Louis and his wife Berdeane began the custom of putting up a map on which fair visitors pinpointed their hometowns.

Courtesy of SFA

SANDWICH FAIR VISITORS OF 1987 CAME FROM 43 STATES AND 41 FOREIGN COUNTRIES

on this map place a pin in

Since 1958 the map in the Horticulture building has been used to pinpoint fairgoers' hometowns.

Louis also increased the number of categories in the premium book. He once said that C. R. [Brady] hit the roof when he presented all the additions to the premium list, but Brady went along with his ideas. Wagner resigned his position in 1983 and was succeeded by his son John. He said, "I think I've been at it long enough, so this is my last year. I hope they'll let me retire."

In a July 1, 1987, news release published in the *Mid-Week*, Fair Association Past-President Carlton "Dutch" Hough recognizes Louis's contribution to the Fair: "Our fair really didn't start to grow until about 35 years ago when Louis Wagner became interested in making our exhibits the best in the state." He "created the atmosphere in the exhibit buildings that left people thunderstruck when they entered because it was such a beautiful sight."

Appearance was important to Louis. After all the entries had been checked in and judged, with the help of his family and department workers, he stayed through the night arranging and rearranging the displays.

Louis also served as a director from 1955-1985. While on the board, he was vice president from 1962-1984.

These unique animals continue to interest fairgoers. They are at the Fair for one day only—Saturday. The current superintendent is Jeff Hoyt who is assisted by Mary Hoyt.

4-H Club Fair and Junior Fair Livestock

A forerunner to the Junior Shows at the Fair was the 4-H Club shows that were supervised by Ben Eade. The 4-H shows ceased in 1948; the Junior Fair started in 1949 with Eade and Elmer Henderson as Superintendents of Livestock. The livestock classes were steers, beef and dairy heifers, sheep, and hogs. No stall fees or entrance money was charged in 1949.

Eade and Henderson were superintendents of the Saturday and Sunday shows for two years; then Don Stahl replaced Henderson. By 1953 Stahl was the superintendent. In 1954 LaVerne Johnson started working in the Junior Fair with Stahl. In 1956 Johnson and Henderson worked together as Junior Fair General Livestock Superintendents. Beef, dairy, sheep, and hogs each began with their own department heads.

Henderson remained two more years as Livestock Superintendent until Ed Duvick took over in 1961. In 1963 Milford Clausen was department head; he was in this position until 1973 when Junior Livestock Superintendent was no longer listed in the premium books. The Junior Livestock Show is held on Saturday and Sunday of the Fair.

Junior Fair Livestock Sale

The first record of a Junior Livestock sale was in 1971 with Gene Darfler and Buck Nesson as superintendents. Jerry Davis replaced Nesson by 1973, and by 1977 Darfler was no longer helping with the sale. Davis was superintendent through 1982. In 1983 Joye Gommel took over the position. After 1985 the junior sale was not listed.

HORTICULTURE DEPARTMENT

Superintendents and their areas are John and Kathy Wagner, Open Show Plants and Flowers, also Open Show Grains, Fruits and Vegetables; Jeff Wilson, Junior Show Grains, Fruits and Vegetables; and Cathy Meyer and Lisa Meyer, Junior Show Plants and Flowers.

For the first Fair in 1888, David Harmon was Superintendent of Grains and Vegetables. The Fruit Superintendent was Jacob Budd, and Flower Superintendent was Lottie Logan. In 1893 Miss Minnie Kennedy was Plants and Flowers Superintendent. In mid 1890's, Mrs. James Castle was listed in charge of flowers. Dan Knight, then Thomas Mercer was in charge of grain, grass, seeds, and vegetables. George Kleinsmid, C. M. Yearley, and Thomas Mercer were Fruit Superintendents respectively.

In 1900 D. K. Crofoot became Superintendent of the Horticulture building. He supervised the grain, vegetable, fruit, cooking, baking, sewing and flower departments. Dwight Crofoot was an early organizer and promoter of the Fair. He also was a partner in a Sandwich dry goods, shoe and boot business. After his death in 1905, George McDonald served until 1918 when tall and lanky Charles Howison started his term that spanned three decades, 1918 to 1947. Howison was an architect and native of the United Presbyterian Church area. He was a 20-year member of Sandwich High School Board of Education and an alderman on the city council.

After the war many changes took place. In the Horticulture Department, Louis Wagner became Superintendent of Fruits, Vegetables and Grain in 1947, taking over from Charles Howison. Frances Toombs took over the floral displays in 1948. Toombs and her husband owned and operated a local flower shop. As a team Toombs and Wagner helped give the department the notable reputation it has today. In 1982 Ramona Butler assumed Toomb's responsibilities. In 1988 Susan Cromwell, who had helped for five years, became Open Show Flower Superintendent. She held the position until 1998 when Kathy Wagner, Ginger Wagner Smith, and Nancy Glover became the assistants to John Wagner.

The Wagner family has been actively involved in the Horticulture Department since 1947 when Louis became building super-intendent. Berdeane Wagner worked beside her husband, and their son John started helping when he was very young. John became building superintendent in 1984 when his father retired.

The Wagners expanded the categories for exhibitors. They started the bundled grain and herb shows and organized the displays for attractiveness and uniformity. In 1980 John added one of the most popular exhibits—the decorated pumpkins—to the Junior Fair entries.

Frances Toombs
Floral Superintendent 1948-1981

Courtesy of F.T.

Frances "Fran" Toombs and her husband Jack owned a floral shop in town. They exhibited in the Industrial Hall. Fran says, "Going in the south door, we were just to the right."

Fran remembers, "In 1949 C. R. Brady asked if I would take over the flower show. It was 1951 when I actually started." Looking back on her term as superintendent, Toombs says, "Those 30 years were the most pleasant years of civic work I've ever done. I loved the flowers and the people."

"The first year we had so few entries; we brought flowers from our shop to help fill up the pyramid. Louie [Wagner] brought in the model windmill that graced the top for several years." Fran, along with Mrs. Louis Wagner and friends, made beautiful wreaths for the entrance and seasonal decorations for the walls.

In an effort to build up the show, Fran encouraged her friends and even customers to bring their flowers to the Fair. Before her retirement, the shelves of the circular pyramid in the center of the room, overflowed with arrangements.

The camaraderie was strong between the superintendents and the volunteers. The crew has fond memories of a customary potluck held on Sunday night after the building was emptied and the flower vases were all washed. "I always managed to have good help. In fact, Ramona Butler had helped me so many years, it was a very smooth transition when she took over."

Courtesy of M.C.

Millie Carter
Needlework Superintendent 1960–1995

Millie (Watt) Carter, Sandwich, was active at the Fair long before she became a superintendent. She remembers "hanging out" in the Federated Church food stand while her mother worked, and she also exhibited as a young girl. Later she entered carved and tooled leather, etched aluminum and other craft items, and needlework projects.

In 1954 Needlework Superintendent Pauline Newton asked Millie if she would help her at the Fair. She accepted and worked with Pauline until her retirement in 1960; then Millie became Needlework Superintendent. In an interview in December 1999, Millie talked about her job as department supervisor. She said, "I never had the fair out of my mind. You had to keep thinking where you wanted to change this and that . . . ." Throughout the years, she has been involved in planning for better use of display space, one of her ideas being the slanted shelves used in the Home Arts building.

Like the families of other superintendents, Millie's family has been very supportive. She says her children have been helping "from the time they could breathe." She also relied on the help of her friends. She jokes, "If you knew me five minutes, I got you working."

Even though Millie retired a few years ago as superintendent, she stays busy at Fair time. Each morning she unlocks and helps tidy up the inside of the Home Arts building. She says she likes to remove the first layer of dust to make it easier to get the glass cases clean.

During the Fair she enjoys "the entries in the Arts and Craft building and in the Home Arts building; I don't seem to go any other place. I also like seeing the people, especially the ones I only see once a year." Millie also has a "Sunday job" at the Fair; she helps her son Doug and daughter-in-law Nancy with the Antique Auto Show.

Millie is still an active exhibitor. In 1989 she started painting and has won many ribbons in the last few years with her watercolors. Her favorite subjects are barns, covered bridges, mills, and lighthouses.

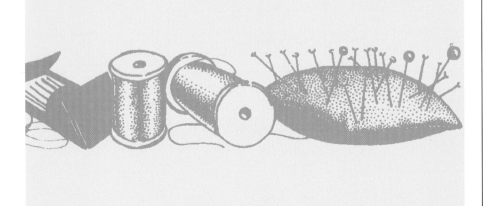

For the 100th fair in 1987, he returned some heirloom vegetables to the premium book. John's wife Kathy, their children, and now their grandchildren are all involved in the Horticulture Department.

Junior Fair Grains, Seeds, and Vegetables

There have been very few superintendents for the horticulture Junior Fair since its beginning. In 1949 Louis Wagner was named the first Junior Fair Grain, Seed and Vegetable Superintendent. It was a Saturday and Sunday show until 1957 when an addition was added to the east side of the Horticulture building. The show then expanded to five days.

In 1967 John Wagner became Junior Fair Superintendent and continued through 1983. Byron Curnutte filled the position from 1984 to 2000 assisted by Kathy Wagner through 1991 and assisted by Jeff Wilson beginning in 1992. Wilson became the department head of Junior Fair Grains, Seeds, Forages, Vegetables and Fruit in 2000 following Curnutte's death.

Junior Fair Plants and Flowers

Also in the east addition to the Horticulture building are the Junior Fair Plants and Flower entries. This department began in 1949 with Frances Toombs as superintendent. She continued in that position for 31 years. In 1982 Joan Curnutte took over for Toombs and was superintendent through 1999. Cathy Meyer assisted Curnutte through 1987. Meyer is the current Junior Fair Plants and Flowers Superintendent; Lisa Meyer assists her.

HOME ARTS DEPARTMENT

The current superintendents and their areas are Renee, Pam, Penny, and Karen Monkemeyer, Open and Junior Show Foods, and Junior Show Home Economics; and Donna Leonard and Pat Redden, Open Show Needlework.

Items now exhibited in the Home Arts building were once included in other exhibit buildings. As early as the 1888 Fair, kitchen, dairy and pantry entries headed by Superintendent Mrs. E. Coleman and needlework headed by Mrs. G. Walter were with grain, vegetable, fruit, and

Photo by J.A.D.

flower departments in Floral Hall.

By 1893 Mrs. James Howison was Superintendent of Kitchen, Dairy and Pantry; she was followed by Mrs. Edwin Wright and later by Mrs. M. Nathan as Superintendents of Needlework, Household Fabrics and Manufactures. In 1897 local dry goods merchant D. K. "Dwight" Crofoot was named Superintendent of Floral Hall. George McDonald followed him in 1905. By then the food and needlework entries were located in the new Horticulture building. McDonald served until Charles Howison took over in 1918. Howison retired in 1947.

In 1948 the Kitchen, Pantry and Dairy Departments moved from the Horticulture building to the Industrial Arts building (a.k.a. Home Arts). Needlework had already made the move to the building that was under the supervision of Pauline Newton and Lila Belden. Many people in the area remember Pauline and her dog Skipper; until her retirement in 1960, both were familiar sights at the Fair. Newton helped start the Sandwich Public Library and was librarian for forty years, retiring in 1966.

In 1954 Millie Carter started working with Newton in the needlework exhibits. Upon Newton's retirement in 1960, Carter became Superintendent of Open Show Needlework. Carter was an exhibitor for a number of years and still has the stuffed animal she entered as a girl in 1928 when it won a blue ribbon. Later she entered a variety of crafts. Today she enters watercolor paintings, one of her hobbies since 1989. After working with Carter for a number of years, Donna Leonard succeeded her as superintendent in 1996. Carter still works in that area at Fair time. Pat Redden assists Leonard.

Today the building is shared with Open and Junior Show food entries under the direction of Superintendent Renee Monkemeyer. In 1953 Louis Wagner asked Renee Doderlein (nee) to help with the Food Department in the Home

Arts building. She accepted and became the superintendent in 1955 when Nan Jean Beck resigned after being superintendent from 1952 to 1954. The Fair became part of her family as she married and had three sons. Today they all help, including her six grandchildren. There is a job for everyone; the smaller girls climb into the display cases to wash the glass on the inside. Monkemeyer's goal is to be superintendent for fifty years; then her sons and daughter can take over her job. Monkemeyer is also superintendent of Junior Show Needlework and Clothing entries. Daughters-in-law Pam, Penny, and Karen Monkemeyer assist her.

Monkemeyer has seen multiple changes in her department. One of the most dramatic was extending the Open and Junior Shows through Sunday. At one time she shared the Home Arts building with Arts, Crafts and Photography. It was a big change when those departments moved into their own building. Monkemeyer notices that there are families of exhibitors. She says it isn't unusual to see girls exhibiting in the Junior Department today whose mothers started out there; also there are more entries from boys and men, especially in foods.

Junior Fair Home Economics

Junior Fair Home Economics included clothing and foods. Helen Ogilvie was the first superintendent in 1949. By 1952 Ruth Gerlick had taken over the department, and in 1955 Renee Monkemeyer joined Gerlick. Monkemeyer was named Junior Fair Home Economics Superintendent in 1956 and still holds that position. Pam and Penny Monkemeyer joined her in 1994; Karen Monkemeyer in 2000.

PHOTOGRAPHY DEPARTMENT

Current superintendents and their areas are Becky Morphey and Jodi Brummel, Open and Junior Show Amateur Photography.

Photography leadership in 1888 was Mrs. Frank Barnes, assisted by Mrs. Cora West in charge of painting and photographing. The next

left: (l. to r.) Pat Redden and Donna Leonard

Photo by B.V.

Home Arts
Front row: Carrie Dew, Penny Monkemeyer, Renee Monkemeyer, Pam Monkemeyer, Shelia Perkins, Row 2: Louis Thurow, Marge Thurow, Sheila Summerson, Becky Rosenwinkel, Brian Monkemeyer, Row 3: Bruce Monkemeyer, Karen Monkemeyer, Not pictured: Bob Monkemeyer, Judy and Dave Klussendorf, Kathy Augsburg, Kris and Claire Swenson, Lyn Smith, Beth Thanepohn, Kris Larson

Photo by B.V.

**Open & Jr. Photography,
Open & Jr. Ceramics, Jr. Art**
Front row: Rosemary Wiley, Debbie Vaughn, Jackie Morphey, Laura Winebaugh, Joanne Johnson, Row 2: Rick Shaw, Chris Wahlgren, Becky Morphey, Bonnie Sharp, Betty Hargraves, Row 3: Jodie Brummel, Row 4: Rick Morphey, Howard Rosenwinkel, Justin Brummel, Gary Brummel, Bill Johnson, Not pictured: Jill Stege, Dale Stege, Doug Stahl, Linda Stahl, Brian Ruddy, Stephanie Wayne, Terry Voga

Photo by B.V.

Arts and Crafts
Front row: Beverly Vilmin, Lorraine Carlson, Magdalene Haas, Ruth Nelson, Carol Pruski, Row 2: Peggy Gilbertson, Lois Ronning, Paula Moore, Mike Pruski, Row 3: Albert Carlson, Rita Ferguson, Jan Miernicki, Chris Butler, Nancy Butler, Pam Nelson, Not pictured: Kathy Barry, Margie Butler, Joan Hardekopf, Hellen Hill, Mary Ellen Huss, Tim Huss, Sue Huss, Ryan Kellogg, Margaret Knutson, Gary Moss, Lori Nelson, Marcia Nelson, Diane Stahl, Tom Stejskal, Kim Nilles

available records in 1893 show Miss Lizzie Abbott was superintendent and by mid 1890's Mrs. Kate Smith, followed by Mrs. R. C. Cook. By 1897 D. K. Crofoot was in charge of all Floral Hall exhibits, the building where this department was located. Following him was George McDonald then Charles Howison. For a time in the 1920's and the early 1930's, photographs were not listed. It was not until 1947 that photography appeared again in premium books and was listed with paintings.

In 1948 when Pauline Newton was Photography Superintendent, the department title was changed to Art and Photography. Virginia Bark became superintendent in 1949 and served through 1956 when Helen Slauf took over for the next two years. Mrs. Otis Ivie followed in 1959. Harlan Walley was in charge until Renee Monkemeyer became superintendent in 1962 until 1971. Starting in 1972 Marilyn Popp served as superintendent until her death in 1985. Karen Monkemeyer then took over. In 1992 when she moved away, her assistant Becky Morphey became superintendent with Jodi Brummel as her assistant. Morphey and Brummel handle the Open and Junior Photography Shows. They have had to deal with the growing number of exhibits in their department as well as the possibility of changing rules to compensate for new methods of photography. Superintendent Morphey says, "The Fair gets in your blood. Even though by the end of the Fair, you don't want to think about it, by the next year you are excited once again it is here."

Junior Fair Photography

This department started in 1950 with Pauline Newton and Virginia Bark as superintendents of the Art and Photography Department. In 1956 Bark was superintendent when the department name changed to Photography and Hobbies. Following Bark was Helen Slauf in 1957 and Harlan Walley in the early 1960's.

By 1964 Renee Monkemeyer was in charge of photography along with food and clothing, and in 1972 Marilyn Popp became Junior Fair Photography Superintendent. Popp was department head until her death in 1985. At that time Karen Monkemeyer took over until she moved away in 1992.

Becky Morphey was the new superintendent in 1992; her assistant was Jodi Brummel. They are the current Junior Fair Photography Department heads.

EDUCATION DEPARTMENT

Current superintendent: Nancy Lou Rex
In 1888 this department was called Educational, Natural History and Musical Instruments and was headed by Henry Hess. By 1893 Professor W. W. Wirt was in charge followed by Professor Hubbard in 1895 and Professor Cross in 1896.

Entries in 1888 covered map drawings, penmanship, composition, collections of minerals and fossils, taxidermy or birds, manufactured marble and stone, pianos, reed organs, and best display of manufactured upholstery goods, and household furniture.

In 1903 the department name changed to Educational, Natural History; it changed again in 1931 to Educational and again in 1946 to Education Department. Education superintendents were not always listed in the premium books even though the department existed. At one time educator and school administrator L. G. Haskin headed it. From 1950 to 1964, local teacher Agnes Stahl was in charge. Plano educator James C. Goodie followed her in 1965. From 1966 to 1994, no Education Department existed. In 1994 the description of this department changed when the current department head Nancy Rex took over the duties. Today the department's focus is school groups that visit the Fair.

Industrial Arts

From 1950 until 1965, there was an Industrial Arts Department headed by local Industrial Arts teacher David Graf. After Graf,

Louis Wagner took over in 1966 until 1971 when Industrial Arts became part of the Arts and Crafts Department. For a time from 1967 until 1971, there was also a Woodworking and Handicrafts Department headed by Louis Wagner. That also became part of the Arts and Crafts Department in 1972 when the new Arts and Crafts building opened.

ARTS AND CRAFTS DEPARTMENT

Current superintendents and their areas are Ruth Nelson and Pam Nelson, Open Show Art; Ruth Nelson, Pam Nelson, Margi Butler and Jan Miernicki, Open Show Crafts; Ruth Nelson, Mary Ellen Huss, Diane Stahl, Junior Show Crafts; Becky Morphey and Joanne Johnson, Junior Show Art and Ceramics; Becky Morphey, Ceramics.

In 1972 a new Arts and Crafts building opened to accommodate the increasing number of exhibits. Ruth Nelson, who had worked at the Fair since 1960 in the Home Arts building, became building superintendent. Cheryl Hearn assisted her in Art from 1988 to 1994 and Julia Baker in Crafts from 1992 to 1996. Her responsibilities included over 600 exhibiting categories in Open and Junior Arts and Crafts. Nelson has continued as Arts and Crafts Superintendent and is assisted by Pam Nelson, Margi Butler and Jan Miernicki in Open Show entries.

Junior Fair Arts and Crafts

Junior Fair Art started in 1950 with photography. Pauline Newton and Virginia Bark supervised it. From 1956 to 1960 no Junior Art was listed in the premium book. Junior Fair Arts and Crafts appeared in the premium book again in 1961 under Millie Carter's leadership in the Home Arts building. Carter was superintendent until the exhibits moved to the newly opened Arts and Crafts building in 1972. At that time Ruth Nelson was head of Open and Junior Fair Arts and Crafts.

In 1978 because the number of exhibits had grown, Art was separated from Crafts. Rachel Schmidt was named Junior Art Superintendent and was in that position until 1994. Joanne Johnson became her assistant in 1992. Schmidt retired in 1995. Jane Jacobson then joined Johnson as a Junior Art Superintendent. Jacobson resigned in 1997, and Becky Morphey

became superintendent; Johnson is her assistant. In 1998 the department was changed to Art and Ceramics.

Junior Fair Arts and Crafts was headed by Ruth Nelson through 1999. In 2000 Ruth stepped aside to become assistant with Diane Stahl. Mary Ellen Huss, who had been helping since 1986, became Junior Fair Craft Superintendent.

COLLECTIONS DEPARTMENT

The current superintendents are John Wagner assisted by Bess Moss and Mary Lou Moris.

In addition to Arts and Crafts, Ruth Nelson supervised 74 categories of collections until 1973 and again in 1977. From 1973 to 1976 Alberta Barker was Collections Superintendent. Rachel Schmidt was appointed superintendent in 1978 and served until she retired in 1995. Schmidt was also head of Open Ceramics and Junior Art; Juanita Anderson assisted her. After Schmidt's retirement, Jane Jacobsen served as superintendent until her resignation in 1998. John Wagner is the current Superintendent of Collections, assisted by Bess Moss and Mary Lou Moris.

Photo by B.V.

Collections, Craft Demonstrations
Front row: Bess Moss, Pauline Moris, Ardath Fritsch, Row 2: John Wagner, Eileen Weber, Barb French, Joyce Tyrrell, Mary Lou Moris, Row 3: Wilma Simms, Ron Adrian, Joanne Adrian, Judy Larson, Martha Sampson, Don Sampson, Alonzo (Bud) Burgin, Not pictured: Linda Floyd, Edie Weeks, Pamela Miles, Duane Miles, Ralph Wallis, Dorothy Benjamin

OPERATIONS DEPARTMENT

The current superintendents and their areas are Donald and Dan Bark, Concessions and Displays; Nancy Lou Rex, John Hallaron, and Roy Wahlgren, Ticket Sales; Ginger Dannewitz, Office and Data Manager; Jim Webber, Caretaker; Andy Krafft, Assistant Caretaker; Harold Dannewitz and Reed Johnson, Electricians; Scott Breunig and William Haag, Parking and Police; Karen Breunig and Cheryl Augustine, Information and Souvenirs; and Barbara Hoffman, First Aid.

Concessions and Displays

This department evolved from the original

Armand "Doc" Legner, DVM
Director 1961-1981

Veterinarian Armand Legner, DVM was almost a legend at the Sandwich Fair and in the surrounding community. He began veterinary practice in Sandwich in 1937. He founded the Sandwich Veterinary Hospital in 1957, operating it until his retirement in 1983. In the 1940's Henry White, President of the Fair Association, asked him to check the health papers of the livestock. He made sure the cattle, hogs, and sheep were free of disease before entering the shows. He served on the Fair Board of Directors from 1961 to 1981.

He held two jobs: veterinarian for the Fair and Superintendent of Parking and Police for the west end from 1967 to 1979. Doc, as he was fondly known, continued to check the health papers for the growing numbers of livestock entries in both the Open and Junior Shows until 1994.

In a newspaper interview, Doc cited three reasons for the Sandwich Fair's success: dedication, volunteers, and the independence the board gives to the superintendents to govern their respective areas. Doc Legner had a special quality of caring for his fellowman wherever he was. He always made individuals feel special and needed. Those who knew him gained from his example. In the fullness of life, he found simplicity. In day-to-day life, he found enjoyment.

(l. to r.) Kenneth Klotz, Robert Reid of Reid's Entertainments, Louis P. Brady in front of the Concession Office.

top right: Donald Bark, Director since 1978

Privileges Department that was supervised by A. Gage as early as the 1893 Fair. In 1899 F. A. Pratt held the position alone until 1916. The September 15, 1904, Sandwich *Free Press* reported, "Fred Pratt is doing his best to make the fair a success and is one of the busiest men on the grounds. With a chart in one hand, a receipt book and pencil in the other and his pockets groaning because of the weight of money, he has filled the Midway space to overflowing."

P. S. Lindner joined Pratt in 1916. They worked together for several years. By the early 1920's, Lindner was superintendent; he served until mid 1930's.

A. O. Fosse followed in 1936. Superintendent of Privileges was no longer listed in the premium books after 1937. During the time from about 1937 to the early 1940's, C. R. Brady was in charge.

The next records available listed Midway and Concessions Superintendent in 1944 as Charles Fish. William Dillon followed from

1945 through 1952. By 1953 Louis P. Brady was the Superintendent of Concessions and Display Space.

In 1961 area auctioneer Kenneth Klotz joined Brady. The two of them headed the department until 1966 when Fred Kinchner replaced Brady working with Klotz. Kinchner became active on the Fair Board in 1966 after receiving a share of Fair stock as a gift from his wife Marie. Klotz and Kinchner worked together as head of Concessions and Display Space until Kinchner's death in 1971. At that time Donald Bark came into the department.

Bark has headed the department since 1978; his son Dan has been his assistant since 1998. They assign display spaces and food concessions to over 300 clubs, organizations, and businesses at the Fair. During the Fair their headquarters is in the Round Office.

Ticket Sales

Superintendent of Ticket Sales was previously called Superintendent of Outside Gates. This name change took place in 1966 when Fair Treasurer Lewis Rex was superintendent. Rex was a local insurance agency owner, who held the position until his untimely death on Saturday morning of the Fair in 1968. Nancy Rex recalls how much he enjoyed the Fair; her last conversation with her father the night before his death was about the tractor pull. Jack Norling, son-in-law of Rex, became Superintendent of Ticket Sales in 1969. He held that position and that of Fair treasurer until the 100th Fair in 1987. He became Fair Board President at that time and gave up ticket sales. In the August 27, 1980, *Fair Times*, Norling said,

"The hardest thing for me is getting enough people to handle the sales and to collect the tickets from the people. I used to have a lot of college kids helping me, but school starts earlier and there aren't as many around to help."

Norling's sister-in-law Nancy Rex and John Hallaron were named Ticket Sales Superintendents in 1988. In 1997 Roy Wahlgren began working with Rex and Hallaron. They manage ticket sales and collection at all entrance gates to the Fair.

Data Management

Audrey Hoffman handled the office and computer work of the Fair from the late 1980's until her death in 1997. Hoffman lived in Hinckley and was active in the community as a Fair helper and fairgoer. Ginger Dannewitz, the current Data and Office Manager, started in 1997.

Dannewitz is a Sandwich native who grew up helping and working at the Fair. She remembers working at the Log Cabin food stand and as an usher at the grandstand. Dannewitz is one of the few year-round employees of the Fair.

Caretakers

According to the 1938 Fair Board minutes, the directors agreed to hire a caretaker. However, the records do not show who, if anyone, was hired before 1946 when Shelby Morris assumed the position. Morris served until his death in 1968. Herman Carlson assumed the duties in 1968 and continued through the 100th Fair in 1987. Andy Krafft took over from Carlson and was the caretaker until 1999 when his assistant Jim "Biff" Webber became caretaker. Krafft is the assistant to Webber.

Electricians

The first electrician listed as department head was Charles Bark in 1989. Before 1989 others were active in doing electrical work about the grounds, namely Carlton "Dutch" Hough and James Anderson.

Bark was the Fair electrician for just two years. In 1991 Harold Dannewitz became the electrician. John Spoor was Dannewitz's assistant in the early 1990's. For several years Reed Johnson has worked with Dannewitz on electrical repairs and upgrades throughout the grounds.

Parking and Police

This department evolved from Fire Protection, Police, and Traffic, which Director Don Stahl supervised from 1956 to 1960. Later, the board saw a need to establish superintendents for the area of Parking and Police. In 1967 Dr. Armand "Doc" Legner and Donald "Did" Breunig were named to the position. They worked together until 1973 when Frederick "Fritz" Lindner replaced Breunig. Lindner was the local lumberyard owner and new on the Board of Directors.

Legner and Lindner headed Parking and Police until 1980. Scott Breunig and Stuart Phillips became superintendents in 1980. Upon Phillips' death in 1988, William Haag was named to the department to work with Breunig. Breunig and Haag are the current superintendents who head up police security and manage the many acres of parking.

Information and Souvenirs

The first year for the Gazebo was 1993. Growing attendance necessitated an easy-to-find information booth. In addition, fairgoers were asking for more souvenirs. Karen Breunig and Cheryl Augustine have headed this department since 1993. At Fair time the Gazebo is located in front of the Home Arts building in the hub of the activity on the grounds.

First Aid

Records from 1918 mention a first aid tent sponsored by the Red Cross near Industrial Hall. In the 1940's a local funeral home provided an ambulance, and by 1945 the area Nurses Club provided first aid. The Red Cross and the Nurses Club provided first aid and cribs for babies in 1948. In 1970 Civil Defense member Earl Tapp was in charge of the First Aid Station working out of an old bread truck backed into a tent.

In 1974 local EMTs and hospital nurses provided first aid under the direction of Kathy Adrian Haggard, R. N. In 1980 Barbara "Boots" Hoffman, R. N., became coordinator and continues in that position today.

Photo by B.V.

Home Arts - Needlework
Front row: Helen Batorson, Donna Leonard, Millie Carter, Pat Redden, Betty Warren, Linda Moran,
Row 2: Eleanor Anderson, Connie Card, Margene Kennedy, Carol Allen, Ruth White, Alberta Clapper, Rita Wiesbrook, Opal Zitka, LuAnn Ladwig, Row 3: Kenny Young, Bonnie Young, Becky Crum, Bonnie Miller, Row 4: Bob Anderson, Spencer Zitka, Don Wiesbrook, Arnold Ladwig, Not Pictured: Ena Carlson, Norma Hough, Les Redden, Jerry Leonard, George Card, Kristy Redden, Bob Barrett, Helen Augustine

Photo by B.V.

First Aid and Paramedics
(l. to r.) Troy Walker, Barbara Hoffman, Brian Voelkel, Jo Anne Parris

Tents and Panels

To provide space for the growing number of exhibits at the Fair, Russell Stahl was named Panels and Tents Superintendent in 1961. During the Fair he helped put up tents to make sure the animals were properly housed and penned. Stahl was a local farmer, who had the Fair "in his blood." He had been a fairgoer since childhood, and he later served 27 years as a Fair Board director. His personality is well remembered by veterans of the livestock area and tractor pull contest. Stahl was seen and heard about the grounds with his familiar cigar and a good story or two to tell with some colorful language. In 1965 his responsibilities also included the tractor pull. After Stahl, Robert Guehler handled Panels and Tents. In 1996 and 1997 Ken Tyrrell was Tents and Panels Superintendent. There is no longer a Tents and Panels Department.

Sheriff's Auxiliary Police
Front row: Bob Browning, Ryan Wallis, Matt Kimmey, Sr., Derek J. Moran, Row 2: Don Frederick, Carol Kimmey, Mark Kimmey, George Schuster, Duane Rapp, Scott Johnson, John Steele, Row 3: Don Kimmey

Grounds and Water

Keeping up the fairgrounds and making sure there is a good supply of water has always been a big job for the Fair Board. In 1897 C. W. LaSuer was in charge of Grounds, and in 1898 F. A. Pratt was in charge. The first water main was extended from the city in 1898, and by 1904 Henry Hennis had taken over the responsibility of Grounds. For the 1900 to 1903 Fairs, C. V. Stevens was in charge of Water. In 1904 Thomas Mercer took over the responsibility. Mercer continued as Water Superintendent until 1911 when Hennis was in charge of both Grounds and Water.

M. E. Lake helped Hennis in 1921 and went on to become superintendent of both departments by 1927. He served in that capacity until the early 1940's when William Dillon took over the job. By 1939 the Fair was again using its own water supply. In 1944 and 1945 Albert Dannewitz was Grounds and Water Superintendent. After 1945 neither Water nor Grounds was listed in the records, but from time to time they were mentioned in Fair publicity. Carlton "Dutch" Hough worked with both water and electric matters for forty years beginning in 1946. Today the Fair Board has an on-going program for the upkeep of the grounds.

Employment of Help

An activity the size of the Sandwich Fair cannot run on volunteers alone. The earliest record of the Superintendent of Employment was in 1897 with Henry Severy. Severy was a Victor Township dairy farmer who later farmed near Sandwich. He was an organizer and president of the former Farmers Trust and Savings Bank in Sandwich. Severy headed the department until 1927 when T. J. Mahaffey joined him. In 1900 Gates and Police were added to this department.

Mahaffey took over as superintendent in 1932, and in 1938 until 1940 the department was headed by L. R. Evans. Art Potter was department head in 1941, and by 1943 L. R. Evans was back as superintendent. Evans was in charge until 1944; Harry Darnell in 1945. This was the last time this department was listed. Today each department is in charge of getting its own workers.

Forage

In the earlier years, food for the livestock entries was either provided or was available. As far back as 1897, F. A. Pratt was Superintendent of Forage. By 1900 Pernett Potter was the head of Forage, and in 1901 when Potter became Cattle/Sheep/Swine Superintendent, John Latham was in charge for a couple of years.

Following Latham in 1903, Chris Suppes took over as the head of Forage. He served for 30 years in this position until mid 1930's when August C. Baie became department head. Baie was the superintendent until 1944; after that

Fire Department
Front row: Bryan Leopold, James Newton, Bob Judd, Dave Jordan, Bill King, Richard Kell, Charles Fish, Gregg Williams, Row 2: Don Rimgale, Jason Weymouth, Tim Kern, Mike Pruski, Brian Voelkel, Chad Johnson, Row 3: Bob Lawrence, Douglas R. Stahl, Jason Pruski, Reed Johnson, Kerry Boring, Dale "DJ" Jordan, Troy Walker, Mike Rettig, Bob Springstroh, Brad Fish

Forage was no longer listed in the premium books. Today's exhibitors provide food for their own livestock.

GROUNDS ACTIVITIES DEPARTMENT

Current superintendents and their areas are Don Augustine and Larry Dannewitz, Grandstand Entertainment; Jim Meade, Harness Racing; Wiley Updike and Gene Frieders, Tractor and Truck Pulls; Scott Breunig and Don Lawyer, Ag Land Stage; Joe Steffen and Scott Breunig, Draft Horse Pull; Doug and Nancy Carter, Fair Auto Show; Dick Delp, Micro-Mini Tractor Pull; Eileen Weber, Crafts and Demonstrations; Mike Krafft, Antique Farm Machinery; Matt Wilson, FFA Farm Zoo; Larry Robinson, Fiddle Contest; Kenny Huff and Fred Morel, Horseshoe Pitching; and Steve and Carole Hilleson, Western Horse Show.

Grandstand Entertainment

As early as 1900, Henry Hennis, D. K. Crofoot, and Fair Secretary Eugene Randall were the committee to secure entertainment. In 1906 George McDonald replaced Crofoot and Fair Secretary, C. L. Stinson became a member of the committee. P. S. Lindner replaced McDonald by 1916, and M. E. Lake replaced Hennis in 1921. Lake, Lindner, and Stinson were in charge until Charles Howison replaced Lindner in mid 1930's. C. R. Brady took over from Stinson in 1941.

In 1944 Ben Eade and C. R. Brady were in charge. Grandstand superintendents in 1946 were George Wahlgren and A. W. Colliflower. Wahlgren was a partner in the local men's clothing store and Colliflower an officer with the local bank. By 1947 Carl Scent was helping in this area. Scent and C. R. Brady worked together on entertainment to mid 1950's when Henry White joined them. At the same time publicity was added to the committee's responsibilities.

The Grandstand and Gates Superintendents in 1959 were Carl Scent and Lewis Rex. When the responsibilities divided, Rex became Gate Superintendent. Louis P. Brady replaced Scent in 1967 working with his father C. R. Brady. In 1970 Kenny Klotz and Wes Scents joined the

Behind the Scenes

President Wiley Updike says one reason the Fair is a success is that it has a working Board of Directors. Much of the work they do is evident; however, like any successful organization, a lot goes on behind the scenes that sometimes calls for emergency action. Louis P. Brady, Secretary Emeritus, says, "We always manage to work around a problem, no matter what it is."

Some of the problems have been challenging. Brady recalls one Fair in which he was in the spotlight more than he wanted to be. An auto thrill show booked to start at 1 p.m. on Sunday was late. A grandstand full of eager spectators waited for the show to begin. They waited and waited. For Fair directors who organize the entertainment, it was an afternoon that lasted forever. Brady remembers taking his turn with other Fair officials in front of the grandstand for five hours trying to keep the crowd calm. No one remembers, or admits, exactly what was said or done during the five hours, but somehow they managed to keep the crowd. The autos finally arrived, and the show started at 6 p.m. It seems the cars and drivers had a show in North Carolina the previous day, and they had stopped to take a nap on their way to Sandwich.

Another time a group of performers for the Friday night show telephoned from Leland; they had driven right through Sandwich. The Fair board sent a sheriff's car to direct them to the fairgrounds.

One year a bus carrying the Nashville Brass broke down in Plainfield. Don Augustine and Donald "Did" Breunig rented a truck and went after them. The show went on—almost on time. One year country singer Eddie Rabbit was almost late for his performance. He decided to go jogging and got a late start from his motel in Morris, IL. Underestimating the entrance lines to the fairgrounds, he arrived on the grounds right at show time.

Another near-disaster involved electrical power. Blomsness Amusements saved the day with its generator when Tammy Wynette's show required more amperage than was available at the time. Sandwich Fair audiences know they will always be entertained well, but they don't always know how hard Fair officials work to make sure they are.

center: Donald Augustine, Director
since 1985

Kendall County Record

Carlton "Dutch" Hough
Director 1946-1988

"The Sandwich Fair was not a seasonal activity. It was a way of life for everyone in the family," remembers Susan Hough Farr Carlton "Dutch" Hough's daughter. She recalls that hardly a day passed that he didn't work on the grounds or plan the next improvement. "Dad always had a project in progress. He wanted the Sandwich Fair to be the best fair in the state."

Hough often involved his whole family in preparing the premium books, driving the water truck for harness-racing events, and documenting Fair highlights by taking numerous pictures and slides. His involvement began in 1942 as assistant Speed Superintendent. Four years later he became a director. He served as vice-president from 1956-1961 and president from 1962-1985.

Being an electrician, he rewired many of the buildings. He also set up a telephone system on the grounds, painted, and did general maintenance projects. Another improvement was the building constructed on the racetrack infield that was used as a dressing room for the grandstand entertainers.

Even when Hough was relaxing, he was working. At the Thursday night dances held during the summer, he arrived early to spread wax flakes on the concrete floor. He helped take tickets and worked the lights, changing the colors that lit up the dancers.

The 1979 Sandwich *Fair Times* documents Hough's energy when it came to helping his friends. Augie Otto explained how Hough helped him finish assembling his new steam locomotive so it would be ready for the 1974 Fair: "Dutch brought out his woodworking tools. Herman Carlson [the caretaker] came with him. That Dutch is a slave driver. Not that he ordered anyone around; it was just that to keep up with him, you've really got to move."

His energy extended beyond Sandwich. Hough served as Director of the Illinois Association of Agricultural Fairs and was elected state president in 1959 and 1960. Although he never owned a racehorse, his enthusiasm for horses was evident; he helped organize the Illinois Valley Fair Circuit. He spent part of many summers at the Illinois State Fair and at five county fairs driving the circuit's water truck. He also served as secretary of the Illinois Valley Trotting Association.

In 1983 Governor Thompson acknowledged his work with country fairs by presenting him with the Outstanding County Fair Award—one of the highest awards of the State Association. A reluctant honoree, he credited the Fair's success to the group effort of the Board of Directors, the workers, the high-quality exhibits, and the visitors who come to the Fair each year.

Bradys with entertainment and advertising. In 1973 Donald "Did" Breunig, who had worked in the area since mid 1960's, replaced C. R. Brady and Wes Scents. Klotz worked in this area until 1977. Don Augustine joined Brady and Breunig in mid 1970's.

Grandstand superintendents in 1990 were Augustine and Breunig. Breunig worked on grandstand events and entertainment for nearly 30 years, and he also served as Fair treasurer.

After Breunig's death in 1992, Larry Dannewitz began working with Augustine on Grandstand Entertainment. Today, as the current superintendents, they share the duties of booking entertainment, selling tickets, supervising ushers, and setting up the grandstand for the shows.

Tractor Pull and Truck Pull Contests

These attractions are grandstand shows. The Tractor Pull began in 1965, and it has become one of the most popular events at the Fair. Local farmer Russell Stahl was the first Tractor Pull Superintendent and the driving force of its popularity. One of the superintendent's responsibilities is to see that competitors abide by the rules of the Tractor Pulling Association and operate the equipment properly. Stahl's longtime assistant was Edwin Tuntland from 1965 to 1979. Four-wheel drive Truck Pull contests were first held at the 1978 Fair; Wiley Updike was in charge of these contests in 1978 and 1979. Stahl and Updike were in charge of the pulls until Stahl stepped aside in 1986 and let current Fair Board President Updike take over. Gene Frieders has been Updike's assistant since 1993. Truck and Super Semi series pulls are Thursday evening; tractor and mini rods are held on Saturday afternoon and evening.

Department of Speed: Harness Racing

This department is notably as old as the Fair and an area that has brought much entertainment to fairgoers. At the 1888 Fair, local livery and feed stable businessman Ira M. Arnold was the Superintendent of Speed. He was followed by local real estate agent Joseph C. Calahan.

By 1893 T. S. Clough, Jr. was Speed Superintendent and C. W. LaSuer by 1895. Soon LaSuer became Horse Stall

Superintendent. Local alderman and saloon owner Henry Hennis was next; he began in 1896 holding that position for many years into mid 1920's. Hennis was an early stockholder and a tireless promoter of the Fair.

By 1927 Thomas Mercer was superintendent. He had been head of horse stalls prior to becoming involved with the Department of Speed. He retired from this position in 1940 at age 82. Mercer assisted in the Department of Speed at the State Fair in Springfield for 40 years. Art Potter followed him. In 1945 Carlton "Dutch" Hough started with Potter in this department. These two men headed the Speed Department until 1959 until V. F. Beck became Hough's assistant.

In the late 1960's when Hough and Beck were in charge, harness racing horses were the only horses at the Fair, except for pony rides for the children. Beck was involved with Speed until 1982 when James Meade started working with Hough. Meade became Superintendent of Speed in 1989 after the death of Hough. There have been only nine Speed Superintendents in the 113 years of the Fair.

Sandwich Fair Auto Show

In 1967 the first Antique "Car Parade" was held east of the Horticulture building; local variety-store owner Robert Loy was in charge. Loy was head of the show through 1982. Following him in 1983, Wiley Updike became superintendent.

Updike was in that position for 10 years when Warren Greenwood of Somonauk joined him in 1993. Greenwood worked with Updike for three years; in 1996 and 1997 Greenwood's wife Ula helped Updike.

Updike stepped aside in 1998, and Doug and Nancy Carter became superintendents. It is now called the "Sandwich Fair Auto Show." The show is held on Sunday in the racetrack infield. Different makes of cars are featured each year.

Micro-Mini Tractor Pull

In 1980 the first Micro-Mini Tractor Pull was held. Dick Delp has been the superintendent of this event since its beginning. This adult hobby uses modified toy tractors on a regulation track with scaled-down skids. Mike and Melissa Miller from Boone County, Illinois, help Delp and also

participate in the event. It is held on Saturday evening in the swine show ring.

Craft Demonstrations

In 1972 Marie Kinchner-Rice was asked to create a Craft Demonstrations Department. The demonstrations began the following year on the tent-covered concrete area on the south side of the Home Arts building. A new building was erected for the crafters in 1987 near the grandstand. Kinchner was head of this department until 1994.

Kinchner's assistant was Ruth Haag from 1972 through 1985. Beginning in 1983, Eileen Weber was also her assistant. Weber took over the department in 1995 when Kinchner-Rice passed away.

Antique Farm Machinery

The Antique Farm Machinery display was started in 1967 with Andy Krafft as superintendent. Krafft was interested in old farm machinery and knew others with the same interests. The display has always been located inside the train track. Willard Schmidt, Alvin Miller, Ed Weismiller and Dave Stahl assisted Krafft in the early years. Krafft's son Michael joined him in 1986. Michael became superintendent in late 1987 when Andy became full-time caretaker of the fairgrounds.

Photo by J.A.D.

FFA Farm Zoo

The FFA Farm Zoo was started in 1967 under the leadership of Milford Clausen of Waterman, Don Wilson of Sandwich, Jack Niles of Shabbona, and Arnie Parchert of Somonauk. These four men headed the department until 1975 when Leland-Somonauk FFA advisor Andy Anderson took over the position until 1979. The current superintendent is Somonauk teacher Matt Wilson who took over in 1979. His assistants are Gary Blankenship and Joe Steffen.

FFA members from Indian Creek, Somonauk-Leland, Hinckley-Big Rock and Newark are involved in the project. They main-

center: Matthew Wilson, Director since 1995

tain the building, the animals, and the area around the building.

Fiddle Contest

The Fiddle Contest was started in 1995 under the direction of Larry Robinson and continues today under his leadership. Fiddle players from a wide area compete in junior or senior division by playing a fast song, a slow song, and one other song for prizes on Wednesday evening at the Ag Land stage.

Horseshoe Pitching

Horseshoe Pitching returned to the Fair in 1986 after an absence of many years. The event takes place every day of the Fair inside the train track. Kenneth Huff of Waterman helped bring it back and has

Photo by V.G.

(l. to r.) Glenn Bower assisted Kenneth Huff with horseshoe pitching in the late 1980's.

been the superintendent since 1986 with Glenn Bower as his assistant until 1990. When he moved away, Charles Hilliard became the assistant. Following Hilliard was Paul Johnson

from 1991 to 1997. Fred Morel has assisted Huff since 1998. Huff is in charge of pitching until the weekend; then Morel takes over. Sometimes Huff and Morel are participants at the Sunday matches.

Western Horse Show

The Western Horse Show started in 1981 with Steve Hilleson and Paul Butler as superintendents. An arena at the west end of the grounds was built for the first show. Butler worked with Hilleson until 1991; Adrian Butler assisted until 1995 when Carole Hilleson was named to head the department with Steve. The Horse Show is held on Wednesday morning with several events for men, women, and juniors. The Hillesons are the current superintendents.

Sandwich Free Press

David Graf
National Teacher of the Year

In 1968 the Fair Association honored Superintendent of Industrial Arts David Graf for his contribution to education. Graf, coordinator of the Diversified Occupations Program at Sandwich High School, was selected as National Teacher of the Year. The ceremony included a parade, a flag raising at the grandstand, and presentation of a plaque.

Editor's Comments in *Sandwich Free Press*
September 12, 1929

We certainly do not agree with those who advocate the abolition of the Sandwich Fair. We feel that it is a very fine thing. Those who argue against the proposition must have failed to notice the joy that was written across the faces of men and women who no longer live in Sandwich but returned for one or more days at the fair to visit their old friends and comrades. Wrinkles were erased from countenances for a day or two when older men and women came together to talk of old times and recalled happy days of yesteryear. One man in particular (almost 90 years old) we noted, who it seemed, had dropped 20 years from his shoulders in a few hours on the grounds Thursday afternoon. We believe—in fact we know—the Sandwich Fair is a mighty fine thing to keep alive.

Ag Land Stage

Ag Land Stage started in 1993 under the direction of Scott Breunig and Don Lawyer as the assistant. Today, Lawyer schedules most of the activities including the bands. Don Stahl handles the arrangements for the fiddle contest. The stage was first built for WGN Noon Show. Later bands were added to attract people to the ag area. In most recent years an awning and dance floor were added, as well as bench seating and shade trees. The stage and seating are disassembled and stored in the livestock barns soon after the Fair.

Draft Horse Pull

Ben Eade was superintendent of this department from 1933 to 1937. The pull contest continued several more years; however, there are no other records of leadership until 1995 when Scott Breunig, assisted by Joe Steffen, headed the department. Steffen's experience with draft horses helped to make this department run smoothly. He had helped with the draft horse pull at the Heart of Illinois Fair in Peoria for a number of years and is now the superintendent of the event. Steffen is also the draft horse pull superintendent at the Kendall County Fair.

Steve Lance of Cambridge, Wisconsin, has supplied the dynamometer, the pull truck, since 1995. Lance's daughter is the announcer and his wife keeps the records.

OTHER SUPERINTENDENTS
Agricultural Implements and Manufactures

A rather short-lived department was that of Agricultural Implements and Manufactures. This apparently was for the commercial equipment and products entered at the Fair. Items listed and judged in 1888 in this department ranged from sulky plows, hand corn shellers, and carriages to churns, washing machines, refrigerators, and even tombstones and monuments. Some items received a monetary prize, some a diploma.

Evan Lewis was its superintendent in 1888, Orlando Slater in 1893, and Philo Slater from 1895 to 1896. Records are sketchy for this department; it was not listed in the premium books after 1903.

Louis P. Brady honored (l. to r.) Frances Toombs, Renee Monkemeyer, and Millie Carter for long-time service in 1970 at the Fair Appreciation Dinner.

Fair Appreciation Dinner

Sandwich Free Press articles in April 1951 and March 1952 report accounts of department dinners at the American Legion for the clerk's [secretary's] office and superintendents of the Horticulture and Women's buildings. After the dinner the group met at the Fair office to discuss plans for the next Fair. Workers have been recognized, thanked, and entertained at the dinners for half a century. It is also a time for honoring long-time retiring workers and leaders and making special presentations.

For the past ten or fifteen years each fall after the Fair, a special appreciation dinner is given by the Sandwich Fair Association for department heads and others who help make the Sandwich Fair successful. Emphasized at the dinner is the teamwork that makes each Fair bigger and better. The guest list has grown from a small group to well over 200. The dinners have been held in several locations: The Manor in Earlville, the Ramada Inn in Ottawa, Edgebrook Country Club in Sandwich, and currently at Pitstick Pavilion in Ottawa. A local theater group, magicians, singers, and comedians have entertained guests.

Photo by S.C.

Aerial view of the grounds in the
mid 1990's

52

Buildings and Grounds:
Built to Last

3

CHAPTER

Longevity is a relative concept. Most of today's European nations measure their existence in hundreds of years. The history of some Oriental civilizations extends back for hundreds of generations. In that context the 113-year track record of the Sandwich Fair may at first glance seem unimpressive. But given that Illinois has only been a state since 1818, that DeKalb County government was first formed in 1837, and that Sandwich, Illinois, was founded in 1854, it is apparent that the Sandwich Fair followed close on the heels of European settlement of the Illinois prairie.

Being "on the map" in the minds of the local population indicates that an organization has attained a degree of permanence. Being "on the map" in the minds of those living beyond the immediate area reflects the achievement of institutional status. Throughout Illinois, the Sandwich Fair is a familiar name. The Sandwich Agricultural Institute first held a fair at the current location in 1860, and the erection of buildings on the site specifically for the accommodation of fair activities was commenced more than a century and a quarter ago. The buildings and grounds of the Sandwich Fair are more than a local landmark, they symbolize the Midwestern county fair movement.

This movement has the dual purpose of promoting agriculture and educating farmers and their neighbors in town. At the same time, the county fair provides its patrons with amusement and camaraderie. From the very beginning, community leaders in the Sandwich area demonstrated commitment to the cause by procuring real estate to facilitate their goals.

Land that is a portion of the present grounds was first acquired in 1859 with a fair being held there the following year. After using the property for five years, the fair was temporarily discontinued, only to be resumed sporadically as availability of funds and the level of citizen interest allowed. In 1877 ten men bought twenty shares of stock for $2,000 and reorganization took place.

The September 14, 1877, issue of the *Somonauk Reveille* calls readers' attention to the approaching Sandwich Fair. The brief article states in part, "Many new buildings have been put up, old ones painted and other improvements added until the grounds are among the finest in the state." The reference to old buildings provides evidence that permanent housing for exhibits and activities had been provided from the fair's first days. The founders of the Sandwich Fair had every expectation that their creation would endure.

During its early history, various associations and individuals owned the Sandwich Fairgrounds and buildings at different times. In 1884 the current Fair Association sold the twenty acres of land to Lewis Dieterich for the Dieterich and Ebinger tile factory. Most of the buildings were removed. Thirteen stables were purchased by a company owning a race track southwest of town and were moved to that location. The dining hall went to a local farm for use as a barn. A chicken house was relocated to another nearby farmstead.

The March 11, 1885, issue of *The Free Press* states, "Mr. Dieterich still owns the fair grounds [sic] and the site of the tile factory." During this period the old fairgrounds was leased by a group of men interested in restoring the track and other facilities. The site was known for a time as the Sandwich Driving Park Association.

The Land

In 1888 twenty acres were repurchased from Dieterich for the original price of $2,500 and another three and one-half acres were added adjoining the racetrack and road. The modern history of the Sandwich Fairgrounds begins with these 1888 purchases, an annual fair having been held there each year since. Financing was made available by the sale of 100 shares of stock at $50 each, providing capital in the amount of $5,000.

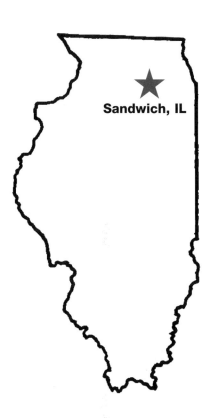

Sandwich, IL

I love everything, but especially the horticulture building with sheaves of grains, gargantuous pumpkins, beautiful flowers (from Illinois, not South America), strange tomatoes, herbs, and peppers, and YUM! Plus, the people are always friendly and happy.

Sharon Gilmour
Montgomery, Illinois

Courtesy of SFA

A 1980's view of the grounds

Land Purchases

1859 - Part of present grounds purchased for $2,500; used five years and discontinued.

1884 - Nearly 20 acres of land sold to Lewis Dieterich for Dieterich and Ebinger tile factory

1888 - Repurchased nearly 20 acres from Dieterich for original purchase price of $2,500; also that year, 3.5 acres purchased adjoining the race track and road

1891 - 16.11 acres purchased from Dieterich for $1,200, and 3.5 acres for $350

1921 - 5 acres purchased from Mike Fanning for $6,500

1943 - 5 acres purchased from Annie Grover Estate for $3,200, including brick caretaker's house

1945 - 3.2 acres purchased from Gilbert Gletty

1947 - 4 acres purchased from Eber Merrick for $800

1949 - Total 60.3 acres

1954 - 3.27 acres purchased from Gilbert Gletty

1964 - 7.5 acres purchased from Clarence Wilkening

1965 - 6.689 acres purchased from Claude and Malinda Gletty

1966 - 22.8 acres purchased from Charlotte Rud; total 100 acres in fairgrounds

1975/1976 - 59 acres purchased from Malinda Gletty farm; total 160 acres in fairgrounds

1990 - 100-foot-wide strip purchased from Robert Guehler for exit to Pratt Road

2000 - Total 170 acres in fairgrounds

Enlargement of the grounds has been an ongoing process. In 1891 the Sandwich Fair Association purchased additional land from Dieterich, adding nearly twenty acres at a cost of $1,550. In March 1921 the Mike Fanning property adjoining the fairgrounds on West Center Street (Suydam Road) was acquired to "square up the grounds." The cost was high— $6,500 for five acres. In 1937 the nearly fifty acres of land and improvements were valued at the depression-era figure of $40,000. No additional land was purchased until the 1940's.

In 1943 five acres were purchased from the Annie Grover estate for $3,200. This included a brick caretaker's house. Two years later the Fair Association bought three and two-tenths acres from Gilbert Gletty. In 1947 with the expenditure of another $800, the total area of the Sandwich Fairgrounds increased to sixty and three-tenths acres when four acres were purchased from Eber Merrick. In small increments, expansion continued through the next two decades.

Another three and two-tenths acres were acquired in 1954 from Gilbert Gletty. In 1964 seven and one-half acres were purchased from Clarence Wilkening. The following year, six and seven-tenths were purchased from Claude and Malinda Gletty. The 1966 purchase of twenty-two and eight-tenths acres from Charlotte Rud brought the total fairground acreage to 100, a five-fold increase from the modest twenty-acre beginning in 1888. Space needs continued to grow, with automobile parking an increasing concern.

In 1975-76 negotiations were completed that increased the size of the grounds by nearly sixty percent with the acquisition of fifty-nine acres from the Malinda Gletty farm. Finally in 1990, a 100-foot-wide strip was purchased to provide a north exit to Pratt Road. It seems appropriate that the Sandwich Fairground now occupies a quarter section of midwestern prairie and woodland.

The founders' twin objectives of promotion and education continue to play out each September on a site that, in regard to size, is typical of a farm of their era. The Fair's originators would surely have deemed a quarter section nearly ideal for the successful pursuit of agriculture in nineteenth century Northern Illinois. Of course, the buildings that have been constructed over the years to house animals and various Fair activities are definitely not typical of a nineteenth century barnyard.

Courtesy of B.H.

left: This judges stand was located to the north of the grandstand, circa 1916. Map location #42B

Courtesy of B.H.

top: This dirt path led into the fairgrounds from the Main Gate past the original Horticulture building in the early 1900's.

bottom: Fair visitors gather near the Main Gate in 1901.

Courtesy of SFA

Attractive Grounds

An attractive premises is essential to any enterprise, but especially for an admission-charging organization. Newspaper reports reflect the efforts of Fair directors to keep the buildings, grounds, and even the routes leading to the site in top-notch condition. In 1891 an article in the *Somonauk Reveille* states: "The judges stand has been fixed up, the fence around the track painted, and, withal, this part of the association's property is absolutely grand and complete." In 1895 the *Daily Argus* reported: "As usual, arrangements have been made to sprinkle the street leading out to the grounds and as usual nothing will be left undone to make the grounds a pleasant and profitable place to spend a few days while the exposition is in progress."

The *Sandwich Free Press* printed the following on May 18, 1905: "The grounds with its wealth of shade and green carpeted lawns is the prettiest in the state and the pride of every resident of this vicinity." In 1915 a four-foot concrete sidewalk was extended from the city limits to the first gate, a distance of 2,100 feet. The Sandwich Commercial Club, Oak Ridge Cemetery, and the Sandwich Fair Association provided funding for the project.

Roadways within the grounds began as dirt paths where dust swirled in dry times and mud splattered during wet periods. The paths were eventually graveled and later covered with ground limestone. The main thoroughfares have now been blacktopped.

Entry Gates

The old, steel-frame entry gates that have greeted visitors since 1897 also stimulate thoughts of Sandwich Fair history. When the twin gates with the top bars boldly proclaiming "Sandwich Fair Est. 1888" came into view, fair-goers who were queued up on Suydam Road knew that their wait to enter the grounds was nearly over. Flanking the old ticket office, these were the main portals for paying customers until 1978. Replaced farther east at that time by a new ticket office and five entrance lanes for improved traffic flow, the ornate gates and old ticket office now grace the west entrance to the grounds—bits of history preserved in a new location.

Distinctive Structures

The landmark status that the Sandwich fairgrounds has achieved in the area and state can be attributed in part to the preservation and distinctive design of many of the buildings. Over time they have been built, rebuilt, remodeled, moved, removed, named and renamed, sometimes resulting in a name game for historians

Courtesy of N.U.

The Main Gate pictured in 1995. A caretaker's residence is pictured in the background.

when they are researching locations and contents of the historic buildings.

At various times flowers have been displayed in Dining Hall, Industrial Hall, Home Arts, and of course, Floral Hall. Baked goods have been exhibited in a variety of places also— Industrial Hall, Home Arts and even the Horticulture building. Livestock is no exception. One year, a barn was used for cattle or horses, and the next year it contained pens for

sheep or coops for chickens.

The shift from one space to another occurred as naturally as creating a new coat from an old one for a growing child. Lack of space was, and still is, usually the determining factor for the shifting and sharing. The continuity achieved by these efforts makes the fairgrounds a familiar, inviting place when Labor Day rolls around each autumn.

Courtesy of SFA

56

View from inside the fairgrounds, behind the Main Gate in 1897

These entry gates have greeted thousands of visitors since 1897. They were relocated farther west on Suydam Road in 1978. Map location #1

The steel-framed gates along with the ticket office were moved farther west to the Gate 5 entrance in 1978.

Ticket seller Virginia Cole preparing for the day. In the background (l. to r.) John Peterson, Scott Norling and Nancy Rex

Photo by K.B.

Main Gate

Main Gate are probably not words that stir up excitement for most people, but they do for Fair Secretary Nancy Rex. Since she was a small child, Nancy has considered the Main Gate to the fairgrounds the opening to an outing full of fun.

For all of the years that she can remember, her family has been involved in the Sandwich Fair. When she was in grade school, her father Lewis B. Rex was the treasurer of the Sandwich Fair. He was in charge of hiring ticket takers and sellers. At an early age, she began begging her father to let her be a ticket taker. He told her that she must wait until she graduated from eighth grade to be a ticket taker. In 1959 she graduated, and she started working in the department that she supervises today. After a couple of years of taking tickets, she decided she wanted to be a ticket seller instead. She persuaded her father to let her sell tickets even though no girl had ever worked in that position previously. Nancy's determination helped begin the practice of allowing both males and females to take and sell tickets.

Ticket sales are the largest of several sources of income for the Fair. When Nancy first started working at the gates, ticket prices were 60 cents for adults, 25 cents for children, and 25 cents for parking. The prices at that time presented a greater challenge for mental mathematics than the current prices of five dollars for adults and two dollars for children. Before the office had a computer—or even a calculator, she remembers her Uncle John F. Peterson working with paper and pencil late into the night tallying the receipts of every ticket seller to arrive at the total gate receipts for the day.

When reviewing some old gate-receipt records from 1962, Nancy commented that the $21,024.85 collected for all five days of the Fair would not be enough to pay the electricity bill for the 1999 fair.

When Nancy started selling tickets in the early 1960's, the Main Gate was centrally located on Suydam Road (location #1). Through 2000 the Main Gate Ticket and Treasurer's Office (location #57) were located at Gate 1 which was originally known as the East Gate. According to Nancy, being assigned to work at the East Gate was like being sent to a distant outpost.

The building that is currently located at Gate 5 (location # 1) was the Main Gate Office. She recalls that the walls were covered with the calculations of past ticket sellers who had counted out their money as they made deposits or checked in for the day. Ticket sellers stood on the centerline of the road on both sides of the office building serving vehicles coming from both directions. The same type of equipment used in 1959 is still used today. In fact, ticket takers still use the same milk cans to collect tickets.

The present Main Gate Ticket Office (location #57) was built in 1972 while Lewis Rex's son-in-law Jack E. Norling was serving as treasurer of the Sandwich Fair. In 1984 under Norling's supervision, ticket sales were computerized. Beginning in 2001, fairgoers will drive onto the grounds via a new north entrance off Pratt Road. After they have parked their cars, they will walk to a booth where they will purchase an admission ticket.

During the years that Nancy Rex has worked with ticket sales, there have been changes, yet the system and atmosphere are much the same. Friendships have developed, and a few romances have sparked among ticket sellers and takers. Parents have started their children and grandchildren working at the gates. The tradition of working at the Sandwich Fair continues.

Fair secretary and ticket superintendent Nancy Rex pictured in front of the Main Gate ticket office in 2000. Map location #57

Building Map Numbers and History

 # 1 **Main Gate ticket office.** The ticket office and gates were built in the late 1800's. They were removed in 1978 from the old Main Gate at the train track to Gate 5 on the west end.

#2 **Draft horse barn.** This barn was originally on the Gletty farm. In 1976 the Fair Association purchased the farm. In 1994 it was cleaned and remodeled for draft horses. When Gletty owned the barn, it was used for racehorses.

#3 **Horse show arena.** This area was built in 1981.

#4 **Dwelling and garage.** These buildings were acquired from the Gletty family in 1975. Today it is a residence for the caretaker's family.

#5 **Ticket office.** Livestock gate #4. It was built in 1945 and moved to this location in the 1970's. Originally it was the grandstand ticket office.

#6 **Beef barn.** This Cleary building was constructed in 1988 as a goat barn. Today it houses beef cattle.

#7 & #7A **Swine barn.** This 44' x 70' structure was built for swine in 1904. The northeast end of the present barn is the original part; it had 56 pens. In 1922 a building was added to the southeast end. In 1956 a 48' x 180' building was added to the west to make a T-shaped building. A covered show ring was added to this complex in 1985 at a cost of $25,500.

#8 & #9 **Sheep barns.** An 82' x 180' shed with a show ring was built in 1979 for $39,560.

#10 **Cattle/Goat barn.** The east end of this structure was built in 1949 as a 38' x 100' cattle barn. The west end, 56' x 170', was built in 1962 for $7,388 from materials purchased from P. S. Lindner. The roof blew off in 1958.

#11 **Livestock barn/Rest pavilion/Agriculture Education and Information Center.** This structure was originally a 4-H Club calf and hog barn built in 1935 with used lumber from sheds torn down in 1934.

#12A **Cattle barn.** This barn was damaged in a 1958 storm.

#12 **Men's and women's restrooms.** They were built in 1977 on the former site of the cattle barn mentioned above.

#13 **Livestock office.** The roof of this structure once sheltered the old, permanent platform scale. It was moved to this location in 1957; an addition was built in 1981.

#14 **Dairy barn.** This structure was built in 1880; in 1925 it was moved 30 feet to the east. An addition was added in 1992 and a lean-to in 1996.

#14A **Milk house.** Don and Doug Stahl built this structure in the late 1960's or early 1970's.

#15 **Sheep barn/FFA Farm Zoo.** This structure was originally built in 1880 as a sheep barn.

It became the Farm Zoo in 1967.

#16 **Horse barn/Ag Land entertainment area.** This area was originally the site of a horse barn that was torn down in 1993. A dance floor was constructed in 1996.

#17 **Horse barn.** This 135' x 40' structure was built in 1914 for racehorses after an old draft horse barn was torn down. Today, the racehorses are relocated during the Fair as the building is used for poultry entries.

#17A **Men's toilet.**

#18 **Racehorse barn.** This 40' x 127' building was constructed of cement blocks in 1908.

#19 **Food stand.** Louis Miller built this structure in 1963 for St. Paul's Catholic Church; a tent was used earlier.

#20 **Men's and Women's restrooms.** They were built in 1982.

#21 **Shower house.** It was built in 1973.

#22 **Metal building.** Sandwich Lions Club built this structure in 1993 to replace a smaller garage-shaped building constructed in 1975. One end has a sturdy pen that holds a steer they raffle each year.

#23 **Maintenance shop.** This 54' x 84' metal structure was built in 1980 for $25,500. It was used for poultry exhibits until the late 1990's.

#24 **Secretary's office.** W. D. Dean built this office in 1892. Tickets were sold there until the 1930's.

#25 **Windmill and well.** L. R. Evans dug the well in 1939. It is no longer used. LaBolle family donated a 1920 windmill in 1970.

#26 **Display pavilion/Commerical building.** This metal structure was built in 1975 as a display and exhibit hall. An open pavilion was originally built on the site in 1900 for Sandwich Mfg. It was badly damaged by fallen trees in a 1974 storm.

#27 **Food stand.** This 30' x 70' building was erected in 1974. It replaced a food building that was damaged by a tornado. Sandwich Methodist Church ladies operated the building in early times. By 1900 the area was an open pavilion for Enterprise Company and Sandwich Mfg. machinery displays. Today, Sandwich Band Association operates the food stand in this location.

#28 **Sheriff's building.** This structure was added in 1975. The Fair Association possibly purchased the building from Louis Miller and placed it here.

#29 **First Aid building.** This structure was added in 1971 and remodeled in 1973. The Fair Association possibly purchased the building from Louis Miller and placed it here.

#30 **Judges stand/Round Office.** This eight-sided building was put up in 1900. Originally it may have been a bandstand near its present location. Many believe it

was used earlier as a judges or timers stand at the racetrack. It was moved to the present location, enclosed and made into the Round Office by 1906. In the 1960's, 3 to 4 feet of the bottom was cut off. It was used as an information center and as an office for the Superintendent of Concessions; today it continues to be the office of the Superintendent of Concessions.

#31 **Rest pavilion/Food stand.** This open Morton building was built in 1983 for $7,000. Earlier there was an American Legion food stand here; and before that, a food stand run by the Federated Church; still earlier, there was a rest pavilion built in 1910.

#32 **ATM building.** A local bank added this portable building in 1996 for an Automatic Teller Machine.

#33 **Public telephones.**

#34 **Display pavilion/Food stand.** Earlier used by the Dorcas Class of the Congregational Church, this food stand has been operated by Joe Kurtz and now by Fox Valley Older Adults. Earlier this area was used for machinery displays of Enterprise Co. and Sandwich Mfg.

#35 **Commercial building.** Morton metal building erected in 1970.

#36 **Commercial building.** This red and white Cleary building was constructed in 1997 over existing blacktop.

#37 **Gazebo.** Scott Breunig built this portable information and souvenir booth in 1993.

#38 **Home Arts building.** The original structure on this site was built in 1892 for $5,000. It was a two-story 100' x 150' x 97' tall building. A porch was added in 1896. In 1905 the building burned. That same year a considerably smaller building, 40' x 100', was rebuilt for $5,000. This building has been called Floral Hall, Industrial Hall, and the Women's Building.

#38A **Original windmill, well, and storage tank.** These improvements were installed in 1897. The windmill collapsed in the 1905 fire.

#38B **Dance floor.** This 40' x 80' area was built in 1954.

#39 **Caboose.** It was obtained in 1997 and remodeled in 1998.

#39A **Transformer building/Storage.** This old transformer building is now used for storage.

#40 **Arts, Crafts and Photography building.** This 50' x 85' metal building was constructed in 1972. An extension was added to the west end in 1982.

#41 **Train depot.** The Otto family built this in 1974.

#41A **Train tracks.** They were laid in 1974.

#41B **Train tracks.** These tracks were used from 1953 to 1974.

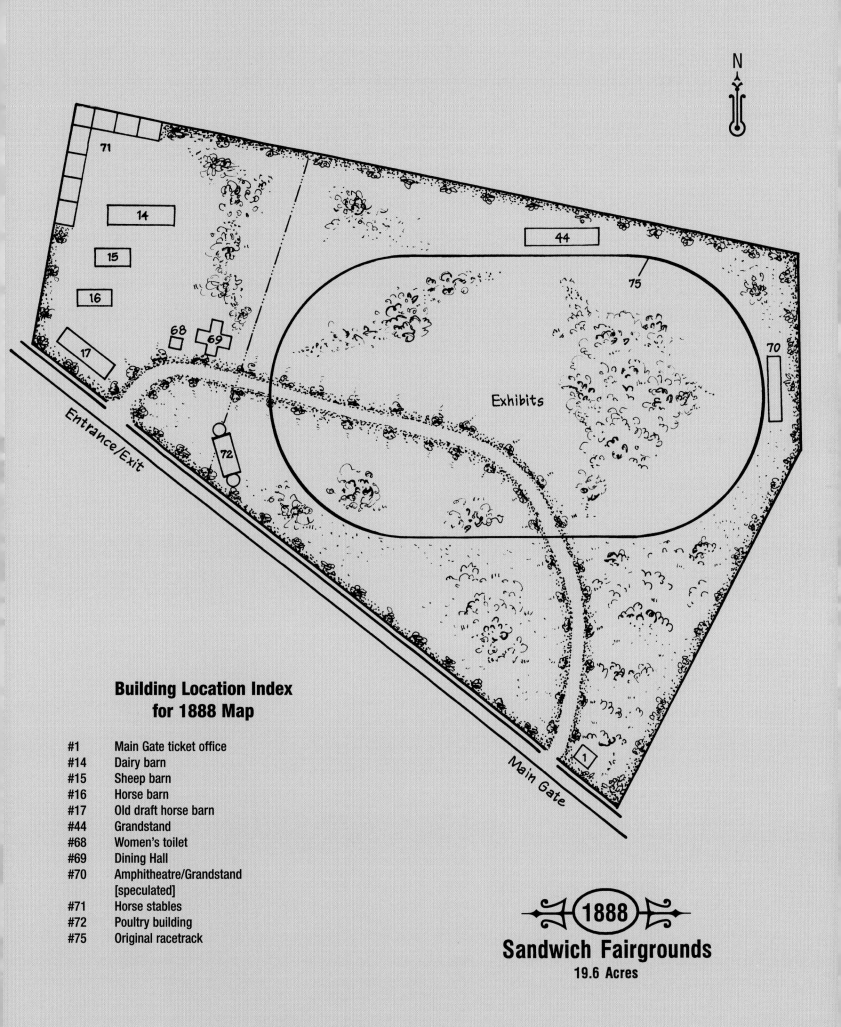

**Building Location Index
for 1888 Map**

#1	Main Gate ticket office
#14	Dairy barn
#15	Sheep barn
#16	Horse barn
#17	Old draft horse barn
#44	Grandstand
#68	Women's toilet
#69	Dining Hall
#70	Amphitheatre/Grandstand [speculated]
#71	Horse stables
#72	Poultry building
#75	Original racetrack

1888
Sandwich Fairgrounds
19.6 Acres

#42   **Storage building.** This building is located inside the racetrack.

#42A   **Quonset hut.** This structure was originally used for first aid; it was located just north of Commercial Building #49. In the early 1950's, it was moved to the racetrack area behind the judges stand where it was used as a dressing room.

#42B   **Judges stand.** This building is located inside the racetrack.

#43   **Judges stand/Dressing room.** The lower level of this structure has been used as a dressing room. It was improved in 1960. In 1997 it was moved 100 feet to the north into the track infield.

#43A   **Stage.** A portable stage was built in 1946. A permanent one was built in 1952; it was removed in 1997.

#44   **Grandstand.** An amphitheatre was built in 1888. Gage replaced the amphitheatre with a new grandstand in 1891. The Fair Association purchased it in 1899. In 1913 a new grandstand was built for $5,250; it doubled the seating capacity. In 1925 additional bleachers, 40' x 60', were added to the west of the grandstand. In 1946 a reserved seating section was added to the front. There is some reference to this "Amphitheatre" facing south onto the original track.

#45   **Food stand.** In 1983 a 54.5' x 54.5' metal Morton building constructed for $16,900 replaced a log cabin built on this site in 1939 and 1940. The log cabin was used by the Methodist Church as a food stand. Today the United Church of Sandwich runs the food stand.

#46   **Grandstand ticket office.** It was built in the 1980's on the site of an earlier ticket office that was built in 1945. The 1945 building was moved to Gate 4 in 1970. An earlier grandstand ticket office was under the grandstand.

#47   **Food stand.** This stand was built in 1955. The Sandwich Moose operated it through 1979. Sandwich Sports Boosters have operated it since 1980.

#48   **Men's and women's restrooms.** They were built in 1977. An addition was added to the east end in 1989.

#49   **Commercial building.** This metal building was put up in 1964 for $11,650.

#50   **Horticulture building.** The original building was built in 1905. A large addition was put on the original building in 1915. It burned in 1931 and was rebuilt that same year. The present structure is the same shape and on the same site as the original octagonal building that was 48 feet across. An addition was added to the east end of the current building in 1957.

#51   **Arts and Crafts demonstrations building.** This metal building was constructed in 1987.

#52   **Collections building.** This 50' x 80' Cleary building was put up in 1997.

#53   **Train shed.** This building, owned by the Otto family, was constructed in 1974. It becomes a tunnel for the train route during the Fair.

#54   **Storage building.** This is the former site of the Main Gate ticket and Treasurer's Office #1.

#55   **Storage building.** This building was constructed in 1948 with bricks from a house that was demolished in 1947.

#56   **Storage building.** In 1997 the Fair Association purchased this metal building from Wick Buildings that had used it several years as their sales location; it was moved west of Gate #1.

#57   **Treasurer's and ticket office.** This office was built in 1974 at Gate #1.

#58   **Dwelling and garage.** This home was purchased from Kenny Morris in the 1950's for the grounds' caretaker.

#59   **Exit ticket office.** Louis Miller used this garage-like building as his sales office at the Fair in 1983. It was originally located near the livestock-racetrack gate. The Fair Association purchased it from Miller after the 1983 Fair.

#60   **Racetrack.** The track was installed in 1891.

#61   **Clay track.** A new 300-foot track was installed in 1997 for tractor and truck pulls.

#62   **Food stand.** This stand was built in 1940. The Yorkville Methodist Church and later individual food vendors used this structure.

#63   **Food stand.** The stand on this site was badly damaged in a 1958 storm and removed in 1995. The Sandwich Sportsmen operated it.

#64   **Dwelling.** This brick home, demolished in 1982, was purchased in 1920 from the Fanning family. It was used as the caretaker's house.

#65   **Dwelling.** This brick home was purchased in 1943 from the Grover family; it was torn down in 1946.

#66   **Women's toilet.** This structure was built in 1910 and refurbished in 1953. It was torn down in the late 1970's.

#67   **Men's toilet.** It was torn down in 1977.

#68   **Women's toilet/Dressing room.** This building was originally a ladies' toilet near the dining hall. It was moved east of the grandstand in 1915 for a dressing room; later it was used for storage. In 1953 it was torn down.

#69   **Dining hall/Storage.** This structure served as a floral hall until 1892 before it was remodeled into a dining hall. It is often identified as the cross-shaped building. One of the three sections was torn down in 1913. Another section became a dwelling and was eventually torn down. In 1957-1958, the remaining section was used for feed storage.

#70   **Amphitheatre/Grandstand.** Some sources believe at one time an amphitheatre may have been located at the east end of the original racetrack.

#71   **Horse stables.** These structures contained space for over sixty horses. They were located along the west fence and were razed in 1934; the lumber was used to build other buildings.

#72   **Poultry building.** The original poultry house was built in 1884. It was destroyed in 1958 by wind.

#73   **Dance pavilion.** Striegel and Stolp constructed this 40' x 60' building in 1922. The sides opened up for ventilation. It was moved in the mid 1940's to South Main Street in Sandwich to be used by the VFW hall; it was torn down in 1996.

#74   **Display pavilion.** This structure was built in 1895.

#75   **Original half-mile racetrack.** This track was in place in 1888; it was referred to as the "speed ring."

#76   **Judges stand.** This structure is located in the horse arena.

#77   **Display pavilion.** This open pavilion was built on this site by 1900 for the Enterprise Company.

Building Location Index for 1910 Map

#	
#1	Main Gate ticket office
#7	Swine barn
#14	Dairy barn
#15	Sheep barn
#16	Horse barn
#17	Old draft horse barn
#17A	Men's toilet
#18	Racehorse barn
#24	Secretary's office
#26	Display pavilion
#30	Round office
#31	Rest pavilion
#38	Industrial Hall
#38A	Windmill, well, and storage tank
#42B	Judges stand
#44	Grandstand
#50	Horticulture building
#60	Racetrack
#66	Women's toilet
#67	Men's toilet
#68	Women's toilet
#69	Dining Hall
#71	Horse stables
#72	Poultry building
#74	Display pavilion
#77	Display pavilion

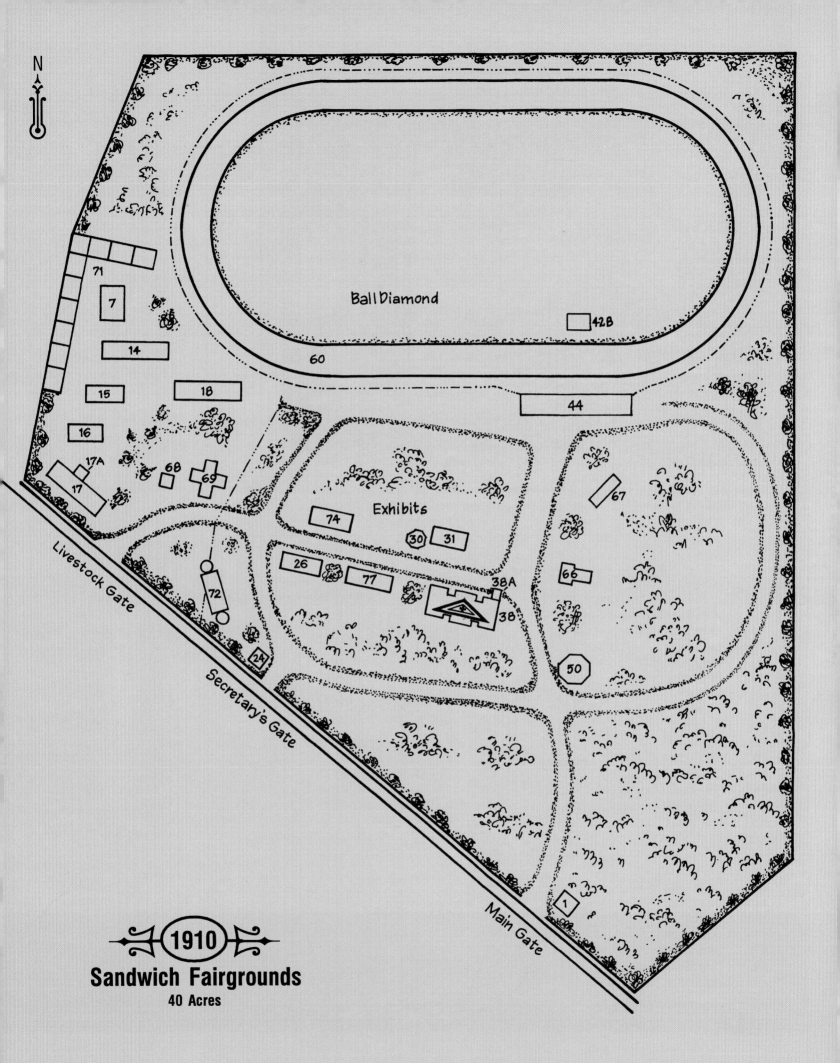

N

Ball Diamond

71

7

14

15

18

16

17A

17

68

69

74

Exhibits

30

31

26

77

72

24

38A

38

67

66

50

44

60

42B

42B

1

Livestock Gate

Secretary's Gate

Main Gate

1910
Sandwich Fairgrounds
40 Acres

61

This line drawing appeared in the *Somonauk Reveille* in August 29, 1890, with the caption "View of the stables and several of the horses in training." It depicts map location #71 on the 1888 and 1910 maps.

Building Location Index for 1950 Map

#1	Main Gate ticket office	#55	Storage building
#7	Swine barn	#60	Racetrack
#10	Cattle barn	#62	Food stand
#11	Calf and hog barn	#63	Food stand
#12A	Cattle barn	#64	Dwelling
#14	Dairy barn	#65*	Dwelling
#15	Sheep barn	#66	Women's toilet
#16	Horse barn	#67	Men's toilet
#17	Horse barn	#68	Dressing room
#17A	Men's toilet	#69	Storage
#18	Racehorse barn	#72	Poultry building
#24	Secretary's office	#73*	Dance pavilion
#26	Display pavilion	#77	Display pavilion
#27	Food stand		
#30	Round office		
#31	Food stand		
#38	Women's building		
#39A	Transformer building		
#42A	Quonset hut		
#42B	Judges stand		
#44	Grandstand		
#45	Food stand		
#46	Grandstand ticket office		
#50	Horticulture building		

*Built after 1910—torn down before 1950

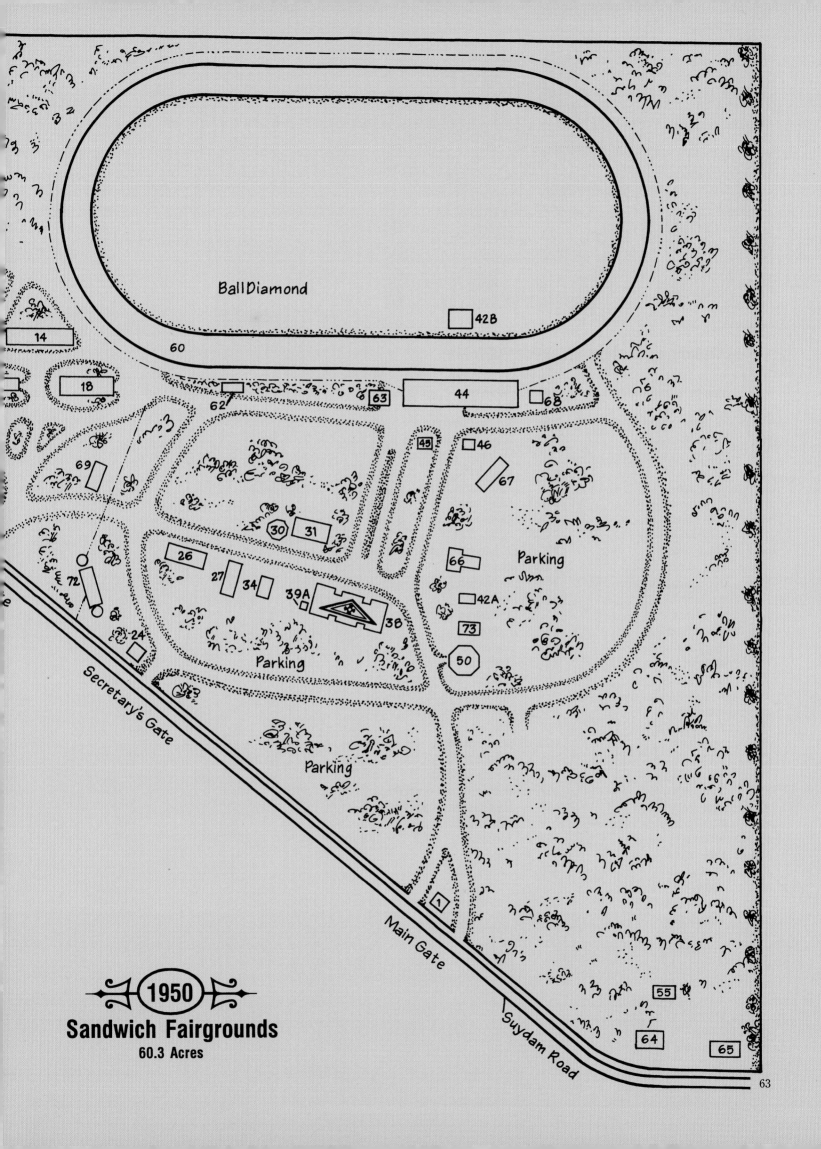

Ball Diamond

42B

14

18

60

62

63

44

68

45

46

69

67

30

31

Parking

26

66

27

34

72

39A

42A

38

73

24

50

Parking

Secretary's Gate

Parking

Main Gate

1

55

64

Suydam Road

65

1950

Sandwich Fairgrounds

60.3 Acres

Courtesy of SFA

1984

Building Location Index for 2000 Map

#1	Original Main Gate ticket office	#38B	Dance floor
#2	Draft horse barn	#39	Caboose
#3	Horse show arena	#39A	Storage building
#4	Dwelling and garage	#40	Arts, Crafts, and Photography building
#5	Ticket office	#41	Train depot
#6	Beef barn	#41A	Train tracks
#7	Swine barn	#41B*	Train tracks
#7A	Swine barn	#42	Storage building
#8	Sheep barn	#42A*	Quonset hut
#9	Sheep barn	#43	Judges stand/Dressing room
#10	Goat barn	#43A*	Stage
#11	Agriculture, Education, and Info Center	#44	Grandstand
#12	Restrooms	#45	Food stand
#13	Livestock office	#46	Grandstand ticket office
#14	Dairy barn	#47	Food stand
#14A	Milk house	#48	Restrooms
#15	FFA Farm Zoo	#49	Commercial building
#16	Ag Land Entertainment	#50	Horticulture building
#17	Horse barn	#51	Arts and Crafts demo building
#18	Racehorse barn	#52	Collections building
#19	Food stand	#53	Train shed
#20	Restrooms	#54	Storage building
#21	Shower house	#55	Storage building
#22	Metal building	#56	Storage building
#23	Maintenance shop	#57	Treasurer's and ticket office
#24	Secretary's office	#58	Dwelling and garage
#25	Windmill and well	#59	Exit ticket office
#26	Commercial building	#60	Racetrack
#27	Food stand	#61	Clay track
#28	Sheriff's building	#76	Judges stand
#29	First Aid building		
#30	Round office	*Built after 1950—torn down before 2000	
#31	Rest pavilion		
#32	ATM building		
#33	Public telephones		
#34	Food stand		
#35	Commercial building		
#36	Commercial building		
#37	Gazebo		
#38	Home Arts building		

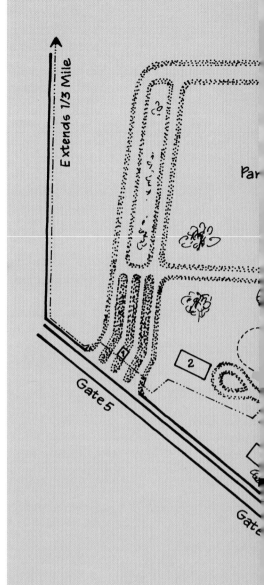

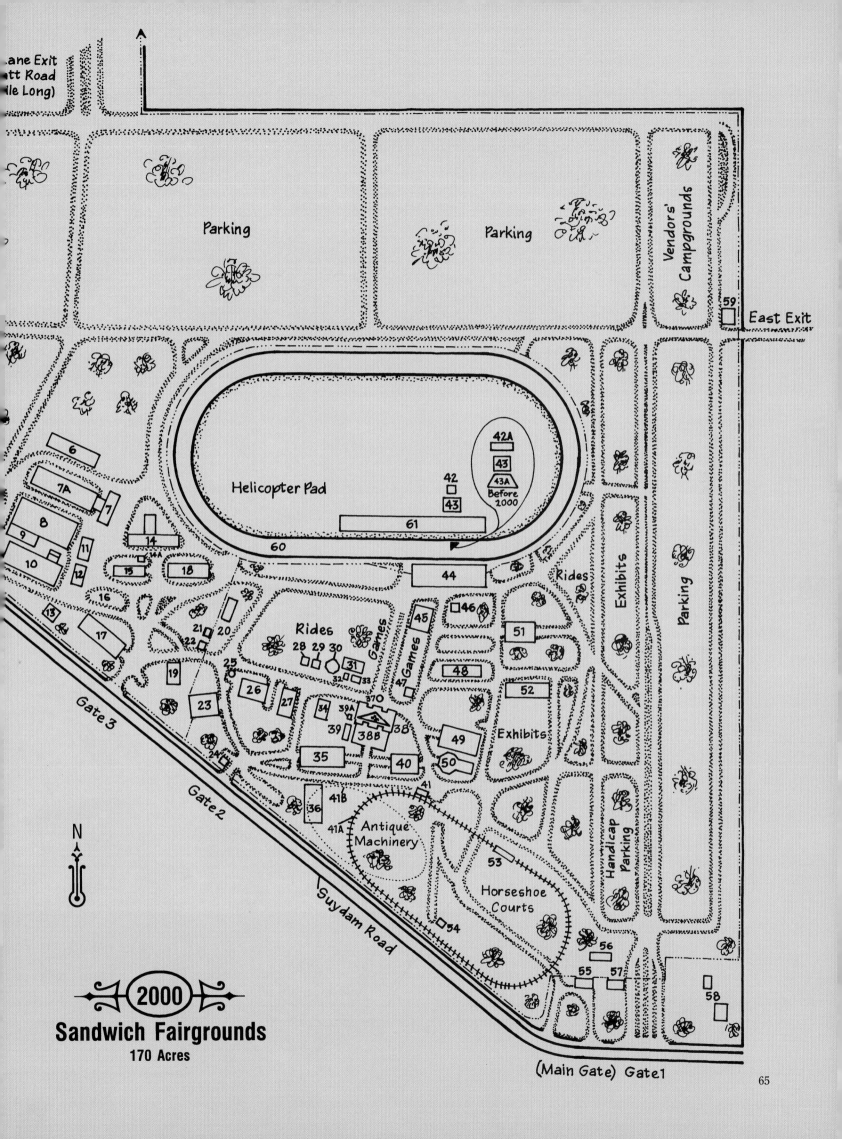

Lane Exit
att Road
le Long)

Parking

Parking

Vendors' Campgrounds

East Exit

6

7A

7

8

9

11

10

12

14

14A

15

18

16

13

17

19

Gate 3

Gate 2

Suydam Road

Helicopter Pad

42A

42

43

43A
Before 2000

61

60

44

Rides

Exhibits

Parking

46

45

Rides

51

Games

Games

48

21 20

28 29 30

31

32 33

47

52

Exhibits

22

25

26

27

34

39A

39

38B

38

49

Handicap Parking

23

35

40

50

24

41

41B

36

41A

Antique Machinery

53

55 56 57

58

Horseshoe Courts

54

N

2000

Sandwich Fairgrounds

170 Acres

(Main Gate) Gate 1

65

Photo by J.E.H.

Courtesy of B.H.

Courtesy of SFA

top left: The Secretary's Office was actually built in 1892 even though the sign on the building shows 1900. Map location #24

top center: The judges stand, circa 1891, was later converted to the Round Office. Map location #30

top right: This early 1900's photograph shows the four steps leading up to the door of the Round Office.

previous pages: Photo by S.B. **pages 66-67:** A 1990's aerial view of the fairgrounds.

below: The Round Office in 1994

Photo by S.B.

Secretary's Office

The Secretary's Office (location #24), adjacent to Gate 2 has the distinction of being the oldest structure on the grounds that is still being used for its original purpose. The Secretary's Office dates from 1892. Modernized and equipped with computers, the building continues to be the nerve center of Fair activities. Tickets were also sold here until the 1930's.

Round Office

For several decades, attendees at the Fair could not escape becoming familiar with the name of another structure which actually predates the Secretary's Office, but which has been utilized for several different purposes during a span of more than 110 years. From at least the 1940's into the 1980's when the Fair was in session, the public address system broadcasted a seemingly unending stream of requests for various individuals to "please come to the Round Office." The Round Office (location #30), actually an eight-sided structure also called the Round House, was originally the judges stand at the racetrack. The original tower boasted several extra feet of height; it was located on the north side of the racetrack opposite the grandstand. From this vantage point, judges would rule on the fairness of starts and visually determine the finish order of each horse race.

Rebuilding and reusing is a Sandwich Fair tradition. An undated photo in the *Fox Valley Shopping News* September 1, 1993, shows the considerably shortened building relocated among the trees away from the racetrack and recommissioned as the Department of Concessions. Four steps lead to the door, which is about two and one-half feet above ground level.

Another photograph in the 1985 *Sandwich Fair Times* shows the red-painted structure minus the bottom three to four feet, which eliminated the steps. This remodeling was done in the 1960's. John Kell of Sandwich was hired to cut off the building and put it on a cement slab. At that point it was still serving as the Concessions Office. The caption accompanying that photo suggests that around 1901 the building may have been used as a bandstand near its present location. The unique little Round Office retains its place of honor across the street northwest of the Home Arts building, invoking memories of Fair times past.

Courtesy of SFA

There is speculation that the Round Office may have once been used as a bandstand. Map location #30

Courtesy of SFA

Livestock Buildings

A fair could hardly be a fair without livestock. The animal structures are among the oldest on the grounds. The whitewashed, wood-frame dairy barn (location #14), which dates from 1880, originally had an interior open-loft area over the stalls on each side of the center alley. Besides its use as a storage area for feed, bedding, and equipment, the loft provided livestock owners, professional herdsmen, and Junior Fair exhibitors with convenient quarters near their stock. Bales of hay and straw serve as mattresses for rolled-out sleeping bags at Fair time. This barn was moved 30 feet to the east in 1925, and in 1992 a wing was added and the stalls were remodeled. A lean-to was built on in 1996.

The Open Show swine barn was erected in 1904, providing fifty-six pens. In 1922 twenty-four pens and space for a show ring were added at the south end. Concrete was poured in the pen and alley area in 1944, and a concrete wash apron was added at the north end of the building several years later. In 1956 a 48' x 180' hog barn (location #7) was completed.

In the opinion of pork producers, one of the most important improvements in the swine department came in 1985 with a $25,000 expenditure for an addition to the swine barn, a covered judging area, and spectator bleachers. The twin show rings feature permanent pens for confining the animals as they are placed in each class. The stress and strain on the animals, on the exhibitors, and on the judges has been significantly reduced with this modernization.

Until Allied victory in World War II allowed new construction to resume at the fairgrounds, the livestock buildings were tightly clustered around a central plaza that served as a judging

area for everything but the hogs. The open-class swine barn with its own show ring was at the north end of the plaza with the dairy barn following to the east. Proceeding on clockwise, the old sheep barn, built about 1880 that is used today for the FFA Farm Zoo (location #15), was next. Some small horse barns, a cattle barn, and the 4-H swine barn completed the circle. The Farm Zoo was started in 1967 and is a popular place for young and old during the Fair.

The cattle barn, badly damaged by a windstorm in 1958, has since given way to a restroom facility (location #12) while the small hog barn has been gutted and converted to a rest pavilion (location #11). For a number of years, this rest pavilion was maintained by the DeKalb County Farm Bureau as a service to Fair patrons. Today it is used for ag education displays.

Photo by V.B.

Courtesy of SFA

It was often necessary to house overflow livestock entries in tents equipped with temporary tethering rails or steel-post and wood-panel pens. After the war, large pole-type buildings began sprouting just to the west of the old livestock area. In 1949 and again in 1962, cattle barns were constructed, the largest being 170 feet long. In 1979 an even larger structure (location #8) was completed to house entries of sheep. The 180' x 82' building contains 200

left: Dating back to 1880, the cattle barn is the oldest building in use on the grounds. It is used today for dairy cattle exhibits. Map location #14

right top: Many improvements have been made to the hog barn since it was built in 1904. Map location #7

right bottom: New livestock buildings were added as the number of livestock exhibits grew.

Photo of B.R.

top left: The FFA Farm Zoo is located in a building once used for sheep exhibits. Map location #15

top right: The livestock office, constructed in 1968, is a busy place during the Fair. Map location #13

Once used as a hog barn and then converted to a rest pavilion, this building is now used for agriculture education displays. Map location #11

In 1974 this steer shed was ready for livestock to arrive.

pens and a central show ring. As in the swine department, the covered show ring represented another much appreciated improvement over the makeshift, open areas utilized for judging in the past.

With a big increase in the number of goats entered in the show, the southernmost of this row of buildings has now been converted from cattle to goats (location #10). Beef cattle have been shifted to the northernmost building (location #6). From south to north, the buildings now house goats, sheep, hogs, and cattle with some overlapping depending on the number of entries in each category.

Livestock Office

As a convenience to exhibitors, the Livestock Office (location #13) was constructed in 1968. It contains remnants of the old permanent platform scales used for checking in animals entered in weight-based classes. The scales were located on the west side of the swine barn. They were sold and the roof was moved to

Courtesy of SFA

Photo by V.G.

Photo by V.C.W.

where the present Livestock Office is located. In other words, the south end of the livestock office roof has the original roof of the old permanent livestock scale. To complete the structure, the sides were filled in and windows and doors were added. An addition was added in 1981. Today, portable scales are used.

Horse Barns

In the plaza of the livestock area, a concrete slab was poured in 1996 (location #16) in the area where an old horse barn stood until 1993. Today, it is the site of the Ag Land Stage where adults and children are entertained day and night.

Though a cattle barn and a thirty-two pen sheep shed were erected in 1880, permanent shelter for beef cattle, sheep, goats, and poultry seems to have been secondary to the needs of horsemen in the early years of the Fair. As the nineteenth century drew to a close and the twentieth commenced, horses were the major providers of farm power and the principal means of local transportation. Given these facts in addition to the popularity of racing, it is little wonder that provision of facilities for horses was high on the agenda of the Sandwich Fair Association.

Thirty-five hundred cement blocks were used in the 1908 construction of the 127' x 40' horse barn (location #18). Ten-foot walls erected upon a solid concrete foundation make it a continuing landmark just south of the gate to the racetrack.

An article in the August 6, 1908, issue of the *Free Press* reported that the new horse barn contained twenty-four box stalls, twelve on each side of a fifteen-foot driveway with roomy accommodations and excellent ventilation. According to the same article, "Nearly 300 loads of dirt were required to make the fill and bring the level up above any chance of water running into the

Courtesy of B.H.

left: The cement block horse barn, built in 1908, remains a landmark at the southwest end of the race-track. Map location #18

following pages: Courtesy of SFA
pages 72-73: A 1986 photograph shows horses waiting for the next race. Map location #16

photos below:
top: This horse barn was built in 1914 to accommodate harness-racing stock. Today stalls are rented to horsemen who train their horses on the track year around. Poultry is exhibited in the building during the Fair. Map location #17

bottom: The old Gletty Barn, built in 1914, has been renovated and is used for draft horse entries during the Fair. (Map location #2) The Gletty barn was part of the 1976 acquisition from the Gletty family.

barn." When built, this barn was referred to in the contemporary press as a training barn and was designed to provide accommodations for harness-racing stock. It is still occupied year round by trainers and their horses. Stall rental payments entitle horsemen access to the track for training purposes.

Horseracing has been a major attraction at the Sandwich Fair since its inception. Draft and driving horses also competed for prizes and ribbons at the Fair although in a less strenuous venue of show classes. Horse fanciers not in the racing business had to wait for a few years for their new barn, but in 1914, a 135' x 40' barn was constructed to house both heavy-draft classes and their lighter, sleeker counterparts used by the locals for transportation. This barn, located at the west end of the grounds (location #17), replaced an old draft horse barn at this same location. Since 1997 it has been used as a poultry barn during Fair week, though the stall space is rented to harness racers the rest of the year. The old Gletty barn near the west side of the grounds has been renovated and also provides a few rental spaces (location #2). During the week of the Fair, draft horse entries can be found there.

Except for the Amish communities in the state, most of the draft and buggy horses were relegated long ago to the status of novelties, but the resurgence of equestrian interest in the form of the western riding horse prompted the Fair Association to make another addition to its facilities in 1981. The Sandwich Fair's first Western Horse Show was held that year in a new arena

appropriately situated at the western edge of the grounds (location #3).

4-H Club Buildings

In 1935 a 4-H Club calf barn and swine barn were constructed. These two buildings were part of the federal government's Depression era work relief efforts. They were used for the 4-H

Photo by S.B.

Photo by J.E.H.

Courtesy of E.W.

top: Edna (Miller) Wallis was born
in the L-shaped dining hall on the
fairgrounds in 1913 where her
family was living at the time.

right: Many delicious meals were
served at the dining hall by ladies
from various churches. Map location #69

Club exhibition through 1948. At that time the
show was moved to the DeKalb area but
returned again in the early 1950's.

Dining Halls

The current Fair Association "inherited" a
reputation for good food and attractive buildings
when it bought the grounds in 1888. The
September 10, 1879, issue of the *Sycamore True
Republican* made reference to the "tasteful and
pretty" buildings. "The dining hall is a beautiful
permanent building, costing $600. It is rented
yearly at $125 by the ladies of some church, who
last year made $203 out of it."

The September 11, 1879, issue of the
Sandwich *Argus* served up a big helping of
praise: "Go to the dining hall at the fair grounds
for a good square meal. Anything you want and
all you want can be had at all hours. As the
ladies of the Congregational society never do
anything by halves, you may be sure of something good to eat."

Another advertisement in the same paper
read, "The dining hall has been trimmed and
made specialy [sic] attractive with bouquets of
flowers. The eating is superb at 40 cents a meal,
and the ladies who wait on guests look so happy
that it's a pleasure to patronize them."

Continuing to lease the dining facility at the
fairgrounds each fall, these church women
apparently did quite well financially. A story in
the September 23, 1882, *Argus* reports: "The
dining hall was conducted by the ladies of the
Congregational Church and it was well done.
On Thursday the patronage was immense. The
ladies cleared about $300, but they had to work

hard for the money." In 1884 when the fairgrounds was sold to Dieterich and Ebinger tile
factory, this is the dining facility that was moved
to a local farm to be used as a barn.

Newspaper coverage of the first Fair in
1888 was extensive. The *Sandwich Free Press*,
September 12 reported, "The ladies of the
Baptist Church will have a dining hall on the
grounds . . . where warm meals will be served
within the reach of all. All patronage will be
gratefully received, and no effort spared to ren-
der the table an attractive one." In 1889 there is
reference in the Sandwich *Argus* to a new eating
facility: "The company [Fair Association] has
erected a large dining hall which is under the
care of the young ladies of the Congregational
Church, and a good dinner will they serve each
day." At a later date, September 15, 1892, the
Sandwich *Free Press* reports that a building was
remodeled into a dining hall for the comfort of
fairgoers.

> The building formerly used as floral hall,
> was fitted up with tables and chairs for
> about 200 people; a spacious kitchen and
> a large reception room, and leased to the
> ladies of the Congregational society. Here
> all comers were served with hot meals,
> and lunches. The patronage was more
> than liberal, and every one spoke in high-
> est terms of the meals served and the
> attendance.

A reference is also made to this structure
much later in an article written during the 50th
anniversary of the Fair. It was noted in the
Sandwich Free Press September 2, 1937, that
"The old dining hall was a large structure built
in the form of a cross. The Fair Association had
this building completely equipped for serving

Courtesy of SFA

Courtesy of SFA

Photo by J.E.H.

left: The Sandwich Methodist Church operated a food stand known as the Log Cabin for over 40 years. Note the tree growing through the roof. Map location #45

right: This building replaced the original Log Cabin. It continues to be operated as a food stand by members of the United Church. Map location #45

following page: Courtesy of B.H.
page 76: Circa 1888

meals, including chairs, tables, dishes and silverware. It would seat 400 persons at a time." The article says that the building was finally abandoned because it was such a large undertaking to rent it.

Part of the building was torn down in 1913. The rest was converted into a dwelling for a number of years, but it was eventually torn down after being used for feed storage.

There is an interesting side note concerning Dining Hall when it was used as a dwelling. Edna Miller Wallis relates that in 1913 her father Albert Miller sold their home (the first place west of the fairgrounds) to Gilbert Gletty. While the Miller family waited for their new home near Sheridan to be ready to move into, they rented living quarters in the L-shaped dining hall building at the fairgrounds. On July 6, 1913, during the time they lived there, she was born.

Part of it was still a dwelling in the 1940's. Fair directors today recall that it was referred to as the "Stein" house because the Stein family lived there and trained horses at the fairgrounds.

As the years passed, other church and civic groups seized the opportunity to earn money by catering to the food needs of Fair patrons. By 1922 the Federated Church (location #31) was delivering gustatory pleasure during the Fair. The Methodist Church's "Log Cabin" just south of the grandstand was a familiar sight to fairgoers for many years. A group called the Log Cabin Class at the Sandwich Methodist Church constructed it of telephone poles in 1939 and 1940. Originally the cabin had a dirt floor with a tree growing against the northeast corner of the building. When an annex was attached for food preparation and storage, it was built around the tree. Top-hinged shutters opened to serve the public on three sides. It was razed in 1983, and the Sandwich Fair Association replaced it with a 3,000 square foot steel building (location #45) that is used as a dining facility during Fair week and throughout the year when the fairgrounds are utilized for various other functions.

Entrepreneurial spirit has steadily increased the number of food vendors who set up shop on the grounds each September. They dispense their products from permanent buildings (locations #19, 27, 34, 45, 47), tents, trailers, and mobile homes. From barbecued chicken and pork chops to cream puffs and funnel cakes, there is something to satisfy every one's taste.

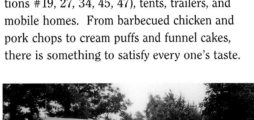

Photo by J.E.H.

The St. Paul's Catholic Church stand has been a favorite place to eat since 1959. Map location #19

Photo by S.B.

The Sandwich Band Association has used this building since 1967. Map location #27

Photo by S.B.

One of the permanent food buildings on the grounds is currently used by the Fox Valley Older Adults Services. Map location #34

Photo by J.E.H.

This building, formerly used by the Sandwich Moose Lodge, has been the location of Sandwich Sports Boosters since 1980. The Boosters have been selling pizza logs at the Fair since 1976. Map location #47

Floral Hall

The current Fair Association also "inherited" from the previous fair owners a reputation for beautiful displays. The *Sycamore True Republican,* September 10, 1879, described Floral Hall as "a cruciform structure, with an elegant floral pyramid at its apex. . . . There is a handsome stand for speakers, and for the band."

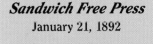

Courtesy of SFA

The September 23, 1888, issue of the *Argus* stated that "The display of fancy work, pictures and flowers was very large and elegant" in Floral Hall (location #69). The newspaper gave a detailed description of wares displayed by local merchants. In the early days, the booths of businessmen were awarded ribbons for attractiveness. This building was probably the same cross-shaped structure used for Floral Hall at earlier fairs. The best reference to the shape is made in the *Argus* in 1892 when the building was converted to Dining Hall, which was cross-shaped.

Courtesy of C.A.

In 1891 the *Free Press* reported "Floral Hall was altogether too small for what was brought for exhibition there and even with the great tent annex it was too crowded for comfort, convenience or profit." The shortage of exhibit space led to the construction of a large, 100' x 150' two-story, barn-like building in 1892. The new Floral Hall was constructed at a cost of $5,000.

Among other things the new hall housed fruit, grain, vegetable, and floral exhibits; the work of local public school children; fancy work and oil paintings; literature from the Women's Christian Temperance Union; and merchandise from local businesses. The new building received laudable comments in newspaper accounts, but the necessity of climbing stairs to view the items displayed on the second floor was a problem for some.

In 1896 M. A. Hendricks was granted permission to add a porch to the north side of Floral Hall. Although he built the porch for his commercial display area, it became the property of the Fair Association.

In May of 1905, just thirteen years after construction, Floral Hall was struck by lightning and destroyed by the resulting fire. This was a significant financial setback for the Fair Association that had just become free of debt after struggling through several years of rainy Fair weeks that had reduced attendance.

Including contents, the loss was estimated at $7,000 since items such as chairs for the grandstand and dining room, and dishes were stored there. Manure spreaders owned by the Enterprise Company were also stored there. After the fire all that remained were nails, the foundation, and the steel wheels of the spreaders standing in rows in the ashes. The stalwarts serving on the Sandwich Fair Board met within a week and decided to postpone the construction of a new horse barn in order to replace Floral Hall in time for the eighteenth Fair the following September.

Construction costs had apparently held reasonably steady or else much of the labor was donated because the 1905 rebuilding was bid at $5,000—the same as for the 1892 construction. To ensure better accessibility for older and handicapped visitors, the new structure was built on one floor instead of two.

The building has had a number of names at various times: Floral Hall, Women's Exhibit Hall, Grand Dame, Industrial Hall, Women's Building. Today, most people call this majestic structure the Home Arts

Sandwich Free Press
January 21, 1892

". . . we are glad the stockholders have voted to build a floral hall for the next exhibition. We suggest they make it large, for it will be one of the main features of this fair as it is of all others. The women take great pride in the floral hall and they will make it a great success. In the Walworth county, Wisconsin, fair, it grew to be *the* feature of the fair, and added greatly to the causes which made that county fair superior to the state fair. Let us have a good large floral hall.

top center: The two-story 100' x 150' Floral Hall was constructed in 1892 at a cost of $5,000. It was destroyed by fire in 1905. Map location #38

bottom center: A new Floral Hall built in 1905 (also known as Industrial Hall) replaced the 1892 building at the same cost of $5,000. Map location #38

below: The Home Arts building, photographed in 1996, remains a well-known landmark.

Photo by S.B.

Courtesy of B.H.

top: The original Horticulture building, built in 1905, was an octagonal structure 48' in diameter. It housed exhibits of fruits, vegetables, grains, floral arrangements, baked goods, and needlework. Map location #50

right: The Horticulture building as photographed in 1995.

bottom: The Horticulture building burned in 1931.

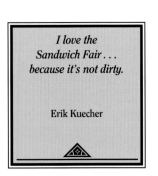

Courtesy of SFA

building (location #38). It has been used for commercial displays as well as exhibitor entries such as flowers, food, needlework, photography, and school exhibits. The 40' x 100' building is one that both local residents and visitors identify as a year-round landmark of the grounds.

Horticulture Building

When the Floral Hall was replaced in 1905, it was recognized that provision of separate areas for different types of displays would be beneficial, so $2,000 was expended for a building specifically dedicated to horticulture and agricultural products.

This original Horticulture building was an octagonal structure forty-eight feet in diameter. It housed exhibits of fruits, vegetables, grains, floral arrangements, baked goods and needlework. Having a hall specifically dedicated to horticulture has contributed further confusion to the potpourri of building names. In the minds of some, it properly became Floral Hall since it now housed the flowers. A large addition was added to this building in 1915.

In 1931 leaf burning was cited as the cause of a fire that destroyed the hall. Firemen quickly arrived on the scene, and they thought they had the smoldering fire under control; however, the tinder-dry frame structure suddenly burst into flames. The firemen's efforts were turned to saving nearby buildings.

Photo by V.G.

In Sandwich Fair tradition, the Horticulture building (location #50) was quickly rebuilt. Still in use today, it resembles the previous structure, being eight-sided with a cupola at the top. In 1957 an addition was made to the east for Junior Fair horticulture entries. During Fair week the Horticulture building is a favorite haunt of the green-thumb crowd.

Arts and Crafts and Collections

In 1972 to relieve crowding and to further separate types of exhibits, a 50' x 85' Arts and Crafts building (location #40) was constructed across the street west of Horticulture Hall. This building provides space for photography, paint-

Photo by M.E.B.

Photo by M.M.

ings, ceramics, handicrafts, woodworking and other fine arts. It was enlarged in 1982. Collectors were provided their own exhibit space in 1997 with the construction of a 50' x 80' beige and green building (location #52). From antiques to the latest craze, the Collections building provides a museum atmosphere and gives fairgoers a glimpse at American culture. Collections of all sorts from Indian arrowheads, carnival glass, porcelain dolls, to belt buckles are increasingly popular.

Photo by J.E.H.

Windmill

In 1970 the Roy LaBolle family gave an Aeromotor windmill, circa 1920, to the Sandwich Fair Association. The windmill has an eight-foot fan. It was used on the LaBolle farm south of Somonauk for many years. Erected between the Home Arts building and the livestock area (location #25), it is another icon of an earlier

period in the ever-evolving agricultural heritage of the Fair. The rainbow hues of the blades are a reminder of the value of diversity.

Caboose

In 1997 Burlington-Northern donated for display a caboose (location #39), a relic of the nation's railroad age. It is located just southwest of the Home Arts building. In 1998 it was completely remodeled to serve as an office for the electricians.

Dancing Areas

A 40' x 60' dance pavilion (location #73) built in 1922 and privately owned by Striegel and Stolp was damaged during the 1931 fire. This pavilion which operated on the grounds for about twenty years was located north of Horticulture Hall. It had sides that could be propped up creating an open-air floor where the fox trot was a popular exercise for paying customers. The charge was a dime for each dance, and the floor was cleared after every dance. In the 1940's this building was moved to South Main Street in Sandwich and used as a VFW hall until 1996.

Years later in 1954, the Sandwich Fair Association began sponsoring dances that

top left: The spacious 50' x 85' Arts and Crafts building was built in 1972. Map location #40

top right: The windmill, donated by the LaBolle family in 1970, has become a landmark on the grounds. Map location #25

Photo by M.M.

right: The Burlington-Northern caboose was brought to the Fair in 1997. It sits southwest of the Home Arts building and serves as the electrician's office. Map location #39

left: Collectors were provided their own building in 1997 when this 50' x 80' building was constructed. Map location #52

Electricity

Jim Anderson

Until 1923 the fairgrounds was quiet when darkness fell. It was not until the Fair directors added night entertainment that electricity became a necessity. Director Carlton "Dutch" Hough and James Anderson were responsible for much of the early wiring. According to Director Harold Dannewitz, who has been electrician at the Fair since 1991, they made improvements even when money was not available in their department. Anderson convinced ComEd to let him use old poles, transformers, and other equipment.

The original system was upgraded in 1939 when many of the buildings were rewired, and wires that had been strung from tree to tree were re-strung to poles. Additional upgrades were made in 1953 with better lighting along the roads and parking areas.

Maintenance is on-going. At one time three transformers fed the entire grounds; today there are 28 transformers. The 2,400-volt system is in the process of being transferred to a 7,200-volt system. Mercury vapor and sodium vapor lights are gradually replacing incandescent light bulbs.

Dannewitz says, "We start right after the Fair . . . adding new wires and bigger transformers for next year to accommodate the load." Nevertheless, the unexpected is inevitable. A few years ago, the carnival supplied a generator for emergency power so a Friday night show at the grandstand could go on as scheduled. The next year a three-phase line was installed into the grandstand area.

To prepare for the actual five-days of the Fair, Dannewitz and fellow electricians Reed Johnson and Frank Moran start weeks before the Fair. "It's like moving in a small town . . . [with] 70-80 house trailers that the carnival people bring in." All of the tents also have to be wired.

During the Fair the electricians work 18-hour days. They replace bulbs and troubleshoot problems for the vendors. They keep close voltage checks on the transformers. Despite the long hours, Dannewitz enjoys doing his part to keep the Fair tradition going.

Beacon News

Carlton "Dutch" Hough

Courtesy of H.D.

Harold Dannewitz

Courtesy of SFA

Courtesy of SFA

This ticket booth was the entrance to the dance floor on the south side of the Home Arts building.

catered especially to area teens. A 40' x 80' concrete slab was poured on the south side of the Home Arts building (location #38b). During the Fair and on Thursday nights from mid-June through August, a local band provided dance music in a well-supervised setting. Bub and His Boys, a local combo, was the featured band during most of the period when dances were held. Later, space for craft demonstrations was created by placing a tent over the former dance floor. That was the site of woodcarving, spinning, candle making, and other handicrafts until a permanent shelter (location #51) was provided for those activities in 1987. Today the concrete area is used for a square-dancing exhibition during the Fair.

Poultry Exhibits

Through World War II, nearly every farm had a poultry flock to supply the family with eggs and regular main course meals. Entering the best from those flocks in competition at the county fair became a time-honored tradition in

Courtesy of PF

The original, octagonal poultry house was cut in two and lengthened into this building to accommodate more poultry entries. It was destroyed by wind in 1958. Map location #72

Photo by N.U.

rural communities. One of the earliest newspaper accounts of buildings on the Sandwich fairgrounds mentioned an octagonal chicken house. It was built in 1884 (location #72).

A *Free Press* article in the September 15, 1904, edition reads as follows: "One of the most attractive exhibits on the grounds is seen in the big, roomy, well-ventilated poultry house. Wm. Fraser has charge of this department and has his troubles locating the big rooster and the little, strutting bantam."

In 1914 new, collapsible-steel poultry coops were purchased for the department. By 1937 William Fraser had been poultry superintendent for fifty years. Contagious disease problems prompted the suspension of all live poultry shows in the United States in 1946. The building was destroyed by wind in 1958. The Sandwich Fair poultry show resumed in 1967 in a tent, and in 1980, the Fair Board expended $25,500 for a 54' x 84' poultry building (location #23) that would also serve as a workshop and storage area for the grounds-keeping crew.

During the last few years, because of the annual inconvenience of emptying the building of maintenance equipment, the poultry show has utilized the horse barn located just inside Gate 3 (location #17). Horse owners must vacate the premises during the Fair.

Racetrack and Grandstand Area

Horseracing has always been a popular pastime in rural America and is an integral part of the Sandwich Fair's history. Some of the

Sandwich Free Press

earliest photographs and sketches of the Sandwich Fair portray the racetrack (location #60) and race horses. Newspaper clippings contain a great deal of commentary on the condition of the track and the results of races.

A few paragraphs about the Sandwich Fair published around 1965 include information that in 1888 when the Sandwich Fair Association bought out the holdings of an earlier fair, the Agricultural Institute, the racetrack (location #75) was near the road behind the present location of the Secretary's Office. A grove of trees was enclosed by that racing oval. Former groundskeeper Herman Carlson states that roadways to the south of the current grandstand mark this earlier location of the track and that there was an earlier grandstand facing south, opposite the direction of the current one.

The August 29, 1890, edition of the *Somonauk Reveille* has an artist's rendition captioned "The Judges Stand and Amphitheatre." Presumably, this would be the "amphitheatre"

top: In 1980 the maintenance-poultry building (Map location #23) was constructed (building on the right). On the left is the Secretary's Office. Map location #24

center: An artist's rendition captioned "The Judges' Stand and Amphitheatre" in a 1890 *Somonauk Reveille* newspaper. Map location #44

bottom: An early photo of horse racing at the grandstand. Note the timers stand directly in front of the grandstand.

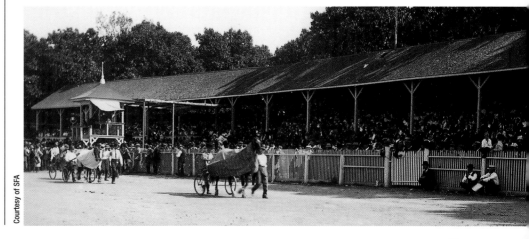

Courtesy of SFA

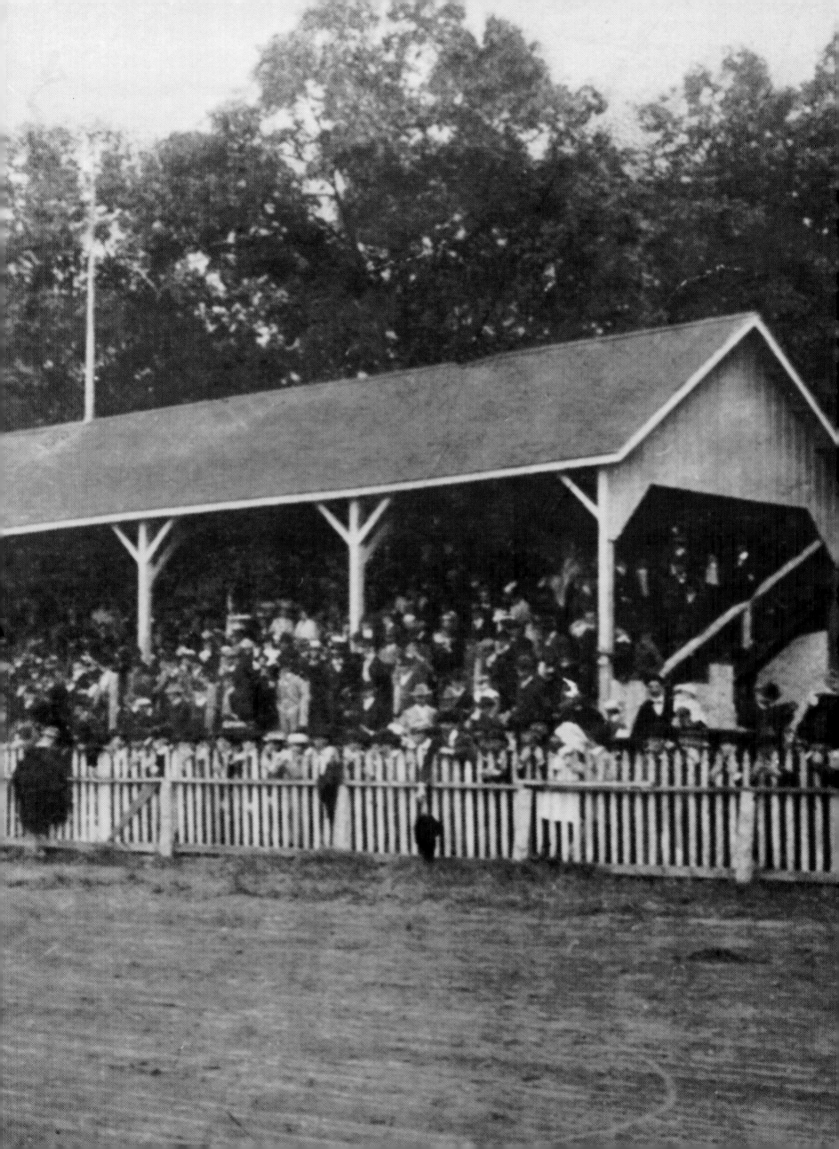

Courtesy of B.H.

top: An early glimpse of the grandstand from the southwest. Map location #44

previous pages: Courtesy of SFA pages 82-83: Old grandstand, circa 1900

bottom: The grandstand as it looked in 1998. The present grandstand was constructed for the 1913 Fair. Map location #44

constructed in 1888 that was replaced by a "Gage" grandstand in 1891 and purchased from a private party in 1899. A photograph printed in a Sandwich Fair premium book shows the back of the Gage grandstand in 1909. It is believed by some that an amphitheatre may have been located on the east end of the original racetrack.

The present grandstand (location #44), slightly longer and much deeper than the first one on the same site, was completed in time for the 1913 Fair season. There was space for about 2,100 chairs giving this grandstand more than double the capacity of the one it replaced. The cost was $5,250.

According to long-time groundskeeper Herman Carlson, the grandstand originally had a pull-down stairs to provide access to a walkway on the roof. It was from this walkway that the finishes of races were photographed to determine the winners in close heats. Mr. Carlson added that pigeons, raccoons, and other creatures made a real mess up there. Photo finishes are still taken from the upper area of the grandstand.

In 1925 to further increase seating, a 40' x 60' bleacher area was added just west of the grandstand. The bleachers held 500 people. More spectators would line the fence extending west from the bleachers where they would have an outstanding view as the drivers turned their sulkies for the start of each race. The bleachers were later removed.

The track itself was an object of considerable interest to racing fans, the news media, and especially the men who maintained it. Groundskeeper Shelby Morris's grandson Larry D. Warrington writes of his grandfather's work: "Granddad took so much pride in the racetrack.... The grounds always looked neat and clean, but the track was pristine. The lime was always white and the drag marks perfect lines, no swiggles or wavers."

Another of Morris's grandchildren, Sandra Warrington Granholm, comments: "One of

Photo by N.U.

Caretakers

Courtesy of S.G.

Caretaker Shelby and Mrs. Morris
pictured in June 1967

Courtesy of SFA

Herman Carlson assumed the caretaker
duties in 1968.

Photo by S.B.

James "Biff" Webber (l.) assumed the
caretaker position in 1999 from
Andy Krafft (r.). Krafft took over the
position from Carlson in 1987.

The Sandwich Fair Board of Directors has always been a working board. In an 1898 Sandwich *Free Press*, Fred Pratt, who was Superintendent of Grounds, was singled out for his contributions: "Fred Pratt has done a most excellent job of cleaning up the grounds; gravel has been hauled, trees trimmed and underbrush and rubbish picked up and hauled away."

In 1908 a *Free Press* article gave more information: "Fred Pratt and Henry Hennis went to Joliet on Monday to see about buying a picket fence for the south side of the home stretch. They were after a fence similar to that used at the state fairgrounds at Springfield."

In the July 1938 Fair board minutes, the board agreed to hire a custodian for the grounds and "to take the charge at picnics." The duties of the Sandwich Fair caretaker were from the beginning, demanding and varied. The head groundskeeper is a permanent resident on the fairgrounds, and his duties continue year round. Besides regular maintenance, there are numerous events other than the Fair that require his presence and assistance.

Shelby Morris served as caretaker from 1946 until his death in an automobile accident in 1968. His grandson, Larry Warrington writes: "When Granddad would mow, he started out in a different spot each time so that it never looked the same all over. The cars parked on the grass, but it always looked like a lawn—no ruts or bare spots. . . . During the fair week it was nonstop work, sunrise to late at night. Granddad had to see to everything from garbage pick-up to manure hauling."

Herman Carlson assumed the duties of Morris. Herman, a talented carpenter, worked on buildings and fences at the Fair. One of his more notable accomplishments was a 1:16 scale model of the Home Arts building; he mounted it on wheels so it could be towed in local parades. The *Sandwich Fair Times* printed a photograph of Carlson and an interview:

> 'I'm just the groundskeeper,' is how Herman Carlson describes his job. But what grounds they are! Imagine the endless repairing, cleaning, and mowing Herman is responsible for! A permanent resident on the grounds, Herman is the guy that every director, every supervisor, every employee of the fair has depended on for the past 19 years. During fair week Herman's work day averages around 16 hours . . . now that's commitment.

Herman continued as groundskeeper through the one-hundredth celebration of the Sandwich Fair in 1987, initiating Andy Krafft to the job during the last year of his tenure.

Andy Krafft worked at the fairgrounds for many years before assuming the role of groundskeeper. Like many farmers in the Somonauk-Sandwich area, he helped out during Fair week. In 1959 Andy helped in the hog department and in 1967, board member Louis Wagner recruited him to organize an antique machinery show. He worked with the antique machinery until 1987 when he retired from farming. His retirement from farming left him available for the head groundskeeper job that he held through 1998. During Andy's tenure off-season events held during the summer greatly increased in number and size. New parking areas and show areas were opened as the size of the Fair grew. The job changed the most while Andy was groundskeeper. Besides the Fair, there are events nearly every weekend, such as Sandwich Antique Shows, Blue Grass Festival, Early Day Engine Club, 4 x 4 Jamboree, 4-H Fair, motorcycle events, craft shows, and picnics.

Jim "Biff" Webber, assistant under Andy Krafft, assumed the caretaker position in 1999. He has been involved in the Fair most of his life, starting as a night watchmen after completing high school. After All-Steel closed, he started working for the Fair during the summer season. In the off-season, Webber keeps busy doing maintenance on equipment and buildings.

Granddad's main jobs during the fair was readying the race track for the horse races. He hated what the demolition derby did to 'his' track."

It has always been difficult for the groundskeepers to maintain the condition of the harness racing track when it was used for other things. Gnashing of teeth by groundskeepers has only recently been somewhat relieved by the installation of a new, clay truck- and tractor-pulling track inside the racetrack oval (location #61). Way back in 1891, a writer for the *Somonauk Reveille* in a column titled "This Year's Fair," extols the merits of a ". . . race course that is not surpassed in this neck of the woods. . . ."

In 1898 the *Free Press* refers to the track in an article about the upcoming Fair: "The track should be fast and some very fast miles paced and trotted." An article in the *Free Press* of April 16, 1908, indicates how much work went into keeping the Sandwich Fair racetrack in good condition:

> Of interest to horsemen and those who enjoy seeing the harness races, will be the improvements to the race track [sic] which will be practically a new one. Last fall the track was given a heavy covering of manure and plowed up and now teams and men are at work leveling it down. The sag at the beginning of the home stretch is to be filled up, making practically a dead level track and a fast and safe one. When the track was first built, a cover of dirt was placed upon it and which was never thoroughly mixed with the clay and dirt below it and for that reason would cup out or give way under the feet of the horses. By plow-

ing it up, the directors hope to obviate this handicap to fast times and have as good a track as there is anywhere in the state.

During the 1940's, a number of improvements were made to the track and grandstand complex. An east-end exit from the stands was added and the west-end gate enlarged in 1942. In 1945 a new grandstand ticket office was built, and the gate and track crossing to the east of the grandstand was improved. The 1945 ticket office was moved in 1970 to Gate 4 for a ticket office. A new, larger grandstand ticket office was then built (location #46).

In following years lights and a new front section were added to the grandstand, and a large stage was constructed across the track from the spectator seating. At this time the front portion of seating was designated as "reserved." Also in 1945 a concrete floor was poured below the west section of the grandstand, and the area was leased to vendors.

In 1947 the number of lights on the grandstand was doubled. A picket fence was erected around the track in 1948. For more durability, agricultural limestone is now used to surface the track. The stage in front of the grandstand was used for band concerts, for performances by National Barn Dance and Grand Ole Opry stars, for the Roxyettes, for vaudeville, a circus and numerous other shows.

Outstanding patron response to these productions prompted the Fair Association to build a "permanent" stage in front of the grandstand in 1952, and in 1960 this stage was updated (location #43a). However, nothing is forever. In 1997 the grandstand stage was removed to make way for the tractor- and truck-pull track. The judges stand was moved back to the north side of the new pulling track by a crane donated by County Crane to make more room for the

top left: The 1945 grandstand ticket office was moved in the 1970's to Gate 4 and is used for storage. Map location #5

bottom left: In the 1970's a new, larger grandstand ticket office was built. Map location #46

right: A temporary stage is shown being used in front of the grandstand in the late 1940's. A permanent stage was built in 1952 and used through 1996. Since 1997, temporary stages have been used when needed. Map location #43A

Photo by J.E.H.

Photo by J.E.H.

Courtesy of SFA

Courtesy of SFA

pulling track. Drainage was installed to accommodate the track, and many loads of clay were hauled to make an excellent pulling track.

Continuing the tradition of making the best better, the grandstand itself was renovated in 1996 with installation of aluminum seating. In 1999 the front, reserved seating was completely redone. The entire roof was also replaced, and an area for wheelchairs was added. Portable stages are now used when needed.

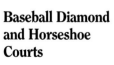

Photo by B.V.

Photo by M.M.

Baseball Diamond and Horseshoe Courts

During the first half of the twentieth century, baseball truly earned its label as "America's pastime." Community-sponsored teams throughout the Midwest proudly carried the names of their towns emblazoned across their uniforms. A baseball diamond in the racetrack infield was the site of invitational games each year during Fair week, and the box scores vied with racing results for space in local newspapers. In 1915 the Fair Association relocated a building east of the grandstand to serve as a dressing room for ball players (location #68).

Horseshoe pitching is another participation sport sponsored by the Fair Association. The game has come a long way from the days when real horseshoes were tossed at a steel post. In high-level competition these days, it is not unusual for all four shoes pitched to be ringers. Today the horseshoe courts are located inside Otto's train track.

top: An 1890's baseball game held in the racetrack infield shows the baseball games drew large crowds.

top center: The judges stand on the north side of the racetrack that is used today. Map location #43

bottom center: In 1999 the reserved seating at the grandstand was completely redone.

Commercial Exhibit Buildings

Provision of permanent facilities specifically for the use of commercial exhibitors began as early as 1895 when an open-display building was constructed for Betz John Deere implement company of Somonauk (location #74). By 1900 two other open-display buildings had been constructed—one for the Sandwich Manufacturing Company (location #26) and the other for The Enterprise Company (location #77). Besides protection from the elements on rainy days, these structures offered shade and free movement of air.

They were popular spots during hot weather. Plank benches connected the outside framing posts and many individuals looked over the machinery on display while resting their weary feet. Much of the machinery continued to be exhibited in the open. In 1904 a *Free Press* writer wrote metaphorically: "Machinery Hall, its sides the horizon, its roof the heavens, is attracting the farmers and a big crowd is always around. Both the Sandwich Mfg. Co. and Enterprise Wind Mill Co. are making excellent exhibits, besides numerous other companies of some special piece of machinery."

While a couple of purveyors of farm equipment could count upon occupying the same fixed locations each year, local merchants increasingly relied upon tents to house their wares. Both individual-sized units and large tents shared by several interests lined the avenues.

In the Depression year of 1930, it was decided that henceforth the exhibitor would pay for the space for commercial displays. Not until 1964 did the Fair board venture to erect a permanent, closed building specifically for rental to firms desiring to show their wares to the public.

An open-display building was constructed west of the Round Office in 1895 for A.H. Betz Implement Company of Somonauk. Map location #74

Courtesy of SFA

By 1900 this open building had been constructed for Sandwich Manufacturing Company. It was a popular place for men to gather. This photograph is from the 1904 premium book. Map location #26

Courtesy of SFA

The Sandwich Enterprise Company had an open-display building by 1900 in the implement display area west of Floral Hall. This photograph is from the 1904 premium book. Map location #77

Courtesy of SFA

Commercial building #4 was built in 1997 east of the Secretary's Office. Map location #36

Photo by J.E.H.

Courtesy of SFA

Aerial view of the tented commercial area. The tent was replaced in the early 1960's by a permanent metal building. The building proved a popular alternative to five days in a tent. Map location #49

The first commercial building proved to be a popular alternative to spending five days in a tent. Not only did the building remain dry during inclement weather, it could be locked at night providing security for valuable merchandise and display hardware. Four commercial buildings (locations #26, 35, 36, and 49) now shelter the displays of various businesses, but many tents are still needed to handle the overflow.

Miniature Train Track Area

First operated in 1953, Augie Otto's steam train has become another Fair landmark. A station-house ticket booth (location #41) has been erected as well as a storage shed (location #53) for the locomotive and passenger cars. Enlargement of the track layout and introduction of a bigger locomotive in 1974 necessitated shifting the main Fair entrance to the east end of the grounds. The area inside the track is utilized for the antique machinery display, melodramas, pony rides, and horseshoe pitching.

Photo by J.E.H.

Otto's station-house ticket booth was erected in 1974. Map location #41

Photo by J.E.H.

Otto's storage shed was built in 1974 to house the locomotive and passenger cars. Map location #53

89

Midway Area

The carnival and entertainment section of the fairgrounds has traditionally occupied the space surrounded by the roads that trace the path of the original horseracing track south of the present grandstand. In general terms the midway was set up from in front of the Home Arts building to the Grandstand ticket office. A double midway is still there, but rides and entertainment booths now have expanded out of the old track oval and extend a considerable distance east. Some space previously used for visitor parking is now occupied by the carnival.

Improved Facilities for Larger Crowds

The Sandwich Fairgrounds used to be a quiet, relatively deserted place most of the year; today, however, there is an activity almost every weekend. Around Labor Day each fall, the grounds assume the character of a small city with many of the same needs for services as a small city. Water, sewer, lighting, power, law enforcement, waste disposal, and communication are suddenly in demand. Though they are all required services today, in earlier years it was possible to sidestep most of them.

Visitors to those first expositions got into their buggies and headed home to do the evening chores before the setting sun made artificial lighting an imperative. As far as energy was concerned, there was little need to reach beyond the manpower and horsepower supplied by individual exhibitors and show patrons.

At the turn of the century, communication was not expected to be instantaneous and worldwide in scope. Word of mouth and a weekly

Courtesy of SFA

top: A view of the 1901 midway; note the clothing styles worn to the Fair at that time.

Courtesy of SFA

bottom: The midway, as shown in the 1940's, has traditionally been located in the center of the fairgrounds.

previous pages:
pages 90-91: Courtesy of SFA
A recent night photo of the midway looking south to the Home Arts building

Sandwich Free Press

The original Main Gate is believed to have been built in 1876 by the Union Agricultural Institute.

newspaper got the job done. In fact, one of the attractions of the Fair was the opportunity to visit with folks and catch up on the news. Sanitation was not ignored, but because the population density was much lower than today, less sophisticated means of waste disposal sufficed. The Fair board modernized essential services as patronage grew, as funds were available, and as the public demanded it.

Restrooms

"I remember holding my mother's hand and entering what was, from a child's viewpoint, a very large outhouse," recalls Sandra Warrington Granholm, granddaughter of Shelby Morris, long-time caretaker at the fairgrounds.

The time was the 1950's and while most of the facilities at the Fair had been kept up-to-date, restroom accommodations for both men and women were still in a nineteenth-century mode. For the convenience of the men in the livestock area at the west edge of the grounds, there was a lean-to attached to a horse barn. The interior featured an eave trough extending along two sides of the room draining into a pit topped by a communal multi-holer on a raised platform—another very large outhouse. The records show that outhouses at the fairgrounds had a long history.

According to minutes of the Fair Association, on November 5, 1895, the board directed that a building committee was to "put privies in repair." When the board revisited the subject of public restrooms seventy-three years later, it was still necessary to put privies in repair. At their regular meeting on February 9, 1968, a special committee reported on an engineering study of the feasibility of installing flush toilets at the fairgrounds.

It was estimated that the cost of such a project would total around $75,000 and because of the large cost, it was decided to postpone any decision and continue to study the problem.

At long last in 1976, in an interview, Fair Secretary Louis Brady said that one major complaint of fairgoers—the lack of flush toilets— was being addressed. A city sewer line had been extended to the grounds and modern restroom facilities would be ready for the ninetieth renewal of the Sandwich Fair in 1977. Good riddance to the Fair's very large outhouses! More modern restrooms were constructed east (location #48) and west (location #12) in 1977,

photo 1: It wasn't until the mid 1970's that flush toilets were installed. The photo shows the east men's toilet in 1977. Map location #67

photo 2: The old east women's restroom. The front part of the building was a room with rocking chairs for mothers with children. It was torn down in the late 1970's. Map location #66

photo 3: Modern restrooms were constructed northeast of the Home Arts building in 1977; an addition was added in 1989. (Map location #48) The Women's toilet on the right was later torn down.

photo 4: North of the windmill is a shower house (l.) for exhibitors and vendors and a public restroom (r.) Map locations #21 and #20

and in 1982, another facility (location #20) was added near the middle of the exhibit area. An addition was made to the east restrooms in 1989.

Courtesy of R.P.

top: This late 1890's photograph shows a windmill near the northeast corner of Floral Hall. It collapsed along with the water tower in the 1905 fire of Floral Hall. Map location #38A

right: Public pay telephones are located near the Round Office and Rest pavilion. Pay phones are still used by some, but personal cellular telephones have become the communications method for many people. Map location #33

Water Sources

A reliable source of water is a basic requirement when large numbers of people and/or animals are brought together in a small area. In 1897 the California Windmill Company was secured to supply water for the Fair. Presumably they were to provide equipment to pump water from a well into an elevated storage tank.

Photographs of the 1892 Floral Hall show a windmill near the northeast corner of that building (location #38a) and reports of the fire which destroyed the hall in 1905 tell of the windmill and water tower collapsing into the burning building. Whether the wind didn't blow enough to operate the windmill or whether the well was overtaxed is not explained in the article.

Following the 1898 Fair, the *Sandwich Free Press* announced that because of "a big shortage of water" at the Fair that just closed, the Fair Board of Directors voted to appropriate $1,000 to extend a water main from Third and Castle Streets to the fairgrounds. In 1907 the *Somonauk Reveille* reported the satisfactory result of this expenditure. The article titled "Fair Will Soon Open" says in part "The water mains from the city of Sandwich run into the grounds, insuring an abundant supply of good, pure, cold water." However, by 1939, the

Sandwich Fair Association decided to once again depend on its own water supply. Their decision was prompted at least in part by the city wanting to install a water meter at the fairgrounds. The *Sandwich Free Press* account on August 17, 1939:

> A new deep well is being dug on the grounds by Lawrence Evans. This well will be deep enough to strike good water and will supply the new bubbling fountains on the grounds. This will be another feature much appreciated by the fair patrons. The water will be pumped from the well by a pump recently invented by Mr. Evans. This pump will be so stationed that it will not only supply the water for the entire grounds, but will also form a part of Mr. Evans display. This will give everyone a chance to see it in operation (location #25).

Eventually, demand for water became too much for the deep-well approach. In an interview with the *Aurora Beacon News* in 1962, Fair President Carlton "Dutch" Hough said that $6,000 from the previous year's receipts had been invested to bring a water main out to the fairgrounds from Sandwich.

Telephones and Safety Buildings

With cell phones in their pockets and their purses, today's fairgoers are linked to the world. As recent as ten years ago, conversation at a distance usually went through copper wires and instantaneous personal communication was not taken for granted. A photograph in the *Sandwich Fair Times* of 1983 shows a telephone bank (location #33) that had recently been installed near the Round Office by General

Photo by J.H.

Courtesy of SFA

left: The first aid building west of the Round Office was added in 1971. It is staffed during Fair hours. Map location #29

bottom: The Gazebo first appeared at the 1993 Fair as an information booth and dispenser of official Sandwich Fair souvenirs. Map location #37

Telephone, the local service provider. Since they were first made available, public telephones at the fairgrounds were generally considered to be for emergency use.

Public safety is always of primary concern where large numbers of people congregate. While the DeKalb County Sheriff's Department has law enforcement responsibility at the Sandwich Fairgrounds year round, during Fair week uniformed officers are on site to provide security and prevent interpersonal disputes from getting out of hand. They also enforce regulations against alcohol consumption on the grounds and deal with various other issues of crowd control.

According to Sheriff Roger Scott, one of the department's most important functions at the Fair is reuniting parents and lost children. The sheriff emphasized that his officers specifically volunteer for duty at the fairgrounds and find it to be an enjoyable experience. The Fair Association reimburses the department for expenses incurred, the officers being paid time and a half for their service. In addition to the uniformed officers, the Sheriff's Auxiliary assists with traffic flow into and out of the fairgrounds. While the Fair is in session, the Sheriff's Police (location #28) are headquartered west of the Round Office.

Information and Souvenirs

In 1993 a new structure appeared on the grounds that is reminiscent of the first Sandwich Fair back in 1888. It is an eight-sided structure, approximately twelve feet in diameter with a cupola, a shake roof, and trim that matches the Home Arts building. Built by Director Scott Breunig and painted by Director Don Augustine, the portable Gazebo is placed at the center of the Fair's pedestrian traffic flow (location #37) just north of the Home Arts building during the week of the Fair. The Gazebo serves as an information booth and a dispenser of official Sandwich Fair souvenirs.

Courtesy of SFA

Courtesy of SFA

1897

Courtesy of B.H.

circa 1890

Sandwich Fair Trees

The Sandwich Fair has always been known for its cool, shaded grounds. As early as November 14, 1885, even before the current Fair began, Directors H. Hennis and F. A. Pratt were instructed by the board to plant shade trees upon the fairgrounds. Again in November 1899, Hennis and Pratt were instructed to plant shade trees. Many of these original trees provide some of the best shade on the grounds today.

In 1902 the *Free Press* advertised the coming Fair: "The grass is like a well-kept lawn, and the great, sturdy oak trees provide ample shade." The next record of tree planting took place in 1947. One hundred shade trees were planted in the east part of the grounds. Unfortunately many of them were American elms that died from the Dutch elm disease in the 1950's. There has been a concerted effort by the Fair Association throughout the years to plant new trees and protect the old ones.

In the mid 1970's, caretaker Herman Carlson planted several ash trees just northeast of the racetrack in a grove known informally today as Herman's woods. Ponderosa pines were grown from seeds and planted near the entrance. In 1984, 1985, and 1986, Director Don Stahl and his son Doug planted one hundred twenty small cottonwood saplings in the west parking lot north of the livestock buildings. These trees have grown to shade the parking area and provide sought-after parking spots.

A tree spade was used to transplant 20 large trees on the fairgrounds for the first time in 1993. These trees were of various species and large enough to avoid being run over by the increased traffic. This planting program has continued with about 20 large trees being relocated annually to fill empty spots on the grounds, to expand the shaded areas in the parking lots, and to replace trees that die.

In 1995 the family of Dr. A. A. Legner, a veterinarian and

Courtesy of B.H.

1953

well-known board member who began working at the Fair in the 1960's, donated two trees in his name. Today a plaque commemorates people who have had trees donated in their honor. To date, there are about 25 names on the plaque. During the Fair the plaque is located on the corner near the windmill.

Flagpoles and Memorials

Several memorials, special gifts, and commemorative markers dot the grounds. In 1943 L. M. Hubbard, L. R. Evans, and Carlton "Dutch" Hough donated a flagpole and flag. The pole was first erected in front of the grandstand but later moved to the livestock area. In 1971 a flagpole was installed at the Main Gate on Suydam Road honoring the late Lewis B. Rex, who served as Treasurer of the Sandwich Fair Association from 1957 to 1968. Another flagpole was installed in 1979 at the west gate on Suydam Road as a memorial to the Gletty family who over a period of thirty years sold parcels of their land to the Association enabling expansion of the fairgrounds. The Glettys formerly owned nearly half the present acreage.

In 1962 a rock garden and monument was placed just inside the perimeter fence near the Gletty Road/Center Street intersection. Plaques there honor two, long-time members of the Board of Directors: Louis Wagner for his thirty years of service and Carlton Hough for his forty years as officer and director. In front of the Round Office is a granite monument commemorating the Fair's 100th anniversary. King and Sons Monuments, Sandwich, contributed it in the Sandwich Fair's centennial year of 1987.

The flagpoles, the memorials, and all the reminders of bygone times stand with the well-kept grounds and buildings—old and new—as a monument to the perseverance of the Sandwich Fair Association in continuing the Midwestern county fair movement into the twenty-first century.

top: The flagpoles on the grounds were dedicated as memorials: The east gate flagpole to the late treasurer Lewis B. Rex, and the west gate flagpole to the Gletty family who sold many acres of land to the Fair to enable the expansion of the fairgrounds.

bottom right: The open pavilion on the left was for the New Idea Company which was a successor to Sandwich Manufacturing Company. A rest pavilion is in the location today. Map location #31

Photo by S.B.

The rock garden near the Gletty Road/Center Street intersection honors two long-time directors: Louis Wagner and Carlton Hough.

1950's

Courtesy of SFA

Fair Roads

The Sandwich Fairgrounds has over six miles of roads. Most of them are gravel and are found in the parking areas. The exit road to the north is over a mile long, and the exit to the east is nearly a quarter mile long. Most of the roads in the show area and some of the roads in the livestock area are paved. More will be paved as funds become available.

Except for those in the parking lots, the roads have names. They were originally named by past Fair President Carlton "Dutch" Hough, who took on the task of creating an accurate scale map of the fairgrounds. Every road, every building, tile lines, water lines, electric lines, and even trees were plotted on the map. This map was finished in mid 1970's and is still used today. Since it was Dutch's map, he named the roads. He named them for directors who were on the Fair board at that time and for some other Fair people. The road names corresponded to the part of the fairgrounds where the individuals were involved. New roads have been added since the original names were given; however, none of the new roads have been named for directors.

Departments and Exhibitors: Friendly Competition

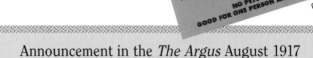

Courtesy of SFA

Courtesy of SFA

September is fair time in Sandwich, Illinois. It is a time when residents of DeKalb and neighboring counties prepare their biggest pumpkins, tastiest pies, best crafts, and finest livestock and transport them to the Sandwich Fair held on the DeKalb County Fairgrounds.

Preparing exhibits is a custom that has been encouraged since the early days of the Fair. In 1915 the *Somonauk Reveille* reminded the community of its responsibility in sustaining the Sandwich Fair: "Everyone within a radius of 20 miles should consider this their fair and should support it by exhibiting the best they have in livestock, grains, seed, vegetables, fancy work, paintings and the product of their dairy, kitchen, and pantry. Good premiums are offered in all these lines, and if we all pull together the 1915 fair will be the best fair ever held."

The communities have been pulling together since 1888 to make every Sandwich Fair the best fair ever held. The first Wednesday after Labor Day, friends, neighbors, and strangers come together as a community to applaud each other's efforts. On opening day of the Fair, they have an opportunity to display their accomplishments and to view the best exhibits of others.

Families of Exhibitors

Some families have been entering their livestock, produce, and handiwork for generations. Joe Steffen, agriculture teacher at Newark, estimates that at least twenty members of his family have been Fair exhibitors. His great-grandfather showed Belgian horses and Hereford cattle. He and his brothers and sisters have carried on the family tradition. While Joe no longer shows Hereford cattle, he is a gladiola exhibitor *extraordinaire* in the Horticulture Department.

Announcement in the *The Argus* August 1917

And Now Comes the 30th Annual

SANDWICH FAIR

September 4, 5, 6 and 7, 1917

And to be successful must have the hearty co-operation and support of every resident of this locality; every man, woman and child living in the district included in this Fair should take a personal pride and interest in this institution. Study the Premium List carefully and see if you can not make an exhibit. There are liberal cash premiums in each department and you can surely find some class in which you can show the results of your efforts. Its greatest purpose is that of education along agricultural lines and the many other interest allied with same. As usual, everything is being done for your comfort, convenience and entertainment. Show your appreciation of our efforts by making this the best Fair we have ever held.

Ira Jones of Hinckley represents another family with a long-standing reputation for exhibiting. He raised livestock and showed ponies and Dorset sheep at the Sandwich Fair for 68 years. His daughter still has his 1902 blue ribbon. Ira spent all but the last of his 96 years on the farm his family settled in 1843. Jones's four daughters all worked on the farm and helped him show livestock. Daughter Florence

opposite page: Courtesy of R.T.D.

left: Nationally-known Belgian draft horses Tom, Dick, Prince, and Bobby owned by Joe Steffen's grandfather Joseph E. Garber of Lowpoint, IL

bottom: Ira Jones of Hinckley poses with two Dorset rams in 1946. Jones exhibited livestock for over 68 years.

Courtesy of J.S.

Courtesy of F.G.

Exhibitors

Oscar W. Anderson Family

The Oscar W. Anderson family exhibited hogs from the 1930's to the 1970's, competing on the local, state, national, and international levels. In the early years, competing at the Sandwich Fair was good advertisement and helped with their income.

Oscar Anderson, the father, was well known in the purebred hog business, producing and selling 1,000 purebreds per year. Oscar's sons, Gerald and Roland, won numerous watches showing livestock at the Sandwich Fair.

Mrs. Herman Friebele

In 1999 Mrs. Herman (Dorothy) Friebele of Oswego was second in the baking championship. She was recognized for fifty years of exhibiting in Home Arts. In 2000 at age 87, she was the Champion Baker. Friebele considers entering at the Fair a real pleasure.

With a big smile, she remembers her first blue ribbon. She received it for a fruitcake that she hadn't planned to enter when she baked it. As a 4-H leader at the time, she encouraged her club members to enter their baked goods in the Fair. They said they would enter their baking if she would enter heres, so she pulled her fruit-cake out of the freezer and signed her name to the entry tag. The rest is history.

Foods Superintendent Renee Monkemeyer considers her an excellent cake baker and the "perfect" exhibitor—never complaining, very patient, and very pleased with her winning ribbons.

Exhibiting at the Fair for the Friebeles is a family tradition. In 1998 her 11-year-old great-granddaughter won a ribbon for a drawing, and in 1999 her grandson won Best of Show for a colored pencil portrait. They both took ribbons in the 2000 Fair as well.

Courtesy of R.M.

Dorothy Friebele (l.) of Oswego was the Baking Champion at the 2000 Fair. Superintendent of Foods Renee Monkemeyer (r.) praises her for exhibiting for over 50 years.

Ronnie Johnson Family

Ronnie Johnson of Leland was the first of three generations in his family to show hogs at the Fair. He showed purebred Polands. In mid 1950's, he received the Breeders Award and silverware that went with the honor. Sons Randy and Brad Johnson showed purebred Spotted Polands and purebred Hamps from the late 1960's to early 1980's. They also won the Breeders Award and the silverware. Amanda Johnson, Randy's daughter, started showing hogs in the 1990's.

Clarence and Gladys LaBolle

Clarence LaBolle of Somonauk started showing purebred Chester White hogs at the Sandwich Fair in 1930 with the Somonauk 4-H Club and also in the Open Class. He won many prizes as he continued showing every year through 1942.

In 1957 Gladys LaBolle started entering flowers. Each year she increased the number of entries in various departments, always winning many blue and red ribbons. She was Grand Champion for three years in the jams and jellies division of Open Show Foods. In recent years she has entered in the Collections Department.

Denise Mestemaker

Denise remembers entering her flowers, sewing, and baking projects. She says it was something her family worked on all summer. The first day of the Fair, Wednesday, the excitement built after school to see if they had won any ribbons. "I'm happy to say we did have success in winning in some categories. I passed this down to my son; he also enjoys entering in the Fair."

Dick and Flo (Jones) Getzelman, sheep exhibitors from Hinckley, display some of their ribbons in 1998 that they have earned since 1933.

Alvin Anderson received 11 first place ribbons and 9 seconds; his daughter Sandra received 14 first place and 15 second-place ribbons as junior champion.

jokes, "We worked so hard, we were known as the Jones boys." Florence and her husband Dick Getzelman continued the tradition as they showed sheep from 1933 through 1999.

Alvin Anderson of Sandwich and his daughter Sandra were recognized in 1956 for their outstanding displays of garden produce. Both were Garden Champions that year. Alvin was a good teacher for his daughter because it was his fourth year to receive the honor.

Another family that has exhibiting in their genes is the Smith family of Rock-I-Farms in Oswego. Patriarch J. George Smith has exhibited dairy cattle for 70 years. Son Kent and grandson Eric follow the family tradition. One of their Brown Swiss cows took four state

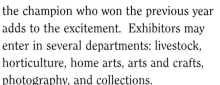

J. George Smith of Rock-I-Farms and his family have been exhibiting dairy cattle for over 70 years.

championships and won the top award for dairy cattle in 1997 at the Sandwich Fair. Another of their animals, a Holstein, was one of only six of its breed in the United States nominated for All-American. Ordinarily the Smiths compete only at state and national shows, but they compete at

Sandwich because, as Kent says, "Victory at this fair means something in the world of dairy farming."

Marion Bazan of Yorkville represents another family that exhibits at the Fair. She was Grand Champion Baker for 11 years. She says when she won her first blue ribbon she was hooked. She has entered baked goods in almost every category. In 1975 her daugher Stephanie won the Junior Grand Champion baking award. Marion believes it may have helped Stephanie launch a career as a high school home economics teacher.

Competition at the Sandwich Fair has always been lively. Since it is the state's last county fair of the year, exhibitors bring their finest to compete. The 1888 Fair awarded $1,390 in premiums; and the 1999 Fair awarded $165,533 in premiums to 1,749 exhibitors. But as one superintendent points out, exhibitors don't value prize money as much as they do a ribbon from the Sandwich Fair. The idea of baking a better cake than the champion who won the previous year adds to the excitement. Exhibitors may enter in several departments: livestock, horticulture, home arts, arts and crafts, photography, and collections.

LIVESTOCK DEPARTMENT

If there is one thing that separates a county fair from a carnival or other local celebration, it is the livestock show. The Sandwich Fair has a history of having one of the best shows in the Midwest. At the first fairs, there were four kinds of livestock: horses, cattle, swine, and sheep. Just like today's shows, the first shows were a big success. Early newspapers attest to the quality and number of exhibits.

The Sandwich *Argus* (1889) reported, "In the cattle department there have been so many entries that an immense new shed has been

Marion Bazan proudly shows off her Grand Champion Baker entry and award at the 100th Fair in 1987.

Ribbons from the Sandwich Fair (photographed in box) are cherished prizes.

Outstanding exhibits are given a large special award ribbon.

Livestock Parade

All prize-winning livestock exhibitors had to parade their animals to collect their winnings. The last parade was held in 1970.

The Open Class paraded on Friday afternoon in front of the grandstand. They returned through the racehorse gate where they chose either a cigar or a candy bar. In 1952 two boxes of cigars and six boxes of candy were used for the Open Class winners.

The Junior Livestock exhibitors were required to parade on Sunday afternoon in front of the grandstand to be eligible for premiums. It took eight boxes of candy in 1952 for the junior winners.

Courtesy of SFA

The livestock parade in front of the grandstand was required of all ribbon winners through the 1970 Fair. This parade was photographed in 1945.

Courtesy of SFA

Four exhibitors proudly display their sheep during the livestock parade.

Livestock Health and Veterinarians

The Sandwich Fair Association requires that all animals exhibited must be free from disease. The State health rules are printed in the premium book. Dr. H. W. Bark was probably the first veterinarian to serve at the Fair.

Dr. Armand "Doc" Legner, who moved to Sandwich in 1937, began checking health papers in the 1940's on Wednesday and Friday of the Fair. Beginning in 1958 Dr. Legner was on the grounds for the entire Fair while his partner Dr. Jack DeVries stayed in the office.

Dr. Craig Stevenson became the Fair veterinarian after Dr. Legner passed away on April 30, 1995. Dr. Stevenson is at the Fair from 4 p.m. to 10 p.m. on Tuesdays and Fridays.

required, and that is over full, with more room called for. There are many specimens of the splendid herds owned all around us, and the outlook is that there will be a good many sales effected on the grounds."

The following accounts appeared in the Sandwich *Free Press*. "What was the most striking in the enormous exhibit of livestock, was the almost entire absence of poor, or even medium animals. Our neighboring farmers and stockmen showed only that which was good, while those from away, who had been attending other fairs, seemed to bring here only those that had taken first premiums" (1892).

"We heard a sheep man say that these were the best sheep in the pens that he ever saw; and forty years among Illinois hogs have never brought us into contact with a better lot than are gathered there" (1896).

"The Sandwich Fair [is a] mecca for all lovers of good stock. Our stockmen who cater to the best in the breeding lines find the Sandwich Fair an excellent place to advertise their stock and open up a new market" (1917).

Today there are nine areas of livestock exhibits: draft horses with 4 classes, beef cattle with 5 classes, dairy cattle with 6 classes, swine with 9 classes, sheep with 10 classes, dairy goats with 7 classes, llamas with 3 classes, rabbits with 37 classes, and poultry with 50 classes.

Horses

At the turn of the century, fairgoers standing near horse barn #1 watched many tons of live horsepower parade before judges. They saw farmers exhibiting their best examples of equine power and transportation.

In the late 1800's and early 1900's, the Fair had 10 classes of roadsters, 2 classes of carriage horses, 11 classes of general purpose horses, and 10 classes of coach horses. There were 10 classes each of Percherons, Englishires, Clydesdales, and French Draft horses. Ten classes of grade [not purebred] draft horses were also offered. First prize ranged from eight dollars for best stallion to two dollars for a yearling gelding. A class for best herd of ponies (no fewer than 10 head) earned thirty dollars for first place.

Apparently there were a few years during the Depression that the draft horse show was discontinued. It appeared in the premium book again in 1935. That year the *Somonauk Reveille*

Photo by V.G.

Audiences enjoyed this demonstration of horsepower by Julie Letry of Long Grove, IL, at the Draft Horse Show in 1997.

Courtesy of SFA

Englishires, Clydesdales, French Draft, and Percherons were popular draft horse breeds at the Fair until the late 1940's. Exactly why they were discontinued at that time is uncertain. When they returned in 1993, they were well received.

noted that the draft horses were outstanding exhibits with over sixty Percheron and Belgian mares and colts. It was noted that only a few years earlier that the draft horse barns had been empty. The horses continued with some variation of classes through 1945. No mention is made of them in the 1946 premium book. They disappeared again in 1948 and returned in 1993.

Through the years there have been classes for Shetland and Welsh ponies, as well as mules, jacks, and jennies. There have been classes of four-, six-, and eight-horse hitches.

Miniature Horses

From 1986 to1989, there was a Miniature Horse Show under the supervision of Joye Gommel. Apparently it was under the direction of the American Miniature Horse Registry and held in conjunction with its national show. Classes were by sizes; the largest was 34" and the smallest was 28" and under. There were 21 halter classes and 12 specialty classes offered. They included the dinner bell derby, jumping, youth showmanship, driving, and multicolored and costume classes. The captivating little horses were popular with photographers and fairgoers. As a result, the show became too large for the time and space allotted and was discontinued.

Photo by V.G.

A well-groomed draft horse waiting to be judged

Exhibitor Tom Hagemann

Oak Hill Farms owned by the Tom Hagemann family started in the 1960's with a love for Belgian draft horses. Within a few years, they started showing at fairs. The family grew to ten grandchildren, the farming operation grew, and the Belgians grew. Before long, what started as a hobby, turned into a family business. They started with halter classes and then purchased a show wagon, which was originally used as an ice wagon years ago in Sterling, IL. They drive all mares in their hitch. The Hagemanns have many mares and colts as well as two Belgian stallions for their breeding service.

Exhibitor Paul McDonald

Paul McDonald of the Mackayr Farm in Princeton began showing Purebred Registered Ayrshire dairy cattle almost 50 years ago; he last showed in 1989. He won the first set of silverware presented to the best three females over all dairy breeds. After the required time lapse of five years before he could enter again, he won a second set of silverware. In all, he won four sets of silverware.

Courtesy of SFA

Judging today is much the same as it was in the past.

Paul's three children—Steven, Paula, and Sue—helped show the family's Ayrshires at the Sandwich Fair. They remember their mother always bringing them to the Fair the Tuesday after Labor Day, which was their first half-day of school after summer vacation. Sue said, "That morning, school couldn't go fast enough! We hurried home, changed clothes, and wolfed down lunch, so we could go to the Fair to see Dad and our Ayrshires, visit our 'fair-circuit buddies,' and help dad with chores." Sue recalls that it was a happy and sad time at the Fair. "We were really happy to be at the Sandwich Fair, but it was also sad because this was the last fair of the year on the county fair circuit."

Special to the McDonald family is a 1979 Sandwich Fair postcard that shows their Ayrshire cow Mackayr Dawn and her twin calves on the bottom half of the card.

McDonald still feels the Sandwich Fair is the best county fair in the state of Illinois because of the beauty and upkeep of the buildings and grounds and the hospitality that the staff always gives to accommodate the exhibitors.

Photo by D.R.S.

In 1964 Douglas R. Stahl proudly showed his prize Angus steer named King Orion.

King Orion

In 1962 young exhibitor Doug R. Stahl wrote to Orion Samuelson to ask if he could name his 4-H steer "King Orion." Orion granted him permission. On the day of the 4-H Steer Show, he was there to see Doug and his namesake.

In 1965 Orion Samuelson and the WGN Noon Show originated at the Fair. It was broadcast from the stage in front of the grandstand. Radio listeners could hear the racehorses going by as they warmed up for the harness races. The WGN "Noon Show" was at the Fair through 1979. By popular demand it returned in 1982 and has been a regular ever since.

To plug the Sandwich Fair, Orion has interviewed Doug, who has been Superintendent of Beef since 1987, and his father Don, who is General Livestock Superintendent, on his "Top O' the Morning" show. The support the Sandwich Fair receives from Orion Samuelson, Max Armstrong, and producer Lottie Kearns is one of the reasons the Fair continues to be well known throughout the Midwest.

Cattle

In the early years, all cattle were listed as thoroughbreds by various breeds. One superintendent handled both the beef and the dairy departments. Perhaps there was no distinction between beef and dairy because several of the breeds were considered "dual purpose." Early Fair books listed dairy cattle as "milch cows." Common beef breeds in the first years were Shorthorn, Herefords, and Angus. Dairy breeds included Holstein, Jersey, Guernsey, and Brown Swiss. The 1888 premium book listed six breeds with nine entry classes.

There are a few noticeable differences between the early years and today. Some early exhibitors transported their cattle to the Fair by rail. They often reserved the same boxcar for the return trip home. Bedding was supplied free until 1930. At the turn of the century, first prize for cattle was seven dollars; whereas first prize was thirty-two dollars for the centennial-year Fair in 1987. The exhibiting classes have increased to six dairy breeds with 24 entry choices each and five beef breeds with 38 entry choices each.

Courtesy of SFA

These Herefords were shown in 1988.

William and Marilyn DeBolt of Plano standing with Sharen (l.) and Karen (r.) in front of the 1,225 pound steer carcass they purchased for 52 cents a pound at the 1975 Fair.

Livestock Carcass Show

Bob Guehler started the Carcass Show in 1966 for swine. Later beef and sheep were included in the contest although sheep lasted for only a couple of years. Exhibitors brought in the live animals, and each one was weighed. They were then loaded onto trucks and shipped to Swift Packing Co. in Rochelle, Illinois. The animals were slaughtered, hung, and graded by Swift. The best grade won first place. The carcasses were transported back to the Fair in a refrigerated trailer for display and an auction.

The show was discontinued when the USDA changed the grading process, but the Fair rules still required a "low choice" grade. Out of a class of thirty-nine head, thirty-five head failed to qualify. The last beef carcass show was held in 1978, and the last swine carcass show was held in 1980.

The Temple Family Exhibitors

Wayne and Marilyn Temple and their son from the LaSalle area spend much of the summer showing their Shorthorn cattle. They consider the Sandwich Fair a highlight in their showing season. During the Fair they live in their camper that they park near the barns. The Temples were one of the first families to camp at the Fair. They recall that at first the Fair provided no electricity or water. They managed by borrowing from the house across the fence. Today, the Fair provides power and water for a full string of campers. Exhibitors need to be near their stock because their day starts around 5:30 a.m. with feeding and washing, preparing the cattle for showing later in the day.

The Temples have fond memories of exhibitors and other people they meet at the Fair. One early morning an older couple sat down at their picnic table, so Marilyn offered them a cup of coffee. They asked to see a menu. She explained they were only camping, but she served them breakfast anyway.

Exhibitors work, play cards, and eat meals together. The meals are usually planned a year in advance because they expect to see each other the next showing season. Fish-fry night usually brings a big crowd. Marilyn has fond memories of showing at the Fair:

> Some of the people are gone, but we still talk about them like Jolly George Aageson the parking man, Dr. Legner, and good ol' Rabbit [Kenny Allen]. He would sit resting and eating his lunch under the awning telling stories about the Fair and the people who make the Fair work. Then there's Doug and Don Stahl who are always the first to buy my Shorthorn Unlimited raffle tickets. They are always there to welcome us and help us get our stalls. You can count on the parking guys to help you out. I remember the year I had surgery and couldn't walk to the cattle barn. Bill and the fellows made sure I had a ride back and forth.

Marilyn says, "Look us up and give us a wave; we're the jolly group by the livestock gate."

Reported in
Somonauk Reveille in 1889

"C. H. White came home from the Kendall County and Sandwich fairs with yards of blue ribbon tied upon his Prairie View head of Shorthorn cattle and his pockets filled with 'filthy lucre' as a result of the premiums awarded him on his exhibit in the different classes. The Sweepstakes prize at Sandwich was captured by his herd, with the excellent animal, Royal Favorite, at the head, and Chas. thinks that would have been glory enough if he had not secured another prize. His stock is all first class and he was justly entitled to all the premiums awarded him."

Courtesy of SFA

John Dolny, "Mr. Showman"

Some people didn't know his name, but they knew the man who rode his champion Duroc in front of the grandstand—and sometimes into the grandstand—during the Grand Parade of Livestock. John Dolny of Plainfield was known to have even stood on his head on the hog's back.

Kids and adults enjoyed him; they looked for him every year. His daughter Mary remembers that he had his own way of entertaining. "If a hog was sleeping, he'd put out a bunch of flowers, a cup, and a sign that said, 'Donate to dying hog.' "

Once he put a mirror inside a box and placed a sign near it: "See the white monkey." Another time he placed some cockleburs in a container and labeled them "porcupine eggs." His good humor was appreciated.

There was more to Dolny than tricks and games, however. His daughter recalls, "He helped 4-H kids and other exhibitors with the fine points of showing, judging, and exhibiting their livestock." At one fair they presented him with a trophy. It was engraved "To John Dolny for Good Sportsmanship. From Exhibitors."

For thirty-three years he competed in the swine department. In 1950 alone, he entered 14 to 20 of his Durocs in fairs at Sandwich, Kankakee, Peotone, Mazon, and Crown Point, IN. He won 10 champion awards, 36 firsts, 25 seconds, and 22 thirds and many lesser ribbons.

A fatal car accident in 1957 ended his exhibiting, but he was remembered at the Sandwich Fair that year. The *Somonauk Reveille*, September 5, 1957, reported, "An impressive tribute is paid to the memory of John Dolny of Plainfield, a premier showman at the Fair. In a prominent pen the Fair Association has placed a large bouquet along with many pictures."

Photo by B.B.

top: Bill Minnegan, an exhibitor for over 50 years from the DeKalb area, in early 1960's

left: John Dolny of Plainfield, Mr. Showman, with one of his champion Durocs

bottom: The livestock parade in front of the grandstand was a tradition for years. John Mahland (l.) 4-H leader of Somonauk, Dale Rogers (m.) of Sandwich with Grand Champion single barrow—purebred Poland China, and Gordon Grose (r.) of Plainfield with Grand Champion pen of barrows—purebred Durocs in 1951.

Exhibitor Dale Rogers
Showing Swine at the Sandwich Fair

Dale Rogers celebrated his eightieth birthday in 1999 and has seen many changes in the livestock barns in the sixty-three fairs that he has attended. When he was sixteen years old, he started showing Poland China pigs. He was in 4-H Club and FFA. He showed Poland China every year for over fifty years and won many hundreds of ribbons. Between 1951 and 1962, he had at least fifteen Grand Champion ribbons.

During World War II, the State Fair was closed as they used the fairgrounds for training troops. Several top hog breeders throughout the country came to the Sandwich Fair during that time to show their pigs. One of the Hampshire breeders asked Dale to show a boar for him. It was the highlight of his Fair week.

Courtesy of RF

In 1951 Dale won Grand Champion Poland China single barrow. Gordon Grose won Grand Champion pen with his Duroc barrows. A tractor pulled them in a wagon in front of the grandstand with other proud winners for the livestock parade.

Even though Dale has not shown pigs for the past few years, he has not missed any of the swine shows. In fact, he has attended every show since 1936. While at the Fair, he spends every day except Friday at the hog barns.

Swine

The 1888 Fair book listed five breeds of swine: Poland Chinas and Magie; Chester Whites and all large white breeds; Berkshires; small breeds, Essex, Suffolk, etc.; and Jersey Reds. Today's Duroc breed went from Jersey Reds to Duroc Jerseys to Duroc.

There were four classes in each breed. First prize was four dollars for a mature boar or sow and two dollars for young stock. The same breeds had unrecorded (no registration papers) classes as well. The popular Hampshire breed didn't appear until about 1925. The once-common Poland China was not listed after 1978. Through the years, there have been classes for Tammworth, Herefords, and Landrace.

In the centennial-year premium book, six breeds of swine listed over 20 classes in each. First prize was eighteen dollars. A carcass show was held from 1964 through 1980, and a feeder-pig class was added in 1981.

The swine registries and individual breeders have offered special awards over the years. The Illinois Swine Herd Improvement Association offered special classes in the 1950's that included litter weights and performance testing. Grades and crosses were allowed to show in these classes.

Sheep

In the early years of the Fair, sheep were listed as fine wool, medium wool, and long wool. There were six entry choices for each type of wool with a first prize ranging from five dollars to two dollars, depending on the class. By 1919 sheep were divided into eight separate breeds. At the Centennial Fair, there were 11 breeds with 13 entry choices for each breed. First prize was eighteen dollars.

In the last two or three decades, sheep entries have increased a great deal. Many families have consistently exhibited for generations. Their support as well as the quality of the exhibits is a major reason for the success of the sheep program. Exhibitors at the Sandwich Fair continue to do well at state fairs and national shows. The Fair has also been honored with nationally known judges. In 1999 the Fair hosted sheep from three states.

Exhibitor Eldon Burger

Eldon Burger from Gardner started showing Cheviot sheep for Jim and Berwyn Johnson of Mazon in 1951 when he was 12 years old. He later got his own Oxford sheep. He remembers when the sheep barn was located where the Farm Zoo is today. He recalls, "Back then you could sleep in the barn. I put my cot in a spot, which got very cold later that night. When I said something to the Fair superintendent about the cold, he laughed and said I was on top of a well. I never put my cot there the next night."

The Coleson Family Exhibitors

In 1975 the Coleson Family, Dale and RoJean and daughters Lisa and Lynn from Varna, started showing sheep at the Marshall-Putnam County 4-H Fair. The girls started out with two crossbred market lambs that their great uncle had given them to show. They enjoyed showing sheep, so they purchased a few purebred Suffolk and started showing at some county fairs. In 1980 they added to the flock with purebred Columbias, so each girl had her own breed. By this time they were showing at ten county fairs. In 1982 after years of helping friends show at the Sandwich Fair, they decided to enter their own sheep. In 1987 they added purebred Dorsets and were showing at twelve fairs with a total of thirty-six sheep at each fair.

Their last show at the Sandwich Fair was in 1997. Since then they have helped others show at the Fair. Coleson says that his grandkids, Lisa's and Lynn's children, are looking forward to following in their moms' footsteps and showing at the Sandwich Fair.

Some of their most memorable moments at the Fair were winning Grand Champion Market Lamb at the 100th Fair in 1987 and showing the Grand Champion Ram and Ewe in the Open Show. Coleson says, "One of the best things about the Junior Show is that champions in each breed get a nice plaque."

Rochelle High School boys showed their champion lambs.

top: This llama enjoys some special care and attention.

left: A young exhibitor shears her sheep before judging.

bottom: Debbie and Kent Paul from Marseilles, IL, have shown cattle at the Sandwich Fair since 1984. They are shown here with the newest member of their Polled Hereford family.

Beacon News

*We attend
several fairs a year,
but this is our favorite.
The superintendents
are very helpful and
assist you with everything
you need. There is so
much to see and do,
and the fairgrounds
are kept so neat and clean.*

Debbie & Kent Paul
Marseilles, Illinois

Beacon News

Photo by P.N.

Courtesy of SFA

Photo by M.E.H.

left: Open Class dairy goat show began in 1980; the Junior Show began in 1985.

right: For the costume entry, both the llama and the handler, Tyler Hoyt, dress in style.

I love the Sandwich Fair because it has such a wonderful variety of activities, buildings, entertainment and livestock exhibits. I remember my son at the age of 10 won grand championship ewe division, and we were interviewed on Farm Town USA Chicago TV.

Marie Wyeth
Aurora, Illinois

Exhibitor Betty Domagala

Betty Domagala from Gardner has shown registered Toggenbrug goats at the Sandwich Fair since 1985. She enjoys going to the Fair, meeting and working with the people, making friends with several of them not only during the Fair but all year long. Betty has good memories of the livestock superintendent welcoming her the first year that she showed at the Fair. "[It] made a good impression on me that he and the Fair cared that I came, and I have been going every year since then."

The first year her goats had to share space with the hogs in the hog barn. The next year the goats had a new barn, and a few years later the cattle and goats switched barns. Every year it seems like there are more goats.

Exhibitors Nancy and Ken Schroeder

Nancy and Ken Schroeder from Emington show Nubian and Oberhasli dairy goats. Nancy says, "The Sandwich Fair is like a small State Fair. We really enjoy coming every year. The people that go through our goat barn really like trying a sample of goat milk or goat milk ice cream." Nancy and Ken have been exhibiting at the Fair since 1991.

Goats

The Open Class Dairy Goat Show began in 1980; it offered five breeds and grade dairy goats with 10 entry choices for each. The 1999 show had seven breeds with 11 entry choices for each and the same for recorded grade goats. The Junior Show began in 1985.

Llamas

Llamas were introduced in 1987. Over 30 llamas were shown the first year. There are three types of llama competition: performance, showmanship, and halter. In 1988 a special costume class was added; both llama and handler were dressed for the occasion.

Rabbits and Poultry

The rabbit and poultry shows have always been popular for fairgoers. Even those who don't know one chicken from another or one bunny from another still enjoy looking at the colorful plumes of the Buff Brahma and the Black Polish and the plush fur of the Palomino and Silver Martins. The eye-level cages make it easy for children, as well as adults, to see the animals up close.

In 1888 there were 39 entry choices for chickens, 11 for guineas, 4 for turkey, 2 for geese, and 3 for ducks. First prize was $1 for chickens and ducks, and $2 for turkeys, geese and guineas.

In the early 1890's until 1937 William Fraser was superintendent of the department as it continued to improve. The entry choices grew

Courtesy of SFA

Beacon News

to 180 for chickens, 20 for turkeys, and 27 for ducks. In the early days, many exhibitors shipped their birds by Railroad Express. It was the superintendent's job to get them to the Fair and ship them back to the owners.

An 1898 news account raved, "One of the most beautiful and attractive places on the grounds is the poultry house. The large building is crowded almost to the roof with coops and pens." The article mentioned names of the big exhibitors and suggests that competition was spirited between Henwood, Howison, and the Arnolds.

In 1914 the department proudly announced, "Handsome new electric-weld chicken coops have been placed in the poultry house, which will make a decided improvement. . . ."

For many years the rabbit show was part of the poultry show. By 1925 there were 27 classes of hares in the premium book. They were not referred to as rabbits in the premium book until mid 1930's.

Photo by J.E.H.

The early 1940's were the heydays for the rabbit and poultry exhibits. In 1940 the rabbit and poultry entry choices took up 12 pages in the premium book with 99 for chickens, 75 for rabbits, 31 for ducks, and 17 for geese. The exhibitors in the 1940's were a fun-loving lot. They were known to have painted a Rhode Island Red with half a dozen colors and labeled it "Ethiopian Caca Snazzy." Another cage—carefully shrouded—was labeled "Irish Bats." The cage contained two pieces of brick—the dictionary definition of a brickbat.

The 1946 and 1947 poultry shows were suspended by order of the Illinois Department of Agriculture in an effort to control the dreaded Newcastle disease in poultry. They returned in 1948 and 1949 but did not have another show until 18 years later.

In 1967 two, long-time poultry exhibitors,

Lyle Troeger and Charles "Cub" Mall, reorganized the poultry show. They listed 64 breeds of chickens with four entry choices for each. They also had one entry choice each for pigeons and rabbits. Prize money, however, had not progressed too far—first place was only $1.25.

Because of limited space in 1996, exhibitors were allowed only two entries per entry choice and were limited to a total of 20 entries. As the show continued to grow, it was moved to the maintenance building; later in 1998, horse barn #1 became the site of the show.

Rabbit exhibits were dropped in 1980 but were brought back with their own show in 1995. Twenty-seven breeds of rabbits and two com-

top left: Young exhibitors prepare their rabbits for judging in the mid 1960's.

top right: The poultry tent was a good place to rest in 1979. Lyle Troeger is on the left.

center: Junior Champion rooster at the 2000 Fair.

Bernice Maness
Best of Show in the Poultry House

Bernice Maness of Sycamore recalls a winning moment in the poultry house in 1977 or 1978. She and her husband always kept a few chickens in the backyard just for eggs and because she liked having chickens around. In particular she was interested in raising black Cochin bantams.

Two young brothers in their foster care had also taken an interest in the chicks. They fed them and cleaned the chicken house. Just for fun they decided to enter one of the little black Cochin hens in the Fair to see how she would compare to the others.

The day came for the judging. The boys could hardly wait. "We followed the judge up and down the rows of cages as he made comments and marked the tags. When he was finished, he went back to the cages of Cochin bantams. We couldn't believe it when he took our little hen out and examined her again."

He also took another chicken out of a cage. "He stood there for a long minute, holding a bird in each hand, looking them over. We held our breath. Finally, he held our little hen up and said, 'The winner.' "

Later in the day, Charles "Cub" Mall and another gentleman presented one of the boys with a trophy for being a young showman. "What a happy kid!"

Courtesy of SFA

(l. to r.) Armand "Doc" Legner, Wiley Updike, and a young exhibitor at the junior livestock sale

mercial entry choices were listed. In five years the show grew from as few as 100 rabbits to over 600 rabbits. In the beginning, Fair personnel caged and cared for the rabbits every day of the Fair. Today, however, only a few examples of all the breeds are kept on display the whole week. The majority of the entries are on the grounds for a one-day show.

Fairgoers return each year to see their favorites. Patches, an English Angora, is popular and so are the large French Lops. A breeder is usually on hand at the display to provide information about buying and caring for rabbits as pets.

Junior Livestock Sale

The First Annual Junior Livestock Sale was held Sunday, September 12, 1971. It was open to all junior exhibitors. Gene Darfler and Buck Nesson started the sale with Eleanor Stahl doing the paper work and organization. The purpose of the sale was to help the junior exhibitors obtain a better price for their animals.

All commercial-fed livestock in fat stock show could be sold in this sale. All livestock had to grade choice according to packer standards. All champions and reserve champions and the first three placing of each class had to be sold. The sale of other animals was optional.

Livestock had to be drug-free. Feed additives containing hormones and antibiotics had to be discontinued 72 hours before the sale. No livestock could receive water or feed after 8 a.m. the day of the sale.

All animals were tagged, and a list of those to be sold was given to prospective buyers on the morning of the sale. A packer bid a floor price for steers, hogs, and sheep before they entered the sale ring, which set a guaranteed price on the animals. There was a charge of three dollars for each steer and a dollar fifty for each hog and sheep. Anyone could buy an animal, keep it, or send it to the packer, paying the difference to the owner.

The last livestock sale was in 1985. It was stopped because livestock bought for home-use did not grade and some exhibitors used unethical means to enter the sale.

CONGRATULATIONS!

To The Following 1953 Grand Champion Winners in the Junior Show

DUANE SCHWINGEL, LaMoille, Illinois, winner of the Elgin watch given for Grand Champion Steer, donated by John Case, North Corn Belt Seed Co., Arthur Walter Seed Co., Pfister Associated Growers.

GLENN TRUCKENBROD, Mendota, Illinois, winner of the Elgin watch given for Grand Champion Beef Heifer, donated by Waterman State Bank.

DALE FRIEMAN, DeKalb, Illinois, Winner of watch given for Grand Champion Dairy Heifer, donated by Oatman Bros. Dairy, Sandwich, Illinois

JAMES BURNIDGE, Elgin, Illinois, winner of watch given for Grand Champion Ewe, donated by Sandwich State Bank.

GORDON OTT, Verona, Illinois, winner of Elgin watch given for Grand Champion Barrow, donated by Somonauk Farmers State Bank.

RICHARD FEIK, LaMoille, Illinois, winner of watch for Grand Champion Pen of Barrows, donated by Leland National Bank.

Courtesy of D.R.S.

This young lady dressed in a wool garment exhibits in the sheep lead class for junior exhibitors. Contestants are judged on outfit (50%), poise and appearance (30%), and sheep's behavior and appearance (20%).

Junior Livestock Show

The Junior Livestock Show began in 1949. It was held on Saturday and Sunday in conjunction with the Sandwich Fair. It was open to all young people under twenty-one years old who lived in DeKalb, Kane, Kendall, and LaSalle counties. In later years, youth from other counties also entered. There were nine steer breeds, nine beef-heifer breeds, ten dairy breeds, and sixteen sheep breeds. The junior swine show had six breeds with two classes in each along with four barrow entry choices.

Cattle premiums were fifteen dollars for first place; sheep and swine were each ten dollars for first place. Various trophies and watches were awarded for champions over the years. To young exhibitors, these are still coveted awards. By 1987 there were seven beef and four dairy breeds with six entry choices for each, for which first prize was eighteen dollars. There were eleven sheep breeds with seven choices for each and four, market-lamb entry choices. Young ladies and gents, who were dressed in wool outfits, competed in sheep-lead classes. The swine show has grown to nine breeds with ten entry choices for each, and a junior goat show was added with six breeds and six entry choices for each.

Courtesy of SFA

Courtesy of JF

Courtesy of D.R.S.

top: Hampshire High School boys and leader showing their champion dairy cattle

middle: (l. to r.) Jessie, Sarah, and Jeremiah, children of Mr. and Mrs. Mike Johnson, pose with their Montadale sheep during the junior sheep show.

bottom: The sheep lead class is a fashion show for junior exhibitors.

Exhibitor N. Stanley Nelson

The first Junior Livestock Show was held in 1949. That year N. Stanley Nelson of Newark was awarded an Elgin watch for his grand champion pen of three, crossbred barrows. Each was 240 pounds. Not only was he thrilled to win the watch, but also he was very pleased that his barrows beat the Illinois State Grand Champion.

Fifty years later, Stanley returned the watch in a display case with pictures and original banner to the Sandwich Fair Association so it could become part of the Fair history.

Don Stahl, Superintendent of Livestock, accepted the watch for the Fair during the WGN "Noon Show" at the Ag Land stage with Orion Samuelson, a well-known agriculture broadcaster. Several hundred people witnessed the event. The watch can be seen at the livestock office during the Fair.

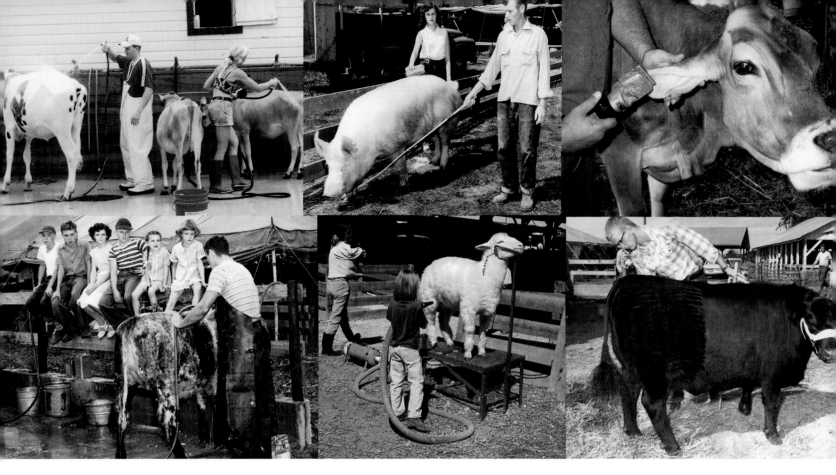

Ready, set, show!

Exhibitors spend hours scrubbing, clipping, curling, or shearing their livestock
to prepare them for the final lineup for the judges.

Changes in the Livestock Department in the Past Century

Photo by M.W.

Several changes have occurred in the past century. Livestock at the turn of the century was large and overfed by today's standards. Today, some of the breeds are listed on the American Livestock Conservatory list as endangered breeds; thus they are no longer listed in the premium book. New classes have been added. In 1938 the Department of Agriculture ordered that all cattle exhibited had to be tested for TB and brucellosis and all hogs had to have proof of vaccination for hog cholera. One of the biggest changes has been in the number of entries. In 1968 pens and stalls were filled with 2,030 head of livestock. Today, there are over 3,261 livestock entries at the Fair.

Photo by M.W.

Another big change is the fairgoers' knowledge of livestock. In the early years of the Fair, a large percentage of the fairgoers lived on farms. Today that percentage has changed dramatically. Although most fairgoers can identify cows, pigs, horses, and goats, identifying specific breeds is like deciphering a foreign language. If asked to match the breed (Charolais, Ayrshire, Belgian, Dorset, Toggenburg, or Chester White) with the species (beef or dairy cattle, horse, sheep, goat, or swine), most fairgoers would be lost. Recognizing this change in the fairgoer, in 1967 the Fair Association added a Farm Zoo sponsored by local chapters of Future Farmers of America (FFA); also, in 1999 barn tours conducted by university students were added to the daily activities [see Chapter 8].

One thing has not changed—the camaraderie among the livestock exhibitors. Because they "live" on the grounds with their livestock, the livestock exhibitors get to know each other better than most exhibitors do.

Many of the exhibitors follow the same fair "circuits." Don Stahl, General Livestock Superintendent since 1966, says that exhibitors come from as far away as Wisconsin, Indiana, Iowa, Missouri, and Minnesota. "It's the Sandwich Fair name that draws exhibitors, not the premium money," Stahl says. "If you can win at the Sandwich Fair, you can go on to national shows." He has heard past exhibitors say that a first place at Sandwich adds money to the auction price of their livestock.

In the 1950's an exhibitor was showing his Poland China hogs. He took second in the boar and gilt classes. When he took first place in the litter class, the second-place showman complained to the judge that his litter had received a first place at the Illinois State Fair. A bystander recalls the judge's calm reply, "But they [your pigs] are not first, today—at *this* fair."

HORTICULTURE DEPARTMENT

The Sandwich Fair has a bountiful history of prize-winning produce. The 1888 premium book listed 10 grain and grass seed entry choices, 24 vegetable entry choices, and 13 fruit entry choices on a small page and a half. The list of 38 flowers took up even less space. Today's listing of 500 entry choices in grains, seeds, forages, fruits, vegetables, and flowers in the Open and Junior Shows covers over 35 pages in the premium book.

opposite page: Photo credits appear in Chapter 11.

top center: Baby animals are the reason some fairgoers call the Farm Zoo the Petting Zoo.

bottom center: The Farm Zoo is a popular place for adults and children who enjoy "hands-on" exhibits.

bottom right: This display at the 1974 Fair is typical of the bountiful harvest displayed in the Horticulture building.

Courtesy of SFA

Exhibitor Frank Reimann

As an exhibitor at the Sandwich Fair for over 60 years, Frank Reimann of Sandwich may have set a record. He was presented a plaque in 1967 for exhibiting fruits, vegetables, and flowers for 50 continuous years.

Frank was proud of his large garden and orchard as well as the site itself. Long before he owned it, his 70-acre farm located on the northeast edge of Sandwich was the site of an early agricultural fair—Union Agricultural Institute—held in 1858 and 1859.

Going to the Fair was a vacation for Frank. He attended every day. He would take his premium book to check off which exhibits brought him ribbons. At the same time, he planned his exhibits for the coming year. The blue ribbons for his fruit basket displays brought him much joy.

Frank passed his love and enthusiasm for the Sandwich Fair on to his children. Daughter Mary Ann (Phillips) remembers helping him dig potatoes and laying them at the edge of the garden so he could select the best ones for his entry.

He loved to talk about his horticulture. He was always glad to give new exhibitors winning tips on how to display their produce and how to choose perfect vegetables and fruits.

Comment by Anonymous Exhibitor

"For 20 years Chuck Pfau beat the socks off me in the hybrid corn show. At first I was sure the judge must have been his brother-in-law, but I soon learned he was a better corn sorter than I was. Maybe I was a slow learner, but I kept trying. Competing with him made me get better."

Exhibitor Helen Bauer

The Bauer Family of Earlville pictured in 1969

Sometimes when one gets started, it's not easy to stop. At least that's the impression Helen Bauer of Earlville gives when she tells about exhibiting at the Fair. She entered her onions in the late 50's and won a red ribbon. Every year thereafter she increased her number of entries until she reached her goal—Garden Champion. She held this title for three years: 1969, 1970, and 1971. Each year she loaded up two trucks and two cars to transport her produce to the fairgrounds. Her husband Ed and her two sons Ed Jr. and Mike also entered items in the Fair. One year Mike was Junior Garden Champion.

Grains, Seeds, Fruits, and Vegetables

In 1888 exhibitors displayed the grains and seeds and some vegetables in half bushels. They displayed 12 specimens of the larger vegetables such as cabbages, pumpkins, and melons. Compared to today's entries that require only three specimens for most exhibits, this is a big difference. Another big difference is the number of squash entry choices. The 1999 premium book listed 53 whereas the 1888 premium book listed only two—hubbard and baking.

An 1888 exhibitor would also see a difference in today's variety of exhibits. Open Show entry choices have grown to include 315 vegetables, 96 fruits, 55 grains and seeds, 34 bundled grains and forages, 6 baled hays, 83 herbs, and 6 types of nuts.

> 60   SANDWICH FAIR
>
> **Special Premiums.**
>
> PRATT FOOD COMPANY, Philadelphia, Pa., offer the following special premiums, which will be on exhibition and delivered by the committee at the time of the Fair to the drawers of same:
>
> No.
> 1. Best display of wheat, one 50c. package Pratt's Animal Food.
> 2. Best display of corn, one 50c. package Pratt's Animal Food.
> 3. Best display of potatoes, one 50c. package Pratt's Animal Food.
> 4. Best display of cabbage, one 50c. package Pratt's Animal Food.
> 5. Best display of apples, one 50c. package Pratt's Animal Food.
> 6. Best display of grapes, one 50c. package Pratt's Animal Food.
> 7. Best display canned fruit, one 00c. package Pratt's Poultry Food.
> 8. Best display jellies, one 60c. package Pratt's Poultry Food.
> 9. Best loaf wheat bread, one 60c. package Pratt's Poultry Food.
> 10. Best layer cake, one 60c. package Pratt's Poultry Food.
> 11. Best silk crazy quilt, one 60c. package Pratt's Poultry Food.
> 12. Best hand embroidered apron, one 60c. package Pratt's Poultry Food.

Another difference is the premiums paid. In 1888, first premium for grains and vegetables was 50 cents; second place was 25 cents. The premium for fruits was a little more: first place was one dollar, and second place was 50 cents. The exhibitor with the greatest assortment of fruit received a diploma. Today's exhibitors earn up to seven dollars for a first place in grain and ten dollars for the largest pumpkin. The premiums for garden vegetables range from $5.50 to $1.

According to an August 1904 Sandwich *Free Press*, "The Floral Hall, as usual, will be a bower of beauty, wherein is housed the exhibits that please the ladies, and where they spend many pleasant hours looking at the diversified number of exhibits that are piled high on the shelves." In the early years of the Fair, garden produce, grains, seeds, flowers and plants, needlework, foods, paintings, photos, and commercial exhibits for the home were all in Floral Hall.

In 1905 after fire destroyed Floral Hall, it was replaced with two smaller buildings, which are today's Home Arts building and the Horticulture building. This was the first step in separating the horticulture and domestic departments. Under the management of George McDonald, the Horticulture building flourished with displays of culinary art, flowers, garden produce, grains, fruits, and agriculture products. Then, as now, one of the first areas visitors noticed was the tall pyramid in the center of the building. Around it were formal arrangements and informal bouquets, making a majestic presentation of local gardeners' efforts.

The 1915 *Free Press* reported that a large addition was added to the horticulture building: ". . . with the additional and increased premiums offered, the building should contain the finest display of grains, seeds, and vegetables ever seen at the fair." Everyone in a 20-mile radius of Sandwich was encouraged to support the Fair by exhibiting the best they had in all areas.

In 1922 the DeKalb County Farm Bureau made a well-received display of grains, grasses, and seeds, as well as a display of various weeds found in the county. At the 50th Fair in 1937, the *Free Press* wrote, "The collection of vegetables and farm products was unusually good, while fruit was so tempting that our scribe came near forgetting the eighth commandment." At this time, bakery goods and canned fruits, vegetables, pickles, and jellies were still being exhibited in the Horticulture building.

In 1943, influenced by World War II, the Fair Board voted extra appropriations to cover a special department for Victory Gardens as requested by the State Department of Agriculture. There were several Victory Garden entry choices: 1) Best display of produce and orchard ready for storage. This display included home-canned or processed foods. First prize was fifteen dollars. 2) Junior display for age 16 or

Courtesy of SFA

under. First prize was also fifteen dollars.
3) Market basket: best display of vegetables.
4) New England boiled dinner: best display of potatoes and three other boiling vegetables.
5) Best group of six storage vegetables (potatoes, sweet potatoes, root crops, onions, pumpkins, squash, etc.).

The Fair Board also planned special exhibits demonstrating how to can and dehydrate foods to support the war effort in conserving all food supplies. The program was known as Governor Green's Cooking School. It was organized by a local home economics teacher and sponsored by the local electric company, Illinois Northern Utilities Company.

Several changes were made for the 1948 Fair in the horticulture area. Louis Wagner, who had been an exhibitor for several years, became the superintendent. In cooperation with various seed corn companies, he initiated a seed corn show. This has continued to the present with seed corn companies furnishing the premium money and the Fair furnishing the ribbons and trophies.

At that time the entire kitchen, pantry, and dairy departments were moved to Industrial Hall (Home Arts building) where new cases were made for the exhibits. This made room for the additional displays of corn and the new junior vegetable display. Viewing hours in the exhibit buildings were extended from 6 to 9 p.m. Long shelves were constructed to provide more display space; baskets and vases were purchased to give

Photo by T.M.

top: The bushel basket display must contain at least 15 fresh vegetables grown by the exhibitor.

bottom: The vegetables at the Sandwich Fair are a sample of the best produce in the Midwest.

Exhibitor Hazel Miller

Hazel Miller of Sandwich received a savings bond for her Victory Garden entry in the 1940's. She had the best display of canned goods, vegetables, fruits, jellies, and jams. The prize was given to encourage women to can as much of their own food as possible during World War II. When Hazel and her family moved to Sandwich in 1958, she cashed in her bond and used the money to make improvements on their home.

I love all the rural displays and the awards given. They are so beautifully displayed.

Anna Hill
Fullerton, California

top left: Al Lower of Somonauk (l.) received a helping hand from Ken Schwemlein of Plano (r.) in 1989 when it came time to place his pumpkin in the Horticulture building.

The largest pumpkin in the Horticulture building is a traditional site for photographs for many families.

center: Cartoonist Bob Montana left this compliment in the comment box in the Horticulture building.

bottom: Bob Montana captured the spirit of exhibiting at the Sandwich Fair in this Archie cartoon originally distributed by King Features Syndication in 1974.

a more uniform and attractive appearance.

The Wagners, Louis and son John, are credited with expanding the entry choices for exhibitors. They started the bundled grain and herb shows. For the 100th Fair in 1987, John returned some heirloom vegetables to the premium book. To qualify, the produce must be grown from seeds that have at least a 100-year history.

A big attraction in the building is always the large pumpkins and squash. The large ones are weighed at the grain elevator in Sandwich and handled by a skid loader, which barely fits inside the building. The largest pumpkin, weighing 670 pounds, was exhibited in 1998.

Judging is done on Wednesday morning of the Fair. One of the judges in the Horticulture Department commented that Sandwich has the best show in Illinois, perhaps because it is later in the season. He also noted that the display of entries is a "visual treat" and there are more peppers today. Maybe this is a trend or maybe it is a "cultural change."

Today, there is an entry choice for every gardener whether it is one of the fifty-three varieties of squash, traditional tomatoes and green beans, or oversized vegetables and garden freaks. The Horticulture building is a gardening lesson for the novice as well as the experienced gardener.

Oops!

John Wagner, General Superintendent of Exhibit Buildings, remembers when the staff used to park on the south side of the Horticulture building. He says, "We had everything on the shelves and all neatly arranged when all of a sudden we heard a big bang, then a crash, splat. The largest watermelon sitting on the shelf hit the floor." One of the workers had misjudged her parking space and bumped the building just hard enough to jar the watermelon off the shelf. John says, "Needless to say it wasn't judged yet, but it took first place by all who enjoyed it, for there wasn't any sense in letting it go to waste."

Courtesy of G.L.J.

left: At one Fair in the early 1930's, Mrs. Marjory Baird had 45 flower entries. She received 42 blue ribbons and 3 red ribbons. Her prize money was more than her husband Pliny received for his pulling horse team [See Chapter 5].

bottom: All the flowers for the collections, best specimen, bouquets, and arrangements must be grown by the exhibitors. They must be tagged and delivered to the Horticulture building by 8 p.m. on Tuesday before the Fair opens on Wednesday.

Floriculture

The 1888 exhibitors had their choice of only two rose entries: a collection in bloom for amateurs and one for professionals. Today's rose gardeners enter in 25 Open Show choices and 22 Junior Fair choices.

Some other flower choices in 1888 included a single or collection of fuschias, geraniums, cacti, oleander, and carnations. Cut flower entries were dahlias, gladioluses, pansies, and zinnias. In the August 1917 *Free Press,* it was noted, "Over in Horticulture Hall the lover of flowers can spend hours viewing the beauties from the private conservatory and the professional greenhouse, while the exhibit of seeds, fruits, etc. always finds an attentive and keen audience."

At the 50th Fair in 1937, Mrs. Ruth Barker was listed as a winner in the cut flowers division with nine first-place ribbons and two seconds. Her son Franklin received a second on the best-arranged bouquet in the junior department.

Courtesy of SFA

Exhibitor Mrs. Doran (Rose) Greif

Rose Greif began exhibiting at the Sandwich Fair in 1967. She exhibited floral arrangements, won seven ribbons, and received fourteen dollars. She has continued to exhibit every year since in spite of some health problems. Her favorite flowers are roses, of course! She also uses zinnias and asters in her bouquets.

Canning and preserving is another area she enters. She has ribbons for watermelon pickles, best display of fruit, and the entire meal entry. In 1980 she began entering her needlework projects. Rose has won 22 first-prize ribbons for her crocheted afghans. All eight grandchildren have received prize-winning afghans.

Rose keeps her ribbons in a box with the prize receipts. She has the two wooden plates hanging in her home that she received for Grand Champion awards in flowers in 1970 and 1972.

Rose and her sister-in-law Catherine Greif have passed on their love of exhibiting to Rose's grandchildren, who live in Sandwich. With Rose and Catherine's guidance, all four grandchildren have been Floral Champions in the junior division. Rose believes working hard and putting one's heart into the entries is the secret for success.

Exhibitor Carol Swenson

Carol Swenson, Sandwich, has been a floral exhibitor since the early 1960's. She has been Floral Champion over 20 times. She became interested in exhibiting when her husband entered vegetables at the Fair. Her first floral entry was a pink pompon zinnia. "As I walked through the front door, it was the first thing I saw, proudly sporting a blue ribbon. There were other entries that year, but that's the one I remember."

Sweet peas are her favorite flowers because of their fragrance and childhood memories of them. Carol's mother gardened and had a real interest in flowers. Carol is especially proud of a religious entry that depicted the resurrection of Christ. She gardens all summer but doesn't begin preparing her entries until about a week before the Fair. She stores them in a cooler to assure their freshness.

Besides gardening, Carol's hobby is training and showing her two dogs in obedience and agility.

Exhibitor Leonard Hafenrichter

Courtesy of L.H.

l. to r. Ramona Butler, Leonard Hafenrichter, and Nancy Updike in front of the flower display in the Horticulture building during the 1983 Fair.

As a child Leonard Hafenrichter of Oswego enjoyed the Fair. He recalls going to the Fair with his father, mother and two brothers, spending the day looking at all the exhibits and eating the picnic lunch his mother prepared. His enthusiasm continued into his adult life. He grew up on a farm, and he exhibited his first flowers a few years before he entered military service in 1942.

After the war he moved to town, and although he didn't enter flowers for a number of years, he continued to attend the Fair. From 1978 to 1996 he was a regular exhibitor in several departments: flowers, photography, antiques and collectibles, oil paintings, and miscellaneous.

Leonard is proud of his accomplishments: Floral Champion 1983; Photography Champion 1991; best, over-all photography slide in 1988, 1989, 1993, and 1995. As a floral exhibitor he knows that getting ready for the Fair means much weeding, watering, trimming, and transplanting of flowers. Concerning the preparation of his entries, he said he picked the flowers and put them in the cool basement on Monday the week of the Fair. He worked late Monday night and Tuesday, making flower arrangements and packing them in boxes to transport to the Fair.

His advice to young (and old) exhibitors is to "have everything ready that you need for your exhibits before the Fair and follow the rules in the premium book."

Looking back, Leonard says, "It has been a lot of work, but rewarding to have won so many ribbons. I have enough ribbons to make a quilt."

At age 84 Leonard is retired. He still takes pictures, and he belongs to the Sandwich Photographic Society. He plans to attend the Sandwich Fair as long as he is able because he enjoys the exhibits, especially the floral and photography displays.

The best collection of gladioluses, not to exceed ten stalks, is judged on perfection of flower (50%), assortment of varieties (40%), and arrangement and suitability of container (10%).

Courtesy of SFA

Zinnias, asters, gaillardia, and rudbeckia combine to make a beautiful summer bouquet.

By the 1950's other flowers appeared in the entry lists: asters, marigolds, calendula, cosmos, larkspur, nasturtium and petunias. Also listed were phlox, snapdragon, salvia, scabiosa, salpiglossis, verbena, ageratum, everlastings and coxscomb [sic].

The 100th Fair in 1987 listed nine different sections to enter in Plants and Flowers. They included best collections, best one-bloom specimens, bouquets, seasonal arrangements, and special color arrangements. Other entry choices included plants, cactuses and succulents, and roses. In an effort to encourage men to exhibit floral arrangements, separate entries called "Exhibits by a Man" were added to the premium book. A professional division included Victorian bridal bouquets with silk flowers, Turn-of-the Century Garden Party arrangement, and Happy 100th Fair arrangement.

As new varieties of plants and flowers are developed, the "pyramid" in the horticulture building continues to grow with new entries.

Courtesy of SFA

Photo by L.H.

Junior Horticulture Fair

Even though there were entries for a junior division prior to 1949, 1949 was the official date for the first Junior Fair. Entries arrived on Friday evening for a Saturday and Sunday show. All the Open Show produce from the first three days was removed to make room for the junior entries. Department workers stayed late to prepare for the second show. In 1957 a large addition was added to the east side of the building, making it possible to extend the Junior Fair all five days of the Fair.

The quality of the junior exhibits often matches that of Open Show. The distinguishing yellow tags of the junior exhibits help fairgoers tell the difference. Many of the building personnel, as well as Open Show exhibitors, give pointers and encouragement to young exhibitors as they are the future of the Sandwich Fair.

Photo by J.E.H.

Sandwich High School senior John Twait was the 2000 Junior Garden Champion in the Horticulture Department.

Photo by J.E.H.

Junior Exhibitor Eleni Filippi

Exhibitor Eleni Wright Filippi reminisces about her experiences as a young exhibitor: "Rise and shine! It's 6 a.m.—time to start picking the flowers! My mother would wake me up on Saturday before Labor Day," Eleni says. "My mother is such a happy-morning person. She had to be—with an 8-year-old daughter that decides she wants to enter almost every best specimen category and flower arrangement category [in the premium book]."

"Mom had to be prepared for the best and the worst. The worst? Helping me pick flowers for hours—pouring rain or burning sun, biting mosquitoes or annoying gnats, little buds or eaten petals. Trying to choose the best was only the beginning of the three-day process. Mom helped me pick flowers, choose containers for specific themes, soak frogs, keep flowers fresh, and organize vases—the easy part. Then it was time for me to create masterpieces!" Eleni was Junior Floral Champion four years: 1984 through 1987. Today, she exhibits in the Home Arts Food Department.

top left: Junior Fair floral exhibits match the Open Show exhibits in quality.

top right: Decorated pumpkins are a popular entry for Junior Fair exhibitors.

inset: Area-resident Eleni Filippi's awards as Junior Floral Champion include silver trays, dishes, and decorative pieces. She entered her awards and ribbons as "Sandwich Fair Memorabilia" in the Collections Department in 1998 and received another blue ribbon.

following pages: Photo by R.M. pages 122-123: The tall pyramid in the center of the Horticulture building has always been a main attraction.

121

Photo by J.E.H.

Linda Berry of Newark painted the collage that hangs permanently in the Home Arts building.

HOME ARTS

In the center of the fairgrounds is a large, well-known landmark that is a popular meeting place for families and friends. It is the Home Arts building known to some fairgoers as the Women's Building. In earlier years, many area businesses displayed their items for sale, and it was known as Industrial Hall. Even earlier, it was referred to as Floral Hall. Today it is the essence of an old-fashioned country fair with displays ranging from quilts to dainty doilies, and multi-tiered wedding cakes to muffins. A colorful collage (pictured left), painted by local artist Linda Berry in the late 1970's, hangs above the walk area in the center of the building. It illustrates the needlework and foods entries that are displayed in the building today.

Needlework

In 1888 a department called Needle Work, Household Fabrics, and Manufacture was located in Floral Hall and offered 57 entry choices of needlework and 26 for painting and photograph entries. Winners were paid one dollar for first place premium and as low as twenty-five cents for second place. Total premiums for both areas were about $100. On September 13, 1890, the Sandwich *Argus* reported,

> The display in the fancy work department is something 'simply immense.'
> No other year having brought together
> so much exquisite needlework, such

Exhibitor Marilyn Donoho

Marilyn Donoho of Paw Paw has been sewing and entering clothing since she was ten years old as a 4-H Club member in LaSalle County. In 1976 she won all three purple ribbons in Open Class Clothing: "Best of Show" in women's, men's, and children's clothing.

Shortly after that, professional classes were added in clothing, and she has entered in those classes ever since; 1999 was her forty-seventh year to exhibit. She has won championships in her classes almost every year.

She comes from a family of Fair exhibitors. Her mother Rosa Hoffman of Earlville, who celebrated her 90th birthday in 2000, entered many items in sewing and baking until 1997. One year she baked the champion cake.

Marilyn's daughter Anita Donoho is following in the family tradition; she has been entering sewing, cooking, and horticulture for twenty years. As a 4-H Club member she began entering when she was nine years old. She also has won many "Best of Show" awards.

In 1988 Anita received three top honors for Champion Junior Garden, Baker, and Sewer. Since 1988 she has received a champion award in sewing every year.

One More Dress?

In order to facilitate the processing of exhibitors' entries, the Fair board adheres to its policy of not accepting additional entries from exhibitors after their original sheets are turned in to the Fair office.

Secretary Emeritus Louis P. Brady remembers one woman who entered several hand-sewn clothing items. After she turned in her list, she asked if she could add one more garment to her list. When she was told she could not, a housedress was entered in the name of her husband, who was evidently also a seamstress.

Reported in Sandwich *Argus* September 17, 1892

"We were shown one of the handsomest pieces of lace work we have seen for some time by Mrs. C. E. Orr, it being a knitted lace spread made by her niece, Miss Ferris, of Bristol, who is totally blind. This work was awarded second premium at the Fair, the one receiving first being made of finer thread, but the workmanship was no better. Miss Ferriss [sic] is an expert at that kind of work and in order to get the design, the pattern, or stitch, is read to her after which she will do the work neatly as anyone blessed with their eyesight."

Courtesy of SFA

Photo by R.M.

quantities of draperies and other articles for household furnishings. This exhibit has great interest for the ladies who linger long in its vicinity, and occasionally a masculine ventures near and is immediately transfixed with delight and wonder at the gorgeous array before him, especially if his best girl has contributed anything to the harmony of the pictures.

The September 15, 1900, issue of the *Argus* said, "By noon the Floral Hall looked like a large fancy store, filled as it was with all kinds of needlework, pictures, and various exhibits by the merchants of Sandwich and vicinity." Foods and pastries, vegetables, grains, and fruits were displayed in the center of the hall. In 1935 premium money totaled $165 for rugs, quilts, table linens and napkins, and various other fancy stitching. Ninety-seven dollars was awarded for painting premiums. By 1936 the department name was shortened to Needlework.

In contrast to the few entries in the Needlework area in 1888, the 1999 premium book contained over 20 pages of items to enter. Individual premiums ranged from four to eight dollars totaling $6,500 in premium money in this area. Today most of the needlework is in the east half of the building with all the walls and shelves filled with needlework exhibits.

Entries range from quilts, afghans, and clothing, to stuffed animals, embroidery, crewel work, and cross stitching. A number of entries are judged on Tuesday evening and are hung in place before the Fair opens on Wednesday morning. The remaining entries are judged on Wednesday morning before the areas are opened to the public. Open Show Foods and Junior Foods, Clothing, and Needlework entries share space in the building.

Photo by R.M.

Courtesy of SFA

top left: Beautiful quilts and other needlework pieces have always enticed fairgoers to the domestic building that has been called Floral Hall, the Women's Building, and the Home Arts building.

top right: Until 1972 the Home Arts building housed a variety of entries that included craft items, art work, and baked goods.

right: Handmade garments are gradually diminishing in America's fast-paced lifestyle, but quality needlework is still on display at the Sandwich Fair in both professional and nonprofessional classes.

bottom: The Sandwich Fair is a quilter's paradise. Everyone admires the colors while veteran quilters examine the stitches of star patterns and other designs such as log cabin, cathedral window, trip around the world, and flower garden.

Apple, blackberry, black raspberry, cherry, current, grape, strawberry. . . jellies, jams, preserves, marmalades, and butters . . . hmmm . . . by the spoonful or on toast.

Exhibitor Karen Campbell

When Karen Campbell of DeKalb says baking is her hobby, it is an understatement. In 1996 she entered over 100 items in Open Show Foods to claim the title "Champion Baker." Championship was a goal Campbell set for herself in 1993. The first year she says she didn't enter enough items. The second year, she was ahead until the cakes were judged—she hadn't entered any. In the third year, she lost by two second-place ribbons. Finally in 1996, she reached her goal and maintained the title in 1997, 1998, and 1999.

Exhibitor and Judge Bill Gilbert

Bill Gilbert has been judging baked items since 1992.

Bill Gilbert is a familiar face in the Home Arts building as an exhibitor and as a baking judge. He first entered his quilts in the Fair in 1989. He exhibited two that year, one a baby quilt in the "any other crib quilt," and the other a stamped cross-stitch bedspread in the "quilted by hand" category. He took a second place on both entries and was "bit by the ribbon bug." Bill challenged himself to improve his stitching and to win a blue ribbon. Since then he has made thirty-eight quilts and received several first places. Bill gives his quilts away as Christmas and special occasion gifts to his family, and he sells them. One quilt he traded to his neighbor for a sewing machine.

Bill is one of forty-seven Certified Master Bakers in the U.S. In 1992 when he was dropping off his quilt exhibits, he asked Superintendent Renee Monkemeyer if the department needed a qualified judge. He started working the next day. He says he started eating Tuesday night and ate through Wednesday afternoon. He was so full that he didn't eat any Fair goodies that year.

Bill has returned as a judge every year. When he is presented with a large number of items in a class, he says he smells them first and then he tastes them. He groups and narrows his choices, looking for specific characteristics in each category. He says, "Sometimes it's harder to pick the second [place] than the first."

Exhibitor Rhonda Larson

Rhonda Larson, Sandwich, exhibited at the Fair the first time in 1982. Strawberry jellies and jams were her specialty. She says, "I liked to spice up my jellies with peach schnapps to change the flavor a bit. After all, everybody used the same Sure Jel recipe."

Foods

In 1888 there were only 23 entry choices in Kitchen, Dairy and Pantry. They included butter (not less than 7 pounds for each entry), cheese (20 pounds), cider vinegar (one gallon), Illinois flour or cornmeal (100 pounds). Baked items such as loaves of breads, cakes, mince or pumpkin pies were also included.

By 1918 cookies, preserves, jams and jellies, candies, vegetables, and "War Bread" had been added. One-dollar premiums were paid for first place and fifty cents for second place.

The July 22, 1948, *Sandwich Free Press* referred to Open Show exhibitors as "The Cooks of Today" and ages 18 and under as "The Cooks of Tomorrow." The department name was changed to Dairy, Apiary, and Culinary, and commercial displays were removed from the building.

Current Superintendent Renee Monkemeyer described the building as "practically bare" when she first saw it in 1953. At that time all Open Show entries arrived on Wednesday morning and were gone by Friday afternoon because Monkemeyer and other workers sold the items for the exhibitors. When entries came in, the

Reported in the Sandwich *Argus* September 15, 1892

"Miss Laura Walter, oldest daughter of Mr. and Mrs. G. Walter although only 15 years of age, is the champion breadmaker, being awarded the first premium for the best loaf of bread in the general class at the fair last week, and competed with many old bread makers."

Courtesy of SFA

Photo by J.A.

Courtesy of SFA

top left: At one time, entries in the Home Arts building were arranged on steps, making it easy to view the exhibits. Today this isn't possible because of the number of entries.

bottom left: Fairgoers love to look at taste-tempting pies displayed under glass. They marvel at the number of bakers who are willing to give up a whole pie to compete for a ribbon at the Sandwich Fair.

top right: Women as well as men have always enjoyed the handiwork displayed in the Home Arts building also known as the Women's Building.

Courtesy of SFA

Photo by J.E.H.

Courtesy of SFA

exhibitors indicated the price they wanted for the item. Late on Friday afternoon, the buyers picked up their food and the exhibitors collected their money. The building personnel worked at a hectic pace to clear out the Open Show entries to make room for the Junior entries that arrived on Friday evening and Saturday morning.

The 1950's saw the beginning of much-needed changes. Taking advantage of the Fair Association's willingness to have each department write its own section of the premium book, the superintendents reorganized and expanded both the Open Show and Junior needlework and foods areas. The first change was to extend the exhibit days of the Junior Fair to match the exhibit days of the Open Show. In addition,

Exhibitor Margaret DeKing

Herbert DeKing of Yorkville says his wife Margaret filled a small chest with her ribbons. They were her pride and joy. She loved to enter her baking in the Fair; some of her favorite recipes were cherry and mince pies, white bread, brownies, and pineapple upside-down cake. He adds, "We used to take a car full [of baked goods] every year."

workers no longer sold items on display. From that point on, there was tremendous growth.

Monkemeyer recalls the evening she and Millie Carter, who was the assistant to Needlework Superintendent Pauline Newton, changed the way the entries were displayed. After Newton left, they spent hours arranging and organizing all the needlework. The next day there were many positive comments from everyone about the attractiveness of the area.

The appearance of the building interior was one of the changes made from 1955 to 1972. The old stair-step shelving for canned goods was removed. Art was hung high on boards that were placed around the inside. Glass exhibit cases were added and hardware was mounted on the walls to hang quilts, clothing and photography. By 1971 every inch of available space was filled.

In 1972 a new building for Arts and Crafts exhibits and Photography was ready for the growing number of exhibits. At first there were concerns there would not be enough entries to fill the extra space. That worry was short lived because the Home Arts exhibits continued to expand. New entry choices were added and staff was increased. For the 100th Fair in 1987, the name was changed from Open Show Dairy, Apiary, and Culinary to Open Show Foods, and all of the junior entries in the building became part of Junior Home Economics.

The superintendents of the Home Arts Department have memorable stories from working for decades in one of the most popular buildings on the grounds. They have come to know families of exhibitors from many miles away as well as the immediate area. They recall a mother and daughter from Chicago who for several years arrived in a taxicab with their exhibits.

Some exhibitors enter "carloads" of items while others enter only one or two items. They have watched young exhibitors grow up and become Open Show exhibitors, and they see

middle and bottom right: The Home Arts building is a gourmet's delight and a hungry man's horror. Exhibitors may enter every kind of bread from apricot to zucchini. Hours of skillful work are shown in the professional and nonprofessional decorated cakes.

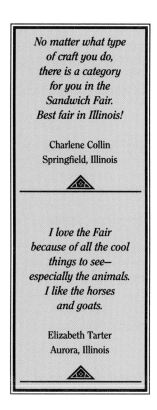

*No matter what type
of craft you do,
there is a category
for you in the
Sandwich Fair.
Best fair in Illinois!*

Charlene Collin
Springfield, Illinois

*I love the Fair
because of all the cool
things to see—
especially the animals.
I like the horses
and goats.*

Elizabeth Tarter
Aurora, Illinois

opposite page: Photo credits appear in Chapter 11.

granddaughters and grandsons of early exhibitors entering needlework and foods today.

Arts and Crafts

Art work was an important part of the early fairs. An 1892 newspaper account mentioned that "The display of pictures in oil, pastel and water colors at the fair was exceptionally fine. There were many gems among the collection that are entitled to consideration." It goes on to say, "We are justly proud of the artistic talent shown by the amateurs of this city and surrounding counties."

In 1898 there were 29 entry choices for art that included oil, watercolor, pencil, crayon, with a few choices in china painting. All of these entry choices are still listed today. The premiums ranged from two dollars to fifty cents for first and second places. By 1900 china painting increased from one entry choice to ten, and it grew to 15 by 1902. Oils and watercolors stayed about the same.

By the late 1800's an Educational and Natural History Department was a part of the Fair. Public school children in DeKalb County displayed their projects. Later, this became part of the Junior Fair. Entry choices stayed the same until around the 1930's. Then the choices began to break into entry groups, starting at kindergarten to eighth grade. By mid 1930's, this department had doubled its entry

categories, but was still restricted to DeKalb County students. The prize money at that time ranged from one dollar fifty cents to fifty cents for first through third places. By 1936 the Fair Association changed its policy and awarded only a blue ribbon for first and a red ribbon for second.

In mid 1930's wood inlay was introduced. Jigsaw puzzles, game boards, and small collections were added. In 1946 art started to expand into oil paintings, watercolors, hand-decorated china, and sculptures.

In 1958 Jewelry was added to Open Art. Today the art entry choices have grown to 170 including china painting, wearable art, oils, acrylics, and watercolors.

In the 1970's the Fair was growing by leaps and bounds. President C. H. "Dutch" Hough had the foresight to realize that as the livestock section was growing so was the so-called women's section. The Home Arts building, for years known as the Women's Building, was bursting at the seams. At the time, it housed Junior Fair arts and crafts, home economics, and photography as well as Open Class crafts, photography, art, needlework, dairy, apiary, and culinary.

Realizing growth would continue, the directors proposed a new building, one that would make more room for all departments. In 1972 building No. 33 opened for art and craft entries. In the early 1980's, an addition to the new building was added for photography exhibits.

In 1996 the building was once again spilling over with exhibits. To correct the situation, a new building was constructed for antique collections and collectibles, which had grown to over 450 entry choices. In twenty-four years, the exhibitors' space grew from one building to three buildings. Yet, there never seemed to be enough room because an increase in entries brought more exhibitors.

Exhibitor Ginny Hann

Ginny Hann of Sandwich has been exhibiting as an amateur in china painting since 1980—to the best of her recollection. She recalls that she received thirteen dollars in premium money that year. Ginny said, "I became seriously interested in china painting several years earlier when I first saw the exhibits of Jean Helm at the Fair, a porcelain art teacher from Plainfield, who entered the Professional Class. I began taking lessons from her, and from that time on, I was 'hooked.' "

It has become a very enjoyable hobby in her retirement because she has met many people who also enjoy china painting. Ginny says that porcelain painting is often mistaken for ceramics. It is quite different, however, because the design is painted on the "bare" piece several times for depth and detail, and it is fired in a kiln to temperatures of approximately 1,350 degrees after each painting.

"Each year I think *no more*, as the kiln never entirely cools off between firings as the Labor Day deadline nears, but there is something contagious about entering in the Fair," comments Ginny.

Photography

Photography exhibits date back to 1896. It was listed with collections of painting and photography. The exhibitor did not necessarily have to take or paint the pictures—just collect them. The premium money was three dollars for first place and two dollars for second place. There were only eight entry choices unlike the 159 in 1999.

*J*udges

taste, smell, squeeze,

measure,

and make

comparisons

as they choose

the best entries

in each department.

right: At one time photography was displayed in the Home Arts building, and exhibitors were not restricted to two inch margins around their photographs.

left: Professional and nonprofessional artists may enter their work in oil, acrylic, airbrush, and watercolor. Shown in the top left is a 1977 painting by Becky Tvrdik Daniels. It hangs in the Fair office at 121 S. Main Street in Sandwich.

bottom right: Arts and Crafts Superintendent Ruth Nelson (l.) and Assistant Mary Ellen Huss check and count entries.

In 1902 photography was still listed with collections. With only two entry choices, it seemed to be dwindling. In 1928 photography disappeared from the premium book even though it was still listed with collections as painting and photography. It wasn't until 1947 that photography started to come back. It reappeared with 15 entry choices, paying three dollars for first, two dollars for second, and one dollar for third premiums.

In 1948 there were several changes. Exhibitors had to list the model of camera used, shutter speed, lens opening, and type of film. Young photographers were encouraged to enter. The age groups were 18 and over and under 18. Black and white film was still the only choice listed. In 1949 new guidelines were developed for Junior Fair participants. Exhibitors could be age 20 and under. Entries were limited to boys and girls in DeKalb, Kane, Kendall, and LaSalle Counties.

New entry choices were added—tinted pictures in 1950 and transparencies with three categories in 1954. Exhibitors could enter two slides for each entry description. The prize money ranged from four dollars to one dollar for first through third places. Transparencies were limited to Open Show. In 1956 there were 44 entry choices for Open Show. In 1999 Photography had a record year of 2,910 photos entered with over 300 exhibitors.

Ceramics

Ceramic pieces were first listed in 1952 in the Art Department. There were eight types of entries: jug, vase, bowl, box, plate, tray, figurines, and any modern not listed elsewhere. In 1960 ceramic entries doubled. By 1969 the entry choices listed were glazed, stained, or original hand-built. First place received one dollar fifty cents and second place received seventy-five cents. A professional class was included through 1984.

Collections and ceramics were listed together from 1984 through 1996. In 1997 ceramic entries were separated from collections when collections moved to a new building. The number of entry choices and premium money has grown since 1997. In 1997 there were 70 different choices to enter. Premium money in 1999 was $834. A special effects class is now offered with entries such as airbrushing and decals.

Courtesy of SFA

Photo by K.L.B.

Junior Arts, Crafts, Photography, Ceramics

In 1949 the Junior Fair was organized and was open to DeKalb, Kane, Kendall and LaSalle Counties. In the beginning there were only 10 entry choices. They included nature study, drawings, kindergarten work, scientific work, manual training, art work, different lines of any school work, set of four drawings exhibited by second-grade pupils, and map drawings. The prize money was one and two dollars for first and second places. The Educational Department disappeared in 1950, and the Industrial Arts Department was started. It was broken into three groups, open to all age groups: exhibitors with one or more years of high school; exhibitors with two or more years of high school; and exhibitors who received 10 or more

class hours per week in instruction in the area entered. The choices were wood, metal, plastics, and drawing.

In 1953 three more counties were eligible to enter in the Junior Fair: Ogle, Boone, and Grundy. Art included ceramics that incorporated pottery, modeling clay, woodcarving—copy or original. In 1955 Industrial Arts added two entry choices: leather and wrought iron. Hobby exhibits were added for ages 16 to 21 years and 15 years and under. The classes were nature, stamp, coin, and other collections.

In 1956 junior photography was listed with hobbies which included collections, nature, stamps, and coins. Color prints were listed with black and white prints, tinted prints, and transparencies. Prize money was four, two, and one dollar for first through third premiums. The entry age was divided from 10-20 years and over 20 years. There were 19 choices for entries.

In 1957 the junior art fair included arts and crafts: pastels, water colors, collections of ceramic pottery, modeling clay, and woodcarving. Prize money ranged from two dollars for first to fifty cents for second. In 1963 hobby exhibits were no longer listed, and in 1967 Industrial Arts Department was no longer listed. Entry choices were now listed in woodworking and handicrafts. This included leather craft, woodwork, mosaics, basketry, and much more. The prize money ranged from one to five dollars. One area that showed noticeable growth was junior ceramics. From 1972 to 1987 the entry choices increased from two to sixteen. In 1999 junior crafts had 444 entries in a limited space, and Junior Art entries increased by 65 entries.

top left: The Home Arts building was literally bursting at the seams prior to building the Arts and Crafts building in 1972.

bottom left: Photography exhibits moved into new quarters when the Arts and Crafts building was erected.

top right: Junior crafter Brooke Updike of Sandwich received a special award ribbon at the 2000 Fair for her craft.

Courtesy of SFA

Professionals and nonprofessionals may enter their woodwork. Because of limited space, no single article may take up more than 12 square feet.

Courtesy of SFA

Photo by J.E.H.

Photo by E.L.F.

top: Since the Collections building opened in 1997, collections have expanded to over 350 types of entries. There are three groupings: Collections 50 years or older, Nature Collections, and Miscellaneous Collections.

bottom: Little Lulu qualified in the "any other not listed" in collections.

right: The ribbon-cutting for the Collections building was in 1997. (l. to r.) Mary Roy, Rebecca Steeves, Louise Glover, Fair President Wiley Updike, Assistant Superintendent Bess Moss, Director John Wagner, Martha Sampson, Superintendent Jane Jacobson, Ida Hanson, and Assistant Superintendent Mary Lou Moris.

COLLECTIONS DEPARTMENT

Collections could be entered at the Fair beginning in 1972 when the new Arts and Crafts building opened. Antique, nature and miscellaneous classes were listed. There were a wide variety of entry choices in these three areas, ranging from antique campaign buttons, small hand tools, and salt dips, to rocks, entomology, and Indian relics, to thimbles and barbed wire.

Premiums totaled $544 for this area; ranging from five dollars to one dollar. Through 1996 there were not many changes except for adding a few entry choices and increasing the premium money. Premium money awarded from 1990 through 1996 was about $1,615 each year.

Many changes occurred in 1997 when the new Collections building opened. More space was available; therefore, many more entry choices were added. Collections became a separate department. Premium money available was $3,652; in 1999 it increased to nearly $5,000. First place premium is six dollars, second place is four dollars, and third place is three dollars. The Antique class has changed to 50 Years or Older. Fairgoers who visit the Collections building experience a small museum of old and unique entries.

School Exhibits

One of the most popular displays for children at the early Fairs was exhibits of their school work. An 1898 issue of the *Sandwich Argus* has a brief account of the display: "The educational exhibit is one that is attractive and is the result of hard labor on the part of pupils and teachers." Later the display was moved to a large tent adjacent to the Industrial Hall. Secretary Emeritus Louis P. Brady proudly tells of his award-winning picture. As a young man, he recalls that he "finally got one picture with a red ribbon."

First place winners in 1927 included Somonauk public school students for their nature-study work and their object-drawing work. The fifteen dollars in premium money was to be used to purchase furnishings for their classrooms.

In 1930 the Sandwich *Free Press* promoted the school exhibits: "It promises to be as good if not better this year and Mr. Haskin, who is in charge of Sandwich schools, is busy preparing the exhibit."

In 1931, ". . .parents, and others who are interested in the schools of this city, will find a most complete display of work that has been and is being done in the local school system. This exhibit is well worth the time of a visit."

Agnes Stahl, former Sandwich school teacher, says, "In later years during the 1940's and 1950's, Sandwich elementary classes displayed art work in the Horticulture building on the entire south wall of the east room."

Art teacher Syranna Kosulic remembers hanging the work of her students as late as the

Sandwich Record

1970's. She says, "Work was hung on every empty space!" No prizes were given but the public showed much interest in the display.

4-H Club Fair

The 4-H Club Fair actually had its beginnings with the pig clubs in the early 1920's and later with the baby beef clubs. Judging contests were held for the young people; trophies were awarded to individuals and to clubs. Records show that Leland and Sugar Grove won at least one time and Waterman won at least twice.

According to a local farmer, "Many of these young people went on to do some pretty good judging." Former DeKalb County Assistant Advisor Raymond Nelson took his dairy-judging team on to win the Illinois State Judging Contest. Ben Eade, 4-H Club Superintendent, took his team on to win fourth in the nation in 1927. Several of the early 4-H members went on to be a part of the Sandwich Fair. LaVerne "Dutch" Johnson served many years as superintendent in both Junior and Open Shows. He was selected for the prestigious Master Farmer Award in Illinois. Elroy Dannewitz also went on to become a club leader and Dairy Superintendent at the Fair.

The official beginning of the DeKalb County 4-H Fair was 1927. It ran simultaneously with the Sandwich Fair from 1927 through 1948. In 1937 the *Somonauk Reveille* reported that "The 4-H Club shed was filled to overflowing and some of the stock had to be kept in outdoor pens. Approximately 300 4-H boys and girls exhibited their projects . . . ."

Beginning in 1949, the DeKalb County

4-H Fair joined forces with the Sycamore Farmers Club Junior Fair, and the Sandwich Fair Association began sponsoring their own Junior Fair.

Looking back, many former members consider 4-H Club a real learning experience and one of the highlights of their summer. Lifetime friendships were formed, and more than a few romances evolved.

4-H Club Hog Auction

One of the main attractions at the 1942 Fair was the 4-H auction of purebred boars and gilts from litters that had raised eight pigs or more to the 56-day age weighing 300 pounds or more per litter. The *Sandwich Free Press* noted that the purpose of the project was to find strains of swine that made quick growth. Two weeks before the sale, competent judges evaluated the litters as to type and breed character. The entire litter had to meet the requirements in order to be sold at the 4-H auction.

DeKalb County boys whose livestock made the preliminary requirements were Ralph DeWerff of Earlville, Hampshire hogs; Stuart Phillips of Big Rock, Hampshire; Lowell Phillips of Big Rock, Hampshire; Kenneth Hjort of Sandwich, Hampshire; Robert Guehler of Somonauk, Poland China; Raymond Mowers of Esmond, Poland China; Wesley Elliott of Kirkland, Poland China; Wendell Hueber of Malta, Spotted Poland China; Allen Twombley of Clare, Duroc Jersey; Bernard Herrmann of Shabbona, Chester White; and Ronald Baie of Hinckley, Berkshire. ⬧

top left: School Exhibits were displayed until the 1970's. Shown arranging the displays are Miss Pearl Scheidecker (l.) of Somonauk who retired as principal of A.E. Woodward School after 47 years in education and Mrs. Agnes (LaVerne) Stahl, a Sandwich teacher.

top right: Armand Dannewitz of Somonauk in 1944 with his 4-H entry

Grandstand and Grounds Entertainment:
Music, Thrills, Crafts, and Comedy

Come one. Come all. There is and always has been something for everyone's enjoyment at the Sandwich Fair. Fairgoers are entertained everywhere at the Fair—in the grandstand, livestock area, around the exhibit buildings, and on the midway.

Grandstand entertainment includes variety acts, harness racing, sky shows, thrill shows and other track events. Grounds entertainment includes a wide range of displays, shows, and participation activities. There is music everywhere at the Fair—sit-down performances at the grandstand and Ag Land stage, strolling performers about the grounds, and lively dance and "boom-box" music from the Midway area.

Some activities like baseball and the queen contest are no longer held, yet they remain vivid in the memories of fairgoers. Horseshoe pitching is an old sport that has returned with a strong following. Some forms of entertainment such as the miniature steam train, antique autos and machinery, and the craft demonstrations evoke memories of bygone days. The midway provides a variety of entertainment all its own, and the entertainment at the grandstand and on the grounds has contributed to the Fair's record-breaking attendance.

At the Grandstand

As it should be at a county fair, the horse events such as harness racing and draft horse pull have large audiences. In addition to the equestrian events, there has always been a wide range of activities for every age group. Most of them can be categorized into two main groups—variety acts and thrill shows. The variety shows include music and animals. The thrill shows contain moments of suspense in the air and on the track. Both types of entertainment pack the stands.

Harness Racing

The longest running and most traditional entertainment at the Sandwich Fair is harness racing. Almost every premium book from 1900 through 1948 had the schedule and prices for races on the front or back cover. The earliest fairs did not have carnivals, stage shows, or even ballgames. Horseracing was the featured entertainment. It offered exciting head-to-head competition, and the crowds loved it.

There were the traditional classes for pacers and trotters, and a class called the gentlemen's driving class. The premium book listed the following requirement: "Not to have been tracked this season and race must be drove [sic] to wagon by owner." This means that the horse was not raced for money that year and the driver must own the horse and the sulky.

Ladies raced too. The 1892 Sandwich *Argus* records that "Miss May Mitten won first place in the Ladies Driving Contest and Miss Minnie Kennedy won second place. There were several other entries and all made a good showing proving that Sandwich has some good lady drivers."

The gentlemen's and ladies' driving events were most likely held between heats of the regular races. Several trick horse acts were used

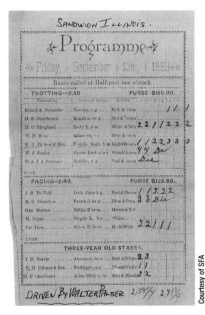

top: Harness racing programs like this were used by 1889 fairgoers.

opposite page: Photo by M.M. 1997

bottom: Horseracing is still a crowd pleaser at the Sandwich Fair. The starting gate folds behind the pace car, and the harness race begins.

"How the Doctor Lost But Won"

Have you ever heard the story of the man who lost but won?
Well, listen, fellow horsemen and I'll tell you how 'twas done.

Back there in the prairie country where the corn grows thick and tall
And where nearly every village has a county fair each fall.
There's nifty little racetrack where they step to beat the band
And a judge that knows his business issues orders from the stand.

Every year the horsey fellows from the city by the lake
Enter for a short vacation and their business cares forsake.
One, a carefree jolly dentist, always "makes" the little town,
Golden Boy he called his pacer, and his name is Doctor Brown.

Now among the other drivers was a chap that we'll call Black,
Though the name was very different that they called him on the track.
And he also had a pacer, quite a fast one rumors ran
Just beneath the Doctor's entry was Black's filly, Mary Ann.

Wednesday brought a crowd tremendous hosts of every creed and kind,
Who intently view the pumpkins, with the races most in mind;
Seven pacers faced the starter in the slow class of the day,
All were on their good behavior and were quickly on their way.

It was everybody's contest 'til they reached the distant stand
Then Black tapped the flying filly and she promptly took command;
Doctor Brown was riding easy, didn't seem to care a whit,
Golden Boy was pacing second and was plainly "on the bit."

Second heat and every starter finished in the selfsame place,
Some declared it good as over, Mary Ann would win the race;
Then a dark horse called The Joker beat them in a furious drive,
Doctor Brown still "buggy riding." Black's bay mare was number five.

Fourth heat and the Doctor's entry quickly grabbed the inner rail,
Black content to take it easy coaxed the little mare to trail;
Then the fifth and at its finish Golden Boy had won two heats
And the crowd now all excited stretched and settled in their seats.

That year's meeting was conducted on a plan that in my mind
Has done more to injure racing than all other things combined;
I may be a bit old-fashioned but the rules that suited me
Held no win-race-record humbug. back in eighteen ninety-three.

Brown and Black who knew the angles, thought no purse could compensate
For the mark they'd get by winning so they planned on "being late."
They alone came out to finish and it readily was seen
That each driver had decided that he'd keep his pacer "Green."

Just three times they scored demurely in a mild half-hearted way
When the judge addressed the driver this is what he had to say:
"Mister Black, you are a fellow that I thought was on the square;
I'm not pleased, I can assure you, with the way you drive your mare.

Now you take the
Doctor's gelding and
I warn you,
Mister Black
It will be your last
appearance if you ever
once look back."
"Doctor Brown," the
judge continued, "You
for years have graced
this course
And no one could
quite convince me that
you'd really pull a
horse.

Yet you seem to fear the record and I've hit upon a plan
That perhaps will "save your bacon" you will drive Black's Mary Ann.
Now you land her here a winner or your patrons by the lake
Won't find you in your office when their teeth begin to ache."

I have seen some famous wrestlers and some bareback riders, too
But I never saw them do the things those drivers tried to do;
Neck and neck they reached the quarter, whips were popping thick and fast,
On into the stretch they struggled, just a question which could last.

Past the half they still were pacing like two demons hitched to pole,
While the drivers' frantic efforts proved each hoped to win the goal.
Side by side the pacers staggered horse by horse and man by man,
But the Doctor won by inches with the filly, Mary Ann.

So the chaps who paid their money for admission at the gate
All agreed it was a corker and that it was simply great;
Black's bay mare had won the battle, Golden Boy had done his best,
And a sort of satisfaction hovered 'neath each driver's vest.

No reward is so enduring as the sense of duty done,
It eclipses all the records and the money that you've won;
Doctor Brown still races horses but he wins whene'er he can
For he don't forget the lesson that he learned with Mary Ann.

Down the street the judge still muses in his spacious dry goods store,
Where he issues daily orders to a dozen clerks or more.
And he still soliloquizes that the rules are not too dense
To be fully comprehended if applied with common sense.

There's a moral to the story, if you'd make the horse game square
Drive your trotter or your pacer as the Doctor drove Black's mare.

—Walter Palmer

Walter Palmer was well known to harness racing fans in the 1890's. He held the pacing record of 2:10 ¼ for a mile in the late 1800's with a horse named "Nellie M." For his accomplishment, the Fair Association presented him with a gold mounted sulky whip. Palmer was well educated and liked to write poetry. The poem, a gift to Tom Mercer, Superintendent of Speed from 1919 to 1940, was printed in the *Sandwich Free Press* September 2, 1937.

in the same manner. Tattersall's Diner of Sandwich owned two high-schooled horses, Golden Duchess and Little Joe. George Ault of Kirkland had another such horse named Eagle the Great. Many things at the Fair have changed, but horses have been part of the entertainment since the beginning.

The first Fair in 1888 took place on a nineteen-acre fairground, much smaller than the present-day grounds. The racetrack was situated around what is now the center of the grounds. Most of the original track is used as roads today. It can still be seen if the fairgoer knows where to look. It ran past the Secretary's Office, around the Horticulture building, over to the grandstand, parallel to the racetrack, and around the windmill. The center of the track was wooded, and it was rumored that some of the drivers took a short cut through the woods. Undoubtedly, it must have been difficult to be a racing judge in those days.

In 1913 the racetrack was moved to the present location, and the current grandstand was built. Traditionally the races began with all the horses in a line attempting to cross the starting line together. The judges decided if the start was good or if a restart was necessary. Restarting caused delays because the horses had to line up again.

The first starting gate was used in 1952 and was attached to the back of a fast car, the same as it is today. As the horses moved into position behind the gate, it folded up and sped away, making the starts easier and fairer.

In 1990 and 1991, night races were held in an effort to increase attendance on Wednesday night. After two years they moved to the daytime and other shows were tried at night.

Old newspaper articles always highlighted horseracing; the results were printed along with stories about the owners and drivers. Several

Compliments Of
FAIRSIDE FARMS
"HOME OF FAIRSIDE PAL"
SANDWICH · 786-7927 · ILLINOIS

Courtesy of J.B.W.

Courtesy of SFA

horses achieved fame at the Sandwich track. A horse named Sandwich received notice in wider racing circles. He and his colts were on display at the 1890 Fair. In 1915 A. E. Tillman of Earlville had a horse named Arwilda. She ran the mile in 2:25 ½. Whether or not this was a record is uncertain, but Tillman had a ruby-stained souvenir cup embossed with Arwilda's name, the date, and her time. In 1959 Sandwich residents took pride in V. F. Beck's famous horse "Fairside Pal" as he set a record at 2:07. Local racing enthusiasts of that day watched the papers for reports as their "native son" competed throughout the state.

In 1888 the top purse was $100 and the winning time was 2:33. In 1907 the purses were up to $350 and the time was around 2:20. In 1917 a purse of $25 and $10 was offered for a half-mile "running mule race." By 1945 purses

top: Harness racing in 1948

left: Fairside Pal, the horse that set a record of 2:07 in 1959, was featured on a 1963 calendar by Fairside Farms.

following pages: *Beacon News* pages 138-139: Fairgoers enjoy the shade of the grandstand as they watch a race to the finish.

Bill Stahl

Ninety-two and one-half years young is the way Bill Stahl of Somonauk described himself in early January 2000. Bill has been a timer in the judges stand for the harness races at the Fair for 18 years. He started by helping Kenny Klotz, Superintendent of Concessions. He still uses the stopwatch Kenny gave him. Bill says it is a favorite watch; other timers ask to borrow it.

Bill's family, natives of Germany, settled in the Somonauk area in 1912. He first remembers going to the Fair in a surrey with his parents around 1915. Later he walked to and from the Fair along the railroad tracks from Somonauk to Sandwich. As a young adult, he was a baseball player at the Fair.

In 1951 he started showing hogs when his oldest son Bill was ten years old. He and his sons showed hogs until mid 1970's. Through his Fair contacts, he sold hogs as far away as Japan. In later years, he helped his son Doug with horses that he boarded at the fairgrounds.

Bill enjoys working at the Fair, and God willing, he will be a timer at many more horse races.

Photo by P.O.

top: Horses coming into the home stretch in 1987

bottom: Charles Lett of Sandwich and his mighty heavyweight pulling team drew enthusiastic fans in the early 1930's.

ranged from $300 to $600, and in 1953 they were up to $500 to $1,000. The top purse in 1975 was $3,500, and the 1980's saw some purses up to $8,500. The top race in 1999 had a purse of $6,250.

Today, although horseracing has declined in some areas because of gambling boats and other pastimes, it continues to draw large crowds at the Sandwich Fair. Fair patrons enjoy sitting in the shade of the grandstand and watching the horses race to the wire. There were ninety-four horses entered in 1999. The current pacing record is 2:00:2 held by Dynamite Springs ('98, G. A. Rath), and the trotting record is 2:04 held by Poco Sidekick ('97, G. Conley).

In 1990 racing fans were introduced to a game called Pick-A-Winner. Before each race, patrons pick a winner using game slips that are included in the racing programs. After each race, two tickets are drawn at random. If the drawn ticket has the winner of the race designated, that person wins five dollars.

A three-year-old filly pacer driven by Jay Garrels set a track record at the 2000 Fair with a time of 1:59:3. She is owned by Ron and Valerie Johnson and trained by Don Brown.

Draft Horse Pull Contest

The horses' powerful legs dig deeply into the dirt. With short, choppy strides, the large Belgian draft horses drag the weights forward. Slowly, slowly, they pull the required 27 ½ feet unless the drivers realize their teams can't handle the load. In that case, they bring them to a stop and their best distance is measured. In contrast to the tractor pull and truck pull, the horse pull contest is relatively quiet. Not that noise makes the horses skittish but the drivers prefer that the crowd be quiet so the horses can hear their verbal commands.

The first horse pull contest was in 1933. Local papers encouraged horse owners to contact Superintendent Ben Eade if they wanted to participate in the horse-pulling contest at the Fair just "for fun." There was no entry fee. The community was told to think twice if they thought there were no good teams left just because they didn't see horses in town any more. Record crowds turned out to watch over 20 teams compete that year. The *Somonauk Reveille* reported, "The grandstand was packed to capacity long before the teams started to demonstrate their strength."

Charles Lett's team won the heavyweight class, teams weighing 3,000 pounds or more. It pulled 3,000 pounds, which was only 250 pounds shy of the state record. In the lightweight class, teams weighing less than 3,000 pounds, the winner was Lewis Rex. Apparently there was some difficulty with the enthusiastic fans crowding onto the track and surrounding the teams. This was indicated in 1934 when a local paper reported that state police would be

Reporter's Comment in Early Newspaper
Sandwich Argus
September 17, 1892

Mr. Clough, the starter at the Fair races, won the good opinion of all. He did not get into quarrels with the drivers, was always fair and just and never lost his head or the control of the track and he has a voice that can be heard.

Courtesy of WF

Courtesy of G.L.J.

Pliny Baird pulled for Cedardell Farms with King and Duke in 1935.

Pliny Baird

George L. Johnson who knew Pliny Baird well tells the following story.

One time after winning the draft horse pulling contest at the Sandwich Fair, Pliny decided to try for a record in an exhibition pull. He had just had his teeth pulled and was wearing his new set of false teeth. Since the fairgrounds was only about four miles from the Baird's home, nearly everyone watching knew Pliny personally, and the grandstand was packed that day.

Just before the horses were ready to pull, the announcer told the crowd over the loud speaker, "Everyone be quiet so that the team can hear their driver!" There was a hush in the stands as everyone complied with the announcer's request.

Pliny started the big pull and called to his horses, "King, Duke, King, Duke, King, D . . . blub." Pliny dropped his lines and grabbed for his teeth. His wife Marj saw what was happening, and in her clear, shrill voice shouted, "Oh, my Lord, Pliny has lost his teeth!" Her voice carried through the whole crowd. The audience instantly burst into laughing so much they almost collapsed the grandstand!

on hand "to keep everyone not assisting with the contest off the track" so that the problems of 1933 wouldn't reoccur.

The 1934 event was as popular as the previous year in spite of the rain. Local papers made no reference to spectators rushing onto the track. Perhaps the state police successfully deterred the crowd, or maybe the mud kept the crowd more orderly.

In the summer of 1935 Lett's team won the state championship at Springfield, weeks before the Sandwich Fair. He had a big team that weighed 3,800 pounds. Apparently only one other team dared to take on his "Goliath." In this case "David" was Pliny Baird of Plano pulling for Cedardell Farms with a pair of roan geldings that weighed 3,500 pounds. Lett's team failed to pull 3,050 pounds in three tries, and Cedardell Farms went on to win in the upset of the year. Some said that Lett's team had been under the weather since returning from Springfield.

In 1937 a loud speaker was mounted to the measuring device to allow all spectators to hear better from their grandstand seats. Records are incomplete, and it is uncertain when the last of these pulls occurred but very likely World War II ended them.

Draft horse pulls returned in 1995 under Superintendent Scott Breunig assisted by Joe Steffen. Although the event is basically the same, some changes are evident. Today, the horses are bigger; teams weigh up to 5,000 pounds and stand 20-22 hands [80 to 88 inches] high. Today the horses are usually Belgians. In the past, audiences compared the strength of Shires, Clydesdales, Percherons, Suffolks, and Belgians.

Today, the weight brackets are broken down to split the teams evenly and are usually around 3,300 and up for heavyweights and 3,300 and under for lightweights. The horses are no longer local teams. Most are part of the horse-pull circuit even though some are used to work the fields in isolated parts of the country.

Enthusiasm for the contest is as great today as it was in the early days of the pull. People still like the strength and beauty of these big horses; they turn out in large numbers to watch experienced drivers encourage their massive teams.

Weights, measurements and measuring devices are keys to determining winners in the pulls. The pull length of 27 ½ feet was determined in the early 1900's by studies conducted

> *I remember the horse pulling contest when Charley Lett beat Pliny Baird of Cederdell Farms. Charley had a big team of dapple greys. He borrowed a heavy harness so he wouldn't tear his old harness up. Each night they would have a parade of champions around the track. I remember the corn games. We would take home our share of blankets as prizes. These were some of my fine memories of the 1930's.*
>
> Robert Thurow
> Hampshire, Illinois

> *I love the Sandwich Fair because of the variety of displays, tractor pulls, antique displays, and the time of year it's held.*
>
> Rich Rezny
> Maple Park, Illinois

Photo by M.M.

top: Today the dynamometer, used to measure the pull of the teams, is mounted on a 1952 truck frame.

opposite page: Variety show advertisements which appeared in premium books

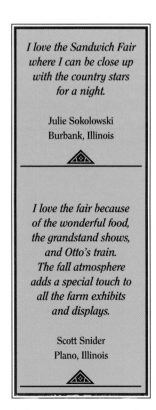

I love the Sandwich Fair where I can be close up with the country stars for a night.

Julie Sokolowski
Burbank, Illinois

I love the fair because of the wonderful food, the grandstand shows, and Otto's train. The fall atmosphere adds a special touch to all the farm exhibits and displays.

Scott Snider
Plano, Illinois

by the University of Iowa. The studies gave farmers an idea of how many horses it took to pull a four- to ten-bottom plow through a field. They also showed that after a horse, or hitch, pulled a distance of 27 ½ feet, it lost maximum power.

Using these studies, officials set the distance for the horse pull contest. From there, it is a process of determining which horses can pull the heaviest load the farthest distance. The teams get three independent chances at the pull. If a team does not succeed, the farthest pull in the three chances is where the team places.

A dynamometer is used to measure resistance. When the horses push into their collars, they pull out a cable attached to weights on the machine. The oil flow opens a valve that lets the weights rise. Unlike the tractor pull where the weights get heavier the farther they are pulled, the dynamometer weights are the same throughout the distance of the pull. When the horses cross the distance, more weight is added for another pull. The term rolling tons is used to describe weight pulled and can be upwards of 75,000 to 80,000 pounds. This is comparable to pulling a semitrailer full of grain.

The dynamometer used to measure the pull of the teams today is basically the same as the University of Illinois model used in 1933. Today, it has been switched to a 1952 truck frame owned and operated by Steve and Wanda Lance of Cambridge, Wisconsin. Only two dynamometers are in use in the Midwest.

Variety Acts

Variety acts include everything from beautiful girls who pose, whirl, adorn, and dance to novelty acts with dancing puppets, flailing whips, and spinning chairs, as well as animals that talk, dance, and dive. They appear in a variety of places. Some are on stage as "stand alone" acts. Others are strolling performers, entertaining audiences all over the grounds. In past years, acts entertained between heats of the horse races. It's no wonder that the shows attract long lines of eager spectators hoping to find the seat with the best view.

Local firemen provided hometown entertainment in 1891 by demonstrating their skill in using fire-fighting equipment. The *Somonauk Reveille*, September 18, reported that "after dinner the Peru, Mendota and Sandwich fire companies took their places on the track to do their part for the amusement of the crowd." The firemen competed in a hose race, Sandwich winning in a "phenomenal time of 34 ½ seconds." The pipeman Guy Eames "made a beautiful coupling," helping to make the victory possible. In the "hub-and-hub race," Sandwich also won.

The "ostrich tent" was a popular attraction in 1892. It housed a creature described in the newspapers as "nine feet from toe to alligator mouth." There were other sideshows in the tent as well. A news reporter of the day suggested that a young man in the tent be given a gold medal because he actually took a distasteful and repulsive 12-inch reptile and "swallowed it down like a peeled banana." After a few moments, the young man took a large swallow of water and out "popped Mr. Snake as bright and fresh as a Morning Glory."

Promotional advertisements provide a glimpse at some of the early performances. A 1915 show bill described the abilities of Pricket, Luster, and Maitland "The Human Frogs." Their act was a "grotesque contortion . . . of realistic fidelity" which far outshone "mother nature in her most brilliant moods."

SANDWICH FAIR
1946
Reserved Seat -- Grand Stand
Established Tax
Federal Tax
ADMIT ONE

Courtesy of SFA

SANDWICH FAIR ASSOCIATION.
GRAND STAND
THURSDAY, SEPTEMBER 10th, 1908.
25 CENTS.
C. L. STINSON,
Secretary

Courtesy of SFA

Famous ★ WHITE HORSE SHOW

World's Greatest Novelty!
CAL & RUTH THOMPSON'S

25 WORLD'S MOST BEAUTIFUL WONDER HORSES 25

Many Other FEATURE ACTS
It's 2 BIG SHOWS in 1

SUNDAY, SEPTEMBER 7

2:30 P. M. and 7:30 P. M.

1947

DAISY and HER PUPS
ONE OF MANY ACTS IN
SUNDAY, SEPTEMBER 13 SHOW
2 Shows Only—2:30 & 8:00 P. M.

1953

Wednesday & Thursday Evenings
In Front of the Grandstand

1946

1958

1962

TELEVISION'S FAMOUS
"PANCHO" LEO CARRILLO
FEATURED
WEDNESDAY
AFTERNOON & EVENING

JONNY RIVERS HIGH DIVING MULES

SEE THE WORLD'S ONLY
HIGH DIVING MULES
Wednesday
Thursday
Friday
Afternoon and Evening

top: Full page 1918 advertisement

bottom: Advertisement for the famous Roxeyettes that appeared in the 1950 premium book.

right: The Fair was a showplace for international performers. In 1953 Armida, the sweetheart of Cisco Kid productions, appeared in South of the Border Fiesta.

Many of the performers were beautiful women. In 1924 the swinging, high flying ladder act of the Earle Sisters entertained the crowds. "Twin sisters costumed in gorgeous attire, their marvelous maneuvers and hazardous gyrations caused gasps of amazement and wonder for astonished audiences. Swinging at great heights, they performed with ease various stunts that even men would not attempt . . . ." The beautiful Dellameade Troupe also performed in 1924. Five elegant women chosen for their perfect figures posed like statues on a huge, revolving stage with special-effects lighting accenting their loveliness.

Still more beauties, the five Ferris Wheel Girls fearlessly performed difficult feats while hanging from bars and whirling at daring speeds around an apparatus modeled after the famous Ferris wheel.

In 1939 a Swing Show presented a Sparkling Girl Review. There was also Gus Sun's Glorified Revue in 1940. It had a glorious cast of stage stars, an orchestra, a line of dancing girls, and a variety of acts.

Direct from the Roxy Theatre in New York in 1951, sixteen gorgeous precision dancers adorned in stunning wardrobe appeared on stage with the famous Roxyettes. They promised audiences unique and varied dancing using every twist of their wrists, ankles, and torsos. In 1953 Alice Morehouse, America's acrobatic dancer, was known for her poise, skill, and outstanding attractiveness which kept her in constant demand in the ballrooms of America's finest hotels. In 1980 the Fabulous Darnells, "three lovely ladies" who performed in perfect unison, complemented their tricks with exotic dog acts.

Undoubtedly, the girls were beautiful and talented; however, those who saw some of the early shows remember details that weren't published. As a teenager Lucile Kegel, who worked in the Secretary's Office, remembers seeing beautiful showgirls painted up like circus horses. She also recalls how dirty their feet were. Her observations remind today's audiences of the realities of earlier times. Most of the walkways and driveways were not paved, and bathing facilities were nonexistent or, at best, primitive. Even though the conditions weren't always accommodating, the show people worked hard to give Fair audiences something to talk about for a whole year—or a whole lifetime.

International Performers

The Fair was also a showplace for international performers. The Australian Waite was a novelty act of flailing whips and spinning boomerangs in 1927. Pedro and Luis, two young Mexican boys, were exceptional acrobats at the 1940 Fair. Skating champions, the Leducs with Scotch figure skater Audrey McColl, were featured in 1959. The life-size puppets from Los Imitados, Spain, were a dance team in 1963.

From Tahiti the "Pearls of the Pacific" performed native dancing. Before the word *Jap* took on disparaging connotation, there were the Mighty Sons of Nippon, the "Three Toki Japs," an early Fair act with foot-juggling, water-spinning, and acrobatic feats of equilibrium on slack wire. Armida, the sweetheart of Cisco Kid productions, appeared in "South of the Border Fiesta."

Circuses and Rodeos and More

Animal shows have always been popular with Fair audiences. Curious onlookers attended Wilber's Society Circus in 1916 and Hill's Great Circus Deluxe in 1918. They were entertained by a talking pony, an intelligent mule, giant baboons, leaping Siberian wolfhounds, acrobatic monkeys, a high-diving monkey, and racing hounds.

In 1921 audiences stood in line to see Delmar, the world-famous dancing horse and a re-creation of a horse thief capture in a show called "Sports of the Plains." Other acts that have performed at the Fair are Lewis Brothers'

144

THE CONLEY TROUPE
With Wonder Bros. Circus & Rodeo
SUNDAY, SEPT. 8, 1946
2:30 P. M. and 7:30 P. M.

1946 Premium Book

DUNVETTE TROUPE
Representative American Aerialists
and Gymnasts
Will give Performances in front of the Grand Stand
on each day of the Fair

These are artists of marked distinction, performing exciting evolutions and dangerous displays that are the marvel of spectators, combining irresistible comedy, and featuring a double full twisting somersault. As added separate features: horizontal bar act by two gentlemen, also flying ring act by lady and gentleman.

Courtesy of SFA

left: Wonder Brothers Circus and Rodeo was a popular show from the late 1940's to the early 1950's.

right: An advertisement in the 1914 premium book announced the performance of the Dunvette Troupe in front of the grandstand on each day of the Fair.

Fire Fly, famous Jumping Horse

—WITH—

105 RANCH RODEO
Wednesday Night, September 9
SPECIAL GRANDSTAND SEATS
ONLY 30c

1953 Premium Book

Fire Fly, the famous jumping horse with the 105 Ranch Rodeo, pleased audiences in 1953. The show was a bargain at 30 cents a ticket.

bottom: One of the more unusual grandstand acts in 1947 featured the Siamese twins Daisy and Violet Hilton.

big three-ring circus (1942), Graham Western Riders with the "world's greatest stunt riders and ropers" (1948), and Wonder Brothers Circus (1951).

Thirty cents in 1953 would buy a ticket to the "105 Ranch Rodeo," a wild west show complete with clowns, trick mules, cowboys, cowgirls, wild bulls, and bucking horses.

The Gene Holter Show delighted audiences in 1954, 1959, and 1972 when local mayors and aldermen rode ostriches and paraded on camels. Fair officials were photographed atop a huge, Hollywood stunt elephant. In 1960 Johnny Rivers' Golden Horse Ranch Thrill Show appeared.

"Uncle Heavy's Burlesque, a Pork Chop Revue," featured Oink the serenading pig in 1963. Trained pigs performed calisthenics, squealed down slides, and pushed newborn piglets in a baby carriage. In 1969 Hubert Castle International Circus entertained audiences.

The Flying Valentines was one of many trapeze and high-wire acts that performed at the Fair. Another was the Dunvette Troupe who did a double, full-twist, horizontal-bar act, and a flying-ring act in 1914. In 1927 the Dixon Riggs Trio, an acrobatic-bicycle act, was on the show-bill. In the 1930's, a lady and three men performed atop a 100-foot ladder without a safety device.

Other unique shows included the Hilton Sisters, known as the Siamese Twins, in 1947; Chicagoan Miss Bettino on the precarious sway pole in 1960; and Trampoline Town USA, a championship versatile tumbling group in 1965.

Comedies, Musicals, and Other Performances

Degen and Bradley's Electric Theater Company was "high tech" in 1910. It was a $2,000 venture with all the latest features that was advertised as one of the best traveling theaters under canvas. The barker enticed his audience, "We carry a $599 piano with mandolin attachment that is worth twice the admission price to hear!"

"If you don't laugh at Joe, there is no other reason than that you can't laugh," said the manager of pantomime comedian Joe Kiljoy in 1924. The Thurston Wonder show promised a gigantic program of illusions and high-class vaudeville acts. *Circus Solly*, a three-act musical comedy, was produced in 1926.

For many years in the 1930's and 1940's, WLS radio artists such as Georgie Goebel, Patsy Montana, Pat Buttram, and the Arkansas Woodchopper were the featured grandstand entertainment every night of the Fair.

A Gay Nineties parade was held in 1942 immediately following the livestock parade. It promised a 100-year-old Victoria drawn by a pair of albino mares and a tandem two-passenger sleigh pulled by a pair of spotted mules. Some of the horse-drawn equipment was owned and driven by local people. Prizes were awarded for the best vehicles if the drivers were dressed in Gay Nineties costumes. In 1951 an honest-to-goodness vaudeville show was presented. Today, Indian Valley Theatre continues the tradition with melodramas under its tent.

A capsule musical-comedy sketch from

Nation's Greatest Drawing Card!
The Only Living
SIAMESE TWINS
Daisy and Violet HILTON
Born Joined Together
AND THEIR BIG VARIETY SHOW
WEDNESDAY, SEPTEMBER 3
Night Show Only

1947 Premium Book

145

Courtesy of EF

The Eakle Family in 1938

Eakle Family Drum and Bugle Corps

In 1938 the Paul and Mary Eakle Family Drum and Bugle Corps from Waterman, Illinois, entertained at the grandstand. At that time they were the only family drum and bugle corps in the National Organization of the American Legion. The seven children performed every afternoon and evening; their warm-up group was the Sons of the Pioneers of WLS Radio. Mary Eakle generally played piano for the family, but that year she was expecting her eighth child, so Allen Yingling of Sandwich accompanied the group on his accordion.

The family began performing in 1933. The corps was made up of Alice, baritone bugler and dancer; Mavis, drum major and dancer; Johnny, snare drummer and dancer; Norma Dea, soprano bugler and dancer; Joan, bass drummer and acrobatic dancer; Nancy, color guard and lyricist; David "Buck" Lee, color bearer and assistant director.

In 1935 Paul Eakle built a self-propelled 42-foot replica of a battleship that appeared in parades throughout the U.S. The American Legion and Legion Auxiliary of Waterman sponsored the float. People did "double-takes" when they saw the battleship on the road en route to parades. At the request of the Canadian government, they participated in a parade at Toronto, Canada, on July 4-6, 1941, with the battleship. They also appeared several times with the battleship in Sandwich parades.

Joan "Joey" Eakle Clark of Sycamore recalls that it rained the year they performed at the Sandwich Fair. Several of the Fair board members helped carry the Eakle children across the muddy racetrack to keep their white slacks clean. After John was drafted in 1941, the family no longer performed.

Photo by B.V.

The Villain of Glitter Gulch was presented in 1999. Front: Frannie Poris (seated l. to r.) Melissa Auer, Allison Auer, Nancy Maroscia, Jenine Johnson, Ken Poris (standing l. to r.) Jim Stott, Tim Flodstrom, Linda Johnson, Jeff Metzger

Melodramas

Boos and hisses are welcome sounds in the Indian Valley Theatre (IVT) melodrama tent located inside the train tracks. IVT, a local community theatre group made up of residents of all ages, has been providing entertainment at the Fair since 1983. Each year, the group performs two different shows with 15 total performances. The cast of the old-fashioned melodramas encourages audience participation by holding up signs to signal appropriate responses: boos, hisses, cheers, and sighs. Popcorn and pop are sold, and the audience is invited to throw popcorn at the villain. Between performances the audience is entertained with olios—short song and dance skits. During the Fair the cast is often seen walking around the grounds, dressed in character, advertising the show. In recent years, IVT has performed for over 1,500 fairgoers each year. Admission is a bargain—one dollar.

Oklahoma entertained audiences in 1957. The Eddie Mack Showboat Minstrels featured a troupe of the finest singing voices in the country in 1958 as well as the famous comedy team of Butterbeans and Susie. Racehorse Williams was also part of the show. In 1959 the grandstand evening show was billed as *Rhapsody in Blue*.

Homegrown, local talent shared the same spotlight as paid performers in 1961. More than 50 contestants vied for 15 slots in the Fair-sponsored Venita Rich Talent Show, competing for a trip to New York to audition for the Ted Mack Original Amateur Hour TV show. On Friday night of the Fair in spite of the rain, talent from the ages of 7 to 70 performed as scheduled. Ann Gaul, marimba player from Shabbona, was selected as the winner.

The New York road show of Meredith Wilson's *The Music Man* was paid $5,500 for two performances in 1964. In 1966 the famous Harmonicats performed.

Photo by B.C.

Korky, also known as Stephen White, began his life as a clown in Morris, Illinois, in 1973.

Entertainment for Children

The Sandwich Fair loves its clowns. Some featured entertainers have been Buttons, KoKo, Korky, and Pudgy. In 1959 Bill "Ko Ko" Alcott returned after a 12-year absence. In 1938 he was billed as "a real circus clown, one of the cleanest and cleverest in the business." Newt "Buttons" Lundquist has been part of the Fair since 1975. In the off-season he is a regular family man who drives a school bus and runs a trophy business; during the Fair he is special to hundreds of children who enjoy his corny jokes and riddles.

Courtesy of SFA

Photo by L.H.

top left: In this 1982 photograph of Dan Barth's Medicine Show, he promised that his stories "would cure your melancholy, purge your gloom, and banish your blues."

top right: One of the earliest mentions of an organ grinder and monkey was in 1941. This photograph taken in 1990 shows the last year a monkey and organ grinder appeared.

Another favorite for children was the "monkey grinder." One of the earliest mentions of this attraction was at the 1941 Fair: ". . . a man with a hurdy-gurdy and a monkey caused considerable amusement for children and grownups." One fairgoer recalls that the monkey in the early 1960's was named Chris; it did 35 different acts. Its owner was Tony. When pennies were tossed at him, he tossed them back because he accepted only silver coins. The monkey and its owner made a final appearance at the 1990 Fair.

Fun makers Murray and Ward were featured with their trick house at an early Fair. Grandpa Cratchet's FarmYard puppet show and Dr. Dan Barth's Medicine Show with magic and ventriloquism have been favorites for many years. Barth performs in an authentic medicine show wagon. He promises that his stories "will cure your

melancholy, purge your gloom, and banish your blues." In 1965 children were fascinated by Daddy Long Legs, a comic on stilts who roamed the grounds and grandstand. Amazing Arthur, another figure on long, stilted legs, entertained children at the 2000 Fair by making balloon animals and hats.

Bob Hamm was a new performer for 1999. He strolled the grounds displaying his "fast and

Photo by P.O.

Grandpa Cratchet's puppet show was a favorite for children for many years.

Photo by V.G.

1999

Buttons the Clown

Appearing at the Sandwich Fair "was like appearing at Carnegie Hall." Buttons the Clown admits that the comparison sounds funny, but that's how he felt when asked to be part of the Fair in 1975. It was "one of the happiest days of my life."

Newt Lundquist of LaMoille, Illinois, created Buttons in the summer of 1974 for an appearance at a Sunday school picnic. He practiced his antics on his wife Mary and their four children.

In those days Buttons looked like a tramp, rather than the white-faced clown fairgoers see today. He wore an orange wig and a checkered pajama shirt. It didn't take long for him to modify the Ping-Pong ball he used for a nose because he recalls that it was very sharp and painful to wear. As part of his original act, he made little animals out of colored balloons.

Buttons believes his audiences are different today. They are in a bigger hurry and are more difficult to entertain because "children today have seen everything." Nevertheless, Buttons the Clown continues to entertain his audiences because he has the greatest requirement of a performer—he enjoys seeing his audiences have a good time.

147

flashy six-gun spinning antics" which included his three-gun barrel flip.

Unique is the only way to describe the variety acts that enticed the crowds then and now to the Fair. Each year visitors to the Fair see their old favorites plus a new act or two.

Thrill Shows

The best thrill shows involve noise and silence. Noise created by revving engines and silence produced when an audience holds its breath—anticipating tragedy or success. Thrill audiences in the grandstand at the Sandwich Fair come alive at the noise of automobile, truck, and tractor engines produced by daredevils and pulling contestants. They follow intensely the cars of local drivers who become daredevils-for-a-day in the Demolition Derby.

Early fairgoers didn't miss a dip or a dive made by the first flying machines and marveled at hot air balloons during the Fair's sky shows. Spectators held their breath when the early contraptions dipped or dived close to the ground.

Auto Racing

Auto racing was one of the earliest thrills on the track. Compared to today's race cars, some of the early racers looked like barrels with wheels on them. Nevertheless, they provided noise, suspense, and anticipation—all the ingredients for a good thrill.

In 1907 the *Somonauk Reveille* highlighted the car races at the coming Fair. "[They] will prove exciting with the people standing on their tiptoes to watch. The race is for blood, as the

manufacturers who have entered their cars will spend every energy to 'do' the other fellow and demonstrate the superiority of their machines."

Auto racing was also held at other times during the year on the Sandwich track. In 1917 two races were held on November 9—one for Ford stock cars and a twenty-five mile free-for-all. Gate admission was charged for nearly two thousand people who attended the event including seventy-five cents for the grandstand. Will Swabe won the five-mile Ford race with a time of eight minutes and four seconds. George Kleinprinz came in second.

Barry Wetzel of Sterling received $200 for first-place in the 25-mile race with a time of 31 minutes. Fair directors served as race officials: P. S. Lindner acted as the starter, C. L. Stinson as timekeeper, and H. A. Severy and Tom Mercer as judges. They considered the race successful enough to schedule another one on Thanksgiving Day.

However, tragedy marred that race. Otto Smith of Peoria, who had finished second in the November 9 race, was thrown from his car when it rolled over twice on the east end of the track. The *Argus* reported, "People ran to assist him, but before they were able to reach his prostrate body the big Ostwig Special came around the turn, and in spite of the efforts of the driver to avoid striking the unconscious man, the big racer . . . hit the unfortunate victim and rolled it [him] several feet." Smith was taken to the Dudley-Wormley hospital in Sandwich where he succumbed to his injuries the next morning. Newspapers do not mention auto racing at the Fair again until 1941.

According to the July 31, 1941, *Free Press*, midget automobile races were taking the country by storm; twelve events were scheduled for the 54th Fair. Leading drivers from all over the US were invited to Sandwich by the American Speedways to make the races one of the big events at the Fair.

Auto Daredevils

"Why Do Ordinary Men Become Daredevils?" queried the 1949 *Sandwich Free Press* headline. For stunt driver Joie Chitwood, it was "new worlds to conquer." For his young drivers, it was money, fame, and applause.

Why did fans pack the grandstand to see drivers in clean-pressed white suits race white Chevrolets up white ramps? They watched for

Three generations of Chitwoods appeared in Auto Daredevil shows at the Fair from 1949 to 1978.

Courtesy of SFA

the thrill of seeing cars airborne, springing from one ramp to another. They watched to experience the impossible and to witness anticipated disasters.

Spine-tingling precision was the name of the game as cars drove through blazing hoops or pools of gasoline, crisscrossed to avoid last-second crashes, or balanced on two left wheels while an announcer wove words like a circus ringmaster. They built nail-biting anxiety, suspense, panic, and appreciative relief in the hearts—and sweaty palms—of vicarious spectators.

Applause and amazement carried the events of the day. The heroes barreled down the track, sprayed clay dirt beneath spinning wheels, and gave a quick crank of their steering wheels to stop within a few feet of the front row of the grandstand spectators. They rested in perfect diagonal parking positions within inches of each other. Every child returned the greeting when the daredevils leaned out their cars and waved or saluted. They knew their names, their hometowns, and their backgrounds. Forget the army, they were joining the Joie Chitwood Show.

"He [Chitwood] came in with an ambition to establish and hold automobile records in daredevil driving," the 1949 *Sandwich Free Press* touted. After all, he held the world record for broad jumping a car through space for a distance of nearly 87 feet. One regular act pitted him jumping a new 1949 Ford from one ramp to another while another daredevil in a second car raced directly underneath.

Three generations of Chitwoods carried the thrill-show banner until silencing the engines in 1978, ending an extravaganza that lasted

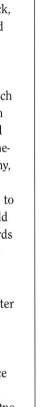

circa 1940's

Courtesy of SFA

over 40 years. Joie, the elder and originator, was a full-blooded Cherokee nicknamed "Wild Indian." He was of Indianapolis 500 fame, finishing fifth on three occasions squeezed around World War II. Chitwood performed at the Sandwich Fair in 1949, 1950, 1965, 1966, and 1978, but he wasn't the only daredevil to thrill Sandwich Fair audiences.

Jimmie Lynch of the "Death Dodgers" successfully drove a stock automobile up an elevated incline and broad jumped a parked auto transport trailer in 1948. The feat had not been as triumphant for Lucky Teter who met his death performing the same thrill stunt in Indianapolis six years earlier.

Other thrill shows included Dick Rogers Motor Maniacs ('40, '52), Ward Beams Auto Thrill Show ('46), Aut Swenson Thrillcade ('51, '54, '58, '59, '63), International Auto Daredevils ('53, '55), Cytrix Motorcycle Daredevils ('56), Transworld Auto Daredevils ('60, '62), Austyns Motor Derby Thrill Show ('61), Johnny King's Auto Daredevils ('64), and Rotroff Auto Thrill Show ('67). On some Fair weeks, three shows were held at two, four and seven p.m. on Saturday or Sunday.

The thrill shows provided a variety of stars and feats. Rocky Fisher performed with the throttle of his automobile pinned to the floorboard. Auto Ball, Blitz Ball, or Auto Polo highlighted four racing cars in action at one time, "continually toying with death." There was a "Slide For Life" feat with a daredevil being pulled behind a car or through a blazing pool of gas. Cars crashed through burning barriers. Motorcycles

top: An early premium book advertisement

following pages: Courtesy of C.A. pages 150-151: Auto racing was an exciting sport to watch in the early 1900's.

bottom: Montgomery Motor Sales of Somonauk printed this advertisement in the 1948 local newspaper when Jimmie Lynch's Death Dodgers were to appear.

Sandwich Free Press

Sandwich Free Press

top: Daredevil Aut Swenson was famous for the Triple Loop-the-Loop Death Car Leap.

bottom: Excited fans pack the grandstand on Sunday afternoon to cheer on their favorite driver. The track is soaked with hundreds of gallons of water to make it slippery before the derby where local drivers repeatedly bash into one another until only one remains.

cleared several parked cars. A deliberate crash-roll contest promised autos flipping over as many as six times. In one promotional photo, the famed Triple Loop-the-Loop Death Car Leap was showcased. In 1959 cars raced over elevated ramps in a Roman Steeplechase. The Aut Swenson show also promenaded "the darlings of daredeviltry." They were billed as the Honey Girls and the Thrillcadettes. Racing star Yvonne LaCost was one of the ladies who catapulted her car through space.

When the fires were extinguished, the smoke and dust were cleared, and the last thrill car was loaded on the trailer, the Sandwich Fair still lived for weeks to follow. Boys and girls pounded the pedals on their Schwinn bicycles, slammed the brakes, and ripped the handlebars to the left. Gravel flew, making the sound authentic. Odds and ends of plywood and large wooden blocks became ramps of flight for selected audiences to watch—usually far from parental supervision. Every neighborhood had at least one famous daredevil practicing for the Joie Chitwood Thrill Show.

Demolition Derby

A long-standing tradition at the grandstand on Sunday afternoon is the Demolition Derby. Fans have their favorite drivers—whether they are their husbands, boyfriends, dads, neighbors or the "guys at the local gas station." They also have the drivers they like to boo—maybe the guy who knocked out their favorite last year. Whatever the case may be, the grandstand seats are always packed on Sunday as the carefully prepared cars slam and bash into one another until, like a gladiator from ancient Roman days, only one remains.

A hired promoter who travels the fair circuit all summer organizes the Demo Derby. His job is more than fun and games. One of his main concerns is the safety of the spectators and the five- or six-man driving team that he brings with him. He also announces the events, cheers the drivers on, and generates enthusiasm and excitement in the audience.

The track in front of the grandstand is prepared for the events by placing large telephone poles around the perimeter and then soaking it with hundreds of gallons of water to make it slippery, slimy, and gooey. When it is ready, the starters and flagmen take their places for another event that has become a tradition at the Sandwich Fair.

Tractor Pull and Truck Pull

Roaring engines, custom paint, flaming pipes, and clouds of smoke create high-powered excitement for devoted fans of the tractor pull and truck pull. Whether seated in the grandstand or pressed against the cyclone fence, fans enjoy the vibration of the earth as engines pull a weighted sled as far as possible down a clay track. From tractors with 60 horsepower at the first pull in 1965, to modified tractors with over 6,000 horsepower and superstock with over 2,000 horsepower today, the tractor pull has come a long way and is here to stay.

The first tractor pull was the Farmer's Stock Class in 1965. It was held on Wednesday afternoon on the limestone-base racetrack in front of the grandstand. Superintendent of the event Russell Stahl liked to remember when the weight of the sled was controlled by 60 men standing at 20-foot intervals on both sides of the track. As the tractor approached the men, they jumped on the "skid." One by one, they

Photo by S.E.H.

Courtesy of SFA

top: The first tractor pull was in 1965. Area farmers brought their tractors and pulled against their neighbors. Rex Wolf of Sugar Grove is pictured here.

increased the weight of the sled as it went down the track. This type of skid was used for three years. Today, tractors pull sophisticated, computerized-hydraulic sleds adding precision to the event but taking away the romance and drama of the "old days."

When the tractor pull was first organized, local farmers brought in most of the tractors. There were four weight classes (three for men and one for women) with a combined purse of $800. All tractors were weighed at Westbrook Grain Company in Sandwich. Ed Tuntland was Stahl's assistant, and Jim Meyer was the announcer. Bob Anderson and Polly James recorded the times and distances of each pull. Roberta Troeger wrote the checks for the winners.

As tractor pulling became more popular, the tractors became more sophisticated and powerful. In 1971 a class was added that introduced "hot rods." These modified tractors were the forerunners of today's classes: Pro-Stock, Super Stock, Modified, and Mini Rod. One of the most popular modified machines was a Minneapolis-Moline tractor with an Allison aircraft engine. The machines still resembled farm tractors, but they were no longer used for farming.

In 1976 the Illinois Tractor Pullers Association (ITPA) was formed. As a member,

bottom: Today tractors pull sophisticated, computerized-hydraulic sleds. The first pulls used a sled with the weight controlled by 60 men standing at 20-foot intervals and jumping on the sled as it came down the track.

Photo by C.L.

God Bless America

One Saturday evening (year uncertain) just before the tractor pull, it began to rain hard. In fact, it poured down. The start of the tractor pull was delayed, and the grandstand audience began to get restless. Russell Stahl, superintendent of the event at the time, began to get nervous. He was afraid he would lose both the audience and the tractor pullers because of the delay. He got on the loudspeaker and asked the audience to sing *God Bless America* with him. Those who recall the scene aren't sure how long the audience sang (if they ever did), but they remember Russ singing a solo—loud and clear. It was a hilarious moment—one that lasted quite awhile. Before long, the rain stopped, and the tractor pull continued.

Courtesy of SFA

top right: The first flying machine caused a lot of conversation at the 1910 Fair. This airship/biplane appeared at the 1920 Fair.

Photo by J.H.

Photograph from the 100th Fair in 1987. Pickup trucks were added to the pulling program in 1978.

Photo by D.S.

The monster "Bear Foot" truck standing 12 feet tall began entertaining audiences at the truck pull in 1987.

the Sandwich Fair conducted the competitions under its sanction. All tractor weights were certified, and the pullers no longer had to "weigh-in" before each pull.

The event continued to grow. In 1978 pickup trucks were added to the program under the supervision of Fair Director Wiley Updike. Local men and boys brought in most of these street-legal trucks. In 1986 Updike became the Superintendent of Tractor and Truck Pulls. In 1987 Fred Shafer's monster "Bear Foot" truck, weighing 15,000 pounds and standing over 12 feet tall, began entertaining audiences at the pull with its truck-crushing demonstrations. In 1990 Art Downs replaced Bob Jones as announcer. About this time Gene Frieders became assistant superintendent. In 1999 a semi-tractor pulling class sanctioned by the National Tractor Pullers Association (NTPA) was added to the competition. In 2000 all of the events were sanctioned by the NTPA, the ultimate in tractor pulling events.

As the "sport" grew, safety measures were introduced for the benefit of the audience as well as the pullers. In 1997 a new, clay-based track was installed on the infield with new lighting and bleachers to accommodate the fans. The judges stand was moved back 75 feet to provide room for the new track.

This event, thought to be a fad when it was first organized, is one of the biggest and longest grandstand draws at the Fair. The fans, participants, and crew are loyal. Some of the track crew members, including Updike's grandson Dan Breunig, have helped since they were in junior high school. Roberta Troeger is still writing checks. Today, her husband Norm helps clerk along with Julie Wilson. Several pullers have

been in the Sandwich competition since its beginning. One competitor was nearly 80 when he made his last pull. If history is an indicator, this event will be even more sophisticated and powerful in the new millennium.

Sky Shows

Not only did autos provide popular thrills but sky shows also packed the grandstands. Daily balloon ascensions were advertised as early as 1895; parachuting in 1899; and flying machines in 1910. In spite of the danger to the performers, audiences loved to watch these men attempting what seemed impossible only a few years earlier.

Some performers suffered serious injuries. In 1895 a Mr. Weaver, an assistant in "Professor" M. M. Forsman's balloon, was seriously injured when he fell 40 feet to the ground. The *Sandwich Argus* reported that the accident occurred when Mr. Weaver loosened himself from his parachute as it entered the timber west of the fairgrounds. His injuries were compounded when he jumped for the branch of a large elm tree and missed. He was taken to his Sycamore home to recover.

Another mishap occurred in 1907 when Henry McAllister was shot from a cannon too low for his parachute to open. McAllister was "dashed" to the ground from 40 feet. Landing on his feet, McAllister seriously sprained his ankles, fell on his back and injured his spine causing partial paralysis from the waist down. He was taken to the Aurora Hospital.

All the buzz at the 1910 Fair focused skyward on a Flying Machine. Only seven years ear-

Sandwich Free Press

left: This early flying machine and the "birdman" pilot gave a two-day presentation at the 1912 Fair. He soared to a height of about 2,000 feet, descended gradually and gracefully brought his machine to earth.

lier, the Wright Brothers had made the first successful flight at Kitty Hawk. Some fairgoers considered the early pilots courageous while others believed they were insane because they considered the flying machines "flying coffins." Newspaper accounts reported that the first "aeroplane" flight at the Fair was an interesting sight for those who had never seen such a machine.

In 1911 the Baldwin Flying Machine, a biplane of Wright distinction, was scheduled to appear at the Fair with Budd Mars providing demonstrations of altitude, dips, volplaning, and all the fancy stunts seen in Chicago. The act never arrived to entertain the huge crowd. A telegram was received that the plane had been wrecked. The Fair board and stockholders published an apology. They attempted to schedule another act, offering a larger cash payoff and a good-sized bonus, but their efforts were in vain. Newspaper stories related that "this is the first time that the association has advertised an attraction that has failed to put in an appearance." It also requested that readers not blame the Fair Association for false hype to attract large crowds.

The next year, printing a letter of confirmation from Chicago in the local paper to give confidence to the crowds, the 1912 Fair Association scheduled a two-day presentation.

He flew in as the largest ever crowds were watching and waiting for the machine to arrive. He landed gracefully in the centerfield on the fairgrounds at half-past ten. The birdman made successful flights in his airship about 3 o'clock and soared to a height of about 2,000 feet. After that he descended

gradually, bringing his machine gracefully to earth. He was watched by an immense crowd that seemed delighted with the daring performance and felt that they were fully repaid for their disappointment of the year before.

In 1913 and 1917, "Dare Devil" Mills performed dips and loop-the-loop stunts in his aeroplane. He was hailed as performing "the most daring and difficult stunts ever undertaken. The airman circled around the grounds several times showing perfect control and making graceful landings." However, on one occasion the performance promised to be too thrilling even for the famous aviator; his flight was postponed because of high winds.

At the 1916 Fair, the mark of showmanship for Selleck-Sinclair Aviators was the DIP O' DEATH! World War I affected the 1918 Fair. The commandant of the Chanute Flying Fields at Rantoul, Illinois, and the government were scheduled to furnish a flyer for Wednesday. However, since troops were being sent overseas at that time, the government reneged saying that the performance would interfere in the training of the men.

In 1919 the famous aviatrix Ruth Law was scheduled for a special attraction at the Fair. She was well known for making a 1916 record flight from Chicago to New York and for offering her services as an aviator at the outbreak of WW I. Being a woman, she was rejected. Unfortunately, at the last minute her appearance was canceled for unknown reasons. She was later rescheduled.

Dick Seal hushed audiences in 1921 with his air acrobatics. The *Free Press* lured audiences by saying, "He performs stunts in the

155

Courtesy of SF

top: This airplane was most likely piloted by an aviator from Peoria who performed at a 1919 sky show. Famous aviatrix Ruth Law was scheduled, but canceled at the last minute.

bottom: The Sugar Squares have demonstrated square dancing in back of the Home Arts building since 1989.

Photo by B.V.

air that makes one's heart stop beating." He was billed as the premier of all air devils from the Sheldon Air Line. Newspaper accounts described Seal hanging by his toes from the landing gear while the plane looped. He also performed tricks in the center of a rope stretched from nose to tail beneath the plane. For his finale, he stood atop the plane while it made loops.

Parachutists continued to be as popular as they were at the earliest fairs. In 1948, reminiscent of earlier sky shows, former army paratrooper Don Wood parachuted from a balloon. His ascension promised to be from an altitude of 6,000 to 9,000 feet. In the 1980's fairgoers witnessed rainbow-colored parachutists landing amid battered wrecks from the Demolition Derby.

Aut Swenson's Thrillcade presented more than fast cars. In 1951 his show included a daring sky escape by French professional Ramon LaRue, protégé of Harry Houdini. Encased in a police-inspected straitjacket, he dangled from his ankles in mid-air from a slender cable attached to a helicopter.

At a 1958 sky show of a different sort was the "death-defying" performance of Bob Top and Lauren who roller-skated on a card table perched 60 feet above the ground. Other sky shows included the Human Torpedo Harry Pollack who was shot from a cannon at the 61st Fair.

In 1963 lovely Miss Anita Conley curled up inside a golden ball that was 40 inches in diameter. She rolled down an incline that exploded with fireworks; then she sped around a loop and jumped through a ring of fire before coming to

rest in a small net. This popular attraction, located at an east coast amusement park during the summer, began touring the U.S. in September, giving one performance per state. The advertisement for the act noted that "the fireworks alone cost them $10 for each show."

People who have attended recent Sandwich Fairs have been able to participate in some of the sky thrills. Fairgoers have taken helicopter rides from inside the racetrack since the 1960's. In the 1990's some watched and others experienced the thrill of bungee jumping from a towering crane.

Music at the Grandstand and on the Grounds

Singers, bands, and dances are a tradition at the grandstand and on the grounds. Even before the official beginning of the Sandwich Fair in 1888, patrons to the grounds were entertained by local bands. A community sponsored Sandwich Band played as early as 1880. Area newspapers reported band uniforms "so attractive that the musicians rivaled the military in attracting the attention of the ladies."

A decade later local entertainment included the Somonauk Military Band, the Plowboys Band of Freeland [Corners], and the Crescent and Union Bands, both of Sandwich. Music groups have continued to entertain patrons with everything from oompah-pahs of marching bands to guitar-picking country stars to accordion-accompanied polkas.

Professor Heun's Aurora Band delighted fairgoers in 1900 and 1901 while the Colored Jubilee Singers performed each day between heats of horse races. The next year featured the National Sewing Machine Band of Belvidere, and in 1910 Round's Ladies Orchestra provided entertainment. In 1919 and other years, the Sandwich Union Band played.

The Depression Era welcomed Chenette's Cadet Band of DeKalb. By the 1950's school bands from Sandwich, Somonauk, Plano, Big Rock, and Hinckley were strutting their musical talents.

Dances

Where there is music, dancing follows. Gents have been swinging their ladies on a Sandwich Fair dance floor since 1922. Juanita

Bark Anderson of Sandwich remembers the "dance hall" owned by George Striegel and Harry "Red" Stolp. Dances cost ten cents each, and "If the crowd didn't get out on the floor, Red would tell Helen McInturf and me to get out there and dance. And the crowd would follow. We danced many nights and never paid," Juanita chuckles.

During the Big Band Era, the Sandwich Fair headlined bands including Falleti's and Glen Victorian, both drawing large crowds. It was with Glen Victorian that one of Sandwich's own, Harold "Bub" Goodwick made his musical fair debut. Goodwick and a group of local boys became celebrities at the Fair with a band called "Bub and His Boys." For years they provided music for dances and later traveled around the fairgrounds playing music from a decorated flat-bed truck.

In the early 1940's the Glenn Miller band was booked at the Fair for a one-night stand. The evening featured many songs that Miller raised to number one on the Hit Parade. Shortly after playing in Sandwich, he and members of his band joined the Air Force.

From the 1960's to 1975 when Bub's band took a leave of absence, rock bands catered to teenage patrons at the fairgrounds. In 1989 dancing prevailed. A square dance club called the Sugar Squares began demonstrations, encouraging fairgoers to join in.

Music of a different sort began in 1988 with the initiation of a friendly contest. Local fiddlers tuned their instruments and tightened their bowstrings for an old time fiddling contest. Monetary prizes are awarded in both junior and senior divisions. Since 1995, Fair patrons have been entertained by John and Toula Pearson and

Toula and John Pearson and their Traveling Bell Wagon Show entertained fairgoers around the grounds from 1995 to 2000.

Bub and His Boys

The Glen Victorians band. (l. to r.) Melvin Eide, Edward Bower, Curtiss Bieritz, Harold Morahn, Orrin Howe, June Winder, Harold "Bub" Goodwick.

The original Bub and His Boys in 1951. (l. to r.) Donovan Goodwick, Ray Voss, Dave Breuer, Ernie Basler, Harold "Bub" Goodwick, Jack Kaiser.

At the 1995 Fair, Bub and His Boys in the "Bubmobile." (l. to r.) Jeff Ford, Donovan Goodwick, Harold "Bub" Goodwick, Ernie Basler, Donna Havasi, Fred Stahl.

Harold "Bub" Goodwick in 1987

Dubbed as one of Sandwich Fair's most memorable entertainers, Harold "Bub" Goodwick began his banjo-strumming musical career in 1927. His first Fair appearance that same year was with the Glen Victorian band, which played the dance hall on the grounds for 10 cents a dance. He performed on WLS Radio from 1930 to 1937.

Following a 15-year musical stint in Cedar Rapids, Iowa, Bub came home to Leland. He collaborated with several young musicians just out of high school and together they formed Bub and His Boys band.

Featuring old time swing, Dixieland, and plain ol' banjo pickin', the group started their Sandwich Fair act in the Baker's Feed tent. Later they moved to the new dance pavilion south of the Home Arts Building. They played there to the delight of dancers until 1968. After that they performed for various sponsors at the Fair until 1975. Then they "toured" the grounds from the back of Fred Stahl's 1937 GMC truck, better known as the "Bubmobile."

The "Boys" continued this tradition for several years following Bub's retirement in 1991, before finally disbanding in 1995. Bub passed away in 1998 at age 92.

The band had 81 different members during the 43 years it entertained. The original Bub and His Boys made their professional debut March 3, 1951. They were Harold "Bub" Goodwick on banjo, Donovan Goodwick on trumpet, Ernie Basler on guitar, Dave Breuer on accordion, Ray Voss on bass, and Jack Kaiser on drums. The most recent members of this show-stopping act included Bub Goodwick on banjo, his son Donovan on trumpet, Ernie Basler on guitar, Donna Havasi on keyboard, Jim Herman on accordion, Jeff Ford on clarinet and saxophone, Fred Stahl on drums, and driver of the Bubmobile Garry Miller.

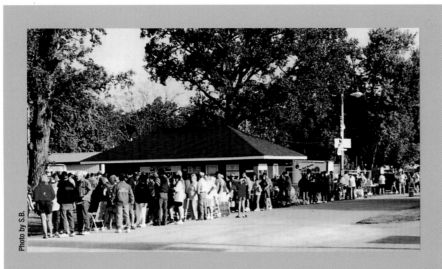

Main gate ticket office in 2000

Labor Day Ticket Sales

In the early days of the Fair, most grandstand events were free so patrons had no need for tickets. When tickets were required, they were usually purchased right before the show. As new shows and events were introduced, fairgoers bought tickets during the Fair at the Ticket Office outside the grandstand.

As Fair attendance continued to grow and popular celebrities were added, the demand for tickets increased and so did the lines to buy them. In 1989 in an effort to make buying tickets more convenient, Fair officials began selling reserved and track seats from the Main Gate Ticket Office on Monday of Fair week. This Labor Day activity evolved into an event of its own. In 1999 and 2000 WCCQ radio personalities and a band entertained long lines of people waiting to buy tickets. Food vendors served coffee and rolls.

In an attempt to keep the county-fair atmosphere, Fair officials continue to sell tickets first come, first served. There are no phone orders, e-mails, or credit cards. People often camp out overnight to get tickets they want for grandstand events they have waited all year to see. Some shows sell out as Fair week progresses, but there are usually plenty of tickets available from the grandstand ticket office during the Fair.

Each year 2,400 tickets are sold for each grandstand show, with the exception of the Friday night show. Since 1987, to accommodate the growing attendance at the popular country music show on Friday night, approximately 1,500 extra chairs are set up on the track.

2000

their Traveling Bell Wagon Show. Sounding a bit like an old-fashioned calliope, the musical twosome play bells and keyboard from a decorated electric bell wagon.

Country Music

Country music has always been popular at the Sandwich Fair. A young Roy Acuff entertained audiences in 1949. Captain Stubby and the Buccaneers headed up the National Barn Dance stars in 1954. In 1957 Grand Ole Opry star Minnie Pearl entertained audiences. Since the 1970's, big-name stars on Friday night have become a tradition [see Chapter 11 for a complete list]. The popularity of the Friday night Country Music Show prompted the Board of Directors to add a Wednesday night show in 1999. The singers and bands draw large audiences from the immediate area as well as fans from Wisconsin and Indiana.

Preparing for the country music shows requires planning months in advance of the performances in September. In fact, as soon as the Friday night show is over, the Fair board begins thinking about the next year. Superintendents of Grandstand Entertainment meet with promoters to select from a list of entertainers who meet the requirements of the board.

After the initial booking, there isn't much to do but wait for the Fair. Director Larry Dannewitz says, "If the weather cooperates, everything usually comes together rather smoothly." On Thursday night after the truck pull, work really begins. The entertainment crew must water, grade, and roll both tracks. When the track is prepared, a semitruck brings in a portable stage. About two hours later, thanks to hydraulics and lots of good help, the semitrailer transforms into a large stage.

**ROY ACUFF IN PERSON—
And His Grand Ole Opry Cast**

Roy Acuff and his Smoky Mountain Boys from WSM and the Grand Ole Opry are scheduled to be at the Sandwich Fair, Wednesday evening, 2 big shows, 6:30 and 8:30 P.M. The whole gang is pictured above: Roy, Pap, Oswald, Jesse Easterday, Joe Zinkan, Jimmy Riddle, Tommy Magness and all the rest. Also on hand will be Dot and Smoky, singers of sweet duets. The Acuff show promises fun for everyone from six to nisty—and older, too, if you can make it!

Roy Acuff entertained at the 1949 Fair.

1949 Premium Book

Friday morning comes early. Sound and lighting crews arrive first. Ground crews and local youth clubs help unload the heavy speakers and sound boards. Grandstand crews begin to unload and arrange chairs for seating on the track.
Promotional agents and road managers arrive next.

By now people begin lining up to buy tickets if they are still available. The entertainment superintendents wait for the bands, roadies, and stars to arrive. If the performers arrive as planned, they spend the afternoon practicing and tuning their instruments. If they don't, that's another story [see Chapter 2 Behind the Scenes]. This can be a tense time. Superintendents Dannewitz and Don Augustine have come to expect "a new challenge" every year.

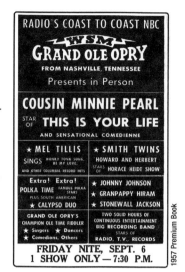

Stars from the Grand Ole Opry entertained at the 1957 Fair.

Meeting the needs of the performers is an important role of the grandstand superintendents as well. Country star Neal McCoy's road manager called a few days before his performance and asked if there was a golf course nearby. Fair officials arranged an 8:00 a.m. tee time for McCoy and his crew. When his bus arrived at 6:00 a.m., he saw the course and headed right over to Edgebrook. He asked gatekeeper Randy Ellis if he would like to join him. Randy declined because he was on duty. By 6:10 McCoy was already golfing.

On another occasion, satisfying the performer wasn't as easy. Singer Lee Greenwood did not like having the bungee jumpers behind him. He said every time someone jumped, the audience would go "whoa," and he thought his drummer had fallen off the stage.

On Friday nights there are usually two shows. This means that the grandstand and the reserved seating on the track must be cleared in a very short time after the first show to make ready for the second show. In 1999 a Wednesday night show was added to the

Grandstand Ushers

Ushering in the grandstand was a role originally filled exclusively by young ladies. They were hired to help patrons find their seats in the reserved section and to "pass the hat" for Pick-a-Winner tickets during the harness races. Even though the girls were paid for their services, they would probably have done the job for free since it was an honor to be chosen to help in the grandstand.

In the 1950's and 1960's

Gordon Johnson (l.) supervised the ushers in the 1950's and 1960's. Bonnie Scents (Miller) (r.) wears the ribbon and pin identifying her as an usher.

the girls dressed in their best clothes—usually wool skirts and sweaters—no matter how high the temperature rose on hot, September days. Today the dress code is a bit more relaxed, but the young teenage helpers still look their best. The Fair hires ten ushers for the grandstand each year.

Gordon "Gordie" Johnson, a barber in Sandwich, supervised the ushers in the 1960's. Those who had the privilege of ushering in the grandstand in those days have fond memories of their experiences. In the '50's and early '60's, the young ladies wore a pin with a ribbon to identify their position. Those who helped include Ginger Phelper Dannewitz, Judy Legner Fish, Betty Kinchner Marsh, Nancy Jo Neuhauser Otto, Dova Jacobs Olson, Bonnie Scents Miller, Joyce Kinchner Smith, and Diane McQuown Woodward.

In the late sixties, the girls wore a beret. They included Karen Updike Breunig, April Vincent Kershaw, Susan Mall Munday, and Linda Vincent. Today the ushers are identified by the special hats they wear.

Margaret "Peg" Dummer started scheduling ushers sometime in the 1970's. Peg says, "I was asked if I would like to get ushers for the grandstand shows, to which I agreed. I wish I could remember all the names of the ushers." Peg says that sometimes girls and boys call her to ask for the privilege of ushering. Today she is using some of the children of her earlier ushers.

Earl "Kais" Wilhelm worked many years at the east grandstand gate. Peg has also worked with Earl Baie, Carl Scent, Wes Scents, her husband Herman Dummer, Donald "Did" Breunig, Frank Ament, Gordon Johnson, Don Augustine, Larry Dannewitz and many more. Peg says, "I have thoroughly enjoyed doing this job through all the years. It's been a joy working with all my co-workers and the fine young people."

schedule of events. It was so popular that the Fair Association continued the extra evening of entertainment in 2000 even though the behind-the-scenes work was increased.

In addition to the country music the directors organize other events at the grandstand such as the truck pull and tractor pull, demolition derby, and harness racing.

Ag Land Stage

The Ag Land Stage is an entertainment area that wasn't really planned; it just evolved over a period of time. After the 1992 Fair, Director Don Bark suggested an old, dilapidated horse barn be demolished to open up sight lines to the livestock area. The objectives were to improve the appearance of the area and hopefully to draw more people to the barns. The Fair wanted to showcase the animals and to educate the increasing number of urban visitors about agriculture.

Prior to this time, the area inside Gate 3 was used mostly for vehicle parking, which unintentionally divided the livestock area from the rest of the Fair. When the sun went down, this part of the Fair looked deserted because the only light in the area was located on the end of the old barn. People walked into this area, looked around, and decided there was nothing more to see. The Fair was growing fast; it needed more room. This space seemed wasted.

The next phase of the Ag Land Stage evolution happened just before the 1993 Fair. The WGN "Noon Show" was planned for Thursday, and a good stage wasn't available. Scott Breunig thought some old cement forms that were stored in one of the barns could be made into risers. The risers could be placed alongside one another to form a portable stage. The idea developed; the stage was finished by Fair time and placed where the old barn had formerly stood. WGN appeared on Thursday, and two local bands, C. C. Cash and Whoa Nellie, were hired to appear on Friday and Saturday nights. This opened up the area and attracted people for the first time at night.

In 1994 a new canvas made a roof for the stage and gave it a more professional look. That year four bands appeared—mostly country and western, and people wanted a place to dance. A plywood dance floor, stored from years before, was set up in front of the stage for dancing. The dance floor also gave the school kids someplace to sit while they watched the magician and medicine show during the day.

A concrete dance floor improved the site in 1996. The area had a full schedule: WGN "Noon Show," bands every night, and stage shows during the day. The stage was drawing many people, lighting was improved, and commercial exhibitors were renting the expanding area. By this time the Ag Land area had become too

much for Scott Breunig to manage because his responsibilites as Superintendent of West End Parking had also increased. Don Lawyer started managing the stage and coordinating the acts.

The Ag Land Stage continues to be a draw with bands every night, The "Noon Show," fiddlers contest, stage acts, and even church services on Sunday. Since the stage was installed in 1993, more people have found their way to the livestock barns, the Farm Zoo, Ag Information Building, food vendors, and commercial exhibits. During the 1999 Fair, one of the food stands even ran out of food on Saturday night.

The Ag Land Stage has served its purpose in connecting the livestock area with the rest of the Fair and giving the Fair more exhibit space. It has become a gathering point on the west side of the grounds for people who come to be entertained and to learn more about agriculture.

Beacon News

Newell Gates of the LaSalle-Peru area was a contestant in the Fiddlers contest at the Ag Land stage.

Old Time Fiddlers Contest

More of a show than a contest, participants in the Old Time Fiddlers Contest entertain fairgoers at the Ag Land Stage. The contest was organized in 1995. There is a junior division for fiddlers up to age 16. The senior division is for fiddlers age 17 and older. In the past, contestants have ranged from five to eighty years old. There are usually around twenty participants in the contest. They are judged on three songs: one slow, one fast, and one personal selection.

GROUNDS ENTERTAINMENT

There are a variety of events and entertainments located throughout the grounds. Some are relaxing like Augie Otto's train and others are competitive like horseshoe pitching and the Micro-Mini Tractor Pull. The antique machinery and cars, Western Horse Show, and craft demonstrations are references to the past. The activities all evoke memories of past times not only because many fairgoers have grown up with the attractions but also because they exemplify a former era.

Augie Otto: The Man and His Train

To many children, as well as adults, Augie Otto's train is synonymous with the Fair. It has fascinated fairgoers for three generations. To understand the essence of this fascination, one must capture the spirit of the man who created it.

August "Augie" Otto III was born on a farm south of Sandwich in 1910. As a boy he preferred his father's machine shop to the games and sports of his peers. He was by nature an independent thinker, ready to try a new adventure.

As a teenager he built an airplane and gave rides at the Fair in the 1920's. An expert welder and machinist, he not only had the skills to build a train, but the love of steam and the sense of adventure required to begin such an undertaking.

In 1943 he began to build his first steam locomotive. He squeezed 2,500 hours into his busy schedule to complete it. By the winter of 1951, he proudly displayed it in the window of the Public Service Company on Railroad Street, Sandwich. A contest was held to name the engine.

Seventh grader Jan Hagar, who had been studying about the "Iron Horse" in her history class, submitted the winning name—"The Iron Pony." The second place entry, the O.T.T.& O, was so good the judges suggested it be put on the coal tender. This coal-burning engine and its cars made their debut at the 1953 Fair running on about 900 feet of 14-gauge track. The engine and tender were 13-feet long and weighed 2,600 pounds. It delighted young and old for over 20 years.

Fairgoers in the 1950's also remember the old steam popper that Augie's wife Dorothy and

Courtesy of R.P.

Augie Otto's first train "The Iron Pony" made its debut at the 1953 Fair. It delighted young and old for over 20 years.

Photo by L.H.

The Burlington 3000 replica made its maiden run at the 1974 Fair. Augie Otto spent seven years building this train.

Photo by M.M.

The train crossing on the Otto train track is staffed by crossing guards. (l. to r.) Richard Byrd, Charles Viriam, George Zimmerman, and Paul Johnson

bottom: Augie Otto is pictured with his grandchildren Augie and Andrea Otto.

Photo by H.W.

family used to pop corn for the passengers.

Starting in 1967 Augie spent another seven years building a second train that is used today. The Burlington 3000 replica weighs over five tons and pulls four cars that weigh 2,100 pounds each. It is a one-quarter scale replica of a passenger engine manufactured by Baldwin Locomotive Company of Philadelphia. When it was finished, Augie sold the Iron Pony to a fellow train-lover who operates it at the Pontiac Threshers Reunion every fall.

When the new engine made its maiden run at the 1974 Fair, it ran on 2,000 feet of 15-gauge track. Augie gave about 5,000 rides on Saturday. *The Sandwich Free Press* records that on Sunday Augie turned over the throttle to a helper because after four days of circling the track, he said it was getting hard to remember whether he had gone around once or twice. A new depot concession area was added that year as well. Popcorn and pop were served from its window.

The 1994 Fair was a hard one for the family, as Augie had passed away only weeks before. Sons Norman and Allen have much of their father's ability, so the train is still in good hands.

Members of the Otto family are always on hand to answer hundreds of questions from curious fairgoers. Q. Where does the train go? Twice around the half-mile track. Q. How long does it take? Five or six minutes plus loading time. Q. Can I sit in the caboose? Wait until the next trip; it's already full. Q. Can we sit together? Four of you will fit in car 2 and three in car 4; or you can wait for the next trip. Q. Is it really steam? Yes, about 195 pounds of pressure. Q. What kind of fuel do you burn? The Iron Pony burned coal; the new train burns diesel fuel. Q. Did you know mommy rode the train when she was little? We hope she still does. Q. Did you find my camera, teddy bear, diaper bag? Check at the concession window. Q. Can we take a picture by the engine with the engineer? You bet.

Horseshoe Pitching

Horseshoe pitching was first introduced to the 1928 Sandwich Fair. The August 30, 1928, edition of the *Somonauk Reveille* reported,

Several regulation courts have been laid out and the elimination contests will commence at 9 o'clock Wednesday morning. This form of sport will appeal to the farmers and others who are particularly interested in the art of putting the horseshoe around the peg. Much time and effort has been spent in making these courts the best there is in the country.

As an added attraction, the Fair hired lady-pitcher Mrs. George Broulette, of Minneapolis, a three-time champion, to do exhibitions the last three days of the Fair. She guaranteed in her contract to pitch at least 50% ringers, which made the contest more interesting to some of the spectators.

After the 1928 Fair in the September 13 edition of the *Somonauk Reveille,* it was stated: "This sport, a new one for the Sandwich Fair, drew a large number of spectators and also a large number of contestants. Mrs. George Broulette displayed her ability several times and everyone watching her was very much impressed."

At the 1929 Fair, horseshoe pitching remained popular. The August 8, 1929, *Somonauk Reveille* reported,

"Putt" Mossman who is the holder of nine worlds records and three times world champion horse shoe [sic] pitcher and at the same time a great trick pitcher will appear on the program. One of his tricks is that of pitching against an opponent while blindfolded. It is said that his stunts are unusual and will entertain everyone who sees them.

Horseshoe pitching continued through the next three Fairs; the 1933 *Somonauk Reveille* said, "The horseshoe pitching contest is attracting the usual number who are interested in this sport. A special attraction at the courts this year is the appearance of the Schultz Sisters of Harvey, one of whom holds the championship for women horseshoe pitching." Horseshoe pitching was discontinued sometime after the 1933 Fair for unknown reasons. There wasn't any organized pitching at the Fair for over 50 years.

Photo by V.G.

The 1986 Fair saw the return of horseshoe pitching to the Sandwich Fair. Ken and Leota Huff of Waterman were appointed superintendents of horseshoe pitching with the help of Herb Strousberger of Waterman and Paul Johnson of Shabbona. Four courts were constructed inside Otto's railroad tracks. Pitching proved to be so popular that two more courts were added the following year.

Each day of the Fair brings a separate category of pitching competition. Wednesday is the DeKalb County Contest when the best pitchers in the county compete to see who's the best. Senior citizens compete on Thursday in the 65 and older class. Friday brings Class "C" competition for those who throw 0 to 19% ringers. Saturday is a double header starting with Class "B" for people who throw between 20% and 35% ringers, and then the Class "A" pitchers compete. Class "A" pitchers throw over 35% ringers.

All entrants must have pitched 50 shoes for a qualifying score prior to the contest. The doubles competition with 24 to 25 teams takes place on Sunday; to keep the competition fair, everyone draws for partners. Wednesday's through Friday's winners are awarded ribbons while the winners on Saturday and Sunday get cash prizes.

The winners in the first horseshoe pitching contest in modern times were Paul Johnson of Shabbona, DeKalb County Tournament; Don Lindholm of Yorkville, Sr. Citizen class; Dale Campbell of Genoa, Class "C"; Henry Slusarik of Peru, Class "B"; Harold Lange of Elgin, Class "A"; and Al Johnson of Millbrook and Ken Kingsbury of Genoa, Doubles.

The horseshoe pitching contest continues to the present time and draws good crowds to the shaded pits inside the train tracks.

Antique Farm Machinery

For more than a century, Sandwich Fair

patrons have enjoyed a display of farm machinery, gas engines, and other agricultural hardware. At early Fairs the farm machinery displayed was the latest thing available. Everything from hay presses, to corn shellers, to gas engines was displayed for farm and city visitors to admire. In 1898 the local newspapers reported that John Betz of Somonauk had an "excellent display." The Sandwich

Photo by J.A.

Manufacturing Company represented its famous line of Southwick hay presses and corn shellers and gave demonstrations of their machinery. The Enterprise Company displayed a full line of steel and wood windmills, aerating pumps, tanks, corn plows, and the Pope Automatic Fence Machine.

Farm machinery has been on display every year since, right up to the present Fair. The machinery is always the latest available. Caterpillar, John Deere, and Case-IH are some of the well-known companies represented.

In the late 1960's, Louis Wagner encouraged Andy Krafft, Alvin Miller, and Ed Weismiller to set up a display of antique farm machinery inside the Otto train tracks. With the help of Red and Ray Barnes of Aurora, who had a collection of old, horse-drawn implements, they put together a display. Krafft remembers returning from Aurora with two semi-flatbeds of equipment and three pickup trucks of odds and ends. This collection constituted the first Antique Farm Machinery Show at the Fair.

According to Krafft, the oldest piece from those first years was a threshing machine made of wood, including a wooden elevator made in the 1800's. Other items displayed included a wooden corn planter, a wood hay rake, and horse-drawn cultivators and plows. A rare six-horsepower gas engine built by the old Sandwich Engine Company was also on display.

Collecting and restoring old engines has become a popular hobby. Those who exhibit at

left: Horseshoe pitching contests are held everyday of the Fair. The horseshoe pits are located inside the train track.

right: One of the oldest pieces of farm machinery on display in 1977 was this horse-drawn plow.

bottom: Sandwich Manufacturing Company made gas engines in the early 1900's. They are sought after by collectors today.

Photo by H.W.

Photo by K.L.B.

top: Katie Kleinmaier of Nettle Creek School near Morris, Illinois, watches first-hand as corn is being ground by antique equipment.

middle: This old steel-wheeled Oliver tractor was on display in 2000 in the antique machinery area.

bottom: A line of Studebakers at an Antique Auto Show

the Fair receive a free pass and the pleasure of talking to fairgoers for five days about their collections. The show has become so popular that it has almost outgrown its space. The display area inside the railroad tracks is shaded and cool. Picnic tables and chairs are scattered around so people can relax, enjoy the Fair, and meet friends away from the action of the midway and commercial buildings.

Photo by J.E.H.

The Antique Farm Machinery area is also an outdoor museum that educates and entertains. Children and adults watch rope being made and corn being ground. Some of the collections have included barbed wire, telephone insulators, and pencil sharpeners.

Following in his dad's footsteps, Michael Krafft took over the superintendent duties in 1987 when Andy became grounds keeper at the Fair. Craig Fox of Somonauk and Bob Miller of Leland help Michael lay out the display. The area continues to grow and offers Fair visitors an opportunity to see antique machines in action and a chance to see some of the changes that have taken place over the years.

Antique Cars Make Way for Classic and Muscle Cars

Old cars, like old photographs and furniture, evoke memories in just about everyone. Maybe it's remembering a ride to town in Grandpa's Model T, a first car purchased, or an unforgettable date in a '57 Chevy. Everyone, at some time or another, feels a special fondness for a certain model or make of automobile.

Sandwich Fair patrons have had the opportunity to admire hundreds of classic automobiles at the fairgrounds since 1967—the premiere year for the Antique Auto Show. Robert Loy and Warren Greenwood, along with David Kolzow and Ronnie Scaggs, organized the first show. Wiley Updike joined this core group in 1970.

At the first show, about 75 cars were displayed on the grassy area between the roads leading to the parking lot from Gate 1.

During its early years, the event was a competition on Saturday afternoons. Today, however, the show is promoted as a Family Day event on Sunday morning. Vehicles are no longer judged. Drawings are held for prizes.

The car show is currently billed as the

Photo by N.U.

Photo by V.G.

Sandwich Fair Auto Show and has been organized by Doug and Nancy Carter since 1997. It is held on the track infield. Each year it focuses on a particular make of car from a certain decade. More than 200 vintage autos that include authentic antiques as well as classic and muscle cars gather at the fairgrounds each year.

Exhibitors from as far as Missouri, Michigan, Iowa, and Indiana meet with the local folks to show off their prized possessions and arouse a few memories of days past.

Crafts and Demonstrations

As the 1960's ended, Americans began to look back to their heritage—their roots. Renewed importance was placed on arts and crafts of bygone days and the artisans who produced them. The Sandwich Fair Board embraced this reawakening, realizing it would enrich the Fair. In this spirit the Fair board asked Marie B. Kinchner to develop a Crafts and Demonstrations Department in 1971. They wanted talented artisans who were willing to demonstrate their skills, sell their work, and talk knowledgeably about their crafts every day of the Fair—rain or shine.

The new department debuted in 1972 under a blue tent that was pitched over the old dance area south of the Home Arts building. Ruth Haag assisted Marie in the department.

Photo by V.G.

The first craft demonstrators provided a variety of talent. They included Jan Sorenson and Glenda Anderson, candlemaking; Sharon Johnson, pottery; Vi Ferden, egg craft; Keith and Jackie Hauser, stained glass; Stan Benson, woodcarving; Mary Jane Huntley and Jean Helm, china painting; Miriam Myers, dough art; Shirley Bohn, weaving; Linda Anderson, flowers; Virginia Olson, macramé; Norma Hughes, ceramics; Mary Ann Polanrek, wire sculpture; Baumey, basket making; Donna Anderson, dolls; Barb Stetz, miniatures; Les Hage, inlay wood pictures; Joyce Sebby, tole painting; Mortons, caning; Becky Morton, muppets; and Howard Davis, pen and ink.

A favorite "tent story" occurred after a torrential downpour one Saturday night in 1979. When Marie arrived to open at 6 a.m., she found the ceiling of the tent touching the ground. The entire expanse of canvas was filled with water. Efforts to lift one side and drain the water failed. Finally, someone crawled under the tent and cut a hole in the tent's center to drain it. Fairgoers that day had no idea there had been a problem!

Wind and heat provided some more memories for the tent demonstrators. When summer storms created high gusts of wind, the sides were lowered and everyone hoped the moorings would hold. In 1988 a heat record was set. When the inevitable storm came through, the tent had to be evacuated. There was damage to

top: One year car enthusiasts came to see the featured car, the Willys-Overland.

center: Janice Sorenson (l.) and Glenda Anderson (r.) were some of the first craft demonstrators. They are pictured here in 1974.

Marie B. Kinchner Rice
Superintendent of Crafts and Demonstrations
1972-1994

Courtesy of B.K.M.

Marie B. Kinchner Rice is known best for the work she did to develop a Crafts and Demonstrations Department in the early 1970's. As interest grew in arts and crafts, the Fair board realized the potential it held for the Fair. Marie successfully searched the Midwest for talented artisans willing to exhibit all five days of the Fair and perform demonstrations daily. She loved the responsibility. It was her "baby."

The craft demonstration tent opened in 1972. It was popular from the beginning as an educational site for children on class trips and for adults shopping for accents for their homes and early Christmas gifts. The popularity and success of this project became evident by the expansion of the department. In 1987 a new, permanent building was constructed for the demonstrators.

Marie Kinchner's term as superintendent came to an end in 1994. She suffered a series of strokes and passed away in November. Her last Fair was a highlight as she had a chance to visit numerous friends made during her 23 years of dedicated service.

Photo by V.G.

Woodcarver Joe Dillett taps out a custom-order in the craft demonstration building.

suppose you tease all the kids like that?"

After 15 years of success, it was evident that the craft demonstrations were a popular attraction. By this time, Eileen "Ike" Weber had succeeded Ruth Haag as Marie's assistant. The Fair board decided to build a permanent building for the craft demonstrations. It opened in 1987 under some of the tallest oak trees on the grounds. Everyone cheered except the squirrels. According to the craft demonstrators, the squirrels showed their displeasure by perching in the overhanging trees and bombarding the roof with nuts!

The new facility had better electrical hookups, doors that locked, and less dust. Five of the crafters who moved from the tent to the new building were still demonstrating in 1999.

the tent, but the crafters were unhurt.

Another time, Shirley Covert, a stone polisher and jewelry maker, recalls losing the diamond from her ring. She speculated that it had fallen into a customer's bag during a sale. However, during the morning cleanup, she saw a sparkle in the dust. She retrieved her stone and snugly reset it.

Joe Dillett, a master woodcarver, was always accompanied by his helper/wife Sharon. They arrived every day with a picnic lunch, blanket, pillow, and a dolly for their daughter who spent the day playing and taking naps behind Joe's display.

Photo by K.B.

Shirley and Wayne Covert demonstrated stone polishing and jewelry making for many years.

Opening day, then and now, has always been exciting for the craft demonstrators. Children on class trips arrive in the morning, and all the exhibitors put on demonstrations and answer questions. Potter Dale Woodworth was demonstrating one day when a student asked how the potter's wheel turned. Dale quickly responded that he had a little squirrel underneath that provided the power. Several children bent down to search for the squirrel. One young lad, with his hands on his hips, confronted Dale, "I

Photo by B.W.

Fairgoers enjoy watching Dale Woodworth use the potter's wheel.

They are Joe Dillett (woodcarver '80), Clyde & Felice Goering (wheat weaving '78), Lois Narog (scratched, carved eggs '78), Bert Strike (calico and gingham patchwork '78), Dale Woodworth (pottery '83).

Many of the artisans have been together for over twenty years. They have developed strong friendships that allow them to have fun together. Lois Narog, the egg lady, says the crafters are "full of the devil," explaining that she sometimes finds Legos and plastic eggs among her carefully designed ones. "Of course, no one knows where they came from." Barb

Clyde and Felice Goering of Kansas demonstrate the delicate art of wheat weaving. These items were for sale at their 1979 craft booth.

Duro, beadwork, echoes Narog's feelings. She says, "Even though we see each other only once a year, it's as though time stops between fairs. We pick up where we left off from the year before."

Eileen "Ike" Weber became superintendent in 1995. Barb French, Joyce Tyrrell, and Linda Floyd assist her. They seek out artisans to demonstrate heirloom crafts as well as the current fad craft. They watch over the department during the Fair, and they make sure everything goes well for the craft demonstrators.

Contestants prepare for Western Horse Show events

Western Horse Show

The area north of the old Gletty barn and west of the other livestock buildings is usually a quieter part of the grounds—away from the midway excitement. Quieter, that is, unless it's Wednesday morning. On Wednesday morning, spectators gather to watch riders compete for the best times in barrel, flag, plug racing, and pole bending in the Western Horse Show. Participants come from Illinois, Wisconsin, Iowa, Missouri, and Indiana.

When Steve and Carole Hilleson and their friend Paul Butler first organized the Western Horse Show in 1980, it lasted only a few hours. Today it lasts from 9 a.m. to almost 7 p.m. Because of the event's popularity, in 1999 it was moved from Sunday to Wednesday morning to help alleviate traffic congestion.

The show has junior divisions for riders 10 and under, 13 and under, and 18 and under in addition to the open show for adult riders. Open-barrel competition for men has 60 classes, and ladies open-barrel competition has up to 40 classes. Most classes have 30 or more entries.

To fully understand this event, one must know the jargon. No matter how it sounds, the "pony plug, 10 and under" competition is a race with one barrel at the end. Young riders must go around the barrel and return with the fastest time. In barrel races, if a rider knocks over a barrel, five seconds will be added to his/her time. Going off course will result in disqualification. In other words, to be successful in the Western Horse Show, a rider must have a fast horse and be able to cut the corners close.

Micro-Mini Truck-Tractor Pull

Another event on the grounds is the Micro-Mini Truck-Tractor Pull. It was started in 1980 on Wednesday night in the old swine show ring where the bleachers now stand. From 1981 to 1984, it was held on Thursday night. In 1985 a new show ring was built between the two swine buildings. The contest was changed to Saturday night in 1990.

Ed Miller from Belvidere, one of the original competitors, still helps organize the event. Toy tractors, modified with gas model airplane engines and special soft rubber tires and weights run on a track that is twenty-four inches wide and sixteen feet long about four feet off the ground. Pullers may compete in one or all six classes. The hot-rod class tractors pull at least 800 pounds.

Spectators usually watch 90 to 100 pulls that are sanctioned by the National Micro-Mini Tractor Pullers Association. The pullers earn points for placing. At the end of the year, pullers meet and honor the top pullers in the nation.

The rider in this 1987 photograph races around a barrel trying to avoid knocking it over. A 5-second penalty is added if the barrel is knocked down.

Started in 1980, the Micro-Mini Tractor Pull is an event held on Saturday night. Mac McLay of Whitewater, Wisconsin, is shown here in 1986.

171

Courtesy of SFA

right: Baseball games were one of the most popular attractions in the early days of the Fair. The semi-pro baseball games were exciting and entertaining.

Past Events

Some events and activities are no longer held at the Fair, but the memories of them are part of the Sandwich Fair tradition. They include baseball, fireworks, queen contest, sheep dog trials, and society horse show.

Batter Up

"Fans came to watch great baseball games, and that is what they received," former player Wendell Smith of Sandwich recalls. "The baseball games were one of the most popular attractions in the early days of the Fair. These games were semi-pro baseball and always exciting and entertaining. The local teams had some rivalries that go way back."

An advertisement for one of the earliest ballgames in 1899 lured the fans: "This is the rubber between the old time rivals, Hinckley versus Paw Paw." Apparently it continued for several years as the 1905 *Sandwich Free Press* reported, "There was much bad blood between these teams."

Fueling these rivalries was small-town pride, a cash purse, and players who may have been swayed in loyalties. Many town teams were a medley of different locales. For example, the 1905 game had rumors flying that Eberly, a former Hinckley player, had quit and signed with Spaulding—a professional team, later of sporting-goods fame—of Chicago. Eberly was supposed to be in the Paw Paw lineup.

Another question was whether or not a former Somonauk star would suit up for Hinckley. Even ten years later, the paper reported Hinckley and Paw Paw being "loaded, having outside battery men." Hinckley won 1-0 when the Paw Paw center fielder threw wildly to third base on a two-base hit.

The love of the game was one reason teams played. Another reason was the money—usually about one hundred green bills. In 1909 the *Somonauk Reveille* headline explained, "Why They Didn't Play." Backing out for being placed in a "slow class," the Somonauk nine, "one of the leading attractions at the Sandwich Fair for several years," refused to play against Plano for a $75 purse. Meanwhile, Fair officials pushed a $100 prize for the games between Mendota, Hinckley, Paw Paw, and Earlville.

The paper's writer, calling the Fair Association's decision a showing of poor grace, pointed to earlier season games with Hinckley and Earlville that "clearly showed them to be the equal of either of these teams." The reporter continued, "Then they got a team from Aurora and that was poor economy for a difference of $25 since the additional gate receipts from this side of the creek would have far more than made up the difference had Somonauk played."

To this day Lyle Fritsch, Sandwich, remembers the neighboring town rivalries. "We always had good games with Newark, who had Dutch and Wes Johnson. We played Plano quite a few times and won a lot of them."

"People would stand close to the baselines and yell like mad," remembers Harold Prestegaard of Sandwich, a catcher on the old field. "Some fans would run right on the base-line. There were a few fights, but not many. It was quite a thing. They billed it up. People looked forward to it." Prestegaard also recalls that if the teams didn't have a mask for the umpire, the umpire stood behind the pitcher and called the balls and strikes from the mound.

The Playing Field

"It was a cow pasture," pitcher Fritsch teases. "They had run the horses out there, so there were some crazy bounces in the outfield. The infield was half green grass and half skin [dirt]."

"It wasn't the best diamond," agrees Prestegaard. "The outfield had a lot of bumps. A line drive might duck off to the right or left if it hit a clod."

While there wasn't an ivy wall or outfield fence, homers were "legged" out as Fritsch recalls. "I watched one game when the ball hit the third base line. It rolled near the parked cars and trucks and onto the track for a homer. My dad told me about players hitting balls over the racetrack."

Today's fans can relive the spirit of the games in old issues of the *Sandwich Free Press* and *Somonauk Reveille*. According to local newspaper accounts, Big Chief Vaught and Louis Ergott on the Somonauk team did effective battery work on Sandwich's Coss and Strong in 1912 by beating them 11-5. "The Somonauk boys had their batting eye with them and landed on Coss's curves for a total of 11 hits."

In 1916 "Friday's game was a battle royal between Hinckley and Plano. . . . A game between these two teams is always fought to the bitter end. . . . Hinckley showed the mastery, and the final summing up showed a score of 3 to 1 in favor of the Hinckley boys." In 1917 the Aurora Tigers and the Sandwich team were pitted against each other. A Fair advertisement touted it as a battle for supremacy. Newspapers highlighted,

> It proved to be the biggest feature of the program and was witnessed by thousands of people. It was a history-making event for the fair, since Sandwich won 2-1 in 11 innings. It was said that this is the best game ever

played on the fairgrounds and was a thriller from the start. The game took one hour and forty minutes with a pitcher's battle between Reiser [Aurora] and Grandgeorge for Sandwich.

Along with local rivalries, the big city, semi-professional teams from Chicago ran onto the Sandwich Fair ball field in 1921. For weeks the fans anticipated the battle between the Armour team and Joe Green's Union Giants, one of the few black teams to ever play at the Fair. According to the Sandwich press, spectators saw the Giants win 11-3. The Armour team was "unable to connect with the offerings handed them by Luther, the ace pitcher of the colored boys."

The *Free Press* reported on a game in 1922 with a $500 purse between Mendota and Aurora. "[The game] kept the fans at fever heat until the last man was out. The Mendota pitcher was shooting them just where the Aurora fellows weren't hitting." Crowds at the 1930 Fair "stayed until the last putout in the ninth inning" to see DeKalb beat Sandwich 5-2 and Lee top Yorkville 3-1.

In 1939, organizer of the games Ernest "Pummy" Heusinger announced that the games would begin promptly at 10:30 a.m. A news release stated if they didn't begin on time, "A penalty of ten percent of the purse for every fifteen minutes delay [would] be charged up against the team causing the delay."

Hometown rooters cheered the Sandwich nine against perennial enemies such as Sycamore, Aurora, and Earlville. In 1941 it was hoped local favorite Lyle Fritsch would arrive in time for the match against Sycamore. He had pitched in the minor leagues for Sioux City in the Western League that summer. A lot of hype surrounded the game. During the season, Sycamore had won the Northern Division of the Amateur League with Sandwich runner-up,

Lyle George Fritsch

Feb. 27, 1920
Born: Sandwich, Ill.
Height: 6' 1"   Weight: 190 lbs.
Pitches: Right   Bats: Right (.255 Avg.)

"Fireman" Fritsch began his pitching career hurling fireballs for the Glendive Montana semi-pro team in 1940. That winter he played ball with the St. Louis Browns in California. His big break came in 1941 with the St. Louis Cardinals' farm team, the Sioux City (Iowa) Redbirds. He ploughed through that season with 11 wins, 10 losses, a 2.1 ERA, and a spot on the All-Star Team. After serving in WWII, Fritsch moved up a step in 1946 to spring training with the Rochester (NY) Redwings. An unfortunate pitching arm injury ended his professional baseball career, one step away from the Majors. Even so, he hurled the Sandwich (Ill.) Cardinals to victory in 1946 with 14 wins, 0 losses and 1.8 ERA, and then again in 1947 with 13 wins, 0 losses and a 1.6 ERA. Both years, he was the league's All-Star Team. © 1948

The 1948 baseball card of Lyle "Fireman" Fritsch of Sandwich. The games may be gone, but the memories live on.

"FIREMAN" FRITSCH

Courtesy of L.F.

Courtesy of SFA

top: Area town teams were old-time baseball rivals. A lot of hype surrounded the games. The last game played in the 1950's was never finished.

Girls' Games

On Sunday afternoon of the 1948 Fair at one o'clock after the 4-H parade, there was a special game between two girls' teams. The "Gau Oil Powder Puffs" of DeKalb and "Refiner's Pride" of Forest Park were two top-rated teams. The girls used a 10 13/16 inch ball and played with regular baseball rules.

The Last Out

Around the early 1950's, interest in the games suffered, and the local towns had trouble finding enough players to fill the rosters. The large crowds eventually dwindled, and the end result was a final out for baseball games at the Fair. Heusinger, director of the games at the Fair for many years, scoured Sandwich for any-one who wanted to play. In the final years of the games, the contests were reduced to only one semi-professional game, while the others were Pony and Little League variety.

"We would pack a picnic lunch and after the game have a picnic in the parking area. This was quite common at that time," Ed Johnson of Somonauk, who played in Little League games, remembers about the 1953 Fair.

A unique twist to sporting events came when softball was played inside the fairgrounds but not in the center of the track. "I came up to bat, and they threw a nice fat pitch over the plate, and I laid into it." Prestegaard tells. "I thought it would sail to the outfield. Instead the ball was a grapefruit. They painted that thing up to look like a softball. It smashed all over."

In later years Fritsch was umpiring a game with Les Rogers, Sandwich. The game was between Earlville and Utica. "It was one of the last games played there and one that never finished. Utica kept arguing with Les at home plate, and he warned them that they could go home. He ended it at four innings, and I remember Dutch Hough saying 'This is it, no more baseball'."

The infield grass grew back and the outfield bumps eventually eroded smoothly. Fans and players were resigned to sit in the grandstand and fondly peer out towards the ol' field during harness racing or other entertainment venues. The games may be gone, but the memories live on. Fritsch recalls,

> It was always a thrill to play there. My dad and my uncles also played at the

splitting a pair of games.

"The Fair Game Will Be the Decisive One," the *Free Press* headlined. "It will be the greatest team since Dan Holm brought such Sycamore stars as Lundgren, Asmusson, Gertenrich, and the Campion brothers down, at the turn of the century." Maketi, who had two no-hitters that season, was on the Sycamore firing line. If Fritsch was unable to play, the Sandwich skipper would turn to University of Illinois's Jack Smiley from Waterman or Thompkins, a nine-game winner. Today, Fritsch can't remember if he made it home to play or not, but he believes that he probably didn't since the game doesn't stand out in his memory.

On Friday of 1941, Elburn was scheduled against the Aurora Tigers, who featured the "old master" Macey on the mound, a 16-game winner from Plano. The fierce competition was a fact when the *Free Press* promoted ". . . and the Tigers will know they have been in a ballgame before they make it seventeen [wins]."

Sandwich Free Press
September 18, 1902

The ball game between Sandwich and Somonauk was—well we haven't yet been able to find a suitable name. The Sandwich boys had the greatest stage fright imaginable and made errors so fast the scorekeeper took to the woods. Both sides played frightful ball, Sandwich beating her neighbor. When Umpire Finnegan said the game is over, Sandwich had sent eight men across the home plate and Somonauk twenty-one.

Fair and not always for Sandwich. They said the crowds were big. One of the reasons, I think, was that there were a lot of ten- and twenty-dollar bills changing hands at the end of the game. I think this was partly why there were a lot of fights. There was still some betting the first years I played, but that soon was down and on the q.t." Fritsch continues, ". . . at that time, if we could play anywhere, we played there [at the Fair]. Nowadays they [professional players] play for millions. We just played for fun.

"It seemed like a treat and honor to play at the Fair," Prestegaard reflects. "It was an old-fashioned get-together. We had great fun."

"It was sad to see the games come to an end," Wendell Smith says. "They will always be remembered."

At the 1998 Fair sitting on a bench outside the Home Arts building, an 85-year-old fan, Charles Harrington, reminisced with a friend, "I wish they'd brought baseball back." That's what the Sandwich Fair has been about all these years—memories and friends.

64   SANDWICH FAIR PREMIUM LIST

Magnificent Display of Fireworks

WEDNESDAY, THURSDAY, AND FRIDAY NIGHT

We are going to give you the best display of FIREWORKS we have ever put on Lot of fine Set Pieces and a Grand Aerial Display

1928 Premium Book

Fireworks

In 1923 the fairgrounds had electricity! For the first time, fairgoers were treated to a night show. Thearle-Duffield Company, one of the largest builders of fireworks in the world, painted the skies with a "mammoth display." On the ground there were elaborate displays with intriguing names such as The Palace of Jewels, The Rainbow Curtain, Death of the Demons, Niagara Falls, and Down on the Farm.

One display, Threshing Time, showed a threshing machine in action; the shooting fire simulated grain pouring into bags, chaff flying from the blower, and a gas tractor operating in the distance.

In 1924 two mighty, throbbing locomotives, outlined in jets of fire, hurled themselves at each other on the Fair's infield. Potts Fireworks Display Co. of Franklin Park, Illinois, designed the 1925 display. A few minutes before the fireworks began, six nine-inch salutes were fired into the sky to announce to the public that the show was about to begin. The titles of the explosions gave the fire-in-the-sky a theme. Some names of the explosions were "Buttercups," "Pansies," "Fields of Clover," "Springtime," and "Forget-me-nots."

In 1928 a Fair advertisement promised audiences three nights of "The best program of fireworks you have seen at a local Fairgrounds."

Queen of the Fair

Ernest "Pummy" Heusinger, organizer of the baseball games held at the Sandwich Fair, thought the Fair needed an official hostess. Officials agreed. From this idea a queen contest developed. Pummy also believed the contest should benefit the Woodward Memorial Hospital building fund. With hospital representatives and the Fair Board in agreement, the first "Queen of the Sandwich Fair" contest was held in 1955.

Selection of the candidates was a multi-step process that began with penny votes. Girls, ages 16 to 25, placed voting jars in their communities. They received one vote for every cent

As a little girl, I remember coming to the Sandwich Fair with my mother and grandparents. My grandfather Geo. Striegel and Red Stolp were partners in a dance pavilion that was torn down in the late 40's. I had the first dance with my grandpa.

Ruth Derby
Aurora, Illinois

left: The 1928 premium book advertised three nights of the best fireworks for audiences at the fairgrounds.

bottom: Candidates in the 1955 Queen Contest were (l. to r.) Helen Johnson, Eleanor Brunton, Patricia Hickey, Sharon Hollenback, Judy Warren, Janice Houghlin, JoAnn Koska, Etta Weber, and Paula Gates.

DeKalb Chronicle

Courtesy of SFA

top: The queen of the 1963 Fair, Virginia Palmatier of Somonauk, received $100 and a three-day trip to Springfield to compete for the title of Miss Illinois County Fair.

bottom: Judy Henrikson of Leland was crowned Queen of the 1956 Fair. The 1955 and 1956 queen contests were sponsored by the Sandwich Hospital Auxiliary. (l. to r.) Judy Henrikson, Pat Hickey and Master of Ceremonies James McKanna

contributed to the hospital building fund in their name.

Each week chairpersons totaled and posted the votes so the girls would know how they stood in the balloting. The contest usually started August 1. Rules of the contest were simple. It was open to any girl, married or unmarried. They had to include a photo of themselves and a completed application. They were allowed to place money jars in as many locations as they chose.

The three top-scoring candidates from each community placed their contribution jars at the fairgrounds where balloting continued until the evening before the crowning. The top-scoring candidate from each community represented her town in a Court of Honor. Each was presented an orchid from a local floral shop.

From this group of popular beauties, judges chose the Queen of the Fair. The final decision was based on popularity, community involvement, poise, and character.

The first queen was Miss Pat Hickey from Waterman. She received a crown, a dozen red roses, two pieces of luggage, and a portable

radio. The other eight contestants each received ten dollars. The Hospital Auxiliary gave prizes to the contestants eliminated from the Court of Honor. Approximately $1,700 was added to the Woodward Memorial Hospital building fund the first year.

The Hospital Auxiliary also sponsored the contest in 1956. The event raised $835.00 after expenses for the building fund. Judy Henrikson of Leland was crowned queen. She was selected from 25 candidates of the ten communities on the basis of community and school leadership, grace, poise, charm, and speaking ability. In a 1998 interview, she said, "After I won, I took off my formal, put on my jeans and went to the "Bub" dance. I wore my crown and got in free."

After 1956 the contests were discontinued until 1961. At that time until 1965, the Fair Association sponsored the queen contests. They were always popular. A local paper recorded that a packed grandstand cheered as the contestants, riding in convertibles, opened the two-hour program. Tension mounted as the girls appeared on stage in bathing suits and formal gowns.

The later contests expanded to include a banquet the week before the contest where the contestants were interviewed for poise and personality. The contest was based entirely on beauty and personality, not on votes as early contests had been. The rules were modified to comply with the Miss Illinois County Fair Queen Contest, and the prizes included a week at a modeling school, a gold bracelet, and a $100 check. In other years the prizes included trophies and plaques, a $200 diamond ring, and a gold charm bracelet.

1955 Fair Queen Contest Committee

Master of Ceremonies:
    Ernest "Pummy" Heusinger
Hospital Auxiliary members:
    Mrs. Thomas Marsh, Jane Werner,
    Charlotte Early, Frances Bagg
Publicity: Mrs. Robert S. Keller, Mrs. I.H. Easter,
    Mrs. Lester Hage, Mrs. Max Bagg
Earlville: Mrs. O.H. Fischer,
    Mrs. Robert Weldner
Hinckley: Mrs. Herbert Best
Leland: Mrs. A.J. Legner
Millbrook: Mrs. Ralph Witte
Millington: Mrs. George Scheidecker
Newark: Mrs. Carl Norgren

DeKalb Chronicle

DeKalb Chronicle

At the last queen contest in 1965, Diane Unick of Oswego was crowned.

Plano: Mrs. C.O. Nelson
Sandwich: Mrs. Harry Britton,
    Mrs. Robert Berge
Serena: Mrs. Ward Hall
Sheridan: Mrs. Harold Morahn
Somonauk: Mrs. F.E. Scheppler,
    Mrs. Howard Marshall
Waterman: Mrs. Don Spooner

1955 Fair Queen Contestants

Earlville: Janice Houghlin, Helen Klatt, Karen Weidner, Barbara Fultz, Delores Claude, Marilyn Gibson, Julie Norton, Mary Agnes Russell
Leland: Karol Miller, Jo Ann Olson, Helen G. Johnson, Gaydeen Horna, Kay Chambers
Millbrook: Sharon Hollenbeck, Jane Stroup, Wilma Hollenbeck
Millington: Paula Gates
Newark: Eunice Osmundson, Jo Ann Koska, Maryon Miller, Carole Knudson, Ann Ingemuson, Annette Hanson
Sandwich: Barbara Troeger, Etta Weber, Sandra Legner, Sue Meilinger, Lois Clausen, Beverly Walseth, Patricia Leifheit, Beverly Tuttle, Molly Mapes, Mary Curran, Joanne Erickson
Sheridan: Ruth Ann Beardsley, Eleanor Brunton
Somonauk: Jonette Wasson, Judy Warren, Carol Miller, Margie Faltz
Waterman: Patricia Ann Hickey, Diana Bremner

Queens of the Sandwich Fair

1955	Pat Hickey	Waterman
1956	Judy Henrikson	Leland
1961	Carol Sue Gibney	DeKalb
1962	Roseanne Petros	DeKalb
1963	Virginia Palmatier	Somonauk
1964	Susan Hundley	Oswego
	Barbara Pierson	
	(1st Runner up)	Ottawa
1965	Diane Unick	Oswego

Sheep Dog Trials

From 1986 to 1996, fairgoers watched dogs maneuver sheep through an obstacle course at the west end of the fairgrounds at the Sheep Dog Trials. In the trials a handler used voice and whistle commands to direct the dog. Border Collie is the most common breed used to herd, but other breeds are sometimes used. The dogs are judged on how carefully they handle the sheep and how well they get the job done. Handlers competed for prize money, ribbons, and trophies and earned points to qualify for National Finals and "Top Dog" awards.

At the trials held in Sandwich, there were four classes to enter: Open Class, Nursery, Pro-Novice and Novice. In 1996 more than 100 dogs from around the nation competed at Sandwich. Trials began Monday before the Fair, and finals were held Wednesday, opening day of the Fair.

Photo by V.G.

Sheep dog trials were held from 1986 to 1996. Handlers competed for prize money, ribbons, trophies, and points for national awards.

Society Horse Show

Walt Nelson and Latham Castle were leaders in the Society Horse Show, which started in 1939 and ran until at least 1951. The first show featured 21 classes with some for draft horses as well. For some reason, perhaps because of the show's popularity, reserve grandstand tickets were higher priced for these shows.

There were varied classes through the years. One of the constants was the Fine Harness Stake Class. This was a driving class to be judged on conformation, finish, style, manners, and all-around action. In some years there was a class for jumpers.

There were classes for three- and five-gaited pleasure horses. There were even pony-pleasure and musical-chair classes. A local stock class was available for residents within a 15-mile

Courtesy of B.H.

The merry-go-round was the first midway ride at the Fair. In early days it was mule-drawn; later it was steam powered and eventually electrified. This photograph was taken about 1909.

opposite page: *Beacon News*
A 1998 glimpse of the Fair at night

> *I have been coming to the Sandwich Fair since I was two months old. My grandmother Clementine Condie was a grand champion cook here for many years. I was junior champion cook the year my grandmother's sister was champion cook. The best county fair in Illinois.*
>
> Charlene A. Johnson
> Aurora, Illinois

radius of Sandwich. There were children's classes, roadster, and parade. In later years, there were also costume, calf roping, and trail ride classes. In 1950 the prizes ranged from twenty-five to fifty dollars, and many classes also awarded a trophy.

Midway

From a mule-drawn carousel and hand-turned Ferris wheel in the early days to today's neon-lit, music-blaring, high-speed rotation rides that are part of a carnival that travels with its own three-phase diesel-powered generators and five-wire electrical system—that's how much the midway rides at the Sandwich Fair have changed in the past century. Today's gravity-defying thrill rides such as the Inverter, Gravitron, and Pharaoh's Fury make yesterday's midway seem like a different world, but a look past the neon and noise reveals that the midway really hasn't changed much.

In the eyes of early reporters, the midway in the late 1800's was much like it is today—large and crowded with a variety of attractions. The *Somonauk Reveille* September 18, 1891, gives today's fairgoers a look at the early midway:

> Notwithstanding the grounds are very large, there did not seem to be room for the eager ones who wanted to sell you lemonade, popcorn, ice cream, peanuts. . . . There is a steam merry-go-

round, and lots of chances to "knock the babies down" . . . "The cane you ring is the cane you carry away," and a hundred and one other chances to secure five dollars worth of goods for one.

The next year the Sandwich *Argus* described the midway in a similar way: "Everybody enjoyed themselves, . . . riding on the merry-go-round, patronizing the 'cane man,' shooting gallery, and the various stands." From the *Argus* in 1898: "They are all there. The odds and ends of creation have camped on the fair grounds for four days. . . .the disappearing lady, the dog show, the merry-go-round, knock the babies down and hit the Spaniards, the only living mermaid and other curios without number."

Managing a midway is still a big job. Present-day Superintendent Don Bark can appreciate the challenges Director Al Gage had in 1898. The *Argus* printed

> Al Gage has had all kinds of trouble during the first of the week locating the attractions for the "Midway." He has been the most sought after man on the grounds. Everybody wanted the same spot, but in the end Gage got them all located and is now closely watching lest some one should throw their belongings over the fence into the cornfield and escape before Mr. Gage had an opportunity

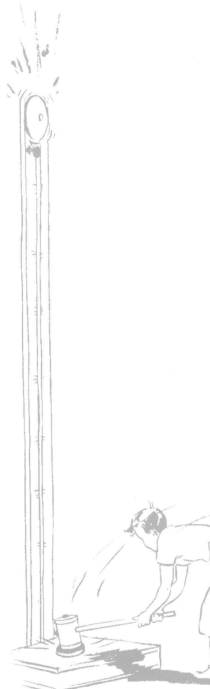

to give them a receipt. . . . Gage will have his hands full to handle this department.

Fifteen years later F. A. Pratt was in charge of midway "Privileges" as the department was called in the early days. He, like Gage, had to be a problem solver. In 1913 the *Free Press* described the midway:

> It's down on the midway where the attractions are and a nickel will never get to the lower end unless in a pocket with a padlock and the key thrown away. Everything the heart could wish for is here. It looks as if everything contrivable [sic] had been brought here to get the nickels. This place was never filled as it is today.

After the Fair that year, the September 25 issue of the *Free Press* addressed the topic of gambling and morality at the Fair. The Rev. J. Franklin Clancy sparked the issue by denouncing the games-of-chance. He was the minister of the Methodist Church in Sandwich that had a food stand at the Fair. In his lengthy article, he gave a thorough review of the activities at the fairgrounds before addressing the real issue of gambling on the midway.

The quality livestock stirred his "farmer-blood," and he saw "evidences of artistic taste and rare execution" at the exhibits. The commercial exhibits showed "fine enterprise among [the] progressive tradesmen," and the local manufacturers gave the "community an enviable reputation for solid worth." He complimented the "excellent provision made to satisfy the hunger and thirst of the thousands without giving them dyspepsia or headache."

As his article chronicles what he alleges to be the negative side of the midway, it also provides a first-hand description of the early games-of-chance. On his stroll about the grounds, Clancy saw games that he considered acceptable. ". . . the stalwart fellows trying to knock a hole through the top of the striking machine and the fellow who was determined to knock the head off the rag doll with a baseball; [and] the fellow who could so gauge sight and muscle as to throw the ring over the right peg . . ." and he said, "I felt like trying a hand at it myself."

Clancy was most critical of the games "in which articles of merchandise were the stake. The articles for which the plays were made were such as appeal especially to women, young people and little children." He cited the Revised

Statutes of Illinois Criminal Code: Section 126 Gaming and Section 137-f, the punishment for gaming. There is an editor's note that he also cited the city ordinances, but since they were not applicable because the fairgrounds was located outside the city limits, they are not included.

Several area ministers, merchants, and Fair officials responded to Clancy's gambling allegations. They all agreed that gambling was wrong; however, the definition of gambling in relation to the fairgrounds was in question. Some doubted that "paddle games" or "throwing rings at worthless canes" or "pelting at dummy figures for vile cigars" was really gambling. Fair Director Fred S. Mosher, who served as treasurer from 1888 to 1924, responded in the same issue of the *Free Press*.

> Sandwich Fair Association does not permit gambling on their grounds, and when the same comes to their knowledge, and to my personal knowledge each year have declined to give permits to people when the device they were to operate was of that character, and this year as heretofore they have removed from the grounds, men, when they found they were abusing their privilege and making use of gambling games.

Mosher goes on to say that a police officer who was hired to attend to such matters was discharged because he knowingly allowed a "crap" game to operate.

The general feeling of midway gambling and the Sandwich Fair Directors was summed up by one writer: "Knowing the managers of the Sandwich Fair as I do, and all of them men of integrity, men of honor and respectability in this community and men at the head of the best families in the city, I am absolutely sure that they would not allow any game device upon the grounds that would come under the head of gambling in violation of the state laws." Later issues of the paper do not address gambling at the Fair, so perhaps the letters from community leaders resolved the controversy.

Another element that has not changed is the suspicion of some of the people who travel with the carnival. Even though many of the carnival families and workers lead lives today just like Mr. and Mrs. John Q. Public, they are sometimes stereotyped negatively as "carnies" and "gypsies." Perhaps it is that carnival employees are an element of the unknown who come to town for only a few days that prompts

Photo by K.L.B.

top: Still popular are games at small booths lined up side by side. Some games test skill, others luck.

bottom: The frogs in this midway game continually move making it a challenge for fairgoers to win a prize.

some parents to warn their children to be careful on the midway. The same suspicion was true of early midways. The people who ran the carnival games were called "fakirs" or swindlers.

The Sandwich *Argus* in an article dated September 14, 1895, gave warning: "There are more fakirs on the grounds than ever before, and they are after the unwary. We did not see any that were unlawful but some of them touch closely on gambling. They are a species to be avoided." Calling the games rigged is probably an unfair generalization, but it is safe to say the odds were heavily in the fakirs' favor.

Apparently not many people took the advice of the early reporter because the number of fakirs seemed to grow. In a later article dated 1897, the *Argus* printed, "As we go to press, Sandwich Fair is in the midst of its annual exhibition. The odds and ends of creation began to gather at the fairgrounds on Monday and today the midway is filled with fakirs of every description, from the cane and ring game to the privilege of throwing last year's eggs at a colored brother for a consideration."

A year later a reporter in the September 10, 1898, issue of the *Argus* had a different slant to the circumstances: "There is a wonderful number of fakirs on the grounds but they add to the show, and mostly sell something the people want. The management has been very careful to exclude all objectionable features and persons."

Not all the carnival games were operated by traveling vendors. Local boys ran at least one booth. In 1907 Ernest "Pummy" Heusinger, an enterprising young man of twenty-two, and his friend Wilson Price operated a duck pond. Customers were invited to buy rings and test

their skills by tossing them around the necks of live ducks that were floating in a large water tank. If a customer succeeded in ringing a duck, he or she could have the duck or a dollar. A news article in 1937 nostalgically quoted Pummy as saying that after the first day the ducks became quite adept at dodging the rings, which was to his and Price's advantage. Their ballyhoo was "Duck in and duck out. You can have noodle, poodle, or kyoodle soup for supper if you win a duck."

Crowds of people still play the games at small booths lined up side by side. Some games test the skills of children and adults: shooting at a target, shooting a basketball, fishing for a box, or throwing a baseball. Other games such as the quarter game are pure chance; still others are pure fun, like the duck game because children always win. The mouse game is one of the oldest and most popular games at the Fair. Players put a quarter on a color and hope the mouse runs to their chosen spot so they can win

Photo by J.E.H.

*I love the Fair . . .
because it has lots of
rides and games.
I like the spook house
and the Tilta-Whirl.*

Ryan Kiest, student
Sandwich, Illinois

Photo by P.O.

top: Fairgoers need a mighty swing to be successful at this midway game.

Photo by V.G.

The Lee Atterbury's from Wichita, Kansas, started with their duck game at the 1947 Sandwich Fair. Today, they operate several games with the help of other family members.

right: A traditional favorite for children is the pony rides located inside the train track.

opposite page:
top: Side-by-side Ferris wheels at a 1930's Fair

bottom: It was a thrill to ride the double Ferris wheel; 1974 photograph

prizes and keep their quarters.

The midway has many vendors who return year after year. Lee Atterbury and his wife from Wichita, Kansas, started at the Sandwich Fair in 1947 with their popular duck game. Over the years they have added seven more games: skee ball, machine guns, a shooting gallery, basketball, a duck hunt, and two balloon games. "As the Fair grew, we grew," says Atterbury, who was a high-pole performer in his younger days in a circus his father started in 1924. The family's horse-drawn circus wagon is now in the Circus Museum at Baraboo, WI.

The Atterbury family has worked fairs from the Mexican border all the way to Alaska; no matter where they roam, they always return to the Sandwich Fair. The Atterburys have two daughters and two sons who leave their professions to spend their vacations each year working at the Sandwich Fair. Atterbury says it is a family operation, and families return to visit them each year because they trust them. People get to know where their booths are, and "They bring their kids and grandkids back to see us." He adds, "That's the way we try to work it. It is a family affair. The Sandwich Fair is great to us."

Over the years the growth of the midway has been steady, but there have been some lean and uncertain years. There was a noticeable difference in the midway in the late 1910's. In 1917 the *Somonauk Reveille* reported that

The one thing that has been neglected this year is the Midway. For

some reason or other the side-shows have passed up the Fair, at least they had not put in their appearance very strongly up to Wednesday noon. There are the usual numbers of fortune tellers but that is about the only place where one has an opportunity of parting with his change outside of the concession stands.

In the World War I year of 1918 it was reported in a local paper that the midway was "sorely lacking and greatly missed." The article continues to say that a ruling by the State Board of Agriculture placed "a ban on this form of amusement." Even the children suffered to some extent that year as the merry-go-round couldn't be moved to the grounds because of a "shortage of help" as the war effort left little time and less manpower for unessential pursuits. However, Sam Dickinson [his name was reported as Sam Dixon in another article] came forward with "a number of beautiful ponies for the children to ride around the circle" at five cents a ride. Dickinson collected forty-nine dollars, which he donated to the Red Cross.

There was also a noticeable setback for the 1920 midway. It was reported that "the old midway seems to have disappeared from the fair, there being no shows along the old familiar alley." However there were still ample places for visitors to "part with their dimes." The souvenir stands "are thick as bees, about three times the usual number on the grounds."

As the 1920's Fairs progressed, the midway was much more than fakirs' games. The *Somonauk Reveille* reported "Midway also leads all previous events in the number of concessions.

Photo by V.G.

There are more shows than usual and the places where one can take a number on about everything from a kewpie doll to blanket are too numerous to mention." The midway continued to grow; according to local newspapers, there was a double midway in 1923.

A 1924 Sandwich *Free Press* article reported that the number of rides increased: "The William Gause attraction which received such favorable comment here three years ago under the auspices of the American Legion, are at the grounds with a chair plane, merry-go-round, the whip, and the Ferris wheel. They shipped from Madison, Wisconsin, to be present at the local fair." In 1925 thrill rides continued to be an important part of the midway. The *Free Press* reported that "The children will enjoy themselves hugely riding the merry-go-round, the Ferris wheel, the chair-o-plane, the whips and the air-o-plane." In 1929 little is recorded about the carnival except that H. H. Webb Shows were responsible for the midway.

Throughout the 1930's Tilley's Amusement took care of the midway. The rides included a merry-go-round and chair planes. The *Free Press* commented on the improvement of the midway in an article dated September 5, 1935:

> During the years of depression the midway was perhaps a shell of what it formerly was. However, this year the midway is filled with various devices of entertainment. There are several new rides that are proving popular and other forms of entertainment are drawing their quotas of patronage. All in all the 1935 Sandwich Fair is one of the most interesting that has been presented to the public in many years.

Another issue quoted Andrew Fosse, who headed the Privileges Department, today's Concessions Department: "This year's fair is assured a live midway."

Some attractions have disappeared from the midway. In the late 1930's and early 1940's the midway had a tent for boxing and wrestling matches. Local men took on the carnival strongmen, and if they lasted for a number of rounds or time, they won a cash prize. Jack Flynn, Ned Flynn, and Jim Wilhelm were some of the local participants.

About the same time, the midway had a tent show advertised as "The Wonders of the World"; most people called it a freak show. There were also "girly" shows, known as "hootchy kootchy" shows. The girls performed private dancing

185

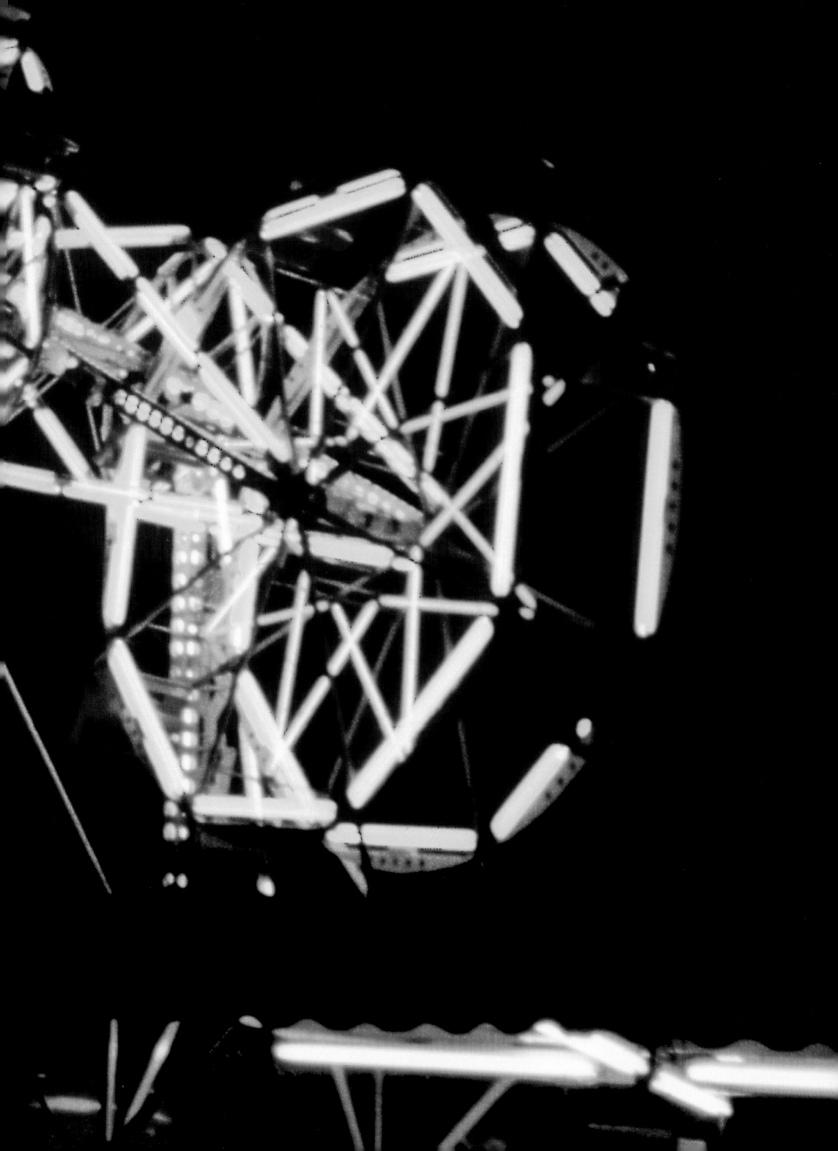

Courtesy of SFA

Photo by B.T.D.

A small fairgoer purchases his ticket for a 1960's midway ride.

top: The Love Barrel ride was popular in the 1940's and 1950's.

bottom: Lois Ann Thorson (Whiteaker) and friend enjoyed a ride in 1944 on the Octupus.

previous pages: Courtesy of SFA
pages 186-187: A 1987 night view of the midway.

Courtesy of B.K.

shows for men who paid admission. It was rumored that shows were put on for Fair directors after the Fair closed. The story goes that in 1946 the "girly" shows became so raunchy and the complaints so many that Fair President C. Howison entered the tent and pulled out the main center pole. With the tent on the ground, the show was over and so were the "girly" shows at the Sandwich Fair.

The Fair provided other amusements in the 1940's. Earl Bunting brought rides, carnival, and the corn game, known today as bingo. People could win brightly colored Beacon blankets as prizes. The 1943 *Free Press* mentioned that there was a little train to amuse the very small folks. In 1944 the midway had a stand where patrons could knock down a "Jap" and win a prize.

In 1946 the Fair went from a three- to a five-day Fair. Growth was evident. Wilson Shows provided five rides for the midway under contract to Bunting. Bunting upgraded his equipment as described in a *Free Press* article: "A letter from Earl Bunting of the Bunting Shows states that he has accepted delivery on four new rides this year replacing equipment that had to be used during the war years. He also states that he has need for all the concession space the board can allow him as the number of people traveling with his shows this year is larger than ever."

The *Free Press* also mentioned a new, streamlined miniature train "which made the younger generation very proud to pass the onlookers." Other riding devices for the young people included an aeroplane ride and flying

scooter. From 1947 through 1975, Wilson Shows provided the midway entertainment. The Wilsons' daughter Lois married Bob Reid of Astoria, Illinois, and then the Reids had the midway rides until 1979. Looking back on earlier fairs, the *Fair Times* in 1979 recorded Reid's reminiscences about the growth of the midway and the life of a midway contractor:

Robert Reid brought five rides to the fair in those days. He remembers, "If we got 20,000 people in five days, it was a good attendance." Now Reid brings 30 rides on 23 trucks to the Sandwich Fair, the biggest they do alone. A double Ferris wheel replaces the old single wheel model that put butterflies in the stomachs of carefree riders. The merry-go-round, twirling rides, little cars and small trains must all be assembled carefully at each move from fair to fair or carnival to carnival for the safety of the riders. They bring their own diesel power to run the rides and machinery, since the pull on the local electrical power here would be too great. Fairs and carnivals are a way of life for the Reids, with the business

Courtesy of SFA

Dellenback sisters Lori (Carey) and Jeanne (Skelton) enjoy a midway ride in 1962.

now bringing three generations on the fair circuit from May through October. The Reids, Robert I and II and their wives, and three children of the third generation. The eldest return to Astoria, the family's hometown when school is in session.

Louis Brady became the Concessions Superintendent in 1949 and continued until 1961 when Kenny Klotz took over. The 1950's and 1960's were years of steady improvement in quality and quantity of the midway's rides and games. Whereas in the late 1940's most of the rides were powered by small, noisy gas motors, which sometimes didn't run well, the newer rides were powered by more reliable and quieter electric motors. In the 1950's a second midway street was opened parallel to the first, which enabled the midway to continue expanding. Besides the merry-go-round and Ferris wheel, rides such as the flying scooters, scrambler, octopus, and tilt-a-whirl were popular at the Fair. On Wednesday, Children's Day in 1952, all rides were nine cents all day and all night. The Sky Wheel and helicopter rides were added later.

The 1965 Fair may seem like ancient history for young fairgoers, but those who worked on

the fairgrounds remember 1965 as if it were yesterday. One word sums it up—*Rain*. It rained on Monday and Tuesday prior to the Fair, and Wednesday, Thursday, and Friday of the Fair. The grounds were so wet that all the rides had to be winched from the road by using cables attached to trees on the grounds. After the Fair the rides had to be pulled out of the mud with large tractors. The midway was a muddy mess, but the Fair went on.

In 1966 the midway continued to grow; it expanded south and east toward the Home Arts building. Opening day of the Fair in 1968 offered fifteen-cent rides on most of the midway thrills. In 1971 there were two big midways. In 1978 Don Bark replaced Klotz as Concessions Superintendent. That same year All Star Amusements was awarded the midway contract. All Star owner Jeff Blomsness and his family brought a bigger-than-ever carnival to Sandwich. The rides included bumper cars, Super Loop, Hurricane, Spider, Tip Top, Cobra, Ferris Wheel, Tilt-A-Whirl, Zipper, Fun House, and kiddy rides like the motorcycle jump, boats, and merry-go-round. The 1983 *Fair Times* gave a little background on Blomsness:

> Nine years ago, Jeff Blomsness was a student at the University of Wisconsin. Like all ambitious young men, he sought summer employment. After reading a want ad in the local newspaper, he applied for a job on a carnival

Photo by J.E.H.

top: This little girl and her father purchased tickets at a recent Fair.

bottom: The Fun House pictured in 2000

Photo by K.L.B.

189

Courtesy of SFA

top: The 1984 Fair version of a roller coaster, one of 35 rides offered

bottom: Steven Curran of Sandwich (in the foreground) is pictured on the swings in 1987.

Photo by M.S.

midway. This temporary position soon led to a lifetime ambition. Today Jeff is the owner and operator of All Star Amusements Company. A supportive family augments Jeff's success in the outdoor amusement field: Arly Blomsness, Jeff's father, assists with office work; Marcie, Jeff's mother, is the company bookkeeper; and Jeff's wife Patti is also the operator of a popcorn stand.

In 1984 the midway had 35 rides including a roller coaster. On Thursday a five-dollar wrist-band allowed unlimited rides on most of the midway thrills. That year the Fair and All Star Amusements hired Richard Keyworth as the Safety Coordinator to insure the safety of the public. In 1991 the midway expanded further east of the grandstand allowing more room for games, rides, and crowds of people.

As the size of the midway has increased, spectacular rides have been added. The tallest and one of the brightest rides, the Giant Gondola, has been at the Fair since 1989. Rising 103 feet in the air with 6,000 lights programmed to offer a brilliant display, it is a popular ride because it offers a breath-taking view of the grounds and can accommodate five passengers at a time in each compartment. At the 1992 Fair bungee jumping offered new excitement on the east end of the racetrack. This attraction allowed thrill-seekers to strap on secure harnesses and free-fall from a platform 175 feet in the air for sixty-five dollars. The Zipper is another ride for the daring who enjoy being locked in a cage that is spinning every which way.

The midway has continued to grow. In 1999

Photo by J.E.H.

Photo by J.E.H.

All Star Amusements brought approximately 125 employees to operate their 20 kiddy rides, 25 adult rides, 63 games, and 40 food concessions. In addition to Blomsness' employees, the 1999 Fair directly booked 18 games, a steam train, a pony ride, and a helicopter ride.

In an effort to offer the latest in thrills, All Star Amusements brings new rides to the Fair every year. The newest ride at the 2000 Fair was called the Inverter. Seating twenty-four patrons at a time, this $600,000 ride lifted those who dared fifty feet into the air then repeatedly flipped them 360 degrees. Young and young-at-heart rode the Inverter and all the other rides all day on Thursday for fourteen dollars by purchasing a wristband. Wristbands were also available during certain hours on Wednesday and Friday.

During Fair week the northeast corner of the fairgrounds resembles a small city. That's where carnival employees and midway people park their trailers and mobile homes. In addition, All Star Amusements brings seven trailers divided into living compartments called bunkhouses for most of its employees.

It's obvious that the midway business has come a long way since the days of the merry-go-round and the single Ferris wheel, but other than the size and the spectacular rides, the midway is about the same. In fact, the merry-go-round and Ferris wheel have been in the same location for at least three-quarters of a century. The midway still gives fairgoers a thrill, a chance to risk a dollar or two, and the only opportunity on the fairgrounds to eat tasty treats in the din of music and flashing lights.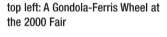

top left: A Gondola-Ferris Wheel at the 2000 Fair

top right: The merry-go-round is always a popular ride for young fairgoers.

In mid 1990's bungee jumping offered new excitement. Thrill-seekers strapped on a harness and did a free-fall from a 175' platform.

Photo by L.H.

Food:
A Taste of the Fair

Fresh-baked pies, barbecued pork chops and chickens, sticky-sweet cinnamon rolls, rich chocolate fudge, spicy tempura, and more and more. It is impossible to go to the Fair without tasting the food. Some fairgoers enjoy full meals in one of the many sit-down eateries sponsored by local organizations and churches. Others "eat their way" around the grounds buying a corn dog at one place, a heaping cup of ice cream at another stop, a mountain of french fries at still another, and a taco on the way to the chocolate-covered frozen banana stand. The Sandwich Fair has so much good food that it is surprising that fairgoers have time to do anything but eat.

The Fair's reputation for good food is older than the Fair itself. When stockholders purchased the Sandwich Fair in 1888, a dining hall was included in the deal. In September of 1879, *The Daily Argus* of Sandwich reported that the hall was decorated with bouquets of flowers, the meals cost forty cents, and the ladies who waited on the guests looked so happy it was "a pleasure to patronize them."

The menu was not included in the newspaper, but the article promised "a good square meal [with] anything you want and all you want . . . at all hours [because] the ladies of the Congregational society never do anything by halves . . . ." In 1880 a "splendid" dinner was offered for fifty cents, breakfast and supper for thirty-five cents in a dining hall that was in "elegant condition." One reporter called the ladies *soldiers* and speculated that they cleared about four hundred dollars.

Dining Hall

After the Fair purchased the grounds in 1888, leasing of the hall changed from time to time; news articles indicate that in 1891 and 1896 the hall was in the hands of the Methodist Church. In 1892, 1895, and 1898, the Congregational Church ladies of Sandwich were once again in charge. In 1893 and 1899, the Presbyterians operated it. In 1902, 1903, and 1905, the Congregational Church of Somonauk was in charge. The Plano Methodists served food in 1907 and 1908.

According to a news article on opening day of the 1911 Fair, the dining hall under the management of Mrs. Fred Shrader served nearly 500 people during a noon rush. The article doesn't make it clear which organization was sponsoring the service; however, it wasn't the Congregational or Baptist Churches or an unnamed church group from Leland because they also did well at their food stands.

Refreshment stands on various parts of the grounds also cashed-in on Fair opportunities. On September 14, 1893, the Sandwich *Free Press* reported, "Will Armstrong and Loren Bliss, two of our enterprising business boys, will conduct a peanut stand at the Sandwich Fair."

opposite page: Courtesy of SFA
The late Wilder Fay of Fay's Bar-B-Que and his family are known for their grilled pork chops and chicken at the Fair.

bottom: A 1940's family brought their picnic lunch and ate under the trees.

Courtesy of SFA

From the *Sandwich Free Press*
Thursday, September 14, 1911

"At the noon hour there was the usual rush for something to eat. The dining hall . . . fed upward of 500." The church lunch counters fed many more "while hundreds had their appetites appeased at the many other lunch counters that dot the grounds down on the midway. Others anticipating the rush for dinner were on their guard and brought their dinner with them and could be seen seated upon the ground under the trees enjoying a family or neighborhood picnic dinner."

Courtesy of SFA

Ladies' groups from area churches leased the dining hall and served meals to hundreds of fairgoers. Map location #69

G. H. Faltz published the following advertisement in the September 11, 1896, issue of the *Somonauk Reveille*: "I will conduct a refreshment stand at the Sandwich Fair next week and respectfully solicit the patronage of those in this vicinity while attending the fair. I guarantee everything to be first class."

The Sandwich *Argus* reported in 1898 that a number of vendors had converged on the grounds. They were selling "red lemonade in glasses the size of a young barrel," red hots, and hot sandwiches. In 1917 the Daughters of the Flag also had a place to eat. Other food stands served "red hots," sandwiches of all kinds, and hot drinks. The Boy Scouts sold light lunches. In 1918 the Red Cross took care of emergencies and were "ready with the finest kind of good things to eat." They made $467 at their lunch stand.

Editor's Comment in the *Argus* September 14, 1895

One of the amusing episodes was when an old lady took her three kidlets to luxuriate on "pop." We promised not to give names but the unusual taste sent a radiance of joy over the countenances of the kidlets that was enjoyable to the outsiders.

Congregational Church of Sandwich

As mentioned earlier, the Congregational Church rented the dining hall for a number of years; they also sold meals in a tent and from a food stand. On September 14, 1889, the Sandwich *Argus* reported that a new, large dining hall had been erected, and it was "under the care" of the Congregational Church ladies. The main dining hall could serve 200 people at one time and was complete with kitchen, tables, and plank seating.

In 1892 the floral hall was converted to a dining hall, and an improvement in seating took place when Jacob Burkhart furnished 200 chairs to replace the old plank seats. According to the Sandwich *Argus*, "The ladies at the dining hall must have taken in $800 for meals and lunches during the fair." As many as 700 or 800 people were reportedly served at one dinner.

The September 10, 1898, issue of the *Argus* reported that the Congregational "ladies worked hard [in the dining hall] but probably did not take in as much money as they donated, but got their pay in a 'tired feeling' and the consciousness they had tried hard to make it a success. We regret that these ladies who are so self-sacrificing have so little compensation." In 1937 Fair Secretary C. L. Stinson reminisced about early Fairs. He told a Sandwich *Free Press* reporter that one year the Congregational ladies cleared $1,200 in the dining hall. Perhaps he

Sandwich Free Press

was referring to their efforts in 1898 because he goes on to say that it was such a large undertaking that they were unable to continue to rent the building.

Early newspapers and childhood memories are the sources for the location of the eating establishments. A 1917 newspaper stated that the Congregational Church ladies had a food tent, and in 1921 a *Free Press* article placed the Congregational folks in the old Enterprise building, which would be west of today's Home Arts building. The customers sat on stools around the stand or at tables placed in the area. In 1921 a 14' by 20' addition was added to the building.

Mrs. Herman Carlson remembers that she washed dishes and peeled potatoes "forever" at the food stand when she was ten or eleven. Both jobs were customary for young people when their mothers or grandmothers helped serve meals at the Fair.

Quen Carpenter of Plano remembers her mother saying that the Dorcas Class, the women's group, started the food stand, and the entire congregation jumped in to help. Pies were made at home; chili, roast beef, and hamburger patties were made in the church basement. Carpenter remembers hordes of city folks arriving on the excursion trains in the 1950's: "We would hear them coming and see all the people walking toward the grounds and think *we can sell them a whole pie for a dollar.*"

According to Violet Lindner of Sandwich, the food stand was going "great guns" in 1938 when she moved to town. As one of the young mothers in the congregation, she took her turn in the food stand with the other young mothers. The hours were long, but everyone had great fun. She recalls that the young mothers didn't

prepare the food; their job was to serve it.

The food stand was, by today's standards, crude; it had a dirt floor. A tent was added to the back so people could sit and eat. When the Congregational and Methodist Churches merged in 1970, this site was phased out. The Methodist site known as the Log Cabin continued.

Log Cabin Food Stand— Methodist Church of Sandwich

Until 1982 the Log Cabin was really a log cabin. Today, when people say they are going to get a bowl of chili at the Log Cabin, they are nostalgically referring to the site, not the 54.5' by 54.5' metal structure that replaced the Log Cabin in 1983. The original structure was built from donated telephone poles in 1939 or 1940 by a group of adults from the Sandwich Methodist Church called the Log Cabin Class.

Janice Kurtz of Sandwich recalls that the Log Cabin Class met every month for a family potluck. Members of the class were Steve and Elna Brimicombe, Bessie Datschefski, Wilbur and Nellie Feehan, Lester and Leah Hage, Chester and Dorothy Hecathorn, Harry and Izetta Hanson, Mr. and Mrs. Jackson, Harold and Mildred Law, Lawrence and Stella Johnston, Pastor Cedric and Martha Pope, Raymond and Frieda Schultz, Bernie and Doris Smith, Orville and Edna Smith, Lester and Nora Updike, Lyle and Grace Walker, Dewey and Emily Walley, and Brad and Ada Ward.

Originally the cabin had a dirt floor with a tree growing against the northeast corner of the building. When an addition was put on the east side for food preparation and storage, the tree ended up inside the structure making the build-

left: The Congregational Church of Sandwich operated a food stand for many years. Pictured here in 1964 are Beth King (l.) and Ruth Derby (r.). Map location #34

bottom: The original log cabin food stand was built from donated telephone poles. Note the tree growing in the middle of the structure. Map location #45

Courtesy of SFA

Chili served by United Church of Sandwich

5 pounds hamburger, browned
1-64oz. can red kidney beans
2-32oz. cans tomato juice
1-16oz. can tomato sauce
2 c. chopped onions
1 T. salt
2 T. chili powder

previous pages: Courtesy of B.H. pages 196-197: Caramel corn, ice cream and candy were at these circa 1915 food tents.

bottom: Still referred to as the "Log Cabin" this metal building was erected after the 1982 Fair to replace the log building. It is operated by the United Church of Sandwich. Map location #45

ing even more memorable for fairgoers.

Top-hinged shutters opened the stand to the public on three sides. There was no seating. The grill and workspace were in the center. Galvanized tubs filled with ice stood under the windows on the north and south sides. They held strawberry, grape, crème soda, and root beer pop. There was a sink in the corner where all the silver-ware and dishes were washed in the days before plastic ware and foam plates and cups.

The menu included hamburgers, barbecue, chili, vegetable soup, and homemade pies. In earlier days, the women of the church canned tomatoes in the church basement for the vegetable-beef soup. Members brought in fresh vegetables from their gardens to add to the soup. Evangeline Gowdy remembers the men had a "secret" recipe for the barbecue they served. It was prepared prior to the Fair and canned at the church. Lester Updike donated the meat. It was ground for hamburgers that were pattied at the fairgrounds until Public Health regulations required that they be made elsewhere.

The Log Cabin was painted pink on the outside in 1966 when the Fair board decided to paint all the buildings different colors. As the years passed, the stand got termites, and the tree

grew bigger and older. After the 1982 Fair, both the tree and the stand were removed. The original log cabin was replaced by a new metal building erected by the Fair Association. Many Fair veterans still refer to the site as the Log Cabin even though a sign is the only remnant of the original cabin. The United Church of Sandwich operates this food building today.

For the 2000 Fair a record-number of 491 pies were served. The pies are still baked fresh at the church each day of the Fair and delivered to the food stand, sometimes still hot.

Yorkville Methodist Church

The Yorkville Methodist Church began its food stand in 1950 to help raise money for a new church building to replace the one that burned in 1947. Adult members prepared the food; younger members served it. As with other food stands, weeks before the Fair men and women donned aprons in the church kitchen and began cutting, chopping, and cooking vegetables and meat for gallons of chili, soup, and barbecue. The week of the Fair, each church family baked an average of two pies everyday. Some were still hot from the oven when they were picked up and taken to the Fair.

The church stand was located just east of the livestock buildings on the north end. It became a first stop for many livestock exhibitors who "lived" at the fairgrounds during Fair week. A fast, hot breakfast at 6 a.m. gave exhibitors time to feed their animals and prepare them for the livestock show later in the morning. Some young people remember sleeping in this stand when they were exhibiting their animals. The stand closed in 1972.

Federated Church of Sandwich

The Federated Church food stand was located near the Round Office where the rest pavilion is today. In 1921 a new stand with the roof projecting out to protect the patrons from sun and rain was placed on the old location. It had a cement floor and a large, roomy kitchen in the rear. Church members served complete meals of roast beef, ham and scalloped potatoes, and homemade pies.

Both the Federated and Methodist food stands recorded "land office" business in 1928. It was noted that a great deal of work went into

Photo by J.E.H.

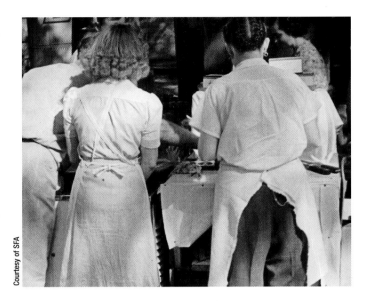

Courtesy of SFA

In earlier days some food was prepared outside. Before disposable dishes and silverware, dishes were washed outside.

Photo by V.C.W.

St. Paul's Catholic Church stand is just inside Gate 3. Many exhibitors and fairgoers start their day here with breakfast. Map location #19

running the lunch stands, a statement that workers at today's food stands agree is still true.

Mary Breunig of Sandwich recalls waiting on tables as a teenager in the 1930's and hearing the nearby merry-go-round music play all day long. Breunig also remembers the delicious, homegrown half muskmelons filled with a scoop of A. B. Henry ice cream that sold for fifteen cents.

Juanita Bark Anderson of Sandwich has fond memories of working at the church stand when her Aunt Clara Elliott was in charge of the kitchen. When she was six years old, she buttered bread and washed dishes outside. Anderson also remembers riding around town

with Charlie Hart of Sandwich in his Whippet car to pick up pies made by church ladies. He removed the back seat of his car and put in shelves to hold the pies. One day on their way to pick up pies, he turned the car over on the fairgrounds. It was up-righted, and they continued on their way for another load of pies.

St. Paul's Catholic Church of Sandwich

St. Paul's Catholic Church food stand, located just inside Gate 3 near the live-stock area, has been a favorite place to eat since 1959 when it began providing food, particularly breakfast, for the live-stock exhibitors. The first shelter was a tent using portable furniture that was stored each

Sandwich Free Press

For several years a tent was used for the St. Paul Catholic Church food stand. Mrs. Frank Ament and Jim Housch were pictured in 1964 preparing breakfast. Map location #19

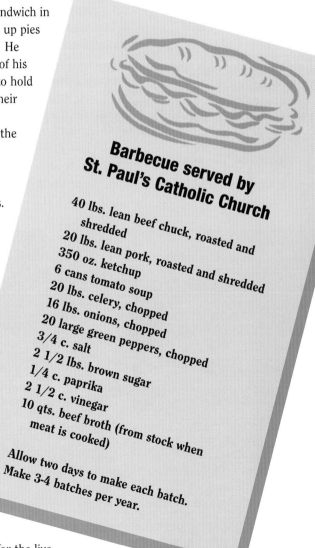

Barbecue served by St. Paul's Catholic Church

40 lbs. lean beef chuck, roasted and shredded
20 lbs. lean pork, roasted and shredded
350 oz. ketchup
6 cans tomato soup
20 lbs. celery, chopped
16 lbs. onions, chopped
20 large green peppers, chopped
3/4 c. salt
2 1/2 lbs. brown sugar
1/4 c. paprika
2 1/2 c. vinegar
10 qts. beef broth (from stock when meat is cooked)

Allow two days to make each batch.
Make 3-4 batches per year.

*The people, the food,
the sights, sounds,
and smells.
The animals,
the family memories.
There is only one fair—
the Sandwich Fair.*

LuAnn Stott
DeKalb, Illinois

top: Al Mueller (l.), Ray Shuck
(c.) and a friend stack
supplies at the American
Legion stand getting ready
for the 1964 Fair. Complete
dinners were offered in their
enclosed stand.

bottom: (l. to r.) Barbara
Fisher, Marion Dannewitz,
Sandra Schultz and Ruth
Reynolds worked at the
American Legion food stand
in the late 1940's.

opposite page: Photo credits appear
in Chapter 11.

year in Jane and Bill Gengler's barn. After water
problems caused by rain flooding the ground
and a leaky tent roof, a concrete slab was
poured. Later, Louis Miller erected a wood-
frame building, and screens were added to make
the area more pleasant. Finally, in order to
serve more people, carryout and picnic areas
were added.

Today, breakfast is still served until
10:30 a.m. Fair patrons fill all the counter stools
and stand in the carryout line for specials such
as "4 Deuces for $4" (a.k.a. 2 pancakes, 2 eggs,
2 strips of bacon, and 2 sausage patties).
St. Paul's still serves a "bottomless" cup
of coffee.

Their menu includes items that have
become a tradition. Karl Rud of Sandwich
makes a blend of sausage especially for St.
Paul's. Their special barbecue is homemade in
the parish kitchen from an old recipe.

Home-baked pies remain a specialty, with
203 served at the 2000 Fair. Rose Grief of
Sandwich still makes grape pies for the farmers.
Since the grapes always ripen after the Fair, she
prepares the fruit a year ahead. She grows her
own blue grapes, pinches the pulp out of the
skins, boils it, and freezes it to be used later. No
matter how many pies she makes, there are
never enough grape pies for the farmers.

It takes 225 four-hour shifts to staff the
kitchen, grill, and counter area. Workers include
many parishioners who have moved away but
return to work at the Fair as a tradition. Father

Sandwich Free Press

Charles McCarren, who started the food stand,
frequently visits during Fair time and puts on a
working apron.

In 1999 members of the church mobilized
the food stand on Labor Day when they began
serving coffee and rolls to people waiting in line
to buy grandstand tickets.

American Legion Auxiliary

The American Legion Auxiliary had a food
stand from 1917 until 1948. Members and
friends served dinners that included meat,
mashed potatoes, gravy, vegetables, and homemade pies. A September 16, 1948, *Free Press*
article indicated the organization did well. In
the article the Auxiliary thanked all of the non-
members who helped make the food stand a
success and explained that all of the profits were
to be used for "carrying out the great program
of peace-time service to America."

Sandwich Sportsman's Club

The Sportsman's Club no longer has a food
stand at the Fair, but the members still remember the good times they had grilling the meat
and serving the food. The men went out early
and started the grills; Artie Johnson always
made egg coffee. The organization bought the
meat and the members donated all the salads
and desserts. Karl Rud made a special barbecue
sauce. Like other food stands, they made
hamburger patties at the booth until health regulations required otherwise. The stand was
located west of the grandstand. Rosemary Wiley
managed the stand from 1960 until 1975;

Courtesy of B.F.W.

The selection and quantity of food are endless. Fairgoers never go home hungry.

Sandwich Free Press

left: Sandwich Moose members Howard Josephson and Violet Kitner worked at the Sandwich Moose Lodge food stand in 1964. Map location #47

right: Funds raised at the Fair by the Sandwich Band Association support the band's activities, buy uniforms and equipment. Map location #27

bottom: Formerly the Moose Lodge building, the Sandwich Sports Boosters have used the building since 1980 to sell pizza logs. Map location #47

Photo by V.B.

"Toots" Gustafson took over in 1975 until it was torn down before the 1995 Fair after it was damaged by wind.

Sandwich Moose Lodge

The Sandwich Moose Lodge began providing food service in the 1930's from a tent. James "Jingle" Allen constructed the permanent building about 1955 just north and east of the Home Arts building. They sold sandwiches and bottled soft drinks from the Mendota Bottling Company. The pop, purchased in crates of 24, was chilled in a horse tank. When the customers failed to return the bottles, the Moose had to pay the deposit on them. The Sandwich Sports Boosters have used the building since 1980.

Sandwich Sports Boosters

The Sandwich Sports Boosters began selling pizza logs in a space under the west end of the grandstand in 1976 in an effort to raise funds to reinstate sports programs at Sandwich High School after a failed referendum. They moved to the Moose Lodge location in 1980. Parents, student athletes, and coaches run the booth. They use the funds to buy athletic equipment and uniforms.

Sandwich Band Association

The Sandwich Band Association food stand is home to more specialties—spaghetti dinners, Italian beef and ribs. The spaghetti sauce is

Courtesy of G.W.

202

Rotarian Dean Holdeman advertised on a bull horn for Sandwich Rotary Club food stand.

homemade from a secret recipe, and the barbecued ribs are fully prepared on site. The menu also includes sandwiches and baked potatoes with chicken a la king or broccoli-cheese topping. Desserts include cakes, brownies, and homemade pies. Parents, grandparents, young musicians, former students, and teachers serve meals in a building west of the Home Arts building.

The food stand opened in 1967 with Norma Holdiman as chair of food preparation. Sandy and Gail Sibigtroth of Sandwich have been organizing the meals since the late 1980's. Funds raised by their efforts support the band's activities as well as buy uniforms and equipment.

Sandwich Rotary Club

The Sandwich Rotary Club has been at the Fair since 1974. The club's first year did not involve food. Members sold tickets and gave out burlap bags for a ride down a giant slide. The following year, they sold brats, cider, and pop from a stationary stand with a canvas top. Originally, Rotary members dispensed apple cider from a barrel. Today, because Health Department regulations have changed, the cider must be pasteurized. Rotary members no longer go to Wisconsin to buy the 500 gallons of cider that used to be in great demand.

In 1980 they remodeled a used travel trailer and sold food from it, adding hot dogs to the

Lines may be long at Fay's tent, but they disappear quickly as they can serve up to 1200 meals an hour.

Fay's Pork Chop Bar-B-Que

Wilder and Martha Fay began Fay's Bar-B-Que as a small business in 1962. Their objective was to promote pork, improve their family farm, and to raise money for their children's college education. Their first year at the Sandwich Fair, they served 1000 meals. In 1999 Fay's served over 26,000 meals. Today, the lines are long at their tent, but they disappear quickly because they can serve up to 1200 meals an hour.

Out of their alliance with the Fair, Fay's Outdoor Catering began. Satisfied customers began asking if Fay's would come to their homes and prepare pork chops for their parties. The basic menu remains unchanged. The family recipes developed by Martha are still being used, along with their original powdered spice that seasons the meat. A Fay Family Cookbook was published in 1986 to commemorate 35 years of operation. It highlights the recipes of twenty family members.

In 1999 Fay's Bar-B-Que used pork chops from 800 hogs, 12,800 chicken quarters, 750 large cans of applesauce, 1,000 large cans of baked beans, 3,600 pounds of cabbage, 244 gallons of Miracle Whip, 4,000 pounds of cottage cheese, 1,800 gallons of lemonade, 900 gallons of iced tea, and 450 twenty-pound bags of charcoal at the Sandwich Fair.

This family business incorporates the talents and abilities of all eight of Wilder and Martha's children, Jackie, Jane, Bob, Marcia, Linda, Tom, Jim, and Joanna. Today, in-laws, grandchildren, friends, and neighbors are also involved.

In 1976, son-in-law Bob Dempsey became manager of the business after the sudden death of Wilder. Dempsey's daughter Krista Mulligan is the office manager and food supervisor.

The Sandwich Fair and the Fay family have grown together making many dear friends throughout the years. In October 1999 Martha Fay died, leaving a thriving business in the competent hands of her family.

I love looking at all the displays of flowers, grains, and veggies. We see our friends from all over the area. I just love everything about the fair!

Martha Grove
Sandwich, Illinois

Courtesy of O.C.

right: Rotary youth exchange students at the Rotary stand in 1980

previous pages: Courtesy of V.C.W. pages 204-205: Sometimes families use benches as substitute picnic tables.

Photo by V.C.W.

top: Grandma's Eatery is the Fox Valley Older Adult stand just west of the Home Arts building. Map location #34

center: Open Door Rehabilitation Center's booth under the grandstand is home of the famous "lemon shake-up."

menu. The club later sold the trailer to the Fox Valley Older Adults, who still use it for food service. In 1993 the Rotary Club purchased a new food-service trailer equipped with shelving, counters, and water heater. They added a commercial grill outside the trailer in 1995. Today, barbecue sandwiches are also available. In 1999 the club served about 300 pounds of brats and 200 pounds of hot dogs. The Rotarians are located on the south side of the Horticulture building.

Fox Valley Older Adults

For a year or two beginning in 1989, the only food item of the Fox Valley Older Adults was rainbow ice cream cones sold at the base of the wind-mill. They also sold handmade crafts in a booth in the commercial building. From about 1991 through 1997, they sold Sandwich's Yum Yum Shoppe ice cream. In 1998 they expanded to a full menu of foods and beverages in a permanent building

west of the Home Arts building. Their food stand, specializing in onion blossoms, steak sandwiches, and breakfasts, is known as Grandma's Eatery.

Open Door Sheltered Workshop

Churches and civic groups are not the only ones to appeal to fairgoers' hungry appetites. Since 1969 many volunteers have sold popcorn and thousands of lemon shakeups at the Open Door booth to raise funds and to make the public aware of the center and its programs. In the beginning the booth passed out brochures and did an occasional raffle. About 1979 the famous "lemon shake-up" was introduced. Their motto is "We make it to your taste; if you don't like it, we will remake it." They rarely have to remake a shakeup. What started with a single booth under the grandstand has grown to a double booth. They also sell bottled water, pizza, nachos, and chili. The Fair Association employs the Open Door residents as the

Photo by K.L.B.

Courtesy of R.P.

left: Alberta Miller of Sandwich is shown in an old popcorn wagon.

Beacon News

top: Cotton candy is spun by Marilyn Sanders of Rockford as fairgoers watch.

bottom: Becky Colby (l.) and June Creed (r.) have been popping and selling corn at the Fair since 1956.

Photo by V.G.

official clean-up crew for the grandstand.

Boy Scouts

Early newspapers show that the Boy Scouts have been part of the Fair since 1917. At that time they sold light lunches. Today Sandwich Troop 45 sells hot dogs and pop from a small travel trailer to raise money for summer camp.

Under the leadership of Scoutmaster Mike Hamer and Jim Gerlick, Somonauk Troop 5 has been selling pop, lemon shakeups, popcorn, and peanuts in the grandstand for McKinney Food Service since 1993. Jim and his wife Sharen supervise the boys during the Fair. They earn a percentage of the sales they make on weekday evenings and on weekends. The money is used for their scout projects.

Forty-Milers and Professionals

Professionals (vendors who travel great distances to fairs) and forty-milers (vendors who travel shorter distances) know that life on the road is hard work. Sometimes "professionals" are on the road eight to ten months of the year, returning to their home base only long enough to repair equipment and take care of personal business.

Since many of the food vendors travel the same fair circuit, they have developed strong friendships. They help each other with supplies and personal needs and enjoy friendly competition among themselves. When new vendors, called "first of May" vendors, join the group, they rely on "professionals" and "forty-milers" for advice on how to succeed at a business that is dependent on the weather and taste buds. Sandwich fairgoers love to eat, and the vendors know how to satisfy their appetites.

Bando Tempura. David Chang of Bando Restaurant in Chicago has been in the food business since the 1980's. Fairgoers have become accustomed to the familiar chants of "tempura, tempura, tempura" to advertise the deep-fried battered vegetables from his two locations.

Cajun Connection. Ron McFarlain, who worked his way up the Mississippi River from Louisiana, started vending at the Fair when he heard that the Association was looking for something different. He serves alligator kabobs, deep-fried battered corn-on-the-cob, etouffee, and jambalaya. His success at the Fair lead to his opening a restaurant in Utica. He serves authentic Cajun food that is spicy—not hot. Manager Amy Martin assists him.

Colby and Creed. The friendship of June Baie Creed and Becky Colby goes back to the days when they played softball together for DeKalb Ag. In 1955 they started selling popcorn together from C. R. Brady's popcorn machine on South Main Street in Sandwich on Saturday nights. In 1956 Brady invited them to sell popcorn and pop at the Fair. When they first started, they sold popcorn for ten cents a bag; today they sell three sizes: $2.50, $1.50, and .50.

Today these two Waterman women have popping machines at two locations near the Home Arts building. They use between 300-350 pounds of popcorn at the Fair each year. They

What's in a Name?

When people think of the Sandwich Fair, one of the first thoughts that comes to mind is food. Fairgoers love to eat ears, feet, pups, dogs, flowers, and even logs. To the outsider who doesn't know Fair-food language, these items may sound far from appetizing, but to native fairgoers who speak Fair-food language fluently, these foods are delicious. Fairgoers learned to speak the food language as small childen strolling with their parents from one food vendor to the next. Now as adults they look forward to speaking their native tongue every September as they order their own favorite foods. However, visitors to future Fairs—perhaps the 3000 Fair—may find it bizarre that the Sandwich Fair natives loved to eat such strange items. The following list of foods will serve as a dictionary for those who may be curious about the appetites of today's Fair visitors.

Fairgoers eat *Elephant Ears* and *Dinosaur Feet*. They aren't as wild or as prehistoric as they may sound. An Elephant Ear is a flattened, deep-fried yeast dough. After it's fried, it's sprinkled generously with cinnamon and sugar. The shape somewhat resembles an elephant's ear; at least it's big—about 8" to 10" in diameter. There are several food stands that sell these popular, warm creations. One food stand alone reports selling 500 a year. Elephant Ears have been available at the Fair since 1975.

Dinosaur Feet are so similar to Elephant Ears that only the experienced hunter can tell the difference. The marketing technique is the biggest difference; a board member's child from the Plano YMCA dressed up in a dinosaur costume to help promote this delicious snack in the late 1980's. Today, the Feet are extinct.

Another favorite, a *Funnel Cake,* is made from donut-like batter swirled into hot oil from a funnel. It is generally about 9 inches in diameter. After being deep-fried, it's topped with powdered sugar or thickened fruit sauce.

Most fairgoers eat at least one *Pronto Pup* or *Corn Dog* and never give a thought to eating a hot poodle even though some people call it a hot dog. This main-meal for many fairgoers is a wiener on a stick that becomes a Corn Dog when dipped into a corn batter or a Pronto Pup when dipped into a flour batter. After the wieners are coated with batter, they are deep-fried and served plain or brushed with catsup and mustard.

An *Onion Blossom* is another Fair favorite. It is a large, sweet onion that is carefully cut almost all the way through from the top. Then it's dipped into a batter and deep-fried. As it fries, it opens up and resembles a large chrysanthemum.

Photo by J.E.H.

A couple at the 2000 Fair enjoy elephant ears.

It's served with a special dipping sauce.

Pizza-on-a-Stick was available a number of years ago. It was a pizza-seasoned sausage with cheese, dipped in pizza sauce and wrapped with puff pastry, then deep fried. *Pizza Logs* are still available today. They are long, chewy buns topped with pizza sauce, cheese, meat, and optional mushrooms.

Tempura, Tempura, Tempura. The words echo throughout the fairgrounds. Vegetables such as onions, sweet potatoes, green peppers, and carrots are coated with a special batter and deep-fried. Fairgoers get a heaping plateful of oriental finger-food—enough to share with a friend. Another favorite that is served mountain-style on a plate is *Slinky Spuds,* spiral-cut deep-fried potatoes.

Some foods are recognizable by their names, yet they are unusual. For example, *Frozen Bananas.* Bananas are peeled, stuck on a stick, dipped in chocolate, and rolled in nuts before they are frozen. About twenty-five cases of bananas are used each day at the Fair to make these tasty, hot-day desserts.

Another cool dessert is a *Buffalo Chip,* not a cow chip or a camel chip. A Buffalo Chip is a hearty slice of vanilla ice cream sandwiched between two giant chocolate chip cookies. *Cotton Candy* may also be classified as a dessert. This old, spun sugar delight is usually made ahead and bagged today because the demand is too great for individual customers to watch the threads of sugar collect around a paper cone.

Drinks such as *Lemon Shake-Ups* and *Black Cows* are also available. Lemon Shake-Ups are made by squeezing a cut lemon into a glass of water to which plenty of sugar has been added. The glass is covered and shaken vigorously. A Black Cow is a concoction better known as a root beer float—vanilla ice cream in root beer. It is an old favorite, so old in fact, that the name discourages some thirsty fairgoers. Another food of the past is a *red hot.* It was a spicy hot dog [wiener] served at the turn of the twentieth century.

So, what's in a name? Hungry fairgoers find their favorite Fair foods no matter what they are called. Perhaps some of these items would be more mouth-watering if they were called by their true ingredients, but fairgoers don't seem to mind. Even if cotton candy were called "puffy or spun" sugar, it would still taste like cotton candy. If asked, most people would probably prefer Elephant Ears to fried yeast dough, or Pronto Pups to batter-fried wieners. So, what's in a name? Tradition—part of the tradition of the Sandwich Fair.

The Sandwich Fair has so much good food that it is surprising that fairgoers have time to do anything but eat.

> *I have been coming to the Fair since 1958; it's a tradition. I now bring my five children. My half-sister had a food stand here— "Bev's Kitchen." She loved working at the Fair and visiting with all the people. The old train brings back wonderful memories.*
>
> Martin Family
> Naperville, Illinois

previous page:
page 209: Photo credits appear in Chapter 11.

believe "If you make a good popcorn, people will come get it." They say they are blessed with family help.

Concessions Unlimited. Marilyn and Gary Sanders of Rockford own three food concessions at the Fair. Mr. Sanders is a former soft drink route salesman. They have been serving pizza, Polish and Italian sausage, corn dogs, hamburgers and hot dogs, cotton candy, caramel apples, and popcorn from their three stands since 1979.

Cooper Family Foods. Miller and Ruby Cooper operate four food stands throughout the grounds with lemon shakeups, sausages, and sandwiches. Their sons Steve and John are part of the operation. This Texas-based family has been coming to the Fair since 1965. Miller started working with his parents when he was 14 years old.

Crystal Clear Ice Company. Providing ice for food vendors at the Fair is no small job. It takes a big company to meet the demand. Crystal Clear Ice Company of Chicago has provided ice for over ten years. In mid 1990's when Fair-week temperatures stayed in the 90 degree range, two semi-trailers of ice (85,000 pounds) were used. Manager Chad Spojic is referred to as the "Ice Man." He and five to seven employees use garden tractors to deliver ice to the food vendors.

Dairy Bar. This stand has been at the Fair since 1969. Marlene of Marlene's Gingerbread originally owned it. Today Andrew Broomfield owns and operates the business. They feature soft serve ice cream, cones, sundaes, shakes, malts, and banana splits.

Eatery Huts. Ralph Pressy of Hobart, Indiana, has been coming to the Fair with his chocolate covered frozen bananas, strawberries, and ice cream for more years than he can remember. He sells approximately fifteen cases of bananas during the Fair.

Enright Foods. The Enrights have been in the concession business since 1961, and they have been at the Fair since 1970 offering corn dogs, hot dogs, and lemonade. William and Sandy each operate a stand as does their son Brett (Blue Ribbon Foods). They plan to open Zachary's Cotton Candy also named for a son. Sandy says, "We love the Fair and the people. It is like coming home."

G & J Concessions. This business was formed in 1979. It came to the Fair for the first time in 1998. George and Joleen Williams are from Saunemin, IL. Their major food products are Italian and Polish sausages and corn dogs.

They use approximately five tons of Italian sausage at each Fair. They plan to buy a new food-service trailer in the near future.

Guido's Pasta. Joe Guido has played the piano at the horse races since mid 1970's. In 1989 he expanded his involvement in the Fair by opening an Italian foodstand near the grandstand ticket office. In 1999 Guido's wife Gloria made 800 pounds of fresh spaghetti sauce for the five days of the Fair. They used 1,800 loaves of bread spread with 150 pounds of garlic mixture. Another specialty is a meatball sandwich. Outside the Fair both Joe and Gloria Guido teach piano. He is a church organist in Lemont; she is choir director at another church.

Hicks Caramelcorn. Hicks Caramelcorn has been at the Fair since 1956. Mr. Landon, the present owner, also sells candy apples and cotton candy.

Hintz Enterprises. Sharon Hintz of Dixon, Illinois, has two food stands. She has been selling popcorn, cotton candy, and corn dogs at the Fair since 1965. Her three daughters sometimes help her.

Illinois Pronto Pups. They have two locations near the Home Arts building and one stand near the grandstand. The business has been at the Fair since the early 1950's, but with different owners.

Irish O'Briens. Irish O'Briens, east of the Home Arts building, offers seating for patrons under a green- and white-striped tent at tables spread with bright green cloths. Since mid 1970's, green and white signs have drawn customers to their specialty of Polish and Italian sausages smothered in onions and green peppers; they also sell complete dinners. The O'Brien family provides food service at fourteen fairs during the year.

Malone's Taffy. Malone's Taffy started at the Sandwich Fair in 1946. When Mr. Long died in 1963, employee Mike Mooney took over the business. The red- and white-striped glass-enclosed trailer has been a favorite stop for half a century for those with a sweet tooth and for those who enjoy watching the putty-like globs of candy change color as it is pulled and folded. A machine transforms the mixture into individually wrapped candies that can be tucked into a purse or a pocket. Mooney sells taffy at 17 fairs from June to October. The Mooneys have two taffy stands at the Fair.

Marlene's Famous Gingerbread. Marlene Holmes has been coming to the Sandwich Fair since 1964. Her specialty is gingerbread topped

Courtesy of SFA

Helen McKinley-Potillo selling her famous fudge

Helen McKinley-Potillo

What do people look for at the Fair? Helen's Famous Fudge, of course. Helen McKinley-Potillo of McKinley Candy Company of Canton, Ohio, has been coming to the Sandwich Fair since 1966. She started with one commercial exhibit–Famous Fudge, of course.

Today she and her two sons Kit and Gary have expanded to four booths and a tent. Along with her natural snacks and nuts, she is Helen of "Helen's Famous Baked Potatoes and Ribs." Her family is part of twenty employees who staff her booths.

At the 100th Anniversary of the Fair, President Jack Norling nominated her to speak on behalf of the exhibitors. In the photo Helen is shown greeting Governor Walker and his family during their visit to the Sandwich Fair. It was quite a day for Helen!

She is also the owner and manager of S & H Cleaning Company that has maintained the restrooms for over ten years.

with whipped cream. Today she lives in Florida, but she used to live in Wisconsin where she served ice cream and frozen bananas in a dairy bar. She commented that of the four fairs she vends, the Sandwich Fair is the best because of the dedicated directors.

McKinney's. The McKinney family operates four food stands around the fairgrounds. Since 1984, this Texas family has sold corn dogs, brats, funnel cakes, lemon shakeups and more. They also handle the sale of food in the grandstand. McKinney food service has been in business since 1927. They raise 450,000 chickens a year on their poultry farm.

Moores. Dick and Lois Moore have been selling thick milkshakes at the Fair since 1978. When they started their business, they couldn't call their product "soft ice cream" because it had

only four-percent butterfat instead of the required six percent to qualify as ice cream. They offer vanilla, chocolate and strawberry because they are the most popular. Some Midwesterners recognize Moore as "Cactus Jim," the host of a children's television show in the 1950's.

Parnell Foods. Ollie and Frank Parnell's family-owned business has been coming to the Fair since 1987. They sell elephant ears with toppings and soft drinks. They are assisted by local employees they like to call the FBI (Fast Boys of Illinois) because they work hard and are very helpful.

Perfection Confections, Inc. James LaFratta and his wife Sissi from Florida are two well-known food concessionaires at the Fair. They started coming in 1974. They are on the road

Photo by J.A.

In 1977 scarecrows Stanley and Sophie were married at the sweet corn stand.

Stanley, You May Kiss the Bride

On September 10, 1977, Secretary Louis Brady performed his first, last, and only wedding at the Sandwich Fair. The marriage was between Stanley and Sophie, scarecrows who lived in the cornfield of Ray and Mary Malewig and their ten children. They had been attending the Fair since 1973 as mascots to the Malewig's roasted corn concession. Stanley and Sophie, dressed appropriately, stood quietly as Mr. Brady began the ceremony in front of the Hot Roasted Sweet Corn stand.

Ladies and Gentlemen,

The Malewig family has called to our attention that these two handsome farm people have been co-habitating in the same cornfield for the past four years.

Now we at the Sandwich Fair Association are willing to overlook this past indiscretion if, and only if, as requested by the Malewigs, their adopted family, they are willing to enter into a more stable relationship than merely standing side by side. We propose to lasso Stanley into the bonds of matrimony.

Thus we are gathered here in the presence of these fairgoers as witnesses to join Stanley and Sophie as husband and wife.

Before we proceed is there anyone here who knows any reason this couple should not be wed? If there be such let him speak now or forever hold his peace.

Who gives this straw stuffed beauty for wedded bliss?
Will the couple please join hands.

Stanley, do you take Sophie to be your wedded wife; in poverty and need; in summer's heat and winter's cold; protecting her always in whatever field you are placed for as long as you both have your stuffing? If so, will you please indicate your acceptance.

Sophie, do you take Stanley to be your wedded husband; in scarcity and want; in summer's rain and winter's snow; through all kinds of harvests, supporting him always, until your straw turns to chaff? If so, indicate your acceptance.

Where is the ring? Place it on her finger, Stanley. Stanley, with this ring as a token of your vows you agree to love her, honor her and to never carry matches.

In the presence of these witnesses, Stanley and Sophie have plighted their troth and will henceforth stand together as one.

Now by the power invested in me by the International Association of Fairs and Expositions and the Sandwich Fair Association, Inc. I declare these two to be scarecrow and spouse. Those who have thus been joined together let no man put asunder.

Stanley, you may kiss the bride.

seven and a half months a year. They sell cotton candy, caramel and red candy apples, popcorn and pop north of the windmill. Among the food vendors, LaFratta is known as the "Ambassador of the Midway" and "Mayor of the Midway" because he enjoys visiting with everyone.

Raymond's Concessions. Owners Andre and Diana Raymond have been coming to the Fair a long time—since before the Fair had flushing toilets. The business was handed down from Raymond's father. It was one of the first food stands to be placed near the animal barns. It specializes in a variety of fresh-made sandwiches from jumbo corn dogs to melt-in-your-mouth Italian beef.

Red Barn Elephant Ears. Sam Coffman and his brother Chris have been selling deep-fried yeast dough sprinkled with cinnamon and sugar since 1975. Sam got the idea from Tiger Ears, a product sold at his church's bake sale. Needing money for college, he renamed the tasty treat and started selling it at local carnivals. Before long he was in business at the Sandwich Fair. Chris says, "People came to the elephant ear stand at first because they didn't know what they were." Now people come because they remember how good elephant ears taste.

Rollin Pin Bakery. Bob Hiller makes crème puffs, eclairs, and crispies "from scratch" at his bakery in Janesville, Wisconsin. Hiller started the business in 1946 for nine hundred dollars. He was in high school when he sold his car to pay for the bakery. The success of his business is based on his belief: "Make it good and make it fresh. Quality is most important."

Scooter's Concessions. Scooter and Bev Ryals and their son Kenny and daughter-in-law Denise have two stands near Ag Land. They started one in 1985 and the other one—Kenny and Denise's stand, "Lemonade and More"—in 1988. They specialize in pasta, pizza, caramel apples, cotton candy, fresh squeezed lemon shakeups, and popcorn. Scooter says his two grandsons, Blake and Grant who are at the Fair everyday, will take over the business someday.

Silver Dollar Bakery. Dan and Don Rowlet and family from Merryville, Louisiana, have been baking fresh rolls and breaking diets every day at the Fair since 1984. Fairgoers watch through a window as they sprinkle cinnamon and sugar on six-foot long pieces of dough before they roll it and cut it into saucer-size pieces for individual baking.

Sun Tea and Onion Blossoms. This booth started in 1979 in the corner of Ferris

Environmentals tent. For several years the only product they sold was sun tea. Over the years the menu has expanded to include onion blossoms and deep-fried turkey legs.

U.S. #1 Taco Stand. The Manuel "CoCo" Venegas family own and operate this popular taco, burrito, taco salad, lemon shakeup, and strawberry shakeup food stand just north of the windmill since 1974. During the five days of the Fair, the Venegas family cooks approximately 500 pounds of beef. They use 350 pounds of tomatoes, 10 cases of lettuce, around 200 pounds of refried beans, and lots of cheese and sour cream. They prepare their own special hot sauce.

Vroman's Lemonade. Fairgoers have enjoyed corn dogs and lemon or orange shake-ups at Vroman's since the late 1940's. Located just inside the midway/livestock-dividing gate, they were once the only place for livestock exhibitors to get a quick bite to eat between livestock shows.

Weber's Incredible Edibles. Perry and Gerry Clauss originally started this stand in 1967. They were the first food vendors to sell Italian sausages at the Fair and the first to have revolving signs and flashing lights on their concession trailer. Upon their retirement in the early 1980's, their daughter Peggy and son-in-law Carl Weber carried on the family business.

After Carl's death in 1986, Peggy continued the business (Weber's Food Service of Seffner, Florida) with her daughter Nicci and her son Tony even expanding to a new product, "Weber's Roasted Corn."

Weber's Roasted Corn. Owner Tony Weber has been coming to the Fair since he was a child with his mother, Peggy Weber of "Weber's Incredible Edibles." He bought the sweet corn business in 1992 from the Malewig family of Leland whom many people remember as having the scarecrow family that Louis P. Brady united in marriage in 1977. Tony specializes in corn on the cob that is slow roasted and dipped in warm melted butter. During the off season, Tony is in the trucking business.

Wentz's Mug and Keg. Owner Ron Wentz from Lostant, Illinois, is a former ironworker who had no retail experience before opening his root beer business at the Fair in 1983. However, he had attended the Fair since 1949, and he knew Sandwich would have a big crowd for his cold drinks. In 1987 he expanded to funnel cakes. He has also sold curly fries and pizza on a stick.

Photo by J.A.

Whitman's. Whitman's of DeKalb have been at the Fair since mid 1980's. They are easy to find southwest of the racetrack between the midway entrance and the livestock area. Their specialty is a butterfly pork chop sandwich; they also serve steak and chicken sandwiches.

Tastes of Yesteryears

Some foods are no longer available, but fairgoers remember them well. The Chandler sisters, better known as the caramel corn ladies, were last at the Fair in the 1970's. They made their caramel corn in a very large old kettle in a food trailer on the north side of the Home Arts building. Sometimes they sang and danced as they worked.

Missing at the 1953 Fair was the little old man who sold cheese chips opposite the Women's Building. Other favorites of the past are Merkt's cheese and sausage and Dutch donuts full of raisins called oliekoekens by the Klepper family. Lee Martin's french fries were also a favorite for a number of years.

For a number of years Barney Storzbach and Joe Kurtz had food stands named Spot #1 and Spot #2. One was west of the Home Arts building (now the Fox Valley Older Adults food stand); the other was formerly the Yorkville Methodist food stand north of the windmill near the racetrack.

The selection and quantity of food are endless. Fairgoers return each year to eat their favorites and seek out new tastes to add to their memories of the Fair. If fairgoers go home hungry, it is not the vendors' fault. ⬙

top: Fairgoers looked forward to sampling cheese and sausage at Merkt's.

Courtesy of G.W.

The Chandler sisters, better known as the caramel corn ladies, retired their business in the 1970's.

213

Commercial Vendors: Something for Everyone

Commercial exhibits have always been one of the main reasons people come to the Fair. In the beginning, the number of vendors may have been fewer and the grounds smaller, but the variety of exhibits more than made up for the size. From early newspaper articles, it is estimated that there were over fifty commercial vendors at the first Fair. There was plenty of time to "see it all" and still have time to visit with friends and neighbors and have a picnic. As the grounds expanded and the popularity of the Sandwich Fair grew, the number of vendors significantly increased. Today's fairgoers must come early and stay late if they hope to visit even a fraction of the commercial vendors during the five days of the Fair.

Managing the food concessions and other vendors has become a large operation that requires attention all year long. According to Superintendent of Concessions and Displays Don Bark, the Sandwich Fair hosted 356 commercial vendors in 2000, which included eighty-two food concessions and six large cafeterias. Secretary Emeritus Louis P. Brady remembers his days as Superintendent of Concessions: "We had plenty of space; we just hoped the exhibitors would see the advantages. We didn't recruit." The increased number of vendors indicate they did see the advantages of displaying their wares at the Sandwich Fair.

At the first fairs, commercial exhibits were sheltered in tents or displayed in the large two-story Floral Hall and later the building that replaced it, the Home Arts building. Farm machinery of area implement dealers such as International Harvester of Plano was located in the center of the old racetrack, which is today's midway area. Today many exhibits are still located in tents and trailers around the grounds, but four permanent shelters protect many of the vendors from the weather. The first building for commercial exhibitors was built in 1964, the last in 1997. The farm machinery display area has expanded to the outer edges of activity on the grounds.

Courtesy of SFA

Commercial Exhibits at the First Fair: 1888

Newspaper accounts of 1888 indicate that the first Fair was an important community event with well-organized commercial displays in a time when lifestyles demanded carriages, hard and soft coal, harnesses, and windmills. Details of the exhibits in early publications serve as a

top: At the early fairs, commercial machinery displays were just west of Floral Hall, some in tents and others in covered shelters. International Harvester Company of Plano was one of the first implement exhibitors.

opposite page: Courtesy of SFA
1960's aerial view of the grounds

Courtesy of SFA

Photo by V.G.

Tents

Berg Industries of Rockford has furnished tents and chairs at the Fair since 1976. At the 1999 Fair, it took twelve men approximately 400 hours to erect about 100 tents for commercial exhibits. Today vinyl tents are used because they provide better protection from the weather than canvas tents.

top: Erecting tents in 1948 required more manual labor than it does today.

bottom: Today, workers use power tools to help erect the tents.

As the grounds expanded and the popularity of the Sandwich Fair grew, the number of vendors significantly increased as seen in this 1945 photograph.

Courtesy of SFA

1911 Premium Book

1888 Premium Book

history of local commerce.

Sandwich Manufacturing Company had a large display of farm equipment. The exhibit was one of the favorites not only because it was probably the largest but also because it was shown in actual operation. Since the company employed many local residents, employees attending the Fair were eager to show their work to their families and friends.

Sandwich Enterprise Company also had a large display. The *Free Press* raved about the Enterprise's Bash Surface Cultivator: It is "conceded by thinking farmers to be the coming implement for the cultivation of corn." The Enterprise was one of the vendors that exhibited its products in competition for premiums. The Company took blue ribbons on all the goods it entered. A *Free Press* reporter regretted that windmills were not part of the premium list because the Enterprise's windmill "showed their 'Enterprise' in methods as well as in name."

There were carriages, surreys, buckboards, carts, and wagons by several Sandwich merchants: Henning and Ross, J. M. Hummel, Kehl Bros., and Gust Walter. One Somonauk merchant, Clark and Company, included two Colorado antelope at his display to attract attention. Gall and Gilchrist displayed "fine work" in marble and granite.

Inside Floral Hall in 1888

Visualizing the merchants inside Floral Hall in 1888 may be easier for today's fairgoers if the hall is compared to a mall. In a sense that's what Floral Hall was—a small shopping mall. It contained a variety of goods to buy as well as exhibits for those who were just window-shopping. Both luxuries and necessities were available. Many came to the Fair to stock up on provisions for the winter. A local reporter wrote, ". . . it is not necessary for any one to go [shopping] out of town."

Courtesy of SFA

Manchester dry goods offered the latest fashions of the day.

The September 26, 1888, issue of the *Free Press* recorded many of the exhibits. Fairgoers who were shopping for furniture visited "our wide-awake C. P. Walter" or Burkhart or Stern. Personal items were also available. Crofoot and Manchester displayed a case of shoes in sizes No. 1 to No. 17. James Warner's "elegant line of clothing and gentle furnishing goods [was] large enough to convince the most fastidious that good goods and good bargains may be obtained at home."

E. F. West had a large display of crockery. Two hardware dealers, George Kleinsmid and Winchell & Abbott, "warmed the hearts of all visitors by their exhibits of stoves."

T. A. Dean and William Hueske "made the hearts of horse owners rejoice" at their excellent display of harnesses and whips.

The photographer C. E. Orr "showed the results of his inventive mind in an electric motor and instantaneous photographic shutter." The ladies loved A. W. Orr's display of plants and flowers from Pearl Street Green Houses in Sandwich. In the home improvement line, Louis Dietrich showed examples of his tile and brick sidewalks.

S. W. Walling was so successful with his demonstration of the Davis sewing machine that he "secured ten orders at the fair." Fairgoers had the option of buying or trading butter and eggs for groceries at H. A. Cox's display. Mrs. M. Butterfield was at the Fair with her fine display of millinery for the ladies. It is not clear what Dr. Charles Winne was vending at his booth, but the newspaper article indicates that he "showed his intention to keep up with the procession, in entering a case of some of the many choice articles which he is selling."

Advertisers in the First Premium Book

Forty-six merchants advertised in the first premium book. Many of them probably exhibited at the first Fair. Businesses from Sandwich included A. A. Jacobs, horseshoeing and general blacksmithing; W. H. Beatty, lightning rods; and Gage & McKindley, groceries. Charles Corlinsky had a variety of goods: groceries, boots, shoes, and dry goods.

Businesses from Somonauk included G. Hess & Sons with general merchandise and John Betz with lumber and agricultural implements. Dr. Molitor's advertisement was printed entirely in German.

Two Northville businesses had advertisements. Northville Roller Mills promoted quality flour and encouraged farmers to exchange their wheat for flour. The Fox River Valley Poultry Yards promised the best strains of fowl.

Cigars had a competitive market in Sandwich in 1888. According to the premium book, there were several dealers and manufacturers. Cigars were available at John Munch's Hive Saloon on Main Street at the tracks, at LeDoyt's News Room on the corner of Main and Center, and at Billy's Place on the North side in Sandwich. T. D. Emerson manufactured his own New Royal, "the best five-cent cigar on the market." P. B. Marrs, proprietor of the Oyster & Ice Cream Parlor, also carried choice Havana cigars.

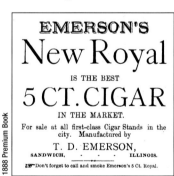

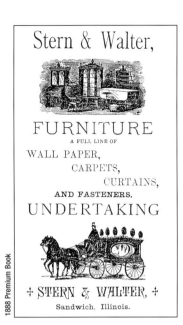

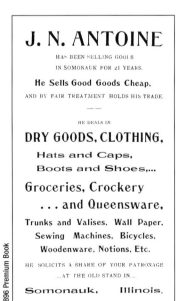
P. S. Fairbanks carried Harvey's and Defiance, also the two best nickel cigars on the market.

Early Sandwich Fairs

Before the second Fair, the Enterprise Company issued invitation cards encouraging fairgoers to visit its display at the Fair. The company was either selling or giving away small windmills because an article in the September 11, 1889, *Free Press* reported that the miniature windmills "take like hot cakes and an Enterprise wind-mill [sic] may be seen in the hands of hundreds, from the youth in dresses to the big fellow's best girl."

By the third Fair, displays were larger. Stern and Walter's furniture display represented four rooms—a parlor, library, dining room, and bedroom. The September 11, 1890, *Free Press* described A. W. Jones as "our popular grocery-man [with] a large display of crockery, glassware, . . . [and a] handsome set of dishes which he has offered as a special prize for the best display of needlework."

Home appliances and furnishings drew admirable attention. Humiston & Son and

Humiston and Son hardware displayed cook stoves, room heating stoves, and other household furnishings in Industrial Hall.

George Kleinsmid, the "old reliable hardware dealer," had large displays of hard and soft coal stoves, cook stoves, gasoline stoves, and general kitchen furnishings. Arthur Orr included palms in his floral display, and Warner's store occupied the entire south half of Floral Hall. J. M. Hummel had the largest display of harnesses, pianos, organs, and musical instruments in Floral Hall.

Somonauk merchants were also well represented at the Fair. J. N. Antoine was on the

The 1890's display in Floral Hall by Warner's Department Store of Sandwich. Warner's had a number of stores within their store, resembling an early day "shopping mall."

second floor of Floral Hall with his clothing and sewing machines. John Betz exhibited buggies and surreys in a tent near Floral Hall. The California Wind Mill Co. continued to do well.

According to the September 15, 1894, *Free Press,* the Fair continued to be a place to shop for luxuries and necessities: "J. Burkhart's display of furniture would do credit to any wholesale house in Chicago. . . . Hendricks needs no other certificate of master in his art

than his display of photos." Many fairgoers bought their groceries from displays that were "endless in quantity." The newspaper listed four grocers: F. H. McKindley, Penniman & Dannewitz, E. Thompson & Son, and Abbott & West. A company from Lake City, Minnesota, displayed seventeen varieties of fall and winter apples grown in northern Illinois.

Newspaper accounts of early Fairs sometimes contain interesting side notes about the vendors. A *Free Press* reporter in the same 1894 issue wrote, "Chas. V. Stevens also of Somonauk, who runs a bank and a windmill factory (queer combination, has to raise the wind to make both go) is on the ground busy explaining the merits of his machines."

The Fair was a show place for new products. In 1890 a new lamp and a razor sharpener attracted much attention at a booth operated by

Courtesy of SFA

The Aurora *Beacon News* occupied the space just west of the Home Arts building for many years so fairgoers could renew their newspaper subscriptions.

William Walling of Martin Bros. O. S. Ferguson exhibited a Mendenhall all-purpose hog trough that "is a success in every way." A new manufacturer in town displayed violins "that some day may make Sandwich famous."

As the Fair grew, area merchants established their "places." A *Free Press* September 15, 1894, article explained that the veteran hardware dealer Kleinsmid occupied "his usual corner with a fine display." In 1895 John Betz erected a building on the grounds to display his large line of road vehicles and farm machinery. At the 1896 Fair, Roy Warner had "a fine exhibit of clothing and shoes at his old place in Floral Hall."

For a number of years, the Aurora *Beacon News* occupied the space just west of the Home Arts building. The news agency gave away blankets and pots and pans to those who renewed their subscription.

Prizes and Gifts from Vendors

In 1892 the *Sandwich Free Press* reported that "Miss Harmon was the happy winner of the $6 pair of shoes, given by Bradley Bros., for the best loaf of bread made from Bradley's best flour. Mrs. Thos. Bryant received the handsome chamber set offered by Gage & McKindley, for the best loaf of bread made from White & Gold flour, sold only at their store."

F. H. McKindley & Company ran an advertisement in the August 31, 1893, *Free Press*: "We will give to the maker of the best loaf of bread made from the famous White & Gold flour—flour to be bought of us and bread to be exhibited at our space in the Floral Hall during the Sandwich Fair—196 lbs. of White & Gold flour put up in a fancy hard wood barrel."

In 1895 Abbott & West offered a bound volume of World's Fair engravings of the buildings and beautiful scenes of the "White City" to the person who baked the best loaf of bread. Each competitor had to present certificates that the flour was either "Washburn Crosby's Superlative" or "Best of All" purchased from them. Their advertisement appeared in the *Argus* August 17, 1895, issue: "Buy the flour now and become expert in the way to use it."

Sandwich Argus

Automobile Exhibits

Automobiles were popular at the Fair. The latest models were displayed with machinery and farm implements. In 1913 the Buick people arranged for parking space near the Secretary's Office and had a man looking after Buick cars free of charge. That same year the Victor Auto Supply Company of Waterman showed Lauson gasoline engines and automobiles. In 1916 automobile exhibits were "without question one of the best and largest that has ever been shown at the Sandwich Fair."

In 1917 the new model 1918 Maxwell with its "50-inch rear spring and latest refinements" was on display west of Floral Hall at the Sandwich Manufacturing Co. They were touted as cars that would withstand punishment "every day in the year." They were available from Edward LeDoyt, The Maxwell Man. Also on display were the Reo and Moline Knight. LeDoyt encouraged fairgoers to make his place their headquarters. At his exhibit fairgoers could rest,

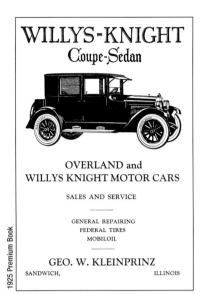

right: A unique exhibit for a number of years was this giant, redwood log made into a home.

opposite page: Photo credits appear in Chapter 11.

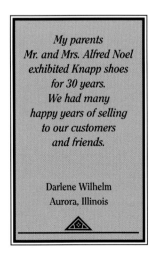

*My parents
Mr. and Mrs. Alfred Noel
exhibited Knapp shoes
for 30 years.
We had many
happy years of selling
to our customers
and friends.*

Darlene Wilhelm
Aurora, Illinois

leave their wraps [jackets], and their lunch baskets.

In 1920 automobiles continued to be a big draw. Dealers LeDoyt and Norem carried Oaklands, Booth-Scripts, and Maxwell cars and trucks. Emory Stockham represented Ford; F. N. King and Sons carried Studebakers; Killey and Kleinprintz had Overlands and Willys Knights; and L. R. Sawyer displayed Stewart trucks.

In 1923 Plano Garage took the lead in the auto exhibits. Their large tent was filled with the latest models of Nash and Chevrolet cars. In 1925 several auto companies reserved space with the tractors for showing the latest models: Buick, Nash, Hudson, Chevrolet, Jewett, Paige, and Studebaker. According to the *Free Press* September 2, 1925, seeing the cars and tractors was worth the price of admission. At the 1939 Fair, Montgomery Motor Sales displayed 1940 Dodges; the Somonauk *Reveille* called them "the luxury liner with the new full-floating ride, and the car of beauty."

Unique Exhibits

Some exhibits were more informative than they were commercial. The headquarters of the Women's Christian Temperance Union (W.C.T.U.) was located in a tent east of the Enterprise building in 1890. They were giving away literature, bouquets, and glasses of cool water. This was the only place on the grounds where everything was free. The September 11 issue of the *Free Press* said they weren't making much money, but they were making lots of friends. In 1913 the Southern Railway Co. exhibited grains, seeds, grasses, and products of the land traversed by their railroad.

In 1919 the Rock Island Arsenal displayed a complete motor train showing whippet tanks "that worked such deadly destruction in the barbed wire entanglements of the German front." It included a complete commissary department, showing the life of the boys in World War I. It also displayed small arms,

bayonets, knives, grenades, uniforms, and "many interesting articles captured in the camps hastily evacuated by the retreating Germans." The Somonauk *Reveille* explained that the exhibit included high-powered guns such as the famous Browning machine gun. "Blank ammunition is carried and this gun will be seen in active use."

In 1923 the State of Illinois had two tent exhibits, which was a compliment to the Sandwich Fair since the larger exhibits were reserved for larger fairs. One tent was for still exhibits and the other was for moving pictures. The still exhibits included a display of noxious weeds and seeds as well as graphic pictures showing road construction in Illinois. Another exhibit promoted better health by offering free medical examinations.

The moving picture tent featured a six-reel film titled "The Organized Good Samaritan." The story was written about various state institutions, including penitentiaries, hospitals and homes for the unfortunate who were wards of

the State of Illinois. The September 13 issue of the *Free Press* stated frankly that the Department of Public Welfare display had "exhibits from all the insane hospitals in the state. . . ."

Well-Established Early Vendors

Betz and Grandgeorge of Somonauk. John Betz's advertisement in the 1888 premium book indicated that he dealt mainly in lumber and building supplies. A sideline was agricultural implements, buggies, and road carts. By 1895 his machinery line had apparently expanded because he built a permanent structure on the

Farm-Related Vendors

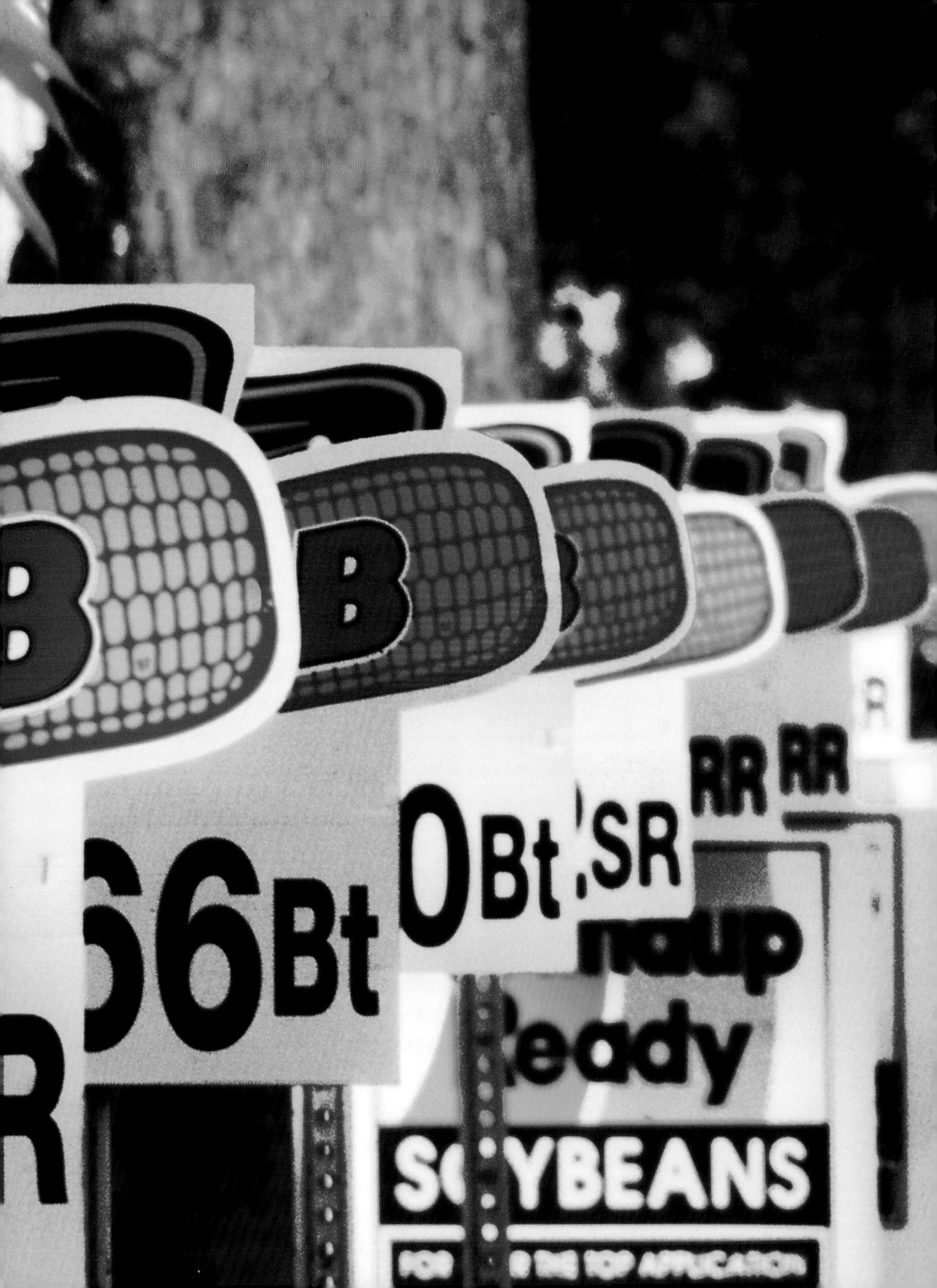
6Bt
0Bt
SR
RR
RR
eady
YBEANS

Courtesy of SFA

Courtesy of SFA

top: John Betz, original owner of this company, was an exhibitor in 1888. This photograph was taken in the 1970's.

bottom: A 1905 postcard of the Sandwich Manufacturing Co.'s display

previous pages: Photo by M.M. pages 222-223: Seed corn vendors have been a common sight for many years.

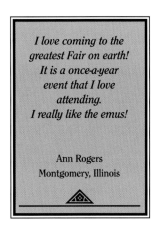

I love coming to the greatest Fair on earth! It is a once-a-year event that I love attending. I really like the emus!

Ann Rogers
Montgomery, Illinois

fairgrounds to display his equipment. John Betz was the sole owner until about 1900. At that time Adolph Betz emigrated from Germany and became a partner in the business. The business became Betz and Grandgeorge in 1926 when Adolph Betz's son-in-law Ray Grandgeorge, Sr. became part owner. Betz-Twait, Inc. and Paul Buck, Inc. later owned the business. Hogan Walker Implement owns the business today.

The Sandwich Manufacturing Company. The Sandwich Manufacturing Company not only exhibited at the first Sandwich Fair in 1888, but it also demonstrated its equipment. The company specialized in corn shellers, horse powers, saws, feed grinders and cutters, Reliance Harvester, and Argentine Mowers. At the 1890 Fair, they demonstrated a new hay-pressing machine. At its peak the company employed 400 workers in Sandwich. It was sold to New Idea of Ohio in 1930 and to Avco Company of New York in 1945. The company continued until 1955

when it became a warehouse.

Wallis Novelties. Dallis B. Wallis of Walnut, Illinois, was a well-known vendor to early fairgoers. His display included fair mementos such as dolls, salt and pepper shakers and other items that children and adults took home as souvenirs. His stand, located on the west end toward the dining hall, had a twenty-five cent spinning wheel and a ten-cent grab bag. For a while he also had pony rides. In 1987 during opening ceremonies, Fair officials recognized him at age 89 for being a commercial vendor for

Dallis Wallis (r.) of Walnut, Illinois, was recognized by Director Don Bark (l.) at the 1987 Fair for being a commercial vendor for 59 years. He continued to operate his booth as late as 1990.

59 years. He continued to operate his booth as late as 1990.

Reymann Gates. Alois "Dutch" Reymann was a local businessman who designed and patented the Reymann Farm Gate shortly after World War II. He manufactured and distributed the "no sag, no drag" gates until the early 1970's. During that time he displayed the gates at the Fair before selling the business to Wiley Fritsch who continued to display the gates for a number of years. After Fritsch's death, Dale and Mary Rogers bought the business and continued making gates until 1987.

Miller's Builders. Louis Miller, known for his Cozy Homes, was the owner and operator of Miller's Builders. His exhibit was located in the northwest corner of the fairgrounds near the livestock area. Miller displayed ready-built chicken coops, garages and other portable buildings that he sold on the fairgrounds. He began his association with the Sandwich Fair in 1936 and continued exhibiting until 1992. In 1983 the Sandwich Fair Association purchased one of his garages and moved it to the Lisbon Street exit. Miller also built a storage shed that stands near the railroad tracks, and he constructed the St. Paul's Church food stand, the Sheriff's Police building, and the First Aid building.

Miller and his wife Edith are remembered for bringing meals to Fair workers and for allowing Junior Fair exhibitors to sleep in their

Local builder Louis Miller displayed ready-built portable buildings in the northwest corner of the midway/concession area from 1936 until 1992.

exhibit building when they stayed overnight to care for their animals. There were chairs at Miller's exhibit for Fair visitors to rest because Edith Miller recalls that many of them would be tired from walking around the grounds. In 1987 the Sandwich Fair Association awarded Miller a plaque for his years of service and hospitality at the Fair.

Fraser Realty. Owned by John and Veronica Fraser, Fraser Realty exhibited under the windmill at the Sandwich Fair from 1976 until 1997. That area is now a park affectionately named Fraser Park. Veronica Fraser fondly remembers her days as a vendor, "I enjoyed the public; I just loved getting out to see the people whatever the weather at the fairgrounds." Although no longer exhibiting, Fraser Realty continues to sell farm and residential property in the Sandwich area under the direction of Veronica Fraser and her son David.

Fraser Realty exhibited in a tent under the windmill at the Fair from 1976-1997. Pictured (l. to r.) are sisters: Maryline Janickic and Veronica Fraser.

Today's Commercial Vendors

Unlike early vendors from businesses within a thirty-mile radius of Sandwich, many of today's vendors come from all over Illinois as well as distant states. For example, American Indian Art is from Arizona, Dom's Sunglasses is from Texas, and Frank's Custom Engraving is from Florida.

Although vendors today may travel more miles, one element has remained the same: The Fair is an exposition of new products as well as time-honored ones. Vendors bring a variety of goods for fairgoers who are comparison-shopping and buying. A typical list might include Flitz metal polish, a new pair of Happy Feet, a new Mack diesel, a four-bedroom log home, socks, and a wrought-iron garden arbor.

Personal items are available from vendors like Midwest Outfitters, Classy Touch, and Buckletown USA. Champion bakers know where to find their favorite bottle of vanilla whether it is Rawleigh or Watkins. The corner booth of the Spice and Grain Shop always has customers buying blends of seasonings for winter soups and other hard-to-find spices and herbs. Seamstresses look for sewing machines at Creative Designs and cloth from the Fabric Store. Fairgoers crowd around the Super Salsa Maker "pitch booth" to hear "it slices, it dices."

Homeowners come with a list of items to find: washing machines and refrigerators at Dock's TV and Appliances, new light fixtures at Unified Supply, and a spa at The Pool Guy. They order large items such as sunrooms from BJ McKay, garages from Coach House, or gazebos from Valkner Nursery and Leisure Woods. In the past few years, landscaping vendors have increased. Flowers, shrubs, and even trees are available from vendors like Winding Creek Nursery and Earth Design.

Just like early fairs, equipment and farming products are big draws. Milam and Wackerline have utility trailers; Ag Tech is a source for fertilizers. DeKane Equipment, Caterpillar, and Hogan Walker display tractors and combines that are larger than a child's imagination. If fair-

Photo by F.T.

Fairgoers could do their annual shopping for Rawleigh spices, flavorings, and household products at the Fair.

Courtesy of SFA

The Fair is an exposition of new products as well as time-honored ones. Fairgoers gather around booths to hear and watch the vendors demonstrate their products.

King and Sons Monuments is the oldest, continuous commercial exhibit at the Fair.

Russell King, William King holding Nathan King, Charles King

King and Sons Monuments

"The oldest, continuous commercial exhibit is King and Sons," say L. P. Brady, Secretary Emeritus and past Superintendent of Concessions. King and Sons Monuments has been at the same location since 1920. It is located west of the Home Arts building across from the Round Office.

The fourth generation of the King family is now running the business which began with Frank N. King, continued with Kenneth King, Russell and Charles King, and now with William King.

Russell King, grandson of the original King, recollects the business "never missed a year even during the war, but we did not give yardsticks away during the war. At first, it was three days and not much of a night fair. [There were] no lights; everyone had a horse . . . and they all wanted to get home by dark. My cousins from Malta . . . took one day to get here, one day at the fair, and one day to get home."

King remembers a simpler county fair than the one today. He remembers horse racing and baseball, the animal exhibits, and the Ferris wheel and merry-go-round.

L. P. Brady said there was no room at such a late date, but if I wanted to tie my balloons to a light pole on the midway, I could give it a try," said Baudino.

The next year, the Baudinos set up a display at their present location outside the Horticulture building. Soon their stock expanded to stuffed animals, celluloid dolls, batons, and pennants. All five Baudino children helped at the Fair. In 1976 they began offering wooden toys patterned after the ones Baudino created for their first grandchild.

For the last twenty years, the Sandwich Fair has been the only fair the Baudinos attend. Although Sue Baudino says, "We don't ever want to quit," she admits that they plan to retire after the 2005 Fair with fifty years of great memories.

Edward Bauntz is shown at his Universal Computer Services booth in a commercial building. He has been analyzing people's personalities from their signatures for over 40 years.

Bauntz Universal Computer Services. This vendor has been analyzing people's personalities from their signatures for over forty years. Fairgoers write their names big, little, plain, and fancy, but they can't fool the computer.

Colonial Kitchen and Bath Cabinetry, Inc. This three-generation business owned by the Jerry Cook family started coming to the Fair in 1976, the first year it opened for business in Sandwich. It specializes in planning, designing, and installing custom cabinetry and counter tops for homes and businesses.

Country Market. Fairgoers can buy all the Illinois Lottery games at this outdoor booth. A variety of other country-store items have occasionally been for sale since the booth opened in 1986. The store is operated by owner Becky Woolsey and Marilyn Lueken.

Hospital Auxiliary. In 1949 the Woodward Memorial Hospital Auxiliary opened its first booth under the grandstand; a local carpenter built it for $1.25 an hour. The Auxiliary volunteers printed 40,000 raffle tickets that sold for

opposite page: Photo credits appear in Chapter 11.

bottom: Since 1955 Jon and Sue Baudino of Marseilles have been selling novelties outside the Horticulture building.

goers need a new building in which to store all their purchases, Morton and Cleary both have several designs.

The list of products is endless. The Sandwich Fair even has emu oil for burns, reconditioned golf balls, and lottery tickets. If it is too overwhelming, visitors can plan a get-away at The Travel Place or Trave*Linn.* One fairgoer said, "If you can't find it at the Sandwich Fair, they don't make it."

Many vendors have been coming to the Fair for decades. Fairgoers return year after year to buy their products. Most of them are located in the same place each year, making it easy to find them.

Baudino Novelties. In 1955 Jon and Sue Baudino of Marseilles began selling novelties, toy trains, and balloons. "On a whim I took my balloons and gas tank to the Fair on Thursday night in 1955.

Photo by J.E.H.

The local hospital auxiliary first operated a booth at the 1949 Fair. They have been at the Fair continuously since 1969. Pictured (l. to r.) at the 2000 booth are Candy Cuneo-Mowinski and Ami Beck.

twenty-five cents each or five for a dollar. They raffled off two bicycles—a girl's and a boy's, a Bendix washing machine, and a TV set. Total receipts were $915.25, but expenses were high at $686.99, leaving a small profit.

The Auxiliary members returned to the Fair in 1955. Ernest "Pummy" Heusinger suggested they sponsor a queen contest to help raise money for the hospital building fund. Young girls from twelve area communities competed in a penny-a-vote contest during August before the Fair [see Chapter 5 Queen Contest]. One young lady was selected from each community for the final phase of the contest held during the Fair. Eighteen hundred dollars was added to the building fund from that contest. The Auxiliary sponsored the contest again in 1956; the profit was $835.

From 1957-1968 the Auxiliary did not have a booth at the Fair. When it returned in 1969 as the Sandwich Community Hospital Auxiliary, the booth was in the original location under the grandstand. That year a pony was raffled. For two more years the Auxiliary was in the same location before moving to the commercial building in 1972.

At the booth in the early 1970's, fairgoers bought baked goods, pledged to give blood, or had a "Sweetheart" photo button or mirror made. In later years other items were sold: Auxiliary cookbooks, silk-screened T-shirts and scrubs, and Auxiliary plates. Thousands of glasses of "low-cal health" drinks (ice water) have been given out and several quilts have been raffled.

Over the years, the Auxiliary has provided health-related services by checking blood pressure, determining blood type, selling hemocult test kits, and giving away anti-smoking buttons and cancer literature. For several years the lung machine from the Cancer Society was on display

The fairgrounds is transformed into a one-stop shopping place for fairgoers during the five days of the Fair.

227

top right: The Sandwich Lions Club raffles a live steer each year.

bottom right: Denny Sorensen, owner of Swalley Music House, is shown at the 2000 Fair.

Naperville artist Marianne Lisson Kuhn offers special pen and ink drawings of the Fair.

showing life-like diseased and healthy lungs. The Auxiliary is sharing the booth with the hospital again; currently, it is known as Valley West Hospital and Auxiliary.

Jo-Cor Ceramics. This Big Rock, Illinois, business has been operating since 1973 and has been coming to the Fair since 1985. It specializes in finished ceramics and dressed animal dolls. It is located in Commercial Building #3.

Artist Marianne Lisson Kuhn of Naperville. Kuhn had been a lifelong Sandwich fairgoer when she decided to become a commercial vendor in 1998. Her love of the Fair prompted her to draw Otto's historic train in pen-and-ink and offer it to fairgoers. Her 1999 drawing was of the Home Arts building and in 2000,

Courtesy of M.K.

Sandwich Fair 2000

the Grandstand.

Kuhn has been an artist for 16 years, working in her home so she can spend time with her family. She is known in the area for her drawings of homes, antique tractors, farm scenes and landmark buildings.

Norwegian Implement. Norwegian Implement began exhibiting at the Fair in 1963 after just one year in business. Originally showing Minneapolis-Moline farm equipment near the chicken house, they moved to the present location east of the Horticulture building in 1980. By 1997 owner Mervin Eastwold was out of the farm machinery business completely and strictly selling chain saws and lawn mowers.

Their exhibit has expanded to include craft items as well as artwork of chain-saw carvers

Courtesy of M.E.

Norwegian Implement Company of Norway, Illinois, began exhibiting at the 1963 Fair showing their farm equipment. They now exhibit chain saws and lawn mowers. A number of years ago Riveland's of Serena, Illinois, shared the tent displaying appliances.

Tim and Karen Barker and Bob and Marie Boyers. According to Eastwold, "While most of our display is 'male oriented,' we like to have something for the womenfolk and kids to enjoy." In the future Norwegian Implement plans to create a fishing lake in the exhibit to promote fishing tours.

The Sandwich Lions Club. The Lions Club Steer Raffle began at the Sandwich Fair in 1961. Members sold tickets from a tent until a

Photo by J.A.D.

permanent building was constructed in 1975. A larger building with ample space for the steer and members working at the booth was constructed in 1993.

The Paperback Encore. Fairgoers step into this tent for romance and mystery and much more that they find in the books they buy to enjoy after the Fair closes. This used paperback bookstore opened for business in Sandwich in 1976 and started selling its overstock at the Fair in 1979. Owner Lois Spizzirri operates the business with her husband Frank and their children and grandchildren.

Photo by J.E.H.

Swalley Music House. According to owner Denny Sorensen, Swalley Music House of Aurora began exhibiting at the Fair in 1961 after just one year in business. Original owner Jerry Swalley enjoyed his association with the Fair until 1970. Today, Swalley's entertains the crowds with beautiful music and gives visitors an opportunity to create their own music.

Sorensen says, "There are some very talented people who walk by and sit down and start playing." Many of the Fair workers and exhibitors will come by to play or sing. He recalls one day when Helen Potillo of Helen's Ribs and Potatoes stopped by and started to sing. She saw a friend in the crowd and hailed him in. "They started singing harmony; it was fantastic!"

Wallenches Family Honey. There has been a honey stand located in the space outside the southeast corner of the Arts and Craft building since 1948. It was originally owned by John and Ada Wetz who sold honey until mid 1980's before selling the specially constructed stand to the Wallenches. The honey stand is built on axles that can be raised to move it and lowered to open it for business. In the early days when the fairground was smaller, their location was on the southern edge of the grounds. Families spent the day at the Fair and when they were ready to go home, they picked up their honey and walked to their cars nearby.

Today's fairgoers are familiar with Wallenches Family Honey stand operated by John Wallenches, his mother Stephanie and his sister Audi. John, who for several years was an apiary inspector for the State of Illinois, currently has approximately 250 hives of bees in the area. The honey farm is located five miles north of Plano, Illinois.

WSPY, Nelson Multimedia, Inc. Larry and Pam Nelson, founders of WSPY-FM Radio, visited the Fair for the first time in 1969. Larry, who was employed by WRMI-FM in Morris, had been in the area covering Bob Hope's visit to the Sandwich Airport in July 1969. In the fall he returned during Fair week with his future wife Pam. He decided this area would be a great place to start a radio station with local programming of news, high school sports, and community events.

Nelson was granted a construction permit for a FM radio station in 1973. WSPY went on the air January 19, 1974. Nelson realized the Sandwich Fair was *the place* to be. He contact-

ed the Fair Association to inquire about a booth. As luck would have it, a business was giving up a space across from the Home Arts building. Fair President Carlton "Dutch" Hough suggested Nelson take the space. He did, and WSPY has broadcast from the fairgrounds during Fair week since 1974.

At the Fair the radio station interviews fairgoers, announces coming attractions, and gives results of judging. It interviews visiting dignitaries, which have included Speaker of the House J. Dennis Hastert and US Secretary of Agriculture Earl Butz. The station's Saturday night play-by-play of the grandstand Tractor Pull was featured for many years.

In 1977 Nelson published the first official *Sandwich Fair Times*, a publication dedicated entirely to the Sandwich Fair. It highlights each year's improvements and attractions. It also includes information about the Sandwich Fair Directors whose hard work and dedication make every Sandwich Fair better than the last. The paper boasts a circulation of 60,000 copies.

In 1990 WSPY started a TV station which has covered many aspects of the Sandwich Fair including a one-half hour special featuring Sandwich Fair Directors, superintendents, workers and exhibitors as well as the sights and sounds of the best county fair in the state—the Sandwich Fair.

Young's Candles. Reta and Don Young started bringing their candles to the Fair in the 1970's. At one time their candle booth was 60 feet long in Commercial Building #1. Later they expanded their business to include spoon rings and moved outside the building. Young says he was the first booth on the backside of the Commercial Building #1.

Vendors know the benefits of returning year after year to the same location. The Sandwich Fair office receives calls throughout the year from Fair visitors who request the names and addresses of businesses that have exhibited. Secretary Emeritus Brady says, "We always tell [our vendors], for your advertising dollar, you will see and talk to more people directly at the Sandwich Fair than you will in any other way. There is no question; we have mighty fine displays!"

Local FM radio station WSPY, owned by Larry and Pam Nelson, has been broadcasting from the Fair since 1974.

left: John Wallenches of Plano is pictured inside the Wallenches honey trailer. It has been located at the southeast corner outside the Arts & Crafts building since 1948; John and Ada Wetz sold the stand to the Wallenches in mid 1980's.

Don Young started bringing candles to the Fair in the 1970's.

Fairgoers: Meet Me at the Fair

You are Invited to Attend
THE GREAT
SANDWICH FAIR
— HELD —
Sept. 14, 15, 16, 17, '97
Increased Premiums and Display!
Railroad Excursion Rates.
$6,000 in Premiums
SEND FOR LIST
E. RANDALL, Secretary,
SANDWICH, ILLS

Courtesy of SFA

8
CHAPTER

The opening stanzas of a poem written by Mrs. Charles Arnold capture the excitement of getting ready for the Sandwich Fair.

The Sandwich Fair is coming,
    Please don't forget those dates.
Come early in the morning
    And stay until it's late.

Bring your fathers, mothers and sisters,
    Your little brothers, too,
And also your wives and sweethearts,
    And all that belong to you.

Bring your sheep and pigs and horses,
    And your cattle, one and all.
Then just watch them take the prizes
    They are giving there this fall.

Your pumpkins, corn and apples,
    Just bring them in a truck.
The roads are now so well patrolled
    You surely won't get stuck.

So come early in the morning
    And come again next day.
See every thing there is to see
    Before you go away.
        — *Sandwich Free Press*
        August 17, 1922

More than likely Mrs. Arnold didn't need to remind readers about the Fair. It was already over a quarter of a century old—an institution in the community. It had established itself for generations to come as a traditional meeting place for families and friends, an exposition of new products, and a showplace for area livestock and harvests.

In the Fair's formative years, however, Fair officials must have felt that citizens needed some persuasion. An article in the 1890 *Sandwich Free Press* reminded readers that they had a responsibility to participate in the Fair. They were

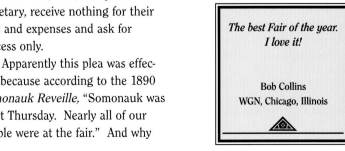

Photo by L.D.

encouraged to exhibit something. If they couldn't do that, they were urged to at least buy an admission ticket.

Let everyone feel that he is, and ought to be, an important factor in the Fair's success. The permanency of the association, and the holding of an Agricultural Fair in Sandwich every fall, are beyond question settled facts. There are many strong reasons why we should have an Annual Fair, and why the whole farming community should take an interest in it. . . . Let every person make an individual effort to exhibit something, and those who have nothing to exhibit can present themselves at the gate and ask for an admission ticket, thereby giving encouragement to the officers of the exhibition, who, except the secretary, receive nothing for their time and expenses and ask for success only.

Apparently this plea was effective because according to the 1890 *Somonauk Reveille*, "Somonauk was quiet Thursday. Nearly all of our people were at the fair." And why

Courtesy of SFA

top: Dressed in their Sunday-best, 1949 fairgoers visit with friends and neighbors on the beautiful oak-shaded grounds.

opposite page: Courtesy of SFA

bottom: Clara Miller of Plano gives a friendly wave in 1987.

The best Fair of the year.
I love it!

Bob Collins
WGN, Chicago, Illinois

231

top center: The Fair was a family affair for George and Sarah Reinhart and their children Clifford, Paul, and Lillian. They walked to the Fair in 1921 with their basket lunch.

Courtesy of SFA

Photo by J.E.H.

top left: In the 1950's young folks came to the Fair with their families, but they soon found their best buddies and enjoyed their favorite foods, rides, and games.

bottom left: Although most families don't bring picnic lunches to the Fair today, there is plenty of food to buy on the grounds, and there is always a place to rest in the shade.

right: Shade trees were gathering places where families and friends ate and caught up on neighborhood news.

opposite page: Photo credits appear in Chapter 11.

232

wouldn't they be? The Fair had a merry-go-round, games of skill and chance, places to have tintypes taken, and hundreds of experiences that daily life didn't offer. Bands played from Somonauk, Freeland Corners, and Sandwich. The exhibits were almost double what they had been the previous year.

A Family Affair

The Fair has always been a "family affair." In bygone days families usually arrived on the grounds together; then they split up. The women, carrying or leading the smaller children, headed for the exhibit buildings and tents, and the men quickly found the machinery exhibits or the livestock barns. Teenagers found their best buddies, their favorite rides, or tried their skill or luck at some carnival games. Everyone promised to meet later at a designated spot that was usually under a large oak tree where Mom would spread a large blanket or tablecloth and open the wicker picnic basket. Delores Devine of Somonauk remembers as a child, "My mother got up early to fry chicken and make pies to pack in our picnic lunch. Then friends would come by and we would all eat together."

Ruth Nelson of Sandwich says the same was

Courtesy of GRF

true of her family. They would meet friends in the parking area, spread blankets on the ground, and eat together. Sometime during the day, she and her dad would ride the merry-go-round because she was afraid to ride alone.

Mrs. Herman Carlson of Sandwich remembers attending the Fair with her family: "We looked at all the exhibits. There was a merry-go-round and different vendors. My favorite thing to buy was peanuts—they smelled delicious, and I could buy a little bag for five cents. I hoped that my dad would buy a big bag for the family to take home for us all to eat."

June Capehart of DeKalb remembers meeting at the Fair early on Sunday morning. Her family and her parents Bertha and Benjamin McNeely parked in a place where they could set up tables and chairs between their cars. For lunch her mother brought fried chicken, potato salad, candy, and gum. June always baked the pies. After lunch her father always handed out quarters to the grandkids Mary Ann and Benj for them to spend on the midway.

For Hendley Hoge of Nettle Creek in Grundy County the Fair was also a family affair—at least for the men in the family. They attended the Fair for the agricultural show. This is evident by the entries in his diary: On

Courtesy of SFA

September 10, 1889, after supper, he and his brother-in-law (or nephew) Will Reardon traveled two and one-half miles north to spend the night at the home of Laura and Fred Stephen, Hoge's daughter and son-in-law. The next morning after breakfast, Fred drove his team to the Fair; Hoge and Reardon rode along. They arrived between nine and ten o'clock. Hoge says it was a very hot day, but "The show was very good." They stayed at the Fair until after sundown, arriving back at the Stephen's home between eight and nine o'clock. They rode home after breakfast the next morning.

Today, even though families don't always ride to the Fair together, it is still a fair for families. Many families use it as a reunion place. Joyce Barrett of Yorkville agrees: "My children who live in Sandwich, Yorkville, Oswego, Montgomery, and Batavia use it as a gathering place each fall."

At the 1999 Fair, Marta Heldenberg and her daughters Rebecca Burke, Laurie Eagan, and Mary Smith were all together for the first time in twenty years. They gathered from Georgia, New York, and Maryland. Family members from Iowa joined them.

Joyce Brandilin of Joliet has been coming to the Fair since she was a child. It's her favorite Fair because it is "a family fair that is safe for children."

Dan Kruep of Downers Grove says, "My entire family loves the Fair. It's a red-letter day on our calendar—for over 50 years. My mom (age 87) still comes, as well as our grandchildren. The fairgrounds with trees and old buildings takes you back to the good old days."

When Theresa Morar of Big Rock started dating her husband, his family introduced her to the Fair. She, in turn, introduced her family to the Fair. Now they are all active in the Fair tradition. She says, "My mother-in-law and I bake cookies, and every year we compete for ribbons."

Illa Thirsk of Sandwich hopes the Fair keeps its family atmosphere. Her family has been coming to the Fair since 1984. Her father who was a baker enjoyed the decorated cakes. When she took her mother to the draft horse competition, it brought back old memories: "It's so interesting listening to her tell about when she drove her dad's teams when they farmed. Seeing those big, beautiful horses up close brought to life all the stories I heard my parents tell as we were growing up."

FAMILY OUTINGS AT THE SANDWICH FAIR

233

Early fairs were a fashion show-place for everyone in the family.

Courtesy of SFA

*I love the
Sandwich Fair
because it is the
"Fair of all Fairs!"
There's a bit of
nostalgia in the air.
There's old farm
machinery, new farm
machinery, livestock,
homemade arts and
crafts, FFA and
4-H exhibits, lots of
great entertainment,
the best pork chops in
the land, and the most
magnificent train ride!
The grounds are
impeccable, and the
staff is extremely
hospitable. Everyone
has fun and gains
a little knowledge of
agriculture. It is truly
a memorable experience.
It is what a county
fair is all about!*

Lottie Kearns, Executive
Production Assistant
WGN Agri-Business Dept.
Chicago, IL

*It is part of my life.
In my travels if Sandwich
is mentioned, they know
about the Fair!*

Mary Breunig
Sandwich, IL

*We feel like we have
stepped back in time;
it has a charming
"old-fashioned" flare!*

Carolyn Finzer
Naperville, IL

Fall Fashions

At one time the Fair was a place for women in the family to wear their new fall fashions. Alice Fitch Zeman of Paw Paw says "Before the fair, the dressmaker came to the house [of my grandparents] staying to make the fall wardrobes for the women and girls of the family." Zeman's mother Blanche Ramer Fitch was born in 1899. She wore her new fall dresses each year to the Fair. Zeman remembers her mother commenting that the Fair was either very dusty or very muddy—not a good place to introduce new fall fashions. She also told Zeman about an embarrassing moment for her as a little girl: "An acquaintance came up and pointed out a small section where the seamstress had not removed the basting thread!"

The fashions changed with the times. When Alice Fitch Zeman was a teenager growing up in Yorkville, young people wore jeans, bobby socks, and saddle shoes to the Fair. In their own way, they continued to make a "fashion statement" even though it must have seemed very relaxed to Zeman's grandmother.

A Tradition

The Fair is an unquestionable tradition in many lives. "The Sandwich Fair" written in 1983 by Joan Sullivan Whitson takes a humorous look at how important Fair attendance is to some people.

He's up all night walking the floor,
When the sun comes up he's out the door;

No time to eat or comb his hair,
He's on his way to the SANDWICH FAIR.

He never worries about his job,
He's on the phone inviting Nels or Bob,
Work piles up but he don't care,
He's got to go to the SANDWICH FAIR.

I'll get things done the best I can,
By now I really understand,
To ask for help, I wouldn't dare,
To keep my Honey from the SANDWICH FAIR.

Last night I dreamed my tires went flat,
The roof caved in, and we lost our cat,
The bird flew away and the cupboards were bare,
But Don went off to the SANDWICH FAIR.

Most of the time he's a real sweet guy,
So for these five days I'll just get by,
If anything happens I'll want him there,
So I hope I don't die during the SANDWICH FAIR.

It is also a tradition in the family of Marilynn Thompson of Newark. She says, "The Sandwich Fair has always been a highlight of the year. We plan our vacations around it. The only time I remember missing it was when our daughter was born. But our family was represented as my husband showed hogs before he came to get us at the hospital."

For Raymond Knutson and his new bride Margaret Whitfield of Sandwich, the Fair became a tradition the first few days of their

Memory—Don Riemensnider

In 1929 when Don Riemensnider was six years old, he went to the Fair with money he had been saving for weeks—probably seventy-five cents. He recalls

It was 9 a. m., and we were on our way to the fair, five miles away. Mother had already fixed fried chicken, potato salad, baked beans, cookies, cake, and coolers of lemonade. Extra blankets were taken so we could sit on the grass. My father was dressed in white duck pants with white shirt and black tie and had on a sailor-type straw hat. My, what a proud looking German man, as he drove our 1928 green Studebaker car with a yellow strip. My mother was dressed in her Sunday best, a long skirt and hat of that time. I sat in front in the middle, and my father was telling me not to wiggle.

In the back seat were my two sisters Ruth and Irene, all in their Sunday best. Also in the back seat was our hired man George Jessel who had worked for our family all his life. George came from Germany and passed through Ellis Island.

As we neared Sandwich, the flag man waved us across the railroad tracks as there were no gates or signals. While we waited in line to enter the fairground, we could see the colorful tents and flags and could hear the buzz of the people and the music of the merry-go-round. I could hardly wait.

We always parked back of King and Sons Monuments because Kenneth King was my uncle. Later in the day, members of our family would gather to eat dinner with them. My father and George had to hurry to get to the draft horse show. Ruth and Irene, with a promise to be back at one o'clock for dinner, went looking for games and rides and boys. That left Mother and me. We met Mother's sister, my Aunt Florence King, and her two boys who were one and two years older than I was. We were such good friends, my city cousins and me, and we were allowed to go on our own.

We rode the whip, the chair-o-plane and the Ferris wheel that took you so high in the sky and then down like you were falling. My, what a ride! Then we had sweet soda, caramel corn, and hot dogs; and it was time for our picnic dinner back at King's Monuments. Mother and Dad, Aunt Florence and Uncle Kenneth, other aunts and uncles, and my grandparents were there and had set up card tables with lots of food. Funny, my cousins and I were not hungry.

After a brief rest, we were ready to go again, but we were out of money. So we went to see the sheep, pigs, chickens, cows, and other things that were free. At last I found my dad, and he gave me money for a couple more rides. Then we went back to King's for supper. After eating and talking of the fair, we went to the amphitheater where the band in their colorful uniforms was playing stirring songs. There were the jugglers and the magician that seemed to cut

Don Riemensnider of Somonauk (center) remembers attending the Fair with his parents Pearl and Elmer.

the lady in two. We saw the beautiful people in their pretty costumes performing high in the sky with the bright lights shining on them as they seemed to float in the air.

By this time it had grown very dark, and it was time for the fireworks show. There were many colorful lights that lit up the sky and the big booms that seemed to shake the earth. The last fireworks was that of the American flag. After that it was time to go home.

On the way to the car, we found George who was at the corn game (bingo) where he had won two red blankets. At the dance pavilion were my sisters. Irene had met her boyfriend and was riding home with him. Ruth had met a boy and was allowed to go with him.

Mother, Dad, George, and I went home. I went to bed, but Dad and George still had farm chores to do. After they checked the chickens and gathered the eggs, they fed the pigs and calves. The cows were milked, their udders, big and full from being milked late, but the Sandwich Fair comes only once a year.

Alma Hartman Burson

Alma Hartman Burson was born in March 1894. She attended her first Fair that September with her family, riding in a horse drawn buggy from west of Hinckley. Her memories of traveling to the Fair each autumn are preserved on audio tape.

> We left home early, for you always wanted to be among the first at the fairgrounds and to be close to the grandstand where the harness races were held. On arrival at the fair, I was given twenty-five cents to spend. It cost five cents to ride the merry-go-round, and that's where all of my money went.

> A picnic dinner was brought from home—fried chicken, potato salad, homemade bread and apple pie, all served on china plates. A white linen tablecloth was spread on the grass, and we settled ourselves around it for the delicious meal, visiting back and forth with other families.

> [After she married, she attended the Fair with her husband Norman "Toomy" Burson.] He was quite an athlete and played baseball against visiting teams at the fairgrounds. As he grew older, Dutch Hough asked him to umpire the games. Our family was given a season pass for the fair because of Toomy's officiating at the baseball games.

Walter Palmer

Walter Palmer, who was a favorite in harness racing circles at the Fair in the 1890's [See Chapter 5 "How the Doctor Lost But Won"], was unable to attend the 1917 Fair because he was in the Army. He mailed a poem to a friend in Sandwich; it was published in the *Free Press*, August 30, 1917. He wrote, "I am mailing herewith a few lines that reflect my innermost feelings this lonely Sunday afternoon."

> O, Autumn, bring me back the days
> I dreamed the dreams of a boy,
> Before I learned the world and its ways,
> When life was one round of joy;
> Bring me a vision of old time friends,
> A handshake and how do you do;
> Bring me one hour that made amends
> For the pain of a whole life through;
> Bring me those moments free from care
> And the patter of feet at the score.
> Bring me one day of the old time fair
> I will never ask for more.
> Bring me a tune from the old time band,
> A glimpse of the old time course;
> Bring the applause of the crowded stand
> At it cheers for the winning horse;
> Bring the chicken dinners rare
> Bring all these I say;
> Revive, O, Autumn, your old time fair
> And bring me one, yesterday.
> —Walter Palmer

marriage. They cut their honeymoon short in September 1939 because they didn't want to miss the open-air dances that were held behind the Home Arts building.

Margaret says, "The Sandwich Fair became a family tradition, second only to Christmas." Their sons Stephen and David entered chickens and hogs as 4-H projects; their daughter Mary Ann entered food and clothing. Stephen began entering paintings and Margaret also entered paintings and crafts. Ray entered grain, hay, and vegetables; in later years he entered antique tool collections. Today, the Fair enjoyment extends to their grandchildren who join the family for a traditional day at the Fair.

She remembers the days before the Fair. "[They were] a hectic time for all, getting those entries in, putting tags with the right items, and packing picnic lunches. But the activities provided great fun and wonderful family memories." Margaret continues to work at the Fair every year in the Arts and Crafts building. The work tradition was begun by her grandfather Joseph Calahan who served as Superintendent of Speed in 1889 and 1890.

Robert Schlapp of Aurora, who has been a farmer all his life, is continuing a tradition set by his father Peter. He comes to the Fair every day to visit friends and neighbors. The Fair is also a tradition for Stacy Christian of Yorkville and her husband. They had their first date at the Fair in 1994, and they "wouldn't dream of missing it now!" For Chris Meduesky of New Lenox, the Fair has been a tradition for twenty-five years. "We look forward to it every year."

A family tradition for Kathy Richmond's family of Plano is to meet at the train on Sunday at four o'clock. When her children were teenagers, they would traditionally buy socks at the tent south of the Home Arts building after the train ride.

"It is a tradition—a 'family affair.' It leaves you with many treasured memories," says Lucille Brockman of Marseilles. In her words, "[I] have always come and always will."

Betty Lankers of Bristol comes to the Fair "to remember the sights, sounds, smells, and touches of [her] life growing up on an Iowa farm." She says, "It is a harvest tradition for me."

"Tradition. It's wonderful," says Suzanne Bradbury of Westchester. Her first visit to the Fair was on the train with her aunt and uncle thirty-some years ago. In 1998 she had her sixteen-month-old triplets with her. She says, "I'm

Photo by L.R.

Family and friends relax at the Fair.

bringing them to the Fair every year."

Karen McHugh of Plano says, "It's a lasting tradition that gets better from year to year! It's a time that families and friends take time to be together."

Memories

Mary Shumway of Sandwich remembers the Fair was only three days long in the 1940's and all the surrounding towns dismissed school on Thursday. She says, "We met our friends . . . and we found our new boyfriends. We rode all the rides—Oh, how I did love the Whip and the Octopus—and had many pictures taken." One time she even went to the dime-a-dance. "It surely was the event of the year! We went all polished up. Oh my, we did go home dirty.

Ron Severson of Minooka

When Ron Severson of Minooka was a young lad, Kendall County did not have a fairgrounds so his 4-H Fair was held in Sandwich. The first time he spent the night away from home without his family he slept at the Sandwich fairgrounds. Enjoying the new-found freedom, he says he and other 4-H youths in the same situation didn't see the need to get to bed before sunrise. He recalls, "What a motley crew [we were] the next day."

During another Fair season, he and a group of friends decided to have a party with a couple of six packs of beer in what was the beef tent before the barn was built. He says Fair officials had been through it all before and showed up with police officers when it seemed to be suspiciously loud. Severson retells the story:

> Roger Hadaway and I ducked out the side and made a straight line run for the semi parked along the fence, figuring we would hide out there till things cooled off. It happened to be a stormy night and about halfway from the tent to the truck a tremendous bolt of lighting lit up the area and we were dead ducks.
>
> The next morning we were to be thrown out of the show and a police report written. But as luck would have it, one of our 4-H leaders, Bill Rushton, persuaded the people in charge that we were a couple of irresponsible teenagers, not the Dalton gang, and that he would personally guarantee it would not happen again.
>
> Bill Rushton is gone now and so is our other leader, Dana Cryder, but at that time they were real heroes in my eyes, and it never did happen again. I would not have broken my word to them for all the money in the world.

According to Severson, there is a big difference between the dedicated exhibitors today and some of the exhibitors of his youth. "[Back] then everybody in the neighborhood showed something just to go to the fair and have a good time. If you won, fine, and if you didn't, you had a fun time anyway."

Photo by M.W.

The late WGN radio personality Bob Collins loved the Sandwich Fair. (l. to r.) FFA members Doug Ness, Scott Wallin, Chris Wilson, Amy Testin, and Greg Anderson

237

Courtesy of SFA

Line drawing by Becky Tvrdik Daniels

A Day at the Fair

Hi. Is this your first time at the Fair? I've been coming to the Fair since I was a small child. I'll be glad to show you around.

It's early; let's start with breakfast. Let's see now—they have eggs, bacon, sausage, pancakes, or just coffee. Don't eat too much, or you won't have room for those huge, hot, gooey cinnamon rolls later in the morning.

I hope you're wearing good walking shoes and have a jacket. It's cool the first thing in the morning. We can start with a walk around the grounds. All the tents and buildings are still closed, but it's fun to walk in the comparative quiet and see the activity. The food trucks are making deliveries, and the concessionaires are refilling their booths in readiness for anticipated sales. The grounds have been cleaned up, and the disposal people have been around emptying the refuse containers and treating them with bee spray. All looks spic and span.

Let's go see what's going on in the livestock area. Everyone is already up and grooming their animals. They give their animals showers, blow them dry, and even brush and curl them sometimes. There'll be judging all day for open and junior exhibitors.

If we're lucky, we'll get to see the horses and sulkies when they take them out to exercise or to race. The sulkies are the little two-wheeled carts that are harnessed to the horses; they have a seat on them for the driver. To race them, the owners—who aren't necessarily the drivers—must call into the "speed office" two days ahead of time to sign them up for a particular race. They're put in a class for their age group. They're either trotters or pacers, depending on the way they're trained. If they're trotters, the legs on the same side move in opposite directions. If they're pacers, the legs on the same side move in the same direction.

You would be surprised how much paperwork there is for all the horses. There are big sheets of paper that have histories like our family trees. Each race they run is recorded as to where they race and who the first three winners are. If a horse isn't a winner, it is noted where he placed and how much money he earned. The paper work takes a lot longer than running the race.

Since the chicken house is on our way back to the main grounds, we'll stop there. We won't have to ask where the building is because when we get near it, we'll hear the clucking and crowing. Have you ever seen so many colors and sizes of chickens?

Let's head toward the commercial section where they cater to our real and fanciful desires. There is everything you can imagine—heating equipment, chimney sweeps, movie videos, redwood signs, hand-powered or electric tools, personalized sweatshirts and T-shirts, pots and pans, and . . . well, we can't see it all today. There are almost 300 exhibitors.

Are you ready for one of those giant cinnamon rolls? We can sit in the rest area or at a picnic table and enjoy our snack while we watch the people go by. There's no better place to watch people. Big and little, short and tall, young and old; you'll see them all at the Sandwich Fair.

We should eat a regular meal for lunch. The churches and service organizations have everything from full meals to quick sandwiches. You can find almost any food your heart or stomach desires. No matter what you decide to eat, save some room for ice cream, pie, fudge, popcorn, cream puffs, and eclairs. It might be a good idea to take some of the extras with us to the grandstand for a couple of hours while we enjoy the entertainment there. At least you can rest your weary feet.

Let your food settle before you start on all those rides. Bouncing up and down and twirling around might spoil your afternoon. Maybe you should try your hand at the sideshow games for a while. Who knows; maybe you'll win a stuffed toy, a dish, or a goldfish.

We still haven't been in the buildings with the exhibits. The Horticulture building has samples of the best flowers and crops in the Midwest. There just isn't any fair better than the Sandwich Fair. There are pumpkins that weigh hundreds of pounds—and little-bitty ones too—ears of corn every color and size, and the most unusual collection of gourds and squashes. The apples are so tempting that I'd like to sneak a bite.

Don't get too tired. We still have to go to the Women's Building—as it is called even though men display their talents there too. There are canned vegetables, fruits, pickles, cookies, pies, breads, and the most gorgeously decorated cakes you've ever seen. At the other end of the building there are quilts, afghans, clothes, and all kinds of fancy work. What a tribute to people's pastimes.

Let's go to the next building where we can see the art work and crafts. Did you see the work of the children? It is an eye-opening experience to see what some young people can do—at least they aren't spending *all* their time watching TV.

There's so much to see and do. You can't possibly do it all in one day. Come again tomorrow. Meet me at the Round Office at eight. Remember your comfortable shoes, and you might want to bring an umbrella, but don't worry if it rains; nothing dampens the spirit of the Fair.

Courtesy of SFA

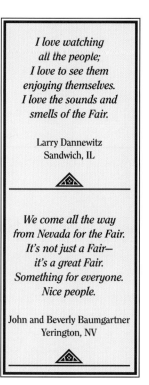

top: Many fairgoers meet at the Home Arts building on Thursday, Homecoming Day, at the Fair.

bottom: Bob Brown, Sr. (l.) known as "Mr. WLBK," broadcast a Noon Show and interviews throughout the day near the front steps of the Home Arts building during the '50's, '60's, and '70's. Pictured on the right is John Riplinger.

There was no blacktopping then."

Joliet resident Dana Bernhard's first visit to the Fair was in 1981. It was the first date with her husband Lanny. "[He] showed me every tractor on display for two hours!" They have attended the Fair every year since.

Becky Kinney of Sandwich says the 1965 Fair is among her most treasured memories.

I was a junior exhibitor, and I entered everything I made that year in 4-H. I couldn't wait to get to the Fair on Wednesday. Back then there were numerous entries; to receive a first or second place was quite an honor, not to mention the prize money that was also important to a 16-year-old. I remember the day like it was yesterday. Mom and Dad were in the Women's Building waiting. I walked up to them and started talking. Dad just smiled and said, "Look." He was pointing to a sign that read, Champion Junior Garment – Becky Thomas, Somonauk. I could hardly believe it; I stood there and cried. My white wool jacket and blue wool skirt had won. I must have checked many times that night to make sure that it had really happened.

Mark Harrington of Batavia says as a boy growing up in the 1960's, he was fascinated with Augie Otto's steam locomotive train ride.

We would race to the front passenger car just so we could watch the man with the bib overalls and striped railroad hat stoke the coal tender. Once the wheels clicked along the rail sections, we watched intensely as it

hugged the curves. The bell and whistle added to the reality of the intriguing moment. After every Fair I would go home and watch my own Lionel train belch out its smoke and shine its light down the track, just like Augie's. It was like having my own Sandwich Fair all year long until next September.

The Sandwich Fair has been a regular event for Lloyd Larson of Earlville since 1935. He remembers the first time he attended the Fair: "I was nine. It was a cloudy, misty day." He stood looking through a picket fence, watching the draft-horse pulling contest. "As they were pulling, someone in the audience clapped real loud; the team stopped. Needless to say the M. C. was not too happy."

Elsie Campbell of Sandwich remembers that her dad was in charge of transporting the fat lady of the carnival from the train to the fairgrounds. He picked her up in his truck because she was too big to ride in a car.

Leonard "Gus" Gustafson of Sandwich remembers when his mother Olive played the piano outside the Home Arts building. In the 1950's and 1960's she played for Wurlitzer on WLBK every day at noon for thirty minutes.

Fair Secretary and Superintendent of Ticket Sales Nancy Lou Rex says, One of the most exciting days of the year for me is still the Wednesday after Labor Day, opening day of another Sandwich Fair. I wake up early in the morning thinking about all the happy fairgoers coming to Sandwich, Illinois, for a good time. I love unlocking the Main Gate, dragging it open, and seeing

Courtesy of BF

Courtesy of SFA

top: Nettle Creek school children at the Fair, circa 1982; (l. to r.) Ryan Florey, Shawn Oelschlager, Matt Haage, parent Jan Torkelson, three unknown children, teacher Donna Kirkpatrick, Danny Eller, Abbie Cutler

bottom: On September 4, 1998, Spike and Donna Loux Johnson were married on the Ferris wheel at the Fair. (clockwise lower left) Grant Burkhart, attendants Keith and Nan Burkhart, Rev. David Kaul of Sandwich, Spike and Donna.

opposite page: Photo credits appear in Chapter 11.

Courtesy of S.D.J.

the smiling fairgoers roll into the fair-grounds for the start of another Sandwich Fair.

In fifty years Victor Stott of Yorkville, who grew up in Newark, has missed the Fair only one year; that was while he was in Vietnam. He remembers "strutting around the grounds" with his high school friends in their letterman jackets. Other memories include twenty years of the children in front of the big pumpkin display.

Ronald Clark, Jr. of Yorkville comes to the Fair every day. In 1988 when his father was 85 years old, he and his brother and his father spent a whole day at the fair—eating, talking, riding rides, and looking! He says, "It was one of the best days of our lives!" Now that his dad is gone, "It's a wonderfully happy memory!"

Memories of the Fair for Larry Bradham of Earlville go back to his school days in Sandwich. "As a child I thought of the Sandwich Fair as the most important event of my childhood." In the 1960's he worked in the church food build-ing so he could spend more time at the Fair. He says, "The Sandwich Fair is the only fair I go to!" He comes to relive his childhood.

Spike and Donna Loux Johnson said their marriage vows on the gondola Ferris wheel on September 4, 1996. Rev. David Kaul officiated. Theirs was the first wedding at the Fair. It was videotaped for television and a radio station interviewed them.

School Children

The gates are open! It's important for every-one to attend the Fair—especially the school chil-dren! Beginning as early as 1889, the *Somonauk Reveille* indicated school closings: "The school was closed on Wednesday to give children an opportunity to attend the fair at Sandwich, that day having been set apart by the association as children's day."

Again in 1891: "Our public school was closed Wednesday and Thursday affording the teachers and pupils an opportunity to attend the fair." In 1896 *Sandwich Argus* reported, "School was kept only Monday and Tuesday this week so as to give the scholars an opportunity of attend-ing the fair."

Long-time Sandwich resident Millie Carter remembers, "The schools would close down, and they'd be out at the Fair from 6 a.m. to 6 p.m." Although it is uncertain if the schools closed in 1948, the September 16 issue of the *Sandwich Free Press* indicated that there was some break in the school schedule for the Fair: "Now—the 61st fair is history, the children have gone back to school, the vacation days are over so we'll all have to settle down into the busy routine of the fall and winter programs."

Michelle Geihn of Aurora used to come to the Fair with her Sandwich elementary class and Miss Hall, the music teacher who taught them a special song for the Fair. Today she still enjoys corn dogs, lemonade, and train rides at the Fair—with her children.

Former Sandwich resident Eleni Filippi of Yorkville remembers the "agony" of being in school on opening day of the Fair.

> While sitting in my fourth grade class during a warm September day, the open windows told me *it's Fair time!* It wasn't the sounds that enticed us 8- and 9-year-olds—it was the *smells*.
>
> They floated across town to Woodbury School, made us squirm in our seats, and dream of foot-long hot dogs, lemon shake-ups, nachos, pronto pups, candy apples, ice-cream cones, homemade pies, spaghetti, buttery corn on the cob, tempura, taffy, popcorn and purple, pink, blue, and yellow cotton candy.
>
> The sweet aromas wafted more than 20 blocks—just to torture us kids. Luckily, when I was in grade school, there were shortened classes during

241

I've been coming to the Fair since I was a child. I love the quilts, cake decorating, taffy, cinnamon rolls, corn dogs, and lemonade shake-ups. My husband Terry and I visit annually with our children to carry on the tradition.

Kathy MacKenzie
La Grange Park, IL

My grandmother Maude Converse won a plaque at the Fair for being the oldest person at the Fair one day in the 1970's. I have been coming to the Fair since 1942. I really love the Fair. It's the best.

Patricia Keierleber
Sandwich, IL

top and bottom right: Political candidates are well represented at the Fair.

previous pages: Courtesy of SFA
pages 242-243: Before the Farm Zoo was established, children were mesmerized by baby pigs in the swine barn.

Fair week. So I could make it to the Fair by three o'clock and satisfy my taste buds with the foods whose smells had distracted me all morning.

Even now—18 years later and miles away—I can close my eyes and smell the Fair.

Beginning in 1998, Sandwich schools no longer had early dismissal for the entire student body during Fair week. However, many school groups schedule field trips to the Fair to participate in activities developed by the Fair's Education Committee, and several area schools continue to excuse students for the Fair if they are involved in FFA programs.

Politicians at the Fair

Politicians are fairgoers too. They come to enjoy the activities as well as to support their political parties. In 1892 Congressman Steward came to the Fair as a participant, and he received a first premium on a fine stallion. Other politicians came to the Fair to make scheduled speeches at the grandstand.

In 1896 according to the Sandwich *Argus*, the speeches at the Fair were "of an unusually high order." Honorable Isaac Clements, a representative for the Republican Party, spoke on Tuesday. Clarence Darrow was scheduled to speak for the Democratic Party on Wednesday; however a recap of the Fair listed Dr. H. Taylor as the speaker. On Thursday, "an admirable

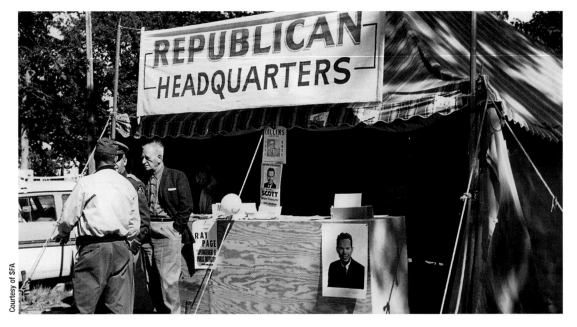

address" was given in favor of full citizenship for women.

The news article does leave some questions as to how many people actually attended the speeches. Some fairgoers apparently had other interests. The *Argus* wrote, "It was impossible to drag many fair visitors from the enchantments of the swing and lemonade long enough to hear."

In 1902 States Attorney A. G. Kennedy and his wife from DeKalb spent two days at the Fair. It was noted in the *Argus* that A. G. held the reins over a "handsome pair of cream roadsters." In 1909 former Representative George M. Tindall of Sugar Grove was at the Fair, and it was noted that he would like another term in the House. Representative Adam Cliffe was also at the Fair in 1909.

In 1923 U.S. Senator Medill McCormick spoke at the grandstand on Thursday about the "Conditions in Europe." There wasn't any charge for grandstand seats to hear the senator.

The custom of designating political days at the Fair existed in the 1930's. In 1934 all of the Democratic candidates spoke in front of the amphitheatre on Thursday. The main speaker of the day was Michael Igoe. A picnic dinner was arranged for 11 o'clock. Friday was Republican Day with former State's Attorney General Oscar Carlstrom as the main speaker.

In 1936 on Wednesday, the Democrats speaking from the judges stand included those running for coroner, state's attorney, and congressman. The principal speaker for the Republican Party on Friday was C. Wayland Brooks, candidate for governor. Naturally, State Representative Henry White, who served as a legislator from 1937 until 1947, was at the Fair—he was a Fair director from 1925 to 1966. Dennis Collins also attended the Fair regularly. He served as State Representative from 1931 to 1943 and as State Senator from 1943 to 1973.

In later years politicians offered services to fairgoers. In 1971 Secretary of State John W. Lewis was at the Fair with a mobile unit where visitors could get information about renewing their drivers licenses, observe a demonstration of vision-testing equipment, and get applications for license plates.

Fair Association President Carlton "Dutch" Hough gave Governor Richard Ogilvie a tour of the grounds in 1972. Secretary of Agriculture Earl Butz told listeners before the Tractor Pull in 1974 not to complain about the cost of products such as milk but to consider the price of soda pop and a six pack of beer. He said if

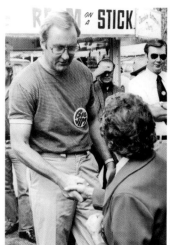

top left: U.S. Secretary of Agriculture Earl Butz drew a large crowd when he spoke in 1974.

top right: Governor James Thompson often attended the Fair.

middle left: Jean and Duane Johnson of Somonauk visit with Congressman Denny Hastert.

bottom: Governor Stratton, Judge Latham Castle, and Senator Paul Simon talk to fairgoers in front of the Horticulture building.

people thought about what they purchased, there would be no food shortages. Governor James Thompson visited frequently in the 1970's and 1980's.

Speaker of the House J. Dennis Hastert (R) 14th District has been a frequent political visitor to the Fair since the 1980's. Even as a child, Hastert spent time at the Fair with his father who had a commercial booth for his feed business.

Courtesy of SF

Early fairgoers crowded around the baseball field to watch the air show.

Traveling to the Fair

An anonymous contributor in one stanza of the poem "Sandwich Fair, 1938" encouraged attendees to get to the Fair early and meet their friends:

So let's get up bright and early
And go there and see the display
And meet all our friends that we know
From near and from far away.
—September 1, 1938
Sandwich Free Press

This 1938 author probably didn't realize the truth of the last line—From near and from far away. When the poem was written, hundreds of miles may have seemed "far away"; whereas today "far away" may mean thousands of miles. Louis and Berdeane Wagner put up three maps—Illinois, world, and US—in the Horticulture building in 1958 for Fair visitors to pinpoint their hometowns. Each year, at least 20 to 30 people from foreign countries mark their home-lands. One year, forty-eight of the fifty states were represented.

The following lines are from the poem "Sandwich Fair, 1930" by Mrs. Chas. Arnold.

The friends we met upon the grounds
And those from far away,
Some we hadn't seen for years

That we saw there each day.
—September 4, 1930
Sandwich Free Press

Judy Popp of Somonauk agrees that is one of the reasons she comes to the Fair. "It's a chance to see old friends and neighbors that you see only once a year. We get caught up on each other's lives and families."

And I think if you do travel
To the fairs this fall
You'll find the good old Sandwich Fair
Just up and beats them all.
—September 4, 1930
Sandwich Free Press

Thirty-seven years later, Jess King shared Mrs. Arnold's opinion in his editorial printed in August 3, 1967, *DeKalb Daily Chronicle.* He encouraged area residents to go to the Sandwich Fair. King, who had attended the 1933 World's Fair, the Montreal Expo in 1967, and numerous other fairs advised readers to avoid the large fairs because they were for those who liked to stand in lines, had loose pocketbooks, oodles of patience, and the herd instinct. In his opinion, local residents didn't need to travel far for a good fair. They had the best fair—the Sandwich Fair—in their own backyard. King said, "It is a gala that I can understand, handle, and pay for." As Mrs. Arnold said, "[It] Just up and beats them all."

The mode of travel to the Fair has changed. In 1891 visitors rode on horses or in wagons and buggies. The *Free Press* printed, "Thursday morning hardly got here soon enough to head off the people, for teams from miles away began to show up around town and on the grounds about as soon as the sun was up and each one brought its load of people. How they came."

Special excursion trains were a popular and convenient way to travel to and from the Fair. In 1896 passenger coaches were attached to freight trains for those who lived east of Sandwich. For excursion rates, they stopped between Sandwich and Aurora.

In 1899, 1900, and 1902, Thursday was Aurora Day at the Fair. Special trains ran from Aurora accompanied by bands, the Aurora Military Band in 1899 and Goddard's Band the other years.

Sycamore Day

For the 1902 Fair, Friday was Sycamore Day. The *Free Press* printed,

> At ten o'clock the special train from Sycamore arrived with nearly nine hundred people and with them the famous National Sewing Machine Band of Belvidere. Headed by the band the entire party formed in line and marched to the groudds [sic]. Sycamore certainly did nobly and the visitors received a royal welcome from Sandwich.

Sycamore Day was Thursday in 1903. Again, a big crowd traveled to Sandwich on the train accompanied by the Belvidere band. Eleven hundred people wearing "Sycamore" badges arrived about eleven o'clock. A large number of school children were in the group. The *Argus* reported,

> After getting off the cars the visitors, headed by their band, marched south to Railroad Street, then west to Main Street, then north to Center Street, then west to the Fair ground where they enjoyed the various attractions, a look at the good stock, a game of ball, and watched the horses go round, leaving for home about 6:30 in the evening.

After a day filled with many activities, their return walk to the train stop was probably a little slower than their arrival.

Thursday was again Sycamore Day in 1904. The *Free Press* reported that a big crowd would be coming on the train. "For years past the merchants and business men of the county capitol [sic] have made this a special day for an outing and to visit with friends at the south end of the county."

In 1905 a special train "large enough to carry all with comfort [ran] to Sandwich by way of Aurora. . . ." The fare was $1.50 round trip. According to the August 24, 1905, *Free Press,* the train ran from Kirkland to Wilkinson, on to Sycamore and from there to DeKalb and over the new I.I.& M. road to Aurora, connecting with the Burlington road. Several weeks prior to the Fair, the *Sycamore True Republican* noted that

Courtesy of SFA

The Sandwich High School band led the way to the fairgrounds from Gletty Road railroad crossing in the 1960's.

247

Photo by J.A.

top: In 1984 fairgoers arrived on the train and walked to the Fair from the Gletty Road crossing.

previous pages: Courtesy of B.H.
pages 248-249: Horse and buggy parking, circa 1897

bottom: A 1974 Midway scene

We loved the FFA petting zoo and the cows getting baths!

Mrs. Russell's Class
Leland Grade School
Leland, Illinois

I like the Sandwich Fair because I get to ride all the rides. I also get to see and pet the farm animals. Love the food! My grandma went for over 80 years, and my parents have taken me my whole life too.

Jessica Noll, student
Sandwich, Illinois

Elephant Ears, Tempura, Fay's Barbecue and all the fuzzy farm animals to look at and pet.

John Walter
Aurora, Illinois

the citizens at the Commercial Club had discussed efforts to make Sycamore Day "more of a success than ever before." Business and professional men were asked to close their shops on Thursday.

Sycamore's efforts were helpful in making the 1905 Fair the best Fair to date. The *Free Press* reported, "They came by train loads, wagons, carriages, and automobiles. Billie's train from the west [named for the popular conductor] unloaded nearly five hundred people. The special from Sycamore four hundred and the west bound trains added hundreds to the mighty throng."

In 1910 and 1911 eastbound trains ran every day; in 1910 Billie's train departed westbound at 6:48 with extra coaches. In 1912 the printed schedule showed the train leaving Sandwich at 8 p.m. and arriving in Plano at 8:09 p.m. and on to Aurora by 8:40 p.m.

Reminiscing about the Fair in 1976, Lorene Stinson, daughter of Charles Stinson, who served as Fair Secretary from 1901 to 1940, recalled some special services that were provided for the safety of fairgoers and to insure the good reputation of the Fair. She said that her father told her a Chicago detective met the excursion trains in Sandwich. It was his job to "spot the hoodlums and tell them to get back on the train."

In 1963 the Blackhawk Chapter of the

National Railway Historical Society arranged a special excursion train from Chicago "To the Best Country Fair in the State"! Included in the $10 adult fare was round-trip rail fare from Chicago to Geneva, charter bus seat from Geneva to Sandwich, admission to the Fair, one ride on Augie Otto's miniature train, and admission to the grandstand for the Demolition Derby.

The CB&Q Railroad made traveling to the Fair easier in 1963, 1964, and 1965 when special trains ran from Chicago on Saturday and Sunday. Sharen Gerlick of Somonauk, a drum majorette for Sandwich High School band, remembers that she and members rode on at least one of the trips into Union Station to play for the visitors prior to their boarding the train to the Fair. When they arrived at the "fairground crossing," the band led thousands of visitors on the two-block march to the fairgrounds—just in time for lunch. They departed at 5 p.m.

Attendance

It is difficult to determine *exactly* how many people attend the Fair each year because in addition to single admissions purchased, some fairgoers buy season and exhibitor tickets. There are also special rates for children on Wednesday, and children ages five and younger are admitted free. Vendors receive Credential Passes, and the Fair

Photo by J.A.

top: The Fair in 1948

bottom: Inclement weather does not discourage fairgoers.

Association also issues a limited number of other passes.

Local newspapers reported attendance numbers some years. The *Somonauk Reveille* reported in 1891 that Thursday was the biggest day ever known in the history of the Fair: "Fully ten thousand people were on the grounds in the afternoon." *The Free Press* estimated the number to be as high as 12,000 on Thursday with an overall total of 20,000 to 25,000 for all four days. The *Hinckley Review* reported, "The Sandwich Fair was a great success. The attendance was phenomenally large. Our Hinckley and Waterman people turned out almost solid."

The 1905 Fair broke all attendance records. Attendance was conservatively estimated at 15,000 on Thursday. The *Free Press* reported

> As usual Thursday was the big day. People passed through the big gates like corn out of the spout of a Sandwich Dustless Cylinder Sheller. Crowds were in every place and everywhere. Not a shady spot anywhere upon the grounds was unoccupied. Hardly before the sun had appeared in the eastern skies people began to arrive. Every avenue leading to Sandwich was crowded. Never was there such a crowd seen here.

The biggest day of the Fair in 1930 was Thursday. According to the *Somonauk Reveille,* ". . . a crowd estimated at 15,000 people surged through the gates. . . ." In 1937 for the three-day Fair the approximate attendance on Wednesday was 3,500, on Thursday between 13,000 and 14,000 and Friday 1,800. The 54th Fair in 1941 also had a big turnout with approximately 25,000 visitors on the grounds.

The first time estimated attendance at a Sandwich Fair exceeded 200,000 was at the 100th Sandwich Fair in 1987. During the 1990's, attendance was 160,000 to 190,000 with the exception of 1997 when an estimated 205,000 people attended the Fair during five days of beautiful Sandwich Fair weather. Attendance at a Sandwich Fair reflects another relationship the Fair has with agriculture since the success of a Sandwich Fair is quite dependent on the weather.

Weather

Researching the weather of Fair week is time-consuming but relatively easy because almost every news story dealing with the event begins with a weather report. A year-by-year chronicle looks like this: rain, rain, rain, sunshine, rain, rain, wind, rain, sunshine, etc. Such a list may seem mundane, but it clearly shows that it usually rains one or two days during the Fair; sometimes attendance is affected, but the spirit of fairgoers is never dampened.

When there was sunshine, the weather was usually summed up in a few sentences saying that the good weather helped make the Fair a success. However, when inclement weather interfered with scheduled Fair events, the wind and rain received columns of coverage, sometimes even more than the planned programs

Sandwich Free Press

During the 1958 tornado, the poultry house was completely demolished when a tree smashed through the roof and supports.

received.

For example, the weather for the 1895 Fair was favorable; the Sandwich *Argus* succinctly reported: "Monday was a beautiful day. . . ." However, when stormy weather postponed the activities of the 1898 Fair, the *Free Press* coverage read like a melodrama with the fairgoers as the heroes and the weatherman as the villain.

The rain Tuesday night was a blessing for the one on Wednesday night was a heart breaker. Hicks, the St. Louis weather prophet, was all right in his predictions this time. There were many unkind things said about him and the weather he was giving us.

Those who had the success of the fair at heart, stood around in the wet grass and muddy roads on Thursday morning and wondered how great the wreck would be. It had the appearance of a disastrous ending.

Wednesday's races had to be postponed until Saturday. The track was wet and soft. Had the rain ended here the damage would not have been so great. But on Tuesday night the rain fell fast and furious. Someone remarked that it rained without a cloud in the sky. Another said "even the stars are leaking."

Thursday morning the clouds had given off all they had, and the sun again peeped out, half ashamed of himself for his long absence. But it was too late for Thursday.

People, in spite of the threatening weather, commenced early in the morn-

ing to gather at the grounds, and at two o'clock there were fully six thousand people on the ground. The races were off and it was too late for the association to provide any entertainment. The big crowd put in the time going from one exhibit to another and back again, sought some dry place and then visited, and talked about the weather and the prospects for Friday.

For the 1915 Fair the *Free Press* reported that the weather was "grouchy," and the prospects of record-breaking crowds were unfavorable. Late Wednesday afternoon a heavy windstorm swept the vicinity followed by a heavy rain on Thursday morning, but it was mild compared to the 1917 rain that shut down the Fair.

The 1917 rain began as a blessing because it drove the farmers out of the fields and to the Fair, but when the rain didn't stop, the Fair finally closed early on the last day. The *Free Press* printed,

As usual the rain jinx struck this section just at the time when everyone was hoping that the weather man would dish out a week of good weather for the Sandwich Fair. The entire week, excepting Thursday, was more or less threatening. On Monday it rained a good share of the day. On Tuesday the weather aspect looked brighter, but early Wednesday morning the storm clouds threatened again to break loose; however, the sun soon dissipated the clouds.

On Wednesday night the storm king again broke loose, accompanied [sic] by lightning, thunder and a veritable deluge of rain, and visions of record breaking attendance at the fair on Thursday faded from the minds of the people of this vicinity, but this rain proved of great benefit to the fair, as on account of the rain farmers were unable to thresh, and hundreds who would have remained at home had it not rained, attended the fair.

The sun came up clear and bright Thursday morning and people began arriving early, until by noon a crowd estimated at about fourteen thousand was in attendance, and over two thousand automobiles were parked about the large grounds, besides there were hundreds of horse and buggy rigs hitched under the trees. It was a beautiful day, and the large croud [sic] enjoyed the program to the fullest extent.

The Sandwich fair was stopped on Friday by a heavy rain that began falling early that morning and continued well into that day. The directors were undecided whether to continue the fair over until Saturday. After dinner, seeing no prospects of a clear up and an opportunity to get the track in proper shape for races on Saturday the directors declared the fair off.

The weather for the 1921 Fair was pleasant; the *Free Press* scripted a bright picture of the grounds and the events:

The weather man either lost his dates or was making a special effort to make Sandwich fair week an ideal one, and he succeeded beyond his expectations. The rain of Sunday night was just what was needed to put the cap sheaf on to make the fair a success. The mornings dawned cloudy, but with little or no indications of rain and before the noon hour the clouds drifted away to be supplanted by a bright September sun. And it was not long before the spacious grounds were filled with automobiles and people.

According to the *Somonauk Reveille*, rainy weather interfered with the races and baseball games for the 1926 Fair:

Rain and threatening weather put

Photo by V.G.

a crimp in the Sandwich fair. . . . The grounds were not fit for the ball game so [they were] declared off early. Toward noon when it was seen that the track could not be put in shape it was decided that the races would also be declared off.

The grounds were in bad shape to get around on account of the heavy rain early Wednesday morning and only a few spectators ventured out. The owners of concession stands and the attractions on the midway were very blue Wednesday.

The show went on for the 1941 Fair in spite of the poor weather; the *Free Press* reported that "Thursday evening Bill Carlsen's band entertained under difficulties during the terrific rainstorm."

The 1948 Fair came close to being washed

top: Strong winds also damaged the New Idea pavilion in 1974.

bottom: An overview of the grounds shows the extensive flooding in the 1980's.

Courtesy of SFA

Courtesy of SFA

A closer view of the flooding shows stranded cars.

out. The *Somonauk Reveille* reported, "Wednesday was one awful day and very few braved the rain to venture into the sodden grounds (we have it on authority that only $22 was taken in at the gate Wednesday) but Thursday and the last days of the week made up for the disappointments of Wednesday."

The major weather news of 1958 didn't occur during the Fair, but it was probably the most talked about subject at the Fair that year because the aftermath of an August 15 tornado was still visible on the grounds. Thanks to crews of volunteers from DeKalb County as well as surrounding counties who helped clean up the wreckage, the Fair opened on time. They removed over thirty fallen trees, the old poultry house, and a food stand, as well as repaired several livestock barns. The devastation created a spectacle. One Sandwich resident took time to count the cars that drove into town to view the disaster:

> In a period of three hours from 6:30 to 9:30 p.m. [on Friday] he counted 1,616 cars coming from the west on the Fairgrounds road. Sunday afternoon from 3 p.m. to 6 p.m. he counted 1,345 cars coming from the same direction.
>
> Sunday night he checked for an

hour and one-half from 7:30 to 9:00 p.m. and checked 605 coming in on that road.

The weather for the 1962 Fair was near perfect. The *Sandwich Free Press* reported that "The weather man was in a generous mood as temperatures under a sunny sky were in the comfortable low 70's." It rained one day but not enough to interfere with any of the activities. Fair officials were happy that the weather for the 1963 Fair was also uneventful, no wind or rain.

On the other hand, good weather was not the forecast for the 1965 Fair; two weeks prior to opening day, the area received fifteen inches of rain. Fair officials were concerned about the "swampy" condition of the grounds and some questioned whether to open as usual on Wednesday since it had rained on Monday and Tuesday of Fair week as well. Unwilling to surrender to the rain, Fair officials worked to accommodate the crowds who hoped the Fair would open as scheduled. They spread nearly 300 tons of gravel throughout the grounds. Carnival rides had to be winched into place using a line truck the Fair Association had purchased from a local electric company.

To add to the existing soggy problems, it rained an additional three inches early Thursday morning turning roadways into soft, gooey muck. It was estimated that there was two feet of water in the midway area. To avoid further problems, Fair officials prohibited parking on the grounds to everyone except workers and commercial vendors. The Fair Association hired two large tractors from McAllister Implement across from the fairgrounds anticipating they would have to pull cars out of the mud.

The downpour didn't discourage fairgoers; however, they arrived with their raincoats, boots, and umbrellas. They parked on both sides of the road leading to the grounds all the way from the cemetery west of Somonauk Creek into Sandwich, and on all the side streets, and then they walked half a mile or more to the entrance gate. Once they were on the grounds, there were enough buildings for them to duck into out of the rain. Although gate receipts were down every day except Sunday, Fair officials said revenues were within $2,000 of the previous year's largest gate receipts.

In 1992, Fair officials worried that they might relive 1965. On opening day a downpour resulted in a record low of 800 ticket sales. Finally the Fair had to shut down Wednesday afternoon because of waterlogged parking areas and lightning. Fair office Secretary Audrey Hoffman told a DeKalb *Daily Chronicle* reporter that workers were using six-inch hoses to suck up the water. Trucks hauled away eleven tankers full of water from the fairgrounds. Fortunately, sunny skies appeared on Thursday, and fairgoers lined up on the grounds.

Even though bad weather makes good conversation, Fair officials are always hopeful they won't have to deal with the inconveniences of rain. They are content to reminisce about 1965, the wettest year, and 1917 and 1992, the years the Fair shut down because of rain.

Admission Costs

In 1898 when a loaf of bread cost five cents, a single-admission ticket cost seven times more— 35 cents. That did not include the admission cost of a horse, which was 25 cents or the cost of a double team, which was 50 cents. Admission rose to 40 cents in 1916 and to 50 cents in 1925. During the Depression general admission dropped to an all-time low of 25 cents in 1932 and finally recovered to 50 cents in 1945. The price of admission rose again in 1951–to 60 cents.

Courtesy of SFA

Though times were prosperous, admission prices held steady for 15 years until 1966. At that time general admission rose to 75 cents—in retrospect that's only a penny a year! Since the 1971 one-dollar admission cost, prices have risen gradually. For the 2000 Fair, a single admission was five dollars, which included parking—in comparison to the price of a loaf of bread, not bad.

Admission prices for children have always been a reduced rate, ranging from 15 cents to two dollars. In 1944 men and women of the armed forces in uniform were admitted free. In 1947 Saturday was Veterans Day; all veterans in uniform or those presenting cards or buttons were admitted to the grounds free. Other spe-cial rates include Senior Citizens who are admitted on Thursday until 5 p.m. for a reduced rate.

Meeting the Needs of Increased Attendance

As attendance increased, so did the need to expand some of the facilities and services to accommodate the crowds. Dealing with the increased attendance has always been a priority of the Board of Directors. As far back as 1892 the Somonauk Windmill company had to supply two hundred extra barrels of water for the growing attendance.

Over the years the first aid facilities and fire protection have been improved; full-time police officers and night watchmen have been hired. For fairgoers' convenience, church services, an information site, more restrooms and rest areas, and organized garbage collection and parking have been added. The Education Committee has expanded to include field trips for school children; the Livestock Department saw a need to include a farm zoo and tours of the livestock barns.

In 1978 Secretary Louis P. Brady said, "We need more places for the people to eat and more place for them to sit." Ironically the Fair Association had to hire more people to handle more people.

First Aid at the Fair

Blisters, bee stings, upset stomachs, headaches, sunburns, minor cuts, weakness, and fatigue. Does this call for a bottle of snake oil? Not hardly. The competent staff of the First Aid Station is on duty to provide necessary relief for fairgoers. Sometimes the cure is as simple as a smile and a cool drink of water. At other times, more advanced medical attention is provided until the fairgoer can be transferred to a local hospital.

As early as 1918, there was aid for fairgoers. A Red Cross tent was located at the east end of the Industrial Hall. The staff was "equipped to meet any emergency." They were also "prepared to take care of the hungry, being ready with the finest kind of good things to eat." They were supported by income from the lunch stand and donations: $467 from the lunch stand; $178.20 from Mrs. Spickerman who sold her plants and cut flower exhibits; $48.90 from pony rides; $6 from bus fares to the fairgrounds collected by

bottom: For the convenience of fairgoers, a first aid station is staffed by nurses and EMT's.

Photo by S.C.

right: Security officers patrol the grounds in golf carts.

bottom: Law enforcement officer Roger Scott

Photo by V.G.

256

Wieman and Werner; and $6 from A. B. Howard from the sale of his chickens.

In 1923 a local paper reported that Miss Rebecca Lockwood was in charge of the emergency tent. In the 1940's Fair Director Don Stahl remembers Sutherland's Funeral Home providing an ambulance. He and Robert "Bertie" Sutherland were the attendants. In 1945 the area Nurses Club had a first aid station. Florence Dannewitz and Wilma "Pete" Fanning were two of the nurses who worked at the station.

Thompson's Children's Shop sponsored a baby clinic. The September 8, 1948, issue of the *Sandwich Free Press* gave more details about this service: "First housed in a tent now housed in a screened building supplied by the Fair Association is the fine place where mothers can let their babies rest in cribs and beds and where first aid can be administered in case of an accident or sudden illness."

In 1970 Civil Defense members and an occasional nurse, under the direction of Earl Tapp, were in charge of the First Aid Station. They worked out of the back of an old, converted bread truck that was backed in under a tent. This arrangement worked for a few years until Fair Director Kenneth Klotz proposed that the current building be erected. A year after it was built, a restroom was installed, making it the first facility on the grounds with a flush toilet.

In 1974 the first, newly trained Emergency Medical Technicians (EMT's) from DeKalb, Kendall, and LaSalle counties and Sandwich Hospital nurses volunteered their services. Kathy Adrian Haggard, RN, coordinated the functions of the building in conjunction with the DeKalb County Ambulance Association. In 1979 Barbara "Boots" Hoffman, RN, became coordinator.

The Emergency Medical Service continues to be housed in the same building surrounded by the Sheriff Department, Sandwich Fire Department, and Round Office. After the DeKalb County Ambulance Association dissolved, area EMT's continued to volunteer their services.

Presently, the free emergency care is a joint effort of the Sandwich Fair Association, Valley West Hospital (formerly Sandwich Community Hospital until 1998), Sandwich Ambulance Service, and area EMT's and RN's.

Photo by G.S.

Police

There is early evidence that police officers were hired to make sure there was no gambling on the grounds, but the 1966 Fair marked the presence of the first full-time police service for the Fair. Off-duty sheriff's deputies were employed by the Fair to provide security during Fair hours. Three men with Sergeant George Shaw in charge made up the detail. Shaw was in charge from 1966 through 1980 when Lt. Roger Scott, the present sheriff, took over. Scott was in charge from 1981 to 1985. Lt. Kevin Hickey commanded from 1986 to 1992, and in 1993 Sgt. Al Newby took charge.

In 1966 the Fair had three sheriffs on duty each day. By 1999 that number increased to four sheriffs on duty during the day and ten to fifteen at night on the weekend. The Fair pays these officers for regular-duty time; on their off-duty hours they volunteer. Their primary duties are to provide crowd safety, grandstand security, and ticket office security and to help find lost children. In 1999 a bicycle patrol enabled the sheriffs to move through the crowds more easily.

The sheriffs are assisted by the Sheriff's Auxiliary, a volunteer organization that directs traffic entering at the Main Gate. They also unlock cars, find cars, and assist the sheriffs in any way they can. The Sheriff's Radio Watch is another volunteer organization that directs traffic entering at the West Gate. The third volunteer organization, Sandwich ESDA, is headed by Don Frederick. ESDA's job is to direct traffic that enters and exits the city of Sandwich. They have people stationed at the stoplights, key intersections, and other places to keep the traffic moving. These three volunteer groups help free the sheriff's police from traffic duties.

Night Watchmen

In 1952 Ray Fox, a farmer from Somonauk, was selected to be the first night watchman for the Fair. That same year, he persuaded Bernell Rhodes, another farmer from Somonauk, to work with him. Their job was to patrol the grounds and call the fire department if they saw any fires. They also called the police if they found any security problems like theft or fighting.

The watchmen worked from 6 p.m. to 6 a.m. patrolling the grounds on foot. On Friday night two more people worked, concentrating mostly on the Junior Fair. Bernell Rhodes recalls Ray Fox liked to walk on the grass instead of the gravel so the noise wouldn't disturb people who were sleeping.

In 1960 Ray's son John took over the night-watch duties. He still heads the crew today. As the fairgrounds increased, the Fair hired more watchmen. In 1990 there were eight watchmen; in 1999 there were 14. Not all the men work the whole five days of the Fair. Some work only the weekends when the crowds are largest.

The watchmen's duties today are much the same as they were in 1952. They close the gates at night, assist people, monitor people entering the grounds after hours, and watch for fires and security problems. One big change that took place in the 1990's was the use of golf carts to enable the crew to patrol a larger area more easily.

Fire Protection

From the early days of the Fair until 1970 the only fire protection for the fairgrounds was provided by the volunteer fire department in Sandwich. In 1970 the Northern Illinois Colt

Association bought a 1,500-gallon tank truck with pump and booster lines. Carlton "Dutch" Hough ran the truck for the Colt Association fairs and kept it at the Sandwich Fair. The Fire District helped to equip the truck with 1-1/2" hose nozzles and other equipment so that the District could use it to haul water to its fires.

In 1984 stand pipes with 1-1/2" hose cabinets were installed in the Grandstand, Home Arts building, and Horticulture building. Today all the buildings have fire extinguishers, and all the livestock barns have fifty-five gallon barrels of water with buckets at each end to extinguish a small fire.

Since the 1990's fire equipment has been on the grounds at all times. For further safety, no open campfires are permitted on the grounds.

Conveniences for Fairgoers

For fairgoers' convenience, church services, an information site, more restrooms and rest areas, and organized garbage collection and parking have been added.

Church Services

The First Twilight Church Service was sponsored by the Sandwich Church Council and the Sandwich Fair Association at the opening of the Fair on September 2, 1945. The guest speaker was Dr. John Holland, "The Little Brown Church of the Air" minister, who was heard over radio station WLS. The Community Chorus Choir under the direction of Grace Mason Frerichs provided music accompanied by Susan Greer. The Rev. Robert T. Frerichs, Chairman of the Sandwich Church Council, was the leader of the service.

Apparently Holland was a popular speaker, as he also conducted the services in 1948. The soloist was Maynard Ferden, Superintendent of Sandwich Schools.

On Sunday, September 4, 1949, the Fair activities commenced with Dr. George M. Gibson of McCormick Theological Seminary as the speaker at the church service. The Kendall County Chorus of the Farm Bureau under the leadership of Royce Duvick provided music.

A community-wide united religious service marked the beginning of Fair week on Sunday, September 3, 1950. The Rev. Raymond H. Laury, pastor-director of St. Paul's Methodist

> *Every year I come to the Sandwich Fair to regain my perspective on real values of life. Simple competition in vegetables, livestock, and home arts. Good entertainment. Great food served the old-fashioned way. A general feeling of "belonging" to a lot of people I've never met. Good parking and a measure of all public events . . . clean and available rest rooms. I arrive pessimistic and depart optimistic about mankind and the entire world. Never ever lose sight of what you contribute to people's lives . . . goodness whether they know it or not.*
>
> David Clopton
> Elk Grove Village, IL

top: Program of the first twilight church service held on the grounds.

left: Sandwich Fire Department is on hand for emergencies.

257

Photo by V.G.

top: Prior to 1993 the Round Office served multiple needs: information site, lost and found center, and Concessions Office.

bottom left: Fairgoers stop at the portable gazebo for information and to buy souvenirs.

bottom right: The old pink outhouse

opposite page: Photo credits appear in Chapter 11.

Church, was the speaker. The Kendall County Chorus sang again this year. In addition, the choir director of St. Paul's Methodist Church Mrs. Perry Saito was the soloist.

On Sunday, September 2,1951, a community church service was held with Professor David E. Lindstrom of the University School of Agriculture as the speaker.

Sunday morning worship services are currently held at the food stand of the United Church of Sandwich.

Information Site: the Gazebo

After the 1992 Fair, President Wiley Updike saw a need for a new information booth. At the time, the Round Office was serving multiple needs: information site, lost and found center, and Concessions Office. Patrons who "grew up" with the Fair knew the little "round" office well. In fact, Margaret Bartel of Plano says her daughter intentionally got lost four years in a row just to hear her name announced over the loud speaker.

Newcomers to the Fair, however, weren't as likely to find the Office. Even though it is painted red and has a unique shape, it had become hidden to some extent by the surrounding buildings. Another problem is that it has only one door, making traffic flow difficult during busy times.

Updike suggested that the new information site be obvious to first-time visitors to the Fair, and if possible, be placed at the busiest place on the fairgrounds. A location near the north exit

Photo by J.E.H.

of the Home Arts building has proved to be a good site. Fair visitors often inquire about grandstand shows and commercial vendors, about the location of the nearest restroom, and even the closest cotton candy stand. The gazebo has also become a popular stop at the Fair for souvenir seekers [see Chapter 9].

Restrooms

If a survey were taken concerning the most noticeable improvement at the Fair, restroom facilities would win by a landslide. Virginia Matthews of Sandwich says, "I remember when the outhouses were the only bathrooms at the Fair. I loved to watch the looks on people's faces when they entered the buildings and found out there were no flush toilets." [See Chapter 3 Buildings and Grounds, Restrooms]

Brent Monteiro of Waterman says,

One thing I remember being scared of as a kid was the men's long narrow bathroom building. Along one side of the building was a row of wooden-seated holes with dividers between them for a little privacy, which wasn't too bad. But, attached to the opposite wall was a long, slanted, rain-gutter urinal that you used according to your height. This put a kid my size all the way down at the low end. So, at that age, I was always too scared to use the bathroom at the Fair. Now, as I look back, I think of how times

Photo by J.A.D.

Courtesy of SFA

have changed in my 40 years, and I long for simpler days like that.

Rest Areas

The Fair has countless exhibits, many performances, abundant displays, and numerous demonstrations—a plethora of activities to exhaust even the most energetic person—thus, increasing the need for resting areas. Wherever there is a place to sit, people congregate to talk and rest.

The Fritsch family helped fulfill the need for resting areas when they converted their commercial tent to a relaxation area. Fritsch Brothers Hybrid Seed Corn originated in 1938 as a family affair started by Wiley and Lyle Fritsch with their dad George doing the pollinating, mostly by hand. The siblings Wiley, Lyle, Helen, Shirley, and Russ detasseled.

According to the Fritsch family, Fritsch Brothers was the first seed company to sell single cross seed to farmers for commercial production. As the business grew, they focused as much on friendship and comfort as they did on product and sales pitch. They provided a comfortable place for friends and strangers to relax.

By the late 1950's the Fritsches had quit raising seed corn, but kept their commercial tent as a resting-place and home base for their youngsters when they strayed. Current fairgoers can still find the tent east of the steam railroad

Courtesy of SFA

259

Photo by J.E.H.

top: Children and adults alike have fun "feeding" garbage to this unique garbage receptacle in Ag Land. The *Wiley* nametag jokingly refers to Fair President Wiley Updike.

bottom: At the turn of the century, cars began to replace horses and wagons in the parking area.

previous pages:
pages 260-261: Courtesy of SFA
Fairgoers take advantage of this rest area near the windmill.

It's a very clean, well-organized Fair. Displays are set up very attractively; workers are very friendly. The Fairgoers seem to be an honest group of people; it amazes me how displays like those in the Home Arts building can be displayed in the open and yet none are stolen. Congratulations on a Fair that has something for everyone from the youngest to the seniors!

Mrs. Doris Kruger
Peotone, IL

tracks near the handicapped parking area; they are still welcome to stop, rest, and visit with fellow fairgoers.

Garbage Collection

Where there are people, garbage is inevitable. The more people there are, the more garbage there is. Because of this fact of life, the Fair Board has had to hire a company to manage the waste that thousands of fairgoers produce. In fact, in 1999 fairgoers produced 63 tons of refuse.

To service the needs of fairgoers, 75 two-yard containers and 14 eight-yard containers were placed around the grounds. The containers are emptied continually during the Fair; each time each container is dumped, it is treated with bee spray. Fourteen gallons of spray were used during the 1999 Fair.

Organized Parking

Increased auto production encouraged traveling which helped attendance soar and made parking an issue. Selected stanzas from "The Sandwich Fair" July 1922 and "Sandwich Fair, 1930" by Mrs. Chas. Arnold printed in the *Sandwich Free Press* focus on the situation.
And the horses and the carriages
Now no more we see.

For the ground is filled with autos,
Just as thick as they can be.

And of course in later years,
There are autos there galore.
The Ford and Packard, side by side
And many, many more.

The weather it was lovely
And the grounds were filled each day
The autos parked in every spot,
In every sort of way.

From 1888 to 1945 there is no record of any organized parking. People attending the Fair paid at the gate, drove in, and parked themselves. The Fair was much smaller then and space wasn't a problem. Mrs. Arnold's poem, however, makes reference to the efficiency or perhaps the inefficiency in which fairgoers parked themselves: "The autos parked in every spot, in every sort of way." As the Fair grew, organized parking was essential. The 70th Fair in 1957 set attendance records; more than 12,000 automobiles were parked during the five days.

Since the responsibilities of parking superintendents extend beyond parking cars, it is surprising that traffic and parking committees were not formed earlier than they were. Armand "Doc" Legner, Parking Superintendent from 1967 to 1979 and a well-known veterinarian from Sandwich, would probably agree. One of his favorite stories was about a couple who lost

Courtesy of B.H.

Courtesy of SFA

Courtesy of SFA

their car. After a long search with his help, the couple found their car only to discover that they had also lost their keys. Alas, after more searching, the keys were found in the passenger door lock.

Stuart Phillips, Superintendent of Parking from 1980 to 1987, explained his extraneous duties in an interview with the *Sandwich Fair Times* in 1986. "One year a visitor was so excited to be at the Fair that he locked his keys in his car—with the engine still running!" Phillips would agree with Legner that fairgoers have a tendency to "forget where they put 'em [their cars]." There are no records of incidents like these prior to the forming of the Parking Committee; however, they probably existed. As the number of cars increased, a traffic committee and eventually a parking committee were needed to organize the parking and help stranded drivers.

Two local merchants from Sandwich, George Wahlgren and Harry Darnell, are listed in the 1946 Fair book as being on the Police and Traffic Committee. They did the parking from 1946 through 1955.

Don Stahl, a present-day Fair board member, was in charge of the parking from 1955 through the 1960 Fair. Walter Ehmke and approximately six other people helped him. Fair patrons entered the fairgrounds through the old Main Gate that was located across from the entrance of the present-day mobile home park. Most of the parking was south of the Home Arts building where the train is located and east of the Horticulture building and north to the racetrack. According to Stahl, his biggest problem was trying to park cars around the many trees in that area.

"Doc" Legner took over parking for the 1961 Fair. He continued to be in charge of parking through the 1979 Fair. Donald "Did" Breunig, who owned a Ford dealership in Sandwich, became a member of the board and helped Legner park cars for the 1964 Fair. In 1965 the parking area was divided. Legner took the west side and Breunig the east side. That same year more land was purchased to increase the parking area on the east side and for the present Lisbon Street exit. The Lisbon Street exit was opened in 1970, giving the Fair a back exit for the first time. Legner and Breunig were in charge of parking through the 1972 Fair when Breunig was put in charge of the grandstand. Frederick "Fritz" Lindner, who owned the lumberyard in Sandwich, with the help of Stuart Phillips, took Breunig's parking job in 1972.

The original Main Gate across from the mobile home park was closed in 1974, and the gate located at the present-day site of Gate 1 was expanded. A new ticket office was built the same year. The train tracks were extended to the east, blocking the old Main Gate. All the east-side traffic entered at Gate 1 and exited to Lisbon Street, making a better traffic flow. In 1976 the Gletty farmland was bought which increased the parking on the west side. At that time cars entering Gate 4 on the west side parked primarily north of the present beef barn. In 1979 the old ticket office and gates were moved to the present site of Gate 5. This gave the Fair a new entrance and more than doubled the parking area.

At the 1980 Fair, local farmers Stuart Phillips from north of Sandwich and Scott Breunig from Newark were put in charge of east and west parking respectively. At that time nearly all the east-side parking was done within an area of the racetrack and south of the Lisbon Street exit. It took a very good attendance day

top left: Prior to 1945, fairgoers chose their own parking spaces.

top right: As the Fair grew, organized parking became essential.

bottom: Scott Breunig has been in charge of the west side parking since 1980.

Photo by V.C.W.

263

Courtesy of SFA

right: By midmorning the parking area is filled.

top left: Bill Haag joined the east side parking crew in 1982 and took charge in 1988.

bottom left: One of the many parking attendants who guide fairgoers to their parking spaces

Photo by J.A.D.

Photo by V.B.

before any cars were parked north of the Lisbon Street exit. On the west side, nearly all cars were parked in an area on the west end of the racetrack. The parking space opened up by the Gletty purchase was seldom needed.

The 1980's were a decade of incredible growth for the Fair. In 1981 John Carls and Joe Marshall became assistants to Phillips and Breunig. In 1982 Bill Haag of Sandwich joined the east-side parking crew. Until then, cars were rarely parked north of the Lisbon Street exit. In the 1980's all of the parking areas were filled on most weekends. For a while the racetrack infield and even the track were filled with cars.

In the early 1980's, there were three, small horse pastures and a camping area for Airstream travel trailers north of the racetrack. According to Superintendent of West Side Parking Breunig, these pastures were a real headache to park cars in because they had small gates and rough ground.

In 1980 parking superintendents borrowed two golf carts from Edgebrook Country Club. Breunig says, "They usually weren't in the best shape, and they seldom lasted the whole Fair without a breakdown." He explained that five or six workers at a time sometimes rode to their work areas on the grounds.

By the end of the decade, parking personnel had radios and six carts which made the job much easier. In some areas fences were removed making areas more accessible and improving the traffic flow. Haag replaced Phillips in east-side parking for the 1988 Fair. Bill Guy of Millington replaced Marshall in 1990.

During this time the Fair had only two exit gates, one at Lisbon Street and the other at Gate 5. Because of the Fair's growth, exit problems were common on the weekends in the late 1980's. To alleviate massive traffic jams, the Fair bought land for a north exit in 1990; the present exit to Pratt Road was opened for the 1993 Fair. Breunig says, "This was a real lifesaver for parking personnel because in the previous two years, some people had to wait over an hour to exit the Fair. Needless to say, a lot of the Fair patrons were very unhappy, and the parking attendants took the brunt of their anger."

The Fair Board knew this situation couldn't continue for long without hurting attendance, so the exit road was built earlier than planned. The north exit road solved most of the problems, and traffic flowed fairly well into the late 1990's. However, the Fair is still growing, and parking space is lost as attractions and commercial ven-

Photo by S.B.

dors are added.

A new parking area was opened in the early 1990's on the northwest side where prairie grass had previously grown. By the later 1990's traffic flow was becoming more of a problem. In 1999 the incredibly good weather contributed to the long lines backed up at the entrance gate. Some people waited an hour to enter the fairgrounds.

In July 2000 to alleviate traffic congestion, the Fair board voted to begin using the Pratt Road exit as the main entrance beginning at the 2001 Fair. The board also approved adding a second lane to facilitate traffic flow. Exiting traffic will leave by way of the present Lisbon Street exit or through Gate 5 onto Suydam Road. The present Main Gate will be open only to pedestrians, drivers with special parking permits, and buses.

Look for the NEW NORTH ENTRANCE to the SANDWICH FAIR beginning *next year* at the **2001 FAIR**

NORTH ENTRANCE beginning *next year* at the 2001 Fair.

Route 30   HINCKLEY   Route 30   To 88 ▶

Somonauk Road

East Sandwich Road

Pratt Road

NEW

Pratt Road

To Route 23

North Fair Entrance

Latham Street

Somonauk Road

Sandwich FAIRGROUNDS   Lisbon St.   6th St.   To PLANO ▶

SANDWICH

Route 34

(Map not to scale)

Route 34

SOMONAUK

FROM ROUTE 34 (EAST)
Turn right at stop light on
  Latham Street
Turn left on Pratt Road
Follow signs to North Entrance

FROM ROUTE 34 (WEST)
Turn left on Somonauk Road
Turn right on Pratt Road
Follow signs to North Entrance

FROM INTERSTATE 88
Take Sugar Grove Exit
Take Rt. 30 West to Hinckley
Turn left on Somonauk Road
Turn left on Pratt Road
Follow signs to North Entrance

Courtesy of SFA

top: Aerial view taken in 2000. The road located in the lower right of the photograph is the road leading to the new entrance on Pratt Road.

drawing: In 2000 the Fair Board voted to begin using the Pratt Road exit as the main entrance in 2001.

265

Courtesy of SFA

SANDWICH FAIR!

Sept 5, 6, 7, 8 and 9 1892

This card will admit any scholar under 12 years of age on Wednesday Sept. 7th, if properly Countersigned by the Teacher.

E. RANDALL, SECRETARY.

TEACHER

Photo by V.C.W.

The Education Committee

For years the Board of Directors of the Sandwich Fair Association, Inc. has encouraged school groups to attend the Fair for educational activities and fun. Students, teachers, and chaperones have been and still are admitted free on Wednesday, Thursday, and Friday of the Fair during typical public school hours.

In 1993 the theme of the convention of the International Association of Fairs and Expositions (IAFE) was "Fairs in a Class of Our Own: Educating and Entertaining." Several board members attended the convention in Las Vegas, Nevada, which featured sessions about the important role fairs play in educating people, especially about agriculture.

Inspired by the 1993 IAFE Convention, the Fair Association formed an Education Committee in 1994. The original committee of Karen Breunig, Jackie Dannewitz, Nancy Lou Rex, and Charlotte Tyrrell continues to meet every year to prepare for school groups that make reservations to attend the Fair.

Since 1994 the Education Committee has mailed informational packets to elementary schools in DeKalb, Grundy, Kane, Kendall, and LaSalle counties in May. A second mailing is sent in August with the reservation form for a school field trip in September.

previous pages: Courtesy of SFA
pages 266-267: A view of the grounds in the early 1960's

top: Directors Don Stahl (l.) and Scott Breunig (r.) accompanied the ICAP Academy class.

right: Sophomores from ICAP Academy, Indian Valley Vocational Center measured their shadows as part of a math exercise.

bottom: Senior English class of Sandwich High School toured the grounds in fall of 1998.

Courtesy of V.C.W.

Photo by V.C.W.

Picnic areas are provided for school groups.

Each year committee members compile an activity booklet for each student who attends the Fair. As students arrive on the school bus, a clown greets them. As part of the welcome, the clown gives the teachers activity booklets that include mathematics problems, language arts activities, a map of the Sandwich Fairgrounds, and other activities based on experiences at the Fair.

The number of students, teachers, and chaperones benefiting from the educational opportunities offered by the Sandwich Fair has increased over the years. Reservations were made for approximately 3,239 people to attend the 1999 Sandwich Fair for "Educating and Entertaining."

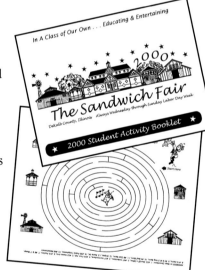

Courtesy of SFA

right columns:
top drawing: Courtesy of K.L.B.
Henry Schmidt, first grade student at Nettle Creek School in the early 1990's, drew this picture after returning from a school trip to the Fair.

middle and bottom: Courtesy of Sandwich School District 430
Acrostic poems were written by fourth grade Project Challenge students Andrew Ruch, Jon Aubry, Jackie Updike, and Trevor Kurtz after visiting the Fair in 1998.

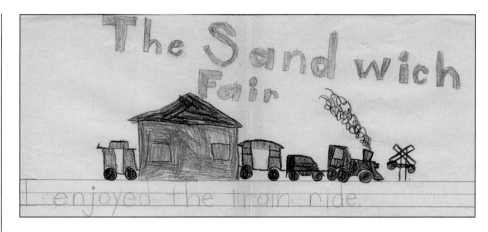

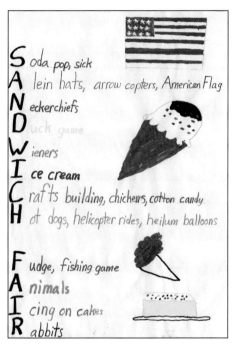

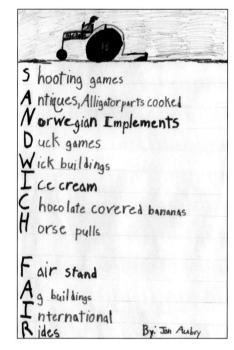

top left: FFA member Nathan Gudmunsen of Somonauk gets a pig ready for a closer view.

top right: Children love to hold the animals at the Farm Zoo.

An FFA member at the Farm Zoo holds a rabbit so children can pet it.

These children admire the chicken held by FFA member Ryan Smith.

FFA members with Orion Samuelson. (l. to r.) front row: Doug Ness, Amy Testin, Samuelson, Greg Anderson; back row: Scott Wallin, Chris Wilson

FFA Farm Zoo

In 1967 Fair Director Milford Clausen established the Farm Zoo in cooperation with the local Future Farmers of America chapters and the vocational agricultural instructors. The original participants were Sandwich, Shabbona, Somonauk, and Waterman FFA chapters.

It was located at the west end of the fairgrounds in the livestock area. Part of an old sheep barn was remodeled to house the zoo.

Sixteen exhibits were on display for children to see close up. They included beef calves, a cow and calf, a ewe and lamb, market hogs, a pony, ducks, geese, chickens, a dairy calf, rabbits, and baby chickens. There was also a display that allowed visitors to watch baby chicks being hatched.

Today, the zoo continues to be a cooperative effort of FFA chapters in Somonauk-Leland, Newark, Hinckley-Big Rock, and Indian Creek. The zoo fills the entire old sheep barn. The exhibits include pheasants, ducks, turkeys, miniature horses, pygmy goats as well as traditional farm animals. The zoo also contains photo collages made by each FFA chapter depicting the yearly activities.

Each day of the Fair, FFA members hold the animals and answer questions about them. The FFA advisors work with their students to select animals and help make the display a success. Generally 45 to 75 students are involved in the zoo, some taking twelve- to fourteen-hour shifts. Former FFA members are also quick to lend a hand for the Fair.

Fair Director and Zoo Superintendent Matt Wilson estimates that since 1988 nearly one hundred thousand visitors pass through the zoo each year. Wilson says, "It is one of the most popular stops at the Fair for children of all ages." Sunday is the biggest attendance day with 25,000 to 30,000 visitors signing the guest ledger, indicating only a percentage of people who actually see the zoo.

Tours of Livestock Barns

The Fair Board added barn tours to its Education Department in 1999 to nurture its agricultural heritage. They saw a need for the tours because many of today's Fair patrons are not from agricultural backgrounds; therefore, many do not feel comfortable touring the barns on their own.

Photo by V.G.

Photo by B.V.

Just as the name suggests, guides escort adults and children on 40- to 50-minute tours through the livestock area. The starting point of the tours was a shiny-red tent located by the Ag Information building behind the Ag Stage. Sondra Wallace of Granbury, TX, founded Barn Tours.[TM] Her objective is to give people an educational and entertaining experience. Barn Tours[TM] hires college students, retirees, and other people from production agriculture who are experts in at least one phase of agriculture. All tour guides go through an extensive training period ending with on-the-job training.

In 1999 the Fair had four college students who conducted tours for eight hours every day of the Fair. The guides were funny and informative.

Sunday Night

On Sunday night the Fair may be almost ready to close the gates on another year, but the grounds and exhibit areas are still busy. At the livestock barns, exhibitors are cleaning the stalls, loading their animals and trunks, and saying goodbye to their friends until the next showing season.

In the exhibit buildings, workers are removing items from the walls and the showcases. Exhibitors are standing in line to pick up their entries, ribbons, and prize money. In the horticulture building, generous exhibitors are giving away fruit, squash, and other exhibits that are too good to toss in the dumpster. In the floral section, vases are being washed and stored for the next Fair.

At the grandstand the track is being cleared

Photo by J.A.D.

Photo by J.A.D.

Photo by J.A.D.

top left: Tour guides with Sandwich Fair Board President Wiley Updike

top right: Livestock is transported home in a variety of vehicles.

(l. to r.) Norma Norling and Nancy Lou Rex are ready to close the ticket office after a successful 2000 Fair.

Director Larry Dannewitz and son Drew of Sandwich are ready to head home to enjoy their Fair food as the 2000 Fair closes.

Roy Wahlgren and John Hallaron close the Main Gate ticket office after the 2000 Fair.

I hadn't been to a county Fair in almost 65 years! But this reminded me of my childhood in Southern Illinois (White County)—the farm smells, the crowds, the animals and sulky races— the midway and the happy people and children enjoying old fashioned entertainment. It was wonderful.

Grace Dahlberg
Sandwich, IL

City folks get to experience country, farm life.

Ron and Joan Sokolowski
Burbank, Illinois

I was about 8 or 9 years old when my parents brought us kids here for the first time. The Fairground is so big, so much to see and do. In 1996 I moved to Wisconsin and have gone to the county fairs up there, but nothing comes close to the Sandwich Fair. I enjoy looking at the photos and farm equipment, and I enjoy eating the different foods.

Michael Brummel
South Wayne, WI

I love the animals and seeing the people I hadn't seen in a while. I think I spent more time talking to people than doing anything else.

Sam Silburn
Sandwich, IL

I love the Sandwich Fair because it's a great connection to the past. I've been coming to the Sandwich Fair with my family since I was a tiny kid, and every year we see old friends, and I learn more about my parents' childhoods coming to the Fair!

C. Bray
Genoa, IL

The Fair makes me smile!

Nancy Morrison,
Morton Grove, IL

I love the old time atmosphere, the pretty Fairgrounds, machinery displays—old and new. I go to 8 to 10 fairs a year. This is my favorite.

Larry Hassinger
Pontiac, IL

It's a great way to officially end the summer. It has great variety of exhibits, food, animals, crafts, gift ideas, and wide open country space. I've been coming for the last 10-15 years. Love it each year.

Sally Frantzen
Elk Grove Village, IL

It is interesting each year— I find something different to see, buy, and experience! We've always come for the past 15 years.

Dorothy Suchomel
Lyons, IL

The Sandwich Fair is one of the last family events free of alcohol. We are so thankful for that.

C. R. Futrell
Sandwich, IL

I love the Fair because it's always on my birthday weekend, and there's no better way to spend the day!

Nancy Kubina
Lisle, IL

It's a close knit, small town fair that's always full of smiling familiar faces. It's taking a walk through the country that's full of glitter.

Becky Mathesius
Earlville, IL

I can't say it any other way: Just the best Fair in the COUNTRY!!! Thanks for creating great memories and continuing to do so in today's day and age. It is an awesome blend of a good old country fair mixed with the vigor of present day life! **KEEP UP THE GREAT WORK.**

Rob Thompson
Ottawa, Illinois

I love the Fair because I grew up in northern New Jersey and went down south every summer to the boardwalk. My dad always won prizes for me at the games. The Fair reminds me of my childhood summers with my family on the boardwalk on the Jersey shore.

Lynn Brooks
Sandwich, Illinois

of demolition cars and reworked for the horses. Popcorn boxes and lemon shakeup cups are being swept from between the benches, and the doors are shut for another year. Food vendors are selling a final meal to fair patrons and tired workers.

Julie A. Twait of Plano says,

> Each year I look forward to the Fair, even though it seems to be a signal to get ready for fall. And I truly feel a pang of sadness as I leave the Fair on Sunday night, knowing a full year will pass before I can come back.
>
> As long as I can remember, I have been coming to the Fair. When I was very young, I went with my parents. I remember holding their hands when we walked through the "Farm Zoo" (one of my favorites) and the barns. My dad had grown up on a farm so he always had things to tell me about the animals.
>
> My family, especially my Grandpa, used to tell stories about when my Dad, his brothers and cousins were in junior high and high school when they stayed at the Fair with the animals they were showing. Quite a lot of *High Jinx* went on in the barns after the Fair closed for the night. Good clean fun, of course!
>
> As time passed, you got to meet your friends at the Fair and walk around by yourself. I always watched how much money I had left because as we left for the night, I bought some taffy or caramel corn to take home.
>
> Now, that I am an adult, I truly appreciate what the Fair has to offer all generations. I see the bench outside the Home Arts building where my Grandma used to sit and talk to people she knew. I see people my age bringing their children to the Fair to enjoy all of its wonders. Seeing children eating their favorite treats and asking to go on another ride or play another game reminds me of when I was their age. I look forward to bringing my own children someday. I hope they grow to love the Fair as much as I do.

Five short days. Children, teenagers, and adults wait all year for five, short days packed full of excitement. It is a busy week; Mrs. Charles Arnold summed up the activities in stanzas from two of her poems that were

Photo by J.A.D.

Electrician Frank Moran disconnects lines on Sunday evening so vendors can move out.

reprinted in the *Sandwich Free Press*.
> And we'll all go home so tired
> But glad we spent the day
> Right at the Sandwich Fair grounds
> In just the same old way"
> —"Our Fair" August 30, 1934

> And the many, many old friends
> That always met us there,
> And planned each year to meet again
> Right at the Sandwich Fair.

> But father, mother and friends are
>   gone,
> And the older ones, just a few,
> Are left to wander in the gates
> Of those that then we knew.

> And I often dream and wonder,
> As I see the fair grounds there,
> If they don't come back in spirit
> And attend "The Sandwich Fair"
> —"The Sandwich Fair"
>   July 1922 ◬

Photo by B.V.

Photo by K.L.B.

top: Superintendents help exhibitors locate their photography entries on Sunday evening.

middle: Jackie Updike of Sandwich proudly shows off her winning junior food entries.

bottom: Clean up in the grandstand after the 2000 Fair

Photo by J.E.H.

Souvenirs:
Keepsakes and Treasures

The number of people who collect Fair memorabilia shows Sandwich Fair pride. It is doubtful that there is another fair in this nation where the competition is so fierce for souvenirs. Collectors of Sandwich Fair treasures are willing to pay top prices for Fair artifacts whether they are rare pieces from the past or just items with the words *Sandwich Fair* written on them. Some of the items such as tickets, Fair ribbons, premium books, and trophies are keepsakes because they signify direct involvement in the Fair. Other items were sold or given away by vendors or the Fair Association.

Some of the items are glass. The oldest and most coveted is the ruby-stained glassware that was available from 1900 to 1915. Other items include ashtrays and a small glass tray with an aerial shot of the Fair. Collectors in the area have ashtrays from 1953, 1954, and 1955 as well as a series of ashtrays picturing the four seasons. In the early 1970's, a local crafter produced a black and white coffee mug featuring Augie Otto's miniature train. Later some of them were colored. Paperweights with the Blue Lady poster image as well as etched plates and mugs were sold at the 100th Fair in 1987. In 1981 a vendor under the grandstand sold glass bells commemorating the Fair. A limited edition of porcelain dolls was available in 1992. The first of a series of ball ornaments was available from the Sandwich Chamber of Commerce in 1994, and paperweights depicting Fair scenes were sold at the 1999 and 2000 Fairs. Other glass souvenirs include pint jar mugs, syrup dispensers, and creamers with Fair scenes and toothpick holders with Otto's train.

Paper collectibles include posters, advertising pieces, matchbook covers, note cards, premium books, and ticket and premium stubs. The 1987 premium book for the Centennial Fair was a large, special gold edition that included vintage pictures. Several collectors have early postcards depicting Fair buildings that no longer exist on the grounds. In 1998 the first of a series of pen and ink drawings of Fair buildings went on sale.

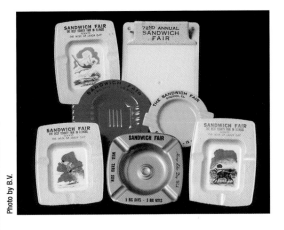

right above: A keepsake trophy awarded at the Fair. The trophy is engraved "Boys Hog Judging Contest First Place Sandwich Fair 1925."

left column:
image one, top: Etched plates and mugs were sold by Fox Valley Older Adults at the 100th Fair.

image two: The 1953 small glass tray, featuring an aerial view of the Fair, and the ashtray are hard-to-find souvenirs.

image three: In past years ashtrays were a common item for sale. Also shown is a small clipboard from the 1960 Fair.

image four, bottom: Fair postal cancellations were used on souvenir glassware.

opposite page: Photo by B.V.
Early 1900's Ruby-stained glass

Collection of Sandwich Fair Posters

right column:
top: A collection of advertising pieces

middle: An original 1958 Fair poster

bottom: Bunting Shows furnished the carnival rides at one time.

left column:
top and bottom: Aut Swenson's Daredevils and Gene Holter's Racing Ostriches were featured on these posters from the 1970's.

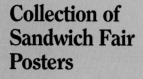

top: The Sandwich Chamber of Commerce started a series of ball ornaments in 1994.

bottom: Mugs were sold in 1974 featuring Otto's train. Paper collectibles include fans, deck of cards and advertising signs.

Glass bells etched "Sandwich Fair 1981" were sold in a booth under the grandstand.

Directors and employees wear Fair patches.

Silver coins about the size of a half-dollar were sold in 1987.

Photo by J.E.H.

Photo by B.V.

Photo by B.V.

Photo by B.V.

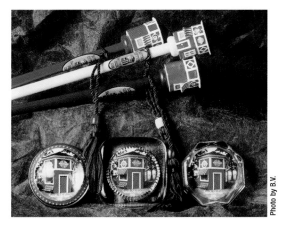

Photo by B.V.

top of page (left to right):
left: Pencils, pens, and pins have been given away or sold at the Fair in the past.

middle: Metal dash plaques are given to auto show participants each year.

right: Fair pennants have been sold through the years.

second column:
left: Collectible Fair memorabilia

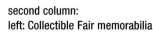

Photo by B.V.

right: Beginning in 1999 a series of walking sticks and paperweights were introduced.

Each year King and Sons Monuments gives away yardsticks.

Since 1977 when Fair officials made arrangements with the Sandwich Post Office to have an official U.S. Postal Station at the Fair the "Sandwich Fair" postal cancellations have become collectibles for many Fair enthusiasts.

Buttons and other metal items are also collected. Buttons have been available such as an orange and black 80th Fair button about two inches in diameter, and ones for the 100th Fair, a Bargain Day, and the 25th auto show in 1991. In 1987 an area coin dealer offered a silver coin the size of a half-dollar. Metal dash plaques have been given to auto show participants. In 1987 a commemorative belt buckle was available. Other items include letter openers, silver spoons, thermometers, and can openers.

Miscellaneous items include first-aid kits, a small clipboard in 1960, fly swatters, a rag ball in 1987, embroidered patches, and pencils and pens. Sandwich Fair pennants have been sold through the years. One collector has a ruler advertising the 1915 Fair. Yardsticks are still popular give-aways at some vendors' booths. Beginning in 1999 a new series of walking canes was a popular item.

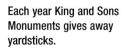

Photo by J.E.H.

The 2000 walking sticks and paperweights featured the windmill.

bottom: Printed on this 1915 ruler: "Ball Games, Races, Free Attractions, etc. Come and Meet Your Friends."

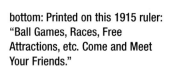

Photo by B.V.

Photo by J.E.H.

Courtesy of B.M.

Photo by B.V.

Photo by B.V.

Photo by .E.H.

Photo by B.V.

Photo by B.V.

Photo by B.V.

Photo by B.V.

Photo by J.E.H.

left column:
top: Hat pins available at the Gazebo from 1993-2000

bottom: One fairgoer has this thermometer in his collection.

middle column:
image one, top: The Gazebo sold a series of Rowe Pottery from 1993-1997.

image two: Items sold at the Gazebo in 1998 featured a farm scene or windmill; 1999 featured a horse barn.

image three: Souvenirs available in 2000 at the Gazebo featured the Home Arts building. A reproduction of the 1900 Premium Book was also sold.

image four: Magnets, matchbooks and a flashlight from the Fair

image five, bottom: Fair hats from around the grounds: antique auto show, tractor pull, and Fair office worn by Fair officials

right column:
image one: Ceramic mugs sold at the Gazebo

image two and three: A sampling of silk-screened t-shirts, sweat-shirts, and hats that have been sold at the Gazebo.

The Gazebo

One place today's fairgoers buy some of these treasures is the Gazebo located just north of the Home Arts building during Fair week. Superintendents Karen Breunig and Cheryl Augustine and their committee are responsible for selecting the souvenirs. A crew of about twelve workers keeps the booth open 12 to 14 hours a day during the five days of the Fair.

For the 1993 Fair, Rowe Pottery designed a crock with a drawing of the Home Arts building; they sold out in two days. Other buildings were commemorated in a series of pieces for the next four years. An aluminum-cast dish by Hanson Casting and Engineering of Sandwich was sold in 1998. Limited-edition pottery pieces by Cloth and Clay of Minnesota were sold in 1999 and 2000. A reproduction of the 1900 premium book and hand-cast pewter medallions depicting the Home Arts building were sold at the 2000 Fair.

Other souvenirs include items with a Fair logo such as T-shirts, sweatshirts, hats, postcards, note cards, magnets, and coffee cups. Lapel pins featuring buildings or historic structures on the grounds have been issued since 1993.

Souvenir Postcards

image one: top: The famous six horse Reminisce Hitch was on a 1997 postcard.

image two: The 1996 Grandstand postcard.

image three: The Home Arts building was featured on the 1998 postcard.

image four: bottom: The colorful windmill as shown on a 1998 postcard is a recognized structure at the Fair.

Photo by C.L.

Photo by M.M.

Photo by M.M.

fanned postcards below, left to right: Postcard from 1979

Gate 5 ticket office and aerial view of the grounds on the 1992 postcard.

Postcard first offered in 1994

The Horticulture building was featured on the 1995 postcard.

Photo by M.M.

Photos by A.Z.

Photos by S.B.

Top Photo by V.G.
Bottom Photo by B.V.

Top Photo by V.G.
Bottom Photo by B.V.

Note Cards by Local Artists

left column:
Sets of six note cards featuring artwork by artist Quen Carpenter.

right column:
A series of birdhouse notecards by artist Jackie Dannewitz were introduced for sale in 1998.

Courtesy of SFA

Courtesy of SFA

Courtesy of SFA

Courtesy of SFA

Courtesy of SFA

Courtesy of SFA

Courtesy of SFA

Courtesy of SFA

Courtesy of SFA

279

SANDWICH FAIR!

Sept. 10th to 13th 1912

H. A. SEVERY
President

C. L. STINSON
Secretary

SANDWICH FAIR ASSOCIATION,
SANDWICH, ILLINOIS.

SEPTEMBER 10, 11, 12, 13, 1901.

SANDWICH FAIR
SANDWICH, ILL.

SEPT. 12, 13, 14, 15, 1905.

THE GREAT
SANDWICH FAIR
SANDWICH, ILL.

Photo by J.E.H.

Sandwich Historical Society

Another source of souvenirs is the Sandwich Historical Society located near Otto's train depot in a wooden wagon booth. Selling souvenir plates, note paper, and memberships, the Society had its first booth at the Fair in 1970. In 1991 members of the group sold one thousand reproduction copies of a 1921 Sandwich Fair poster and iced tea as fast as they could brew it. In 1992 they reproduced another poster and added a souvenir red toothpick holder to their stock. Both items were popular so the group continued to offer a new reproduction poster and one of a series of colored toothpick holders each year. A souvenir goblet was available in 1997, 1998, and 1999. At the 2000 Fair, the Historical Society sold a reproduction of an old favorite—a ruby-stained toothpick holder as well as a covered porcelain dish featuring a carousel.

top: The Historical Society sells souvenirs and iced tea from their wooden booth. (l. to r.) Pat Clapper, Shirlene Peterson, Pat May

Photo by B.V.

Photo by B.V.

A series of toothpick holders were sold at the Fair by Sandwich Historical Society from 1992-1999.

Photo by J.E.H.

previous page: Courtesy of SFA
Posters that have been reproduced by Sandwich Historical Society

top right: Goblets were offered by the group from 1997-1999.

bottom right: The ruby-stained toothpick holder and porcelain dish were offered by the Historical Society at the 2000 Fair.

281

Photo by B.V.

top: Unusual ruby-stained glassware

right: Not all old glass was ruby in color.

previous pages: Photo by B.V.
pages 282-283: Favorite ruby-stained glass pieces from collectors

Ruby-Stained Souvenir Glass

On an oak-shaded Sandwich Fair lane, an itinerant vendor pursued his trade for all to witness; occasionally he hawked his wares with catchy jingles. Women paused, then crowded to gape at the ruby-stained glass creations being etched with words that spelled out wedding anniversaries, "For Mother," a loved one's name or initials, or Sandwich Fair 1912. They marveled at the miniature pitchers, toothpick holders, sugar bowls, and candy dishes.

Today, these ruby-stained souvenirs are coveted finds in antique shops and at auctions. Sometimes they are called ruby-flash glass, but the correct term is ruby-stained because it clarifies the process. Local auctioneers use the glassware as a draw to the auction ring, barking "going once, twice, sold" . . . for hundreds of dollars.

For one collector, the love affair for the Sandwich Fair glass was kindled by his wife, who readily admits to hating auctions, but waited one day to purchase a tiny 1902 goblet with a broken base. "She paid eleven bucks for the thing and surprised me with it," he says with a smile. Now he has a considerable collection, and a lighted showcase displays his favorite pieces: a canoe, a hatchet, and a heart-shaped candy dish dated 1912.

One mug displays a horse's name with its winning time and its owner's name. The horse Arwilda, which was clocked at 2:25.5 at the Fair in 1915, belonged to Earlville veterinarian H. E. Tillman. The present owner of the ruby-stained glass piece says, "Either the horse won and the mug was given to him, or he was so proud, he had one made."

Another piece, a pitcher, celebrates the 79th birthday of Cathleen Laycock, who was born in 1832 and observed the occasion at the 1911 Fair. Some pieces are called "whimsies." One such piece is a 1915 trophy cup with clear handles; another is a derby hat dated 1910. Other pieces include wineglasses called cordials, vases, and small oval dishes (possibly pin trays).

Not all the glass was ruby in color. Collector Clarion "Bud" Anderson, Jr. of Leland owns a 1911 green glass, gold-trimmed

Photo by B.V.

While customers waited, artisans such as this one engraved words on glass items using a foot-pedal powered dentist's drill. Many of these glass pieces sold for 10 cents.

Courtesy of M.A.S.

decorative toothpick holder. "My great-grand-mother was sick the day the family went to the Fair, so her daughter brought home a souvenir [ruby-stained paperweight], and it was inscribed 'To Mother Sandwich Fair - 1906.' That's my pride and joy," Anderson said. "The Sandwich Fair has always been a highlight of my life."

This souvenir craze was sparked by the 1893 Columbian Exposition in Chicago. Its hey-day endured until about 1915. Molten, clear glass was pressed into patterns or blanks of different shapes featuring crystal-cut bases of buttons and arches, upside-down hearts, or truncated cubes. A company purchased the glassware; then girls and women painted on a ruby solution wherever the color was desired. The red color, an imitation of expensive glass, was an extremely thin, surface layer. The pieces were fired in a muffle to affix the color onto the glass. Then they were shipped to dealers like the ones who peddled their trinkets at the Sandwich Fair. With skillful hands, the artisans etched or cut through the red coloring to engrave the words the customer desired, some-thing quaint like "From Aunt Elida and Uncle Bennie To Gurnie, Sept 13, 1906."

Anderson, whose collection includes oval, circular, and rectangular Sandwich Fair paper-weights, has detected some differences in his pieces. He has discovered that the engraver who regularly sold at the Sandwich Fair left a distinc-tive signature mark. He used the same writing style, and he applied three dots above or diago-nally above each capital letter. Another engraver applied a fuzzy outline of letters on some pieces.

Anderson reflects on the people who purchased souvenirs in the early 1900's at the Sandwich Fair: "It was something beautiful, and it caught their eye. Remember, those people did not lead hectic lives like people today. The pieces meant a lot to them. People did a beautiful job on old glass back then."

"I see it as someone going to the Fair and getting a souvenir," says another avid collector. "Certain people had more interest because some families had several or sets. Instead of winning a Kewpie doll, they bought a souvenir. And they were cheap at seven to ten cents, so they were not really a prestige symbol."

They came in a variety of pieces: pitchers with matching tumblers, dresser sets, wine gob-lets, creamers, tiny baskets, toothpick holders, slippers, cake plates, banks and more. Yesterday and today, the crystal and ruby-stained pieces recall memories of the Sandwich Fair.

Photo by B.V.

top and middle: Ruby solutions were painted on glass, then fired for this attractive finish.

Photo by B.V.

bottom: Pitcher and matching tumblers entered as a collection in the 2000 Fair.

Photo by J.E.H.

The Premium Book

The Sandwich Fair Premium Book is the exhibitors' guidebook. It defines the classes and outlines the rules and regulations. Successful exhibitors know the importance of following it closely. Superintendents agree that problems and disappointments occur when someone doesn't read the book carefully.

Changes in the Fair are reflected dramatically in the premium book. A. J. Lukens of Sheridan, Illinois, printed the first book in 1888. It was small, 4 1/2 by 6 1/2 inches, and had 25 pages with fewer than 500 entry categories. Several pages were devoted to local

Photo by B.V.

top: Premium books have changed in size, thickness, and design since 1888.

right: There were 4,200 copies of the 170-page book printed in 2000.

bottom: Archivist Joan Hardekopf was named Fair Historian in 2000.

Photo by V.C.W.

advertising. In 1895 the 64-page book offered $6,000 to exhibitors. Secretary Randall sent out handbills emphasizing the increase in premiums being offered.

Books in the early 1900's included photos of the Fair. By 1907 the books were larger, about 5 1/2 by 8 1/2 inches. During the Depression years, the leaner 28-page book reflected the hard times. There was no advertising, and there were fewer than 500 entry categories. For nearly 50 years, the horseracing schedule and purse were either on the front or the back cover.

While C. R. Brady was secretary, the Fair began to experience tremendous growth. One place this growth was evident was in the premium books. The number of pages doubled, and local merchants were eager to advertise in the book. In the 1940's and 1950's, the pages were printed by the Sandwich *Free Press* and laid out in the lobby of the newspaper office where a group of high school girls, hired at minimum wage, hand-collated the books. Betty Kinchner Marsh said, "This went on for eight hours a day until they were all completed some ten or twelve days later." The books were then ready to be sent out for binding.

The next stage of the process took place in the back room of Brady's Insurance and Realty

office. Each book was hand-addressed with exhibitors' names from the previous year. The books were then sorted by town and bundled for mailing.

Beginning in the 1970's, the cover pictured the "Sandwich Fair" postage-stamp cancellation logo except for three years: 1987, 1996, and 1997. The 1987 Centennial Premium Book was a large, gold edition that included many old photographs. The 1996 and 1997 books had aerial shots of the fair on the cover. The premium books, especially the early ones, are collectors' items. As one Fair enthusiast said, "If it says *Sandwich Fair* on it, it's a collectible."

The format of the books follows a standard. The first pages list the directors and superintendents and give the rules and regulations. Next, there is a listing of entries divided into departments. The livestock classes have always been listed first. Sometimes a schedule of events and entertainment is included. Some past issues had varying amounts of local advertising in the front and back of the book.

According to Secretary Nancy Rex, "The 2000 premium book had more classification entries than any other county fair." It had over 7,000 categories and over $140,000 offered in premiums. A record number of 4,200 copies of the 170-page book were printed.

The Secretary of the Fair is responsible for overseeing the publication of the premium book. An office manager employed at the Fair office does the editing of the book and the processing of entries and premiums. Preparation for the next year's book begins almost immediately after the Fair closes in September. Superintendents meet with their assistants to discuss changes in the premium lists in their departments. During the winter the changes are presented to the Fair Board for approval. The design is finished in early spring and sent to the printer so it will be ready for mailing in July. For the 2000 Fair, 2,400 premium books were mailed to past exhibitors.

PREMIUM LIST
FOR THE
113th
ANNUAL
SANDWICH FAIR

September 6-10
2000

Courtesy of SFA

Photo by C.H.

Quen Carpenter designed many signs throughout the grounds before her 1999 retirement.

Courtesy of SFA

top and bottom: Fair posters and postal cancellation stamps designed by Quen Carpenter.

Quen Carpenter

Quen Carpenter's connection to the Sandwich Fair began over thirty years ago. She entered a button contest in 1968 commemorating the 80th Fair and the Sesquicentennial of Illinois. She won twenty-five dollars for best design. Since then her drawings have become familiar on Sandwich Fair posters, buttons, and commemorative stamp cancellations.

In 1969 she set up an old patio table and a small umbrella under a large oak tree and began sketching faces of fairgoers. Of the uncounted thousands Quen has portrayed from life as a sketch artist, her thirty-year Sandwich Fair career included approximately 2,200 humans, many dogs, a horse, and a ram lamb who posed for her at the Fair. Many who could not be drawn at the Fair made arrangements with her later.

That same year in 1969, she began designing advertisements for the Fair. Fair Secretary Louis Brady called her each spring thereafter to say, "Well, it's time for an ad." She would get busy. She was given free rein. She said, "I could do anything I wanted."

In 1977 Quen was approached by Secretary Brady to design a Postal Cancellation Stamp commemorating the Fair. He asked her to choose an image that residents and visitors could use as a postmark on mail that was sent from the fairgrounds. He wanted something that captured the look and feel of the Fair; Quen chose the historic Home Arts building for her first design.

She expected the cancellation stamp to be a one-time project, but fairgoers and the Fair board were so delighted with the unique commemoration that it became a tradition. Over the years, the stamp featured nostalgic events, people, and buildings.

Besides the Fair ads that Quen created until 1995 and the stamps through 1998, she also designed various signs on the grounds. They include the original sign for the Log Cabin food stand, the sign for Augie Otto's train, the Rotary Club cider and brats signs, and the sign noting the history of the windmill. Quen did all of the signage for Gjovik/Apache Auto Group fair display as well as signs for Dock's TV and Appliance, Swalley Music, The Open Door food stand, and the ATM sign for Castle Bank.

On April 23, 1999, Quen officially retired as Fair artist. She continues to be active in a business she and her husband Bob formed in 1989 and as an officer of the Board of Directors for the Open Door Rehabilitation Center.

Postal Cancellation Postmarks

Since 1977 the Sandwich Fair has had its own postal station and cancellation postmark operated by Sandwich Post Office employees. The first postal station was located in the commercial building west of the Home Arts building. Fairgoers purchase stamps, envelopes, and other philatelic items that can be stamped with a commemorative "Sandwich Fair" postmark.

From 1977 through 1998 local artist Quen Carpenter drew the designs. Students drew the designs the next two years, Pat Molitor in 1999 and Tiffany Johns in 2000. Each design is a familiar building or memory of the Fair.

The postal station moved to a US Postal Station trailer in 1990 just west of commercial building #3 near the windmill. The station is open all five days of the Fair. ◬

Courtesy of SFA

Photo by V.G.

The US Postal Station trailer located across from the windmill

287

The 100th!
The Sandwich FAIR
FIRST FAIR 1888
Sandwich, Illinois
September 9-13
1987
SOUVENIR
ALBUM &
PREMIUM
BOOK

SANDWICH FAIR ASSOCIATION
SANDWICH, ILLINOIS
SPECIAL AWARD

J.M. HUMMEL
Has Knifed the Prices on
Carriages and Harness

1888

PREMIUM LIST
OF THE
FIRST ANNUAL FAIR
OF THE
SANDWICH
Fair Association,
TO BE HELD AT
SANDWICH, ILLINOIS,
September 18, 19, 20 & 21, '88.

Competition Open to All.

Read the Rules and Regulations Carefully, and bring
this List with you to the Fair.

Sewing Machines, Organs, Pianos
Farm Wagons and Machinery
AT RUINOUS PRICES
For Bargains go and see him.
J. M. HUMMEL, Sandwich, Ill.

The 100th SANDWICH FAIRS 1987

Recognition and Celebrations: A Blue Ribbon Fair

The Sandwich Fair is recognized as the oldest and largest county fair in Illinois. It has more exhibits than any fair in Illinois except the State Fair. For many exhibitors the ribbons and plaques are more prestigious than State Fair recognition.

The Sandwich Photographic Society was organized in 1987 to document Fair activities for the Fair's 100th birthday. Since 1998 the Sandwich Fair Association has provided a Reminisce Tent at the Fair where fairgoers share their stories and pictures and learn more about the Fair. In the spring of 2000 the Library of Congress in its bicentennial project to document American culture recognized the Fair as a Local Legacy.

The Illinois State Historical Society and Illinois State Board of Education have recognized the Fair for its longevity and its role in education. It is no wonder that DeKalb County residents are proud of their Fair.

Happy 100th Birthday in 1987

The 100th Sandwich Fair, held September 9-13, 1987, opened with a special ceremony in front of the Round Office. Balloons were released and a special monument donated by King and Sons Monument Company of Sandwich was unveiled.

Fair Board President Jack Norling captured the spirit of the occasion in the address he wrote for the 1987 premium book: "The Sandwich Fair is a lot of things and each person who passes through its gates perhaps has his own definition of what it is; but most of all, it is a community celebration that opens its doors to everyone." On September 2, 1987, prior to the opening, the *Sandwich Record* printed, ". . . she

---

The Board of Directors of
The Sandwich Fair Ass'n., Inc.
cordially invite you and your party
to attend the

100th SANDWICH FAIR

to be held in
Sandwich, Illinois
September 9-13, 1987

Please present this invitation
at the gate

Courtesy of SFA

[the Fair] has aged gracefully. She still doesn't act her age and attracts fairgoers of every age for five full days of family fun."

The 100th Fair Committee, consisting of Louis P. Brady, Carlton "Dutch" Hough, Jack Norling, Wiley Updike and John Wagner, along with the Board of Directors, planned a grand celebration. The nearly 160 acres of fairgrounds had increased almost seven hundred percent from the original 20 acres repurchased in 1888. The committee and directors wanted to make sure the activities and attractions for fairgoers increased at least that much. They planned a bigger Fair than ever before.

Entertainment included Bear Foot Truck Crusher demonstrations; Britt Small and

center: An invitation to the 100th Fair

opposite page: Photo by B.V. Premium book and other items from the 100th Fair

following pages: Photo by J.H. pages 290-291: Balloons were released at the opening ceremony of the 1987 Fair.

Courtesy of SFA

(l. to r.) Director Don Bark presented a recognition plaque to long-time commercial exhibitors William King, Charles King, and Russell King at the 100th Fair.

Photo by B.V.

Photo by S.H.

Photo by B.W.

left column:
top: 100th Fair souvenirs and advertising items

bottom: An eye-catching corn wreath seen at the Horticulture building during the 1987 Fair

Photo by K.B.

right column:
top: Souvenir T-shirts and glassware were available at the Fox Valley Older Adults booth.

middle: The 8th annual Sandwich Fair 10-K race started the activities on Sunday of the 100th Fair.

bottom: A bicentennial group buried a time capsule to be dug up in 2026.

Courtesy of SFA

Singer Marie Osmond entertained in 1987.

Festival; truck, tractor and micro-mini tractor pulls; singer Marie Osmond; demolition derby; western and miniature horse shows and llama shows. Around the grounds were the FFA Farm Zoo, clowns Buttons and Korky, Dr. Barth's Medicine show, Grandpa Cratchet's puppet show, a double midway, and Bub and His Boys band. Activities included a 10-K race.

There was plenty to do, and adults could do it all for a three-dollar general admission charge, and for another dollar, they could park their cars all day. Admission for children ages 6 to 12 was one dollar. To celebrate the Fair's longevity, admission on Friday reverted to 1888 admission prices: thirty-five cents for adults, fifteen cents for children and twenty-five cents to park an auto.

The 100th Fair was special for exhibitors. They received a two-inch pin commemorating the Centennial. A 100th stamp adorned ribbons on winning entries. Entry choices and awards were added to commemorate the celebration. For example, in the Livestock Department, all exhibitors were eligible for breeders' awards, and several grand champions were added to the Junior Show's livestock awards. In the Horticulture Department there were also additions: heirloom vegetables and 100th anniversary flower arrangements. Home Arts and Arts and Crafts added entry choices such as clothing, needlework, crafts, and paintings depicting the 1888 era, old-time Fair photos, and cakes decorated to honor the 100th birthday of the Fair. The Sandwich Fair boasted the largest number of exhibitors of any fair in Illinois outside the Illinois State Fair.

Fair Secretary Louis P. Brady was quoted in the September 9, 1987, Sandwich Record as saying, ". . . the fair has given the town a name." He felt it was the hard work and

Photo by J.A.

Photo by B.V.

dedication of the people involved who made the Fair a success year after year and the reason folks kept coming back.

Brady also complimented the Fair leadership: "Each director strives to make his department the best it can be each year. Everyone wants to be associated with something successful. Each superintendent is striving for excellence in trying to give the public what it wants. I feel they are the backbone of the fair."

An article in the 100th Fair issue of the Fair Times summarized the pride that is felt for the Sandwich Fair.

For to truly understand what makes up the history of the Sandwich Fair is to understand the lives of the people who have made her [the Fair], the generations of farmers who have entered prize livestock and crops, the homemakers who display their best canned goods and needlepoints, the directors, superintendents and committees who have worked year-round to insure her successful growth, and the local school kids who save up a summer's worth of allowances to spend on head-spinning carnival rides, corn dogs and midway games.

These are the people who have made our Fair so distinctive. Generation after generation of families

top right: A monument was placed in front of the Round Office in recognition of the 100th anniversary of the Sandwich Fair. (front row l. to r.) Directors Robert Guehler, Carlton Hough, John Wagner, Louis Brady, Jack Norling, Don Bark. (back row l. to r.) Russell Stahl, Donald Stahl, Donald Augustine, Caretaker Herman Carlson, Donald Breunig, Scott Breunig, Wiley Updike.

Photo by V.W.

Louis P. Brady at the opening ceremony of the 100th Fair

center: A 100th stamp adorned on winning entries. Exhibitors received a commemorative button with a ribbon.

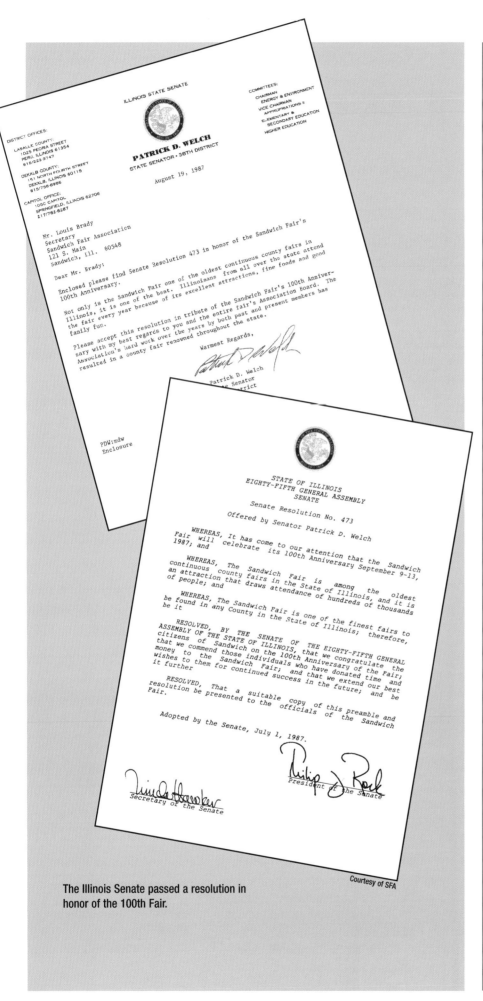

The Illinois Senate passed a resolution in
honor of the 100th Fair.

Courtesy of SFA

Photo by K.B.

Both Leaha Mussleman of Hinckley and the Sandwich
Fair celebrated 100 years in 1987. Horse and buggy
driver was Jim Gunderson.

siastically supported and worked for
the fair, giving it a personality and
flavor that is exclusive to the Sandwich
Fair alone.

The Fair, indeed, had much to celebrate on
its 100th birthday in 1987, as well as on each
succeeding year since then.

The Sandwich Photographic Society

In 1986 Ed Schonfeld, Publicity Director of
the Sandwich State Bank, had the idea of documenting photographically every aspect of the
100th Sandwich Fair to be held in 1987. To prepare for this event, Schonfeld and Joseph Antos
gathered a select group of photographers—Vince
Boland, Paul Gleason, Virginia Grimes, and Curt
Larsen—to do a practice shoot of the 99th Fair.
Pleased with their efforts, the group decided to
form a photographic club, and The Sandwich
Photographic Society (SPS) soon emerged.

The Sandwich State Bank joined forces with
the Sandwich Fair Association to sponsor the
project in 1987, the Centennial of the Sandwich
Fair. SPS members Antos, Boland, Lil
Demichina, Gleason, Grimes, Scott Hanson,
Larsen and Schonfeld planned "Shoot 100."
Schonfeld died suddenly before the 100th Fair
was held. "Shoot 100" was dedicated to his
memory. SPS organized it and called on other

area photographers to join in the effort. About fifty photographers covered everything from paving the roadways on the grounds, erecting the tents, and painting the buildings before the Fair to cleaning up after the five-day celebration. Over 3000 slides and prints were taken at "Shoot 100."

The Sandwich Photographic Society was born of the Sandwich Fair; the life of the club is intimately intertwined with the life of the Fair. The enthusiasm of Boland, the first president, sparked the growth of the club. The club affiliated with the Chicago Area Camera Clubs Association; a junior division was organized later. SPS interacts with other photographic groups; the members lecture, judge competitions, and give courses to other groups.

The club's involvement with the Fair continues. Every year the club sponsors a "Fair Challenge" for its members. They take a single shot of each item on a list of subjects at the Fair from which a committee selects the best pictures. Some photos are chosen for postcards sold at the Fair. Members also submit their best work in the photography competition at the Fair. A ritual has developed among some members the

A 1987 advertising poster

left column:
top: The "Shoot 100" for the 100th Fair was the beginning of the Sandwich Photographic Society.

bottom: Souvenir poster from the 100th Fair

A drawing by Quen Carpenter encouraged Junior exhibitors to enter the 100th Fair.

Photo by J.E.H.

top: The Reminisce Tent has been a memorabilia site since 1998.
(l. to r.) Steve Cromwell, Nancy Updike, Susan Cromwell in 2000

Academy at Indian Valley Vocational Center (IVVC) as exemplary.

Donald Stahl, vice president of the Sandwich Fair Association and Philip Colgan, director at Indian Valley Vocational Center, accepted a plaque from State Superintendent of Schools J. A. Spagnolo at an awards dinner held at the Fairmont Hotel in Chicago.

By studying the Fair as a business, Academy students learned about careers in business contracting, marketing and public relations, sales management, waste disposal, security and policing, food preparation and service, agriculture, horticulture, and animal husbandry.

Reminisce Tent

In 1998 a center was established at the Fair for the purpose of collecting information for the publication of a book preserving the history of the Sandwich Fair. A tent was used at the 1998 through 2000 fairs for fairgoers to congregate and share memories and information. Many of the memories were recorded on audiotape for later use.

In 1999 fairgoers watched videos of previous fairs and viewed a timeline showing information and pictures gleaned by the committee in 1998. The tent was well attended.

At its inception Marie Lindner of Sandwich coordinated all aspects with the help of Nancy Updike of Sandwich. In 1999 Susan Cromwell of Somonauk joined and was again helped by Nancy Updike. In 2000 the three combined efforts for the Reminisce Tent. The entire project was overseen by the History Book Committee that was commissioned by the Fair Board.

day after the judging of the photos. Boland, Peg and Bruce Bartell, Leonard Hafenrichter, and Grimes meet to count their ribbons, have a friendly argument over the judges' decisions, and eat a pile of hot cinnamon rolls.

The Illinois State Historical Society

On September 24, 1988, The Illinois State Historical Society recognized the Sandwich Fair Association at its Centennial Awards Program. This program honors Illinois enterprises that have a century of corporate history.

Sandwich Fair received this honor at the program and banquet held at Oak Brook, IL. Jack Norling, president of the Fair Association at the time, and his wife Norma represented the Fair at the event.

Exemplary Partnership

In the spring of 1998, The Illinois State Council on Business-Education Partnerships recognized the partnership between the Sandwich Fair Association and the ICAP

Library of Congress Local Legacy

The Sandwich Fair was one of the area traditions selected in the 14th District by Speaker of the House J. Dennis Hastert as a Local Legacy to celebrate American cultural diversity as a bicentennial project of the Library of Congress, which celebrated its 200th birthday on April 24, 2000.

Karen Breunig, Jackie Dannewitz, Joan Hardekopf, and Vivian Wright were among 1,700 guests who were invited to the Library of Congress for a celebration on May 22 - 24, 2000. The celebration marked the completion of the

Photo by W.U.

(l. to r.) Joan Hardekopf, Vivian Wright, Jackie Dannewitz, and Karen Breunig work on the history book at the Fair Office.

Local Legacies project, a joint effort by Congress, the Library of Congress and communities throughout the nation to document America's local customs and heritage and send the results to Washington for safekeeping. Scott Breunig, Larry Dannewitz, and Elizabeth Holdeman were also invited to the celebration but were not able to attend. The Sandwich Fair Association sponsored the trip.

The Sandwich Fair was asked to document its activities in photographs, videotape, audiotape and written expression. Folklorists and curators from the Library of Congress provided

guidance and suggestions for the massive documentary project that is now housed in acid-free boxes in the Archive of American Folk Culture at the nation's capital. Visitors to Washington, D.C., may view all the projects at the Library's John Adams Building.

"The Local Legacies project celebrates, and shares with the nation, the grass-roots creativity of every part of America," said Librarian of Congress James H. Billington. "It provides a kind

of snapshot of what Americans thought worth preserving at the turn of the new century and should be a valuable resource for scholars in the future."

Illinois Humanities Council

On October 4, 2000, the History Book Committee received notification that it was the recipient of the Studs Terkel Humanities Service Award. The Illinois Humanities Council initiated the awards program to honor those who have encouraged greater public understanding of the humanities in their communities. Eighty-nine awards were given throughout the state.

Karen Breunig, Jackie Dannewitz, Joan Hardekopf, and Vivian C. Wright were commended for their efforts in organizing the research for publication of a local history book about the Sandwich Fair. The Humanities Council recognized the project as one that documents an American tradition in DeKalb County that involves family gatherings, customs, accomplishments, and local commerce.

Appendix:
It Takes Many People to Operate a Fair

CONTRIBUTORS

History Book Committee
Karen Breunig
Jacquelin Dannewitz
Joan Hardekopf
Donald Stahl
Douglas R. Stahl
Vivian C. Wright, Ed.D.

Writers/Researchers
Karen Breunig
Scott Breunig
Jacquelin Dannewitz
Eleni Filippi
Joan Hardekopf
Mark Harrington
Elizabeth Holdeman
Marie Lindner
Linda Munson
Barbara V. Nadeau
Nancy Lou Rex
Pam Sprague
Donald Stahl
Douglas R. Stahl
Jeff Strack
Marilynn Thompson
Nancy Updike
Wiley Updike
Pat Wallis
Barbara Fisher Weber
Vivian C. Wright, Ed.D.

Contributors
Gerald Anderson
Juanita Anderson
Ronald Anderson
Cheryl Augustine
Donald Bark
Joyce Barrett
Helen Bauer
Marion Bazan
Louis P. Brady
Ruth Breunig
Eldon Burger
A.A. "Bud" Burgin
Karen Campbell
Lori Carey
Dale and RoJean Coleson
Susan Cromwell
Denise Curran
Joan Dannewitz
Larry Dannewitz
Herbert DeKing
Mary Dolny
Betty Domagala
Margaret "Peg" Dummer
Susan Hough Farr
Lyle Fritsch
Russel Fritsch
Bill Gilbert
E.E. Golden
Donovan Goodwick
Sandra Warrington Granholm
Virginia Grimes

Robert Guehler
Tom and Bernice Hagemann
Virginia Hann
Hellen Hill
Barbara Hoffman
George L. Johnson
Ronald Johnson
Becky Kinney
Jim Knox
Margaret Knutson
Janice Kurtz
Clarence and Gladys LaBolle
Marion D. Larsen
Lloyd O. Larson
Marie Lindner
Bernice Maness
Betty Marsh
Sue May
Denise Mestemaker
Renee Monkemeyer
Brent Monteiro
Becky Morphey
Jaye Morrison
N. Stanley Nelson
Pam and Larry Nelson
Norma Norling
Faith Olson
Roger Peterson
Shirlene Peterson
Valerie Kraft Petkus
Mary Ann Phillips
Helen McKinley Potillo
Donald Riemensnider
Dale and Mary Rogers
Dorothy Scent
Nancy and Ken Schroeder
Marilyn Temple
Roberta Troeger
John Wagner
Larry Warrington
Joan Whitson
Pam Kraft Wynne
Alice Fitch Zeman

Student Contributors
Ross Adams
Jennifer Allen
Amber Anderson
Chandra Armstrong
Sarah Bauer
Leslie Beukelman
Ryan Beverly
Will Blanchard
Julia Bousselot
Andy Browning
Josh Burket
Emeri Calvert

Photo by V.G.

The trim around the Round Office clock is an example of the distinctive architecture of the Fair buildings.

BOOK DESIGNER

Olga Lindsay
Lindsay Design Group
Batavia and Marseilles, IL

BOOK PRINTER

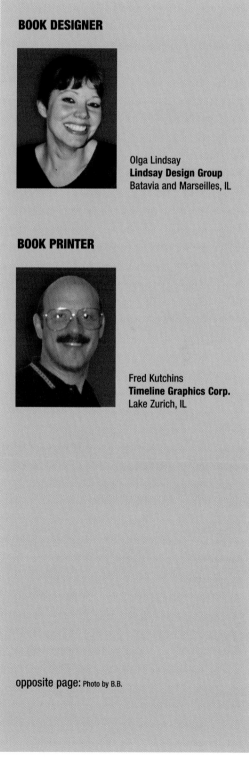

Fred Kutchins
Timeline Graphics Corp.
Lake Zurich, IL

opposite page: Photo by B.B.

299

Courtesy of SFA

1910 Sandwich Fair advertising poster

Christina Patterson
Dusty Pekoc
Jason Riggs
April Roach
Jonathon Smits
Adam Sprague
Jakob Swenson
Sina Swenson
Meredith Szafranski
Luanne Theede
Erin Thirsk
Chris Triantafillou
Keith Vancil
Brandon Voga
Shelly Wilkinson
Frank Williams
Jacob Wilson
Stephanie Wojak
Denise Wright
Mike Zagar

Word Processors
Ginger Dannewitz
Joni Knox
Donna Leonard
Jerry A. Leonard
Amanda MacKenzie
Van Mathre

Proofreaders
Janice Abens
Richard Cook
Gerald Gengler
Mark Harrington
Syranna Kosulic
Marie Lindner
Robert Marsh
Bette Otto
Charlotte Tyrrell

Publicity/Marketing
Eleni Filippi
Marie Lindner
Karen Verda

"Thank you" to all the fairgoers who filled out a "Why I Love the Sandwich Fair" form at the 1998 Fair.

Heather Charapata
Jon Conover
Lorena Corral
Kristen Curtin
Lauren Dannewitz
Jennifer Davis
Jake DeVries
Richard Duffy
Brad Eade
Jason Fatland
Allison Foley
Dan Frantz
Jackie Frieders
Kari Frieders
Jason Gianvecchio
Amanda Gacek
Shelley Gram

Carl Gustafson
Nicole Hardesty
Ben Hay
Alex Hebel
Josh Jandt
Jeremy Jewell
Brooke Johnson
Jenny Jones
Nicole Knight
Jeremy Knobeloch
Eric Koppen
Joe Kotalik
Jack Kubica
Tim Kubisak
Mike Lesus
Philip Lindner
Doug Lueken

Carleen Lurz
Kristen Mall
Sean Maloney
Jennifer Materko
Shawn McDowell
Bob Mendenhall
Ryan Merchant
Mindy Miller
Neal Molnar
Jen Molochnick
Joy Montgomery
Danielle Monti
Kyle Morrison
Melissa Morton
Dan Mowinski
Ryan O'Shea
Colin Orr

PHOTOGRAPHERS, PERMISSIONS, AND COURTESIES

Names for courtesies and families are listed alphabetically by last name; organizations, newspapers, and others are listed by first word. All pages from Premium Books are reproduced courtesy of Sandwich Fair Association. Every effort has been made to accurately credit photographers, and we regret any oversights. The Sandwich Fair Association is grateful for the vast number of photographs and slides donated to the Archives over the years. We are especially thankful to the Sandwich Photographic Society members.

A
C.A.   Clarion "Bud" Anderson
R.A.   Ronald Anderson
J.A.   Joe Antos
B
B.B.   Bruce Bartell
K.B.   Kenneth Bastian
H.B.   Helen Bauer
J.B.   Joyce Bickford
E.B.   Ellen M. Bloomer
V.B.   Vince Boland
K.L.B.   Karen L. Breunig
M.E.B.   Mary E. Breunig
S.B.   Scott Breunig
C
Q.C.   Quen Carpenter
M.C.   Millie Carter
S.C.   Sharon E. Colclasure
D
B.T.D.   Becky Tvrdik Daniels
J.A.D.   Jacquelin A. Dannewitz
J.D.   Joan Dannewitz
H.D.   Harold Dannewitz
L.D.   Lillian C. Demichina
E
M.E.   Merv Eastwold
F
E.L.F.   Eleni L. Filippi
L.F.   Lyle Fritsch
G
F.G.   Florence Jones Getzelman
P.G.   Paul H. Gleason
D.G.   Donavon Goodwick
S.G.   Sandra Warrington Granholm
V.G.   Virginia R. Grimes
T.G.   Tom Grimm
H
L.H.   Leonard Hafenrichter
S.E.H.   Scott E. Hanson
J.E.H.   Joan E. Hardekopf
R.P.H.   Richard & Phyllis Hecathorn
C.H.   Carla Hill
B.H.   Barbara Hoffman
J.H.   John Holbo
S.H.   Shelia Holbo
M.E.H.   Mary E. Hoyt
M.H.   Mary Ellen Huss
J
G.L.J.   George L. Johnson
S.D.J.   Spike & Donna Johnson
K
B.K.   Becky Kinney
A.K.   Andy Krafft
M.K.   Marianne Lisson Kuhn
L
A.L.   Alice Lindner
C.L.   Curtis Larsen
J.L.   James & Siegrid LaFratta

M
M.M.   Michael A. Maroscia
L.M.   Loretta Klotz Martin
B.K.M.   Betty Kinchner Marsh
T.M.   Thomas G. Merkel
E.M.   Edith Miller
K.M.   Karen Monkemeyer
R.M.   Renee Monkemeyer
J.M.   Jack Monsarratt
B.M.   Brent Monteiro
N
R.N.   Ruth C. Nelson
P.N.   Pamela Norpell
O
P.O.   Paul Obis
B.O.   Bill Ostheimer
P
D.P.   Doris Pedigo
R.P.   Roger Peterson
M.A.P.   Mary Ann Phillips
R
L.R.   Larry Raymond
B.R.   Bob Reimann
D.E.R.   Donald E. Riemensnider
S
D.S.   Dan Schleifer
E.S.   Ed Schoenfeld
A.B.S.   Amy Bushnell Scott
M.A.S.   Merwin A. Shaw
M.S.   Matthew Simpkins
G.S.   George Smuckel
D.R.S.   Donald R. Stahl
J.S.   Joe Steffen
T
F.T.   Frances Toombs
U
N.U.   Nancy Updike
W.U.   Wiley Updike
V
B.V.   Bruce VanPelt
W
J.W.   John Wagner
E.W.   Edna Miller Wallis
R.W.   Ron Wallis
J.B.W.   James "Biff" Webber

B.F.W.   Barbara Fisher Weber
G.W.   Gladys C. Wesson
M.W.   Matthew Wilson
V.W.   Vernon Winckler
H.W.   Heath Wright
V.C.W.   Vivian C. Wright
B.W.   Bill Wykes
Z
A.Z.   Allen T. Zagel

Families
BF   Brown Family (Robert C.)
DF   Decker Family
EF   Eakle Family
FF   Fritsch Family (George)
JF   Johnson Family (Michael & Ruth)
KF   King Family (Frank)
MF   Mall Family
PF   Potter Family
GRF   Reinhart Family (George)
RF   Rogers Family (Dale)
SF   Suppes Family
TF   Tuttle Family (Art & Mary)
WF   Wesson Family (Silas Dexter Wesson II)

Newspapers
Beacon News
The Daily Times
DeKalb Chronicle
Kendall County Record
Sandwich Argus
Sandwich Fair Times
Sandwich Free Press
Sandwich Record
Somonauk Reveille

Organizations
SFA   Sandwich Fair Archives

Other
Archie Comic Publications, Inc.
Diary of Hendley Hoge, Grundy County, Illinois
Sandwich High School Yearbook, 1960
Sandwich School District 430

A stilt walker drew the attention of 1965 fairgoers.

SANDWICH FAIR DIRECTORS 1888-PRESENT

Name	Years Served	Office Held
S.D. Coleman	1888-1898	Pres.1888-1895
Wm. Rumney	1888-1890	
T.J. Wright	1888-1890	
Wm. Beveridge	1888-1902	Pres. 1896-1902
A. Gilchrist	1888-1891	
A. Gage	1888-1898	
Louis Rohrer	1888-1895	
Lewis Dieterich	1888-1891	
Gustav Walter	1888-1891	
Lewis Rogers	1888-1896	V. Pres.1888-1893
Eugene Randall	1888-1900	Sec.1888-1900
Fred S. Mosher	1888-1924	Treas. 1888-1924
Chas. H. White	1889-1898	
H.E. White	1892-1893	
Henry Hennis	1889-1924	
C.W. LaSuer	1892-1898,	
	1901-1906	V. Pres. 1892-1898
D.K. Crofoot	1892-1904	
Wm. Foster	1894-1895	
F.A. Pratt	1894-1923	
H.A. Severy	1897-1931	Pres. 1903-1931
J.H. Latham	1897-1911	
L. Hubbard	1898-1900	
Pernett H. Potter	1900-1924	
C.V. Stevens	1900-1903	V. Pres 1900-1903
C.L. Stinson	1901-1940	Sec. 1901-1940; Advisory Sec.1941
Chris Suppes	1903-1935	
Thomas Mercer	1904-1915	V. Pres. 1904-1915
George McDonald	1906-1917	
Wm. Fraser	1906-1937	
S.D. Newton	1916-1926	
P.S. Lindner	1916-1935	V. Pres.1932; Pres. 1933-1935
Charles Howison	1918-1947	V. Pres.1936-1943
		Pres. 1944-1946
Fay Harrington	1923	
W.W. Sedgwick	1925-1930	Treas.1925-1930
M.E. Lake	1925-1943	V. Pres. 1933-1935; Pres.1936-1943
Henry White	1925-1966	Treas.1931-1932
		V. Pres. 1944-1946; Pres. 1947-1961
T.J. Mahaffey	1925-1937	
C.S. Bark	1927-1947	
J.V. Weir	1933-1935	Treas.1933-1935
A.W. Colliflower	1936-1953	Treas.1936-1953
A.C. Baie	1936-1944	
Ben C. Eade	1936-1952	
A.O. Fosse	1935-1936	
Albert Skinner	1937-1939	
C.R. Brady	1938-1972	Sec. 1941-1971; Asst. Sec. 1972
L.R. Evans	1938-1945	
Latham Castle	1944-1963	
Harry Darnell	1945-1955	V. Pres. 1947-1955
C.H. Hough	1946-1988	V. Pres. 1956-1961; Pres.1962-1985
George Wahlgren	1946-1955	
Elmer Henderson	1947-1950	
	1956-1960	
H.W. Bark, DVM	1947-1954	
William Dillon	1947-1951	
Carl Scent	1947-1967	Treas.1957-1966
Douglas Knights	1948-1959	
LeRoy Suppes	1948-1962	
Donald Stahl	1951-1958,	
	1966-present	V. Pres. 1986-present; Acting Pres. 1991
Louis P. Brady	1952-present	Asst. Sec.1966-1971; Sec.1972-1999;
		Sec. Emeritus present
LaVerne Johnson	1953-1957	
David C. Roberts	1954-1956	Treas. 1954-1956
Louis Wagner	1955-1985	V. Pres. 1962-1984
Lewis B. Rex	1956-1968	Acting Treas. 1967; Treas. 1968
Edward Duvick	1960-1965	
A.A. Legner, DVM	1961-1981	
Kenneth Klotz	1961-1977	
Spencer Gord	1962-1972	

Russell Stahl	1964-1991	
Donald Breunig	1964-1992	Treas. 1986-1992
Milford Clausen	1967-1974	
Jack Norling	1969-1991	Treas.1969-1985; Pres.1986-1991
Wesley Scents	1970-1972	
John Wagner	1973-present	
Frederick Lindner	1974-1979	
Robert Guehler	1975-1994	
Wiley Updike	1975-present	Pres. 1992-present
William Mason	1978-1985	
Donald Bark	1978-present	
Stuart Phillips	1980-1987	
Scott Breunig	1982-present	
Donald Augustine	1985-present	Treas. 1993-present
Kenneth Tyrrell	1988-present	
William Haag	1989-present	
Nancy Rex	1992-present	Sec. 1999-present
Larry Dannewitz	1993-present	
Harold Dannewitz	1995-present	
Matthew Wilson	1995-present	

There was no President in 1932
There were no Vice-Presidents 1916-1931 or 1985

SANDWICH FAIR OFFICERS 1888-2000

President

1888-1895	S.D. Coleman
1896-1902	Wm. Beveridge
1903-1931	H.A. Severy
1933-1935	P.S. Lindner
1936-1945	M.E. Lake
1946	Charles Howison
1947-1961	Henry White
1962-1985	C.H. "Dutch" Hough
1986-1991	Jack Norling
1992-present	Wiley Updike

Vice President

1888-1891	Lewis Rogers
1892-1898	G.W. LaSuer
1899	unknown
1900-1903	C.V. Stevens
1904-1915	Thomas Mercer
1932	P.S. Lindner
1933-1935	M.E. Lake
1936-1945	Charles Howison
1946	Henry White
1947-1955	Harry Darnell
1956-1961	C.H. "Dutch" Hough
1962-1984	Louis Wagner
1985-present	Donald Stahl

Secretary

1888-1900	Eugene Randall
1901-1940	C.L. Stinson
1941-1971	C.R. Brady
1972-1998	L.P. Brady
1999-present	Nancy Lou Rex

Treasurer

1888-1924	F.S. Mosher
1925-1930	W.W. Sedgwick
1931-1932	J.E. White
1933-1935	G.V. Weir
1936-1953	A.W. Colliflower
1954-1956	David Roberts
1957	Carl Scent
1958-1968	Lewis B. Rex
1969-1985	Jack Norling
1986-1992	Donald Breunig
1993-present	Donald Augustine

Note: The names listed in the committee and superintendents section may not agree with those listed in the premium books. Corrections and additions were made as they were brought to the attention of the History Book Committee.

BOARD COMMITTEES

1888
Grounds and Improvements: S.D. Coleman, A. Gage, L. Rogers
Premium List and Bylaws: A. Gage, G. Walter, E. Randall

1889
Grievance: Louis Rohrer, G. Walter, Charles White
Finance: William Beveridge, Lewis Rogers, A. Gage
Printing: H. Hennis, William Rumney, A. Gage

1890-1892
No records available

1893
No one listed

1894
No records available

1895-1896
No one listed

1897
Finance: Gage and White
Grievance: Severy and Latham
Printing: Hennis and White
Building: Pratt and Crofoot

1898-1899
No records available

1900
Finance: L. Hubbard, J.H. Latham
Grievance: H.A. Severy, C.V. Stevens
Buildings: F.A. Pratt, D.K. Crofoot
Printing: J.H. Latham, E. Randall
Reception: W.G. Beveridge, C.V. Stevens
Entertainment: H. Hennis, D.K. Crofoot, and Fair Secretary

1901-1902
Finance: C.W. LaSuer, J.H. Latham
Grievance: H.A. Severy, C.V. Stevens
Buildings: F.A. Pratt, D.K. Crofoot
Printing: J.H. Latham, P.H. Potter
Reception: W. G. Beveridge, C.V. Stevens
Entertainment: H. Hennis, D.K. Crofoot, and Fair Secretary (1902 only)

1903
Finance: C.W. LaSuer and J.H. Latham
Grievance: C.V. Stevens and C. Suppes
Buildings: F.A. Pratt and D.K. Crofoot
Printing: J.H. Latham, P.H. Potter, C.L. Stinson
Reception: H.A. Severy and C.V. Stevens
Entertainment: H. Hennis, D.K. Crofoot, and Fair Secretary

1904
Finance: C.W. LaSuer, J.H. Latham
Grievance: Thomas Mercer, C. Suppes
Buildings: F.A. Pratt, D.K. Crofoot
Printing: J.H. Latham, P.H. Potter, C.L. Stinson
Reception: H.A. Severy, Thomas Mercer
Entertainment: H. Hennis, D.K. Crofoot, and Fair Secretary

1905
Finance: C.W. LaSuer, J.H. Latham
Grievance: Thomas Mercer, C. Suppes
Buildings: F.A. Pratt, George McDonald
Printing: J.H. Latham, P.H. Potter, C.L. Stinson
Reception: H.A. Severy, Thomas Mercer
Entertainment: H. Hennis, D.K. Crofoot, and Fair Secretary

1906
Finance: William Fraser, J.H. Latham
Grievance: Thomas Mercer, C. Suppes
Buildings: F.A. Pratt, George McDonald
Printing: J.H. Latham, George McDonald, C.L. Stinson
Reception: H.A. Severy, Thomas Mercer
Entertainment: H. Hennis, George McDonald, and Fair Secretary

1907
Finance: William Fraser, J.H. Latham
Grievance: Thomas Mercer, C. Suppes
Buildings: F.A. Pratt, George McDonald
Printing: J.H. Latham, George McDonald, C.L. Stinson

Reception: H.A. Severy, Thomas Mercer
Entertainment: H. Hennis, George McDonald, and Fair Secretary

1908-1909, 1911
Finance: William Fraser, J.H. Latham
Grievance: Thomas Mercer, C. Suppes
Buildings: F.A. Pratt, George McDonald
Printing: J.H. Latham, George McDonald, C.L. Stinson
Reception: H.A. Severy, Thomas Mercer
Entertainment: H. Hennis, George McDonald, C.L. Stinson

1910
No records available

1912
Finance: William Fraser, C. Suppes
Grievance: Thomas Mercer, C. Suppes
Buildings: F.A. Pratt, George McDonald
Printing: George McDonald, C.L. Stinson
Reception: H.A. Severy, Thomas Mercer
Entertainment: H. Hennis, George McDonald, C.L. Stinson

In 1962 Margo and Marla Anderson of Somonauk were dwarfed by Mr. Farm Bureau.

303

1913-1915
No records available

1916-1917
Finance: William Fraser, P.S. Lindner, C. Suppes
Grievance: P.H. Potter, S.D. Newton
Buildings: F.A. Pratt, George McDonald, H. Hennis
Printing: George McDonald, C.L. Stinson
Reception: H.A. Severy, F.A. Pratt
Entertainment: H. Hennis, P.S. Lindner, C.L. Stinson

1918
Finance: William Fraser, P.S. Lindner, C. Suppes
Grievance: P.H. Potter, S.D. Newton
Buildings: F.A. Pratt, H. Hennis, Charles Howison
Printing: C.L. Stinson, Charles Howison
Reception: H.A. Severy, F.A. Pratt
Entertainment: H. Hennis, P.S. Lindner, C.L. Stinson

1919-1920
No records available

1921
Finance: William Fraser, P.S. Lindner, C. Suppes
Grievance: P.H. Potter, S.D. Newton
Buildings: F.A. Pratt, M.E. Lake, Charles Howison
Printing: C.L. Stinson, Charles Howison
Reception: H.A. Severy, F.A. Pratt
Entertainment: M.E. Lake, P.S. Lindner, C.L. Stinson

1922-1924
No records available

1925-1926
Finance: William Fraser, P.S. Lindner, Charles Howison
Grievance: S.D. Newton, T.J. Mahaffey
Buildings: M.E. Lake, Charles Howison
Printing: C.L. Stinson, Charles Howison
Reception: H.A. Severy, T.J. Mahaffey
Entertainment: M.E. Lake, P.S. Lindner, C.L. Stinson

1927-1931
Finance: P.S. Lindner, William Fraser, Charles Howison
Grievances: T.J. Mahaffey
Buildings: M.E. Lake, Charles Howison
Printing: C.L. Stinson, Charles Howison
Reception: H.A. Severy, T.J. Mahaffey
Entertainment: M.E. Lake, P.S. Lindner, C.L. Stinson

1932-1933
Finance: P.S. Lindner, William Fraser, Charles Howison
Grievances: T.J. Mahaffey
Buildings: M.E. Lake, Charles Howison
Printing: C.L. Stinson, Charles Howison
Reception: T.J. Mahaffey
Entertainment: M.E. Lake, P.S. Lindner, C.L. Stinson

1934-1935
Finance: H.J. White, William Fraser, Charles Howison
Grievances: T.J. Mahaffey
Buildings: M.E. Lake, Charles Howison
Printing: C.L. Stinson, Charles Howison
Reception: T.J. Mahaffey
Entertainment: M.E. Lake, Charles Howison, C.L. Stinson

1936
Finance: H.J. White, William Fraser, Charles Howison
Grievances: T.J. Mahaffey
Buildings and Grounds: M.E. Lake, Charles Howison
Printing: C.L. Stinson, Charles Howison
Reception: T.J. Mahaffey
Entertainment: M.E. Lake, Charles Howison, C.L. Stinson

1937
Finance: C.S. Bark, B.C. Eade, H.J. White

The organ grinder's monkey was trained to pick up coins, but fairgoers were often surprised when it threw back the pennies because It preferred silver coins.

Grievances: T.J. Mahaffey
Buildings and Grounds: M.E. Lake, Charles Howison
Printing: C.L. Stinson, Charles Howison
Reception: T.J. Mahaffey, Albert Skinner
Entertainment: M.E. Lake, Charles Howison, C.L. Stinson

1938-1939
Finance: C.S. Bark, B.C. Eade, H.J. White
Buildings and Grounds: M.E. Lake, Charles Howison
Printing: C.L. Stinson, Charles Howison
Reception: C.R. Brady, Albert Skinner
Entertainment: M.E. Lake, Charles Howison, C.L. Stinson

1940
Finance: C.S. Bark, B.C. Eade, H.J. White
Buildings and Grounds: M.E. Lake, Charles Howison, L.R. Evans
Printing: C.L. Stinson, Charles Howison
Reception: C. R Brady, A.W. Colliflower
Entertainment: M.E. Lake, Charles Howison, C.L. Stinson

1941
Finance: C.S. Bark, B.C. Eade, H.J. White
Buildings and Grounds: M.E. Lake, Charles Howison, L.R. Evans
Printing: C.R. Brady, Charles Howison
Reception: C.R. Brady, A.W. Colliflower
Entertainment: M.E. Lake, Charles Howison, C.R. Brady

1942-1943
Finance: C.S. Bark, B.C. Eade, H.J. White
Buildings and Grounds: M.E. Lake, Charles Howison, L.R. Evans
Printing: C.L. Stinson 1942, C.R. Brady 1943, Charles Howison
Reception: C. R Brady, A.W. Colliflower
Entertainment: M.E. Lake, Charles Howison, C.R. Brady

1944
Finance: Latham Castle, L.R. Evans, A.W. Colliflower
Buildings and Grounds: C.S. Bark, H.J. White, L.R. Evans
Printing: Ben Eade, C.R. Brady
Reception: H.J. White, Latham Castle

Entertainment: Ben Eade, C.R. Brady
Grievance: Latham Castle

1945
Finance: Latham Castle, Harry Darnell, A.W. Colliflower
Buildings and Grounds: C.S. Bark, H.J. White, Harry Darnell
Printing: Ben Eade, C.R. Brady
Reception: H.J. White, Latham Castle
Entertainment: Ben Eade, C.R. Brady
Grievance: Latham Castle

1946
Grounds and Equipment: Darnell, White, Bark, Wahlgren
Buildings and Maintenance: Wahlgren, Castle, Darnell
Electricity and Water: Hough, Darnell, White
Police and Traffic: Darnell, Wahlgren, White
Judging Premiums and Awards: Eade, White, Bark
Entertainment: Brady, Colliflower
Tickets, Admissions and Office Help: Colliflower
Auditing and Finance: Castle, Colliflower, Eade

1947
Grounds and Equipment: Darnell, S. Bark, Wahlgren, Hough
Buildings and Maintenance: Wahlgren, S. Bark, Henderson, Darnell
Electricity: Hough, H. Bark
Police and Traffic: Darnell, Wahlgren, White, Scent
Judging Premiums and Awards: Henderson, S. Bark, Eade, White
Publicity and Catalog: Brady, Scent, H. Bark
Entertainment: Brady, Howison, Scent
Tickets, Admissions and Office Help: Colliflower, H. Bark
Concessions: Dillon
Auditing and Finance: Castle, Colliflower, H. Bark
Forage: Henderson
Score Card and Programs: Scent, H. Bark, Dillon, Brady

1948
Grounds and Equipment: Darnell, D. Knights, Wahlgren, Hough
Buildings and Maintenance: Eade, Wahlgren, Henderson,

Darnell
Electricity: Hough, H. Bark
Police and Traffic: Darnell, Wahlgren, White, Scent
Judging Premiums and Awards: Henderson, D. Knights, Eade, White
Publicity and Catalog: Brady, Scent
Entertainment: Brady, Scent
Tickets, Admissions and Office Help: Colliflower
Concessions: Dillon
Auditing and Finance: Colliflower, Castle, Suppes
Forage: Brady, Suppes
Score Card and Programs: Scent, Dillon, Brady

1949-1950
Grounds and Equipment: Darnell, D. Knights, Wahlgren
Buildings and Maintenance: Wahlgren, Henderson, Darnell, Eade
Electricity: Hough, H. Bark
Police and Traffic: Darnell, Wahlgren, White, Scent
Judging Premiums and Awards: Henderson, D. Knights, Eade, White
Publicity and Catalog: Scent, Brady
Entertainment: Brady, Scent
Tickets, Admissions and Office Help: Colliflower, Hough
Concessions: Dillon
Auditing and Finance: Colliflower, Castle, Suppes
Forage: Suppes, Brady
Score Card and Programs: Scent, Brady

1951
Grounds and Equipment: Darnell, Stahl, Wahlgren
Buildings and Maintenance: Wahlgren, Knights, Darnell, Eade
Electricity: Hough, H. Bark
Police and Traffic: Darnell, Wahlgren, White, Scent
Judging Premiums and Awards: Eade, Suppes, Bark, Stahl
Publicity and Catalog: Scent, Brady
Entertainment: Brady, Scent
Tickets, Admissions and Office Help: Colliflower, Hough
Concessions: Dillon
Auditing and Finance: Colliflower, Castle, Suppes
Forage: Suppes, Brady
Score Card and Programs: Scent, Brady

1952
Grounds and Equipment: Darnell, Stahl, Wahlgren
Buildings and Maintenance: Wahlgren, Knights, Darnell, Eade
Electricity: Hough, H. Bark
Police and Traffic: Darnell, Wahlgren, White, Scent
Judging Premiums and Awards: Eade, Suppes, Bark, Stahl
Publicity and Catalog: Scent, Brady
Entertainment: Brady, Scent
Tickets, Admissions and Office Help: Colliflower, Hough
Concessions: Louis P. Brady
Auditing and Finance: Castle, Suppes
Forage: Suppes, Brady
Score Card and Programs: Scent, Brady

1953
Grounds and Equipment: Darnell, Hough, Wahlgren
Buildings and Maintenance: Wahlgren, Knights, Darnell
Electricity: Hough, H. Bark
Police and Traffic: Darnell, Wahlgren, White
Judging Premiums and Awards: Johnson, Suppes, Bark, Stahl
Publicity and Catalog: Scent, Brady
Entertainment: Brady, Scent
Tickets, Admissions and Office Help: Roberts, Scent
Concessions: Louis P. Brady
Finance and Legal Counsel: Roberts, Castle
Forage: Suppes, Brady
Score Card and Programs: Scent

Grandstand: Wahlgren, Hough, Darnell
Auditing Committee: White, Suppes, Scent

1954
Grounds and Equipment: Darnell, Hough, Wahlgren
Buildings and Maintenance: Wahlgren, Knights, Darnell
Electricity: Hough, H. Bark
Police and Traffic: Darnell, Wahlgren
Judging Premiums and Awards: Johnson, Suppes, Bark, Stahl
Publicity and Catalog: Scent, Brady
Entertainment: Brady, Scent
Tickets, Admissions and Office Help: Roberts, Scent
Concessions: Louis P. Brady
Finance and Legal Counsel: Roberts, Castle
Forage: Suppes, Brady
Score Card and Programs: Scent
Grandstand: Wahlgren, Hough, Darnell
Auditing Committee: Suppes, Scent

1955
Grounds and Equipment: Darnell, Hough, Wahlgren
Buildings and Maintenance: Wahlgren, Knights, Darnell
Electricity: Hough, H. Bark
Police and Traffic: Darnell, Wahlgren
Judging Premiums and Awards: Johnson, Suppes, Wagner, Stahl
Publicity and Catalog: Scent, Brady
Entertainment: Brady, Scent
Tickets, Admissions and Office Help: Roberts, Scent
Concessions: Louis P. Brady
Finance and Legal Counsel: Roberts, Castle
Forage: Suppes, Brady
Score Card and Programs: Scent
Grandstand: Wahlgren, Hough, Darnell
Auditing Committee: Suppes, Scent

1956-1957
Judging Premiums and Awards: Johnson, Knights, Henderson, Wagner
Building and Grounds: Hough, Stahl, L.P. Brady, Suppes

Entertainment and Publicity: C.R. Brady, Scent, White
Finance and Legal Council: Roberts, Castle, Rex
Grievance: White, C.R. Brady, Henderson, Johnson

1958-1959
Judging Premiums and Awards: Knights, Henderson, Wagner
Building and Grounds: Hough, Stahl, L.P. Brady, Scent
Entertainment and Publicity: C.R. Brady, Scent, White
Finance and Legal Council: Scent, Castle, Rex
Grievance: White, C.R. Brady, Henderson

1960
Judging Premiums and Awards: Knights, Henderson, Wagner
Building and Grounds: Hough, L.P. Brady, Scent
Entertainment and Publicity: C.R. Brady, Scent, White
Finance and Legal Council: Scent, Castle, Rex
Grievance: White, C.R. Brady, Henderson

1961
Judging Premiums and Awards: Knights, Henderson, Wagner
Building and Grounds: Hough, L.P. Brady, Scent
Entertainment and Publicity: C.R. Brady, Scent, White
Finance and Legal Council: Scent, Castle, Rex
Grievance: White, C.R. Brady, Duvick
Police and Parking: A.A. Legner D.V.M.
Queen Contest: K. Klotz

1962-1963
Judging Premiums and Awards: White, Duvick, Wagner
Building and Grounds: Hough, L.P. Brady, Scent
Entertainment and Publicity: C.R. Brady and Scent
Finance and Legal Council: Scent, Castle, Rex
Grievance: White, C.R. Brady, Duvick
Police and Parking: A.A. Legner D.V.M.
Queen Contest: K. Klotz

1964-1965
Judging Premiums and Awards: White, Duvick, Wagner

Children at the Sandwich Fair climb over the miniature scale model steam engine made by the Otto Manufacturing Co. of Sandwich. (l. to r.) Karen Jennings, Gary Jennings, Barry Sweeny, two unknown fairgoers

Beacon News

Building and Grounds: Hough, L.P. Brady, Scent
Entertainment and Publicity: C.R. Brady, Scent
Finance: Scent, Rex
Grievance: White, C.R. Brady, Duvick
Police and Parking: A.A. Legner D.V.M., Donald Breunig

1966
Judging Premiums and Awards: D. Stahl, L. Wagner,
H. White, L.P. Brady
Building and Grounds: C. Hough, L.P. Brady, K. Klotz,
D. Stahl
Entertainment and Advertising: C.R. Brady, Carl Scent
Finance: Lewis Rex, Carl Scent
Grievance: L. Brady, L. Rex, K. Klotz, D. Breunig, D. Stahl

1967-1968
Judging Premiums and Awards: D. Stahl, L. Wagner,
C.R. Brady
Building and Grounds: C. Hough, K. Klotz, R. Stahl,
D. Breunig
Entertainment and Advertising: C.R. Brady, L.P. Brady
Finance: Lewis Rex, L.P. Brady
Grievance: D. Stahl, A. Legner, S. Gord, L. Rex

1969
Judging Premiums and Awards: D. Stahl, L. Wagner,
C.R. Brady
Building and Grounds: C. Hough, K. Klotz, R. Stahl,
D. Breunig
Entertainment and Advertising: C.R. Brady, L.P. Brady
Finance: Jack Norling, L.P. Brady
Grievance: D. Stahl, A. Legner, S. Gord, J. Norling

1970-1971
Building and Grounds: C. Hough, R. Stahl, D. Breunig,
A.A. Legner D.V.M.
Entertainment and Advertising: K. Klotz, C.R. Brady,
L.P. Brady, Wes Scents
Finance: Jack Norling, L.P. Brady
Grievance: D. Stahl, A. Legner, S. Gord, J. Norling

1972
Building and Grounds: C. Hough, R. Stahl, D. Breunig,
A.A. Legner D.V.M., D. Stahl
Entertainment and Advertising: K. Klotz, C.R. Brady,
L.P. Brady, Wes Scents
Finance: Jack Norling, L.P. Brady
Grievance: D. Stahl, A. Legner, S. Gord, J. Norling

1973-1974
Building and Grounds: C. Hough, R. Stahl, D. Breunig,
D. Stahl, A.A. Legner D.V.M.
Entertainment and Advertising: K. Klotz, L.P. Brady,
D. Breunig
Finance: Jack Norling, L.P. Brady
Grievance: D. Stahl, A.A. Legner D.V.M., J. Norling

1975-1977
Building and Grounds: C.H. Hough, R. Stahl, D. Breunig,
L. Wagner, F. Lindner
Entertainment and Advertising: K. Klotz, L.P. Brady,
D. Breunig
Finance: Jack Norling, L.P. Brady
Grievance: D. Stahl, J. Wagner, A.A. Legner D.V.M.,
W. Updike
Bicentennial Committee: Jack Norling, L.P. Brady,
D. Breunig

1978-1979
Building and Grounds: C.H. Hough, R. Stahl, D. Breunig,
L. Wagner, F. Lindner
Entertainment and Advertising: L.P. Brady, D. Breunig
Finance: Jack Norling, L.P. Brady
Grievance: D. Stahl, J. Wagner, A.A. Legner D.V.M.,
W. Updike

OFFICE OF SANDWICH FAIR ASSOCIATION
SANDWICH, ILLINOIS
November 2, 1932

As an Exhibitor at the Sandwich Fair this year you were not paid your premium money, amounting to $ 9.25 . This was in accordance with the terms of our Premium list, page 5, which reads, "After all Expenses have been paid, balance of Receipts will be devoted to paying Premiums."

There is no money to pay Premiums at present; however, the State of Illinois will pay us about 50 per cent of our 1932 Premiums provided we can show same as paid.

If you care to give us a receipt in full for 1932 Premiums, and all other Exhibitors will do the same, we can then submit our report to the State and claim our percentage, and whatever we received will be pro-rated among our Exhibitors.

The time is very short and we must have your receipt by return mail if we are going to make this claim.

If this plan meets with your approval, please sign the receipt herewith and return in the enclosed stamped envelope immediately.

C. L. STINSON, Secretary

Courtesy of R.P.H.

In 1932 insufficient funds forced the Fair Association to notify all premium recipients that payments would be deferred. This certificate indicates the exhibitor will receive $9.25 when money is available.

1980-1982
Building and Grounds: C.H. Hough, R. Stahl, D. Breunig,
L. Wagner, S. Phillips
Entertainment and Advertising: L.P. Brady, D. Breunig
Finance: Jack Norling, L.P. Brady
Grievance: D. Stahl, J. Wagner, A.A. Legner D.V.M.,
W. Updike

1983
Building and Grounds: C.H. Hough, R. Stahl, D. Breunig,
L. Wagner, S. Phillips
Entertainment and Advertising: L.P. Brady, D. Breunig
Finance: Jack Norling, L.P. Brady
Grievance: D. Stahl, J. Wagner, W. Updike

1984
Building and Grounds: C.H. Hough, D. Stahl, D. Breunig,
L. Wagner, S. Phillips
Entertainment and Advertising: L.P. Brady, D. Breunig
Finance: Jack Norling, L.P. Brady
Grievance: R. Stahl, J. Wagner, W. Updike

1985
Building and Grounds: C.H. Hough, D. Stahl, D. Breunig,
S. Phillips
Entertainment and Advertising: L.P. Brady, D. Breunig
Finance: Jack Norling, L.P. Brady
Grievance: R. Stahl, J. Wagner, W. Updike

1986
Anniversary: L.P. Brady, J. Norling, J. Wagner, W. Updike,
C.H. Hough
Building and Grounds: C.H. Hough, D. Stahl, S. Breunig
Capital Improvements: W. Updike, D. Bark, D. Augustine
Entertainment and Advertising: D. Augustine,
D. Breunig, L.P. Brady
Finance: L.P. Brady, D. Breunig, J. E. Norling
Grievance: R. Guehler, R. Stahl, J. Wagner, D. Stahl
Off-Season Events: S. Phillips, R. Stahl, R. Guehler
Safety and Security: D. Bark, S. Breunig, S. Phillips

1987
Anniversary: L.P. Brady, J. Norling, J. Wagner, W. Updike,
C.H. Hough
Building and Grounds: C.H. Hough, D. Stahl, S. Breunig
Capital Improvements: W. Updike, D. Bark, D. Augustine
Entertainment and Advertising: D. Augustine,
D. Breunig, L.P. Brady
Finance: L.P. Brady, D. Breunig, J. E. Norling
Grievance: R. Guehler, R. Stahl, J. Wagner, D. Stahl

Off-Season Events: S. Phillips, R. Stahl, R. Guehler
Safety and Security: D. Bark, S. Breunig, S. Phillips
Data Management: Audrey Hoffman

1988
Building and Grounds: C.H. Hough, D. Stahl, S. Breunig,
K.Tyrrell
Capital Improvements: W. Updike, D. Augustine,
C.H. Hough, J. Wagner
Entertainment and Advertising: D. Augustine, D. Breunig,
L.P. Brady, W. Updike
Finance: L.P. Brady, D. Breunig, J. E. Norling
Grievance: R. Guehler, R. Stahl, J. Wagner, D. Stahl
Off-Season Events: D. Bark, J. Norling, R. Stahl,
R. Guehler
Safety and Security: D. Bark, S. Breunig, K. Tyrrell
Data Management: Audrey Hoffman

Committee lists were no longer printed in the premium book after 1988. However, these committees continue to be appointed and to function.

SUPERINTENDENTS OF OPERATIONS AND ENTERTAINMENT

1888
General Superintendent: A. Gilchrist
Speed: I.M. Arnold

1890
Speed: Joseph Calahan

1893
General Superintendent: H.E. White
Privileges: Gage
Speed: T.S. Clough, Jr.

1895
General Superintendent: W. M. Foster
Privileges: Gage
Speed: C.W. LaSuer

1896
Privileges: Gage
Speed: Henry Hennis

1897
Grounds: LaSuer

Privileges: Gage
Forage: F.A. Pratt
Employment of Help: Severy
Speed: Henry Hennis

1898
Grounds: F.A. Pratt
Privileges: Gage

1899
Privileges: F.A. Pratt
Marshal: George McDonald

1900-1901
Privileges: F.A. Pratt
Forage: P.H. Potter 1900, J.H. Latham 1901
Employment of Help, Gates, and Police: H.A. Severy
Water: C.V. Stevens
Marshal: George Owen and E. Kirkpatrick
Speed: Henry Hennis

1902-1903
Privileges: F.A. Pratt
Forage: J.H. Latham 1902, C. Suppes 1903
Employment of Help, Gates, and Police: H.A. Severy
Water: C.V. Stevens
Marshal: George Owen
Speed: Henry Hennis

1904-1906
Privileges: F.A. Pratt
Forage: C. Suppes
Employment of Help, Gates, and Police: H.A. Severy
Water: Thomas Mercer
Grounds: H. Hennis
Marshal: George Owen (No one in 1906)
Speed: Henry Hennis (also 1905)

1908-1909
Privileges: F.A. Pratt 1907
Forage: C. Suppes 1907
Employment of Help, Gates, and Police:
H.A. Severy 1907

Water: Thomas Mercer 1907
Grounds: Henry Hennis
Marshal: Fay Harrington
Speed: Henry Hennis

1910
Privileges: F.A. Pratt
Forage: C. Suppes
Employment of Help, Gates, and Police: H.A. Severy
Water: Records not available
Grounds: Henry Hennis
Marshal: Records not available
Speed: Henry Hennis

1911-1912
Privileges: F.A. Pratt
Forage: C. Suppes
Employment of Help, Gates, and Police: H.A. Severy
Water: Henry Hennis
Grounds: Henry Hennis
Speed: Henry Hennis

1913-1915
No records available

1916-1921
Privileges: F.A. Pratt and P.S. Lindner
Forage: C. Suppes
Employment of Help, Gates, and Police: H.A. Severy
Water and Grounds: Henry Hennis (and M.E. Lake 1921)
Speed: Henry Hennis (also 1919-1925, but not 1921), M.E. Lake 1921

1919-1926
No records available

1927-1931
Privileges: P.S. Lindner
Forage: C. Suppes
Employment of Help, Gates, and Police: H.A. Severy and T.J. Mahaffey
Water and Grounds: M.E. Lake
Speed: Thomas Mercer

1932-1933
Privileges: P.S. Lindner
Forage: C. Suppes
Employment of Help, Gates, and Police: T.J. Mahaffey
Water and Grounds: M.E. Lake
Speed: Thomas Mercer 1932 (No one listed in 1933)
Draft Horse Pull: Ben Eade

1934-1935
Draft Horse Pull: Ben Eade

1936-1937
Privileges: A.O. Fosse 1936 (Privileges not listed in 1937)
Forage: A.C. Baie
Employment of Help, Gates, and Police: T.J. Mahaffey
Water and Grounds: M.E. Lake
Speed: Thomas Mercer
Draft Horse Pull: Ben Eade

1938-1940
Forage: A.C. Baie
Employment of Help, Gates, and Police: L.R. Evans
Water and Grounds: M.E. Lake
Speed: Thomas Mercer (No record in 1939)

1941
Forage: A.C. Baie
Employment of Help, Gates, and Police: Art Potter
Water and Grounds: M.E. Lake
Speed: Art Potter (also 1942)

1942
No records available

1943
Forage: A.C. Baie
Employment of Help, Gates, and Police: L.R. Evans
Water and Grounds: William Dillon
Speed: Art Potter
NOTE: Superintendent of Privileges was probably C.R. Brady 1937-1943

Harness racing is one of the oldest forms of entertainment at the Fair.

Photo by L.D.

A colorful balloon release marked the close of the 1987 auto show.

1944
Forage: A.C. Baie
Employment of Help, Gates, and Police: L.R. Evans
Water and Grounds: Albert Dannewitz
Midway and Concessions (Privileges): Charles Fish
Speed: S. A. "Art" Potter

1945
Employment: Harry Darnell
Water and Grounds: Albert Dannewitz
Speed: Art Potter and Dutch Hough
Concessions and Displays: William Dillon

1946-1948
Grandstand: George Wahlgren and A.W. Colliflower
Speed: Art Potter and C.H. Hough
Concessions and Displays: William Dillon
Caretaker: Shelby Morris

1949-1954
No superintendents listed other than:
Speed: Art Potter and C.H. Hough
Concessions and Displays: William Dillon 1949-1952;
L.P. Brady 1953-1954
Caretaker: Shelby Morris

1955
Speed: Art Potter and C.H. Hough
Concessions and Displays: Louis P. Brady

Speed: Art Potter and C.H. Hough
Caretaker: Shelby Morris

1956-1958
Fire Protection, Police, and Traffic: Donald Stahl
Concessions and Display Space: Louis P. Brady
Speed: Art Potter and C.H. Hough
Caretaker: Shelby Morris

1959-1960
Fire Protection, Police and Traffic: Donald Stahl
Concessions and Display Space: Louis P. Brady
Speed: C.H. Hough and V.F. Beck
Caretaker: Shelby Morris

1961-1963
Concessions and Display Space: Louis P. Brady and
Kenneth Klotz
Panels and Tents: Russell Stahl
Speed: C.H. Hough and V.F. Beck
Caretaker: Shelby Morris

1964
Outside Gates: Lewis Rex
Concessions and Display Space: Louis P. Brady and
Kenneth Klotz
Panels and Tents: Russell Stahl
Speed: C.H. Hough and V.F. Beck
Caretaker: Shelby Morris

1965
Outside Gates: Lewis Rex
Concessions and Display Space: Louis P. Brady and
Kenneth Klotz
Panels and Tents: Russell Stahl
Tractor Pull: Russell Stahl and Ed Tuntland
Speed: C.H. Hough and V.F. Beck
Caretaker: Shelby Morris

1966
Ticket Sales: Lewis Rex
Concessions and Display Space: Kenny Klotz and
Fred Kinchner
Panels and Tents: Russell Stahl
Tractor Pull: Russell Stahl and Ed Tuntland
Speed: C.H. Hough and V.F. Beck
Caretaker: Shelby Morris

1967-1970
Ticket Sales: Lewis Rex 1967-1968,
Jack Norling 1969-1970
Concessions and Display Space: Kenny Klotz and
Fred Kinchner
Panels and Tents: Russell Stahl
Tractor Pull: Russell Stahl and Ed Tuntland
Parking and Police: A.A. Legner and Donald Breunig
Antique Farm Machinery: Andy Krafft, Willard Schmidt,
Alvin Miller 1967-1969; Andy Krafft, Ed Weismiller,
Dave Stahl 1970

Antique Auto Show: Robert Loy
Speed: C.H. Hough and V.F. Beck
Caretaker: Shelby Morris 1967-1968;
Herman Carlson 1969-1970
First Aid: Earl Tapp (Civil Defense) 1970
Farm Zoo: Milford Clausen, Don Wilson, Jack Niles,
Arnie Parchert

1971-1973
Ticket Sales: Jack Norling
Concessions and Display Space: Kenny Klotz and
Donald Bark
Panels and Tents: Russell Stahl
Tractor Pull: Russell Stahl and Ed Tuntland
Parking and Police: A.A. Legner and
Donald Breunig 1971-1972; A.A. Legner and
F. Lindner 1973
Antique Farm Machinery: Andy Krafft, Ed Weismiller,
Dave Stahl 1971-1972; Andy Krafft 1973
Antique Auto Show: Robert Loy
Speed: C.H. Hough and V.F. Beck
Craft Demonstrations: Marie Kinchner Rice and
Ruth Haag 1972-1973
Caretaker: Herman Carlson
First Aid: Earl Tapp (Civil Defense)
Farm Zoo: Milford Clausen, Don Wilson, Jack Niles,
Arnie Parchert

1974-1976
Ticket Sales: Jack Norling
Concessions and Display Space: Kenny Klotz and
Donald Bark
Panels and Tents: Russell Stahl
Tractor Pull: Russell Stahl and Ed Tuntland
Parking and Police: A.A. Legner and Frederick Lindner
Antique Farm Machinery: Andy Krafft
Antique Auto Show: Robert Loy
Speed: C.H. Hough and V.F. Beck
Craft Demonstrations: Marie Kinchner Rice and
Ruth Haag
Caretaker: Herman Carlson
First Aid: Earl Tapp (Civil Defense) 1974, Kathy
Haggard, R.N. (Civil Defense) and local EMT nurses
1975-1976
Farm Zoo: Milford Clausen, Don Wilson, Jack Niles,
Arnie Parchert 1974, Andy Anderson 1975

1977
Ticket Sales: Jack Norling
Concessions and Display Space: Kenny Klotz and
Donald Bark
Panels and Tents: Russell Stahl
Tractor Pull: Russell Stahl and Ed Tuntland
Parking and Police: A.A. Legner and Frederick Lindner
Antique Farm Machinery: Andy Krafft
Antique Auto Show: Robert Loy
Speed: C.H. Hough and V.F. Beck
Craft Demonstrations: Marie Kinchner Rice and
Ruth Haag
Caretaker: Herman Carlson
First Aid: Kathy Haggard, R.N. (Civil Defense) and local
EMT nurses
Farm Zoo: Andy Anderson

1978-1979
Ticket Sales: Jack Norling
Concessions and Display Space: Donald Bark
Panels and Tents: Robert Guehler
Tractor Pull: Russell Stahl and Ed Tuntland
Truck Pull: Wiley Updike
Parking and Police: A.A. Legner and F. Lindner
Antique Farm Machinery: Andy Krafft
Antique Auto Show: Robert Loy
Speed: C.H. Hough and V.F. Beck
Craft Demonstrations: Marie Kinchner Rice and

Ruth Haag
Caretaker: Herman Carlson
First Aid: Kathy Haggard, R.N. (Civil Defense) and local
EMT nurses
Farm Zoo: Andy Anderson 1978; Matt Wilson 1979

1980
Ticket Sales: Jack Norling
Concessions and Displays: Donald Bark
Panels and Tents: Robert Guehler
Tractor and Truck Pull: Russell Stahl and Wiley Updike
Parking and Police: Scott Breunig and Stuart Phillips
Antique Farm Machinery: Andy Krafft
Antique Auto Show: Robert Loy
Micro-Mini Tractor Pull: Dick Delp
Speed: C.H. Hough and V.F. Beck
Craft Demonstrations: Marie Kinchner Rice and
Ruth Haag
Caretaker: Herman Carlson
First Aid: Barbara "Boots" Hoffman, R.N. and local
EMT's
Farm Zoo: Matt Wilson

1981-1982
Ticket Sales: Jack Norling
Concessions and Display Space: Donald Bark
Tractor and Truck Pull: Russell Stahl and Wiley Updike
Panels and Tents: Robert Guehler
Parking and Police: Scott Breunig and Stuart Phillips
Antique Farm Machinery: Andy Krafft
Antique Auto Show: Robert Loy
Micro-Mini Tractor Pull: Dick Delp
Western Horse Show: Steve Hilleson and Paul Butler
Speed: C.H. Hough and V.F. Beck
Craft Demonstrations: Marie Kinchner Rice and
Ruth Haag
Caretaker: Herman Carlson
First Aid: Barbara "Boots" Hoffman, R.N. and local
EMT's
Farm Zoo: Matt Wilson

1983-1985
Ticket Sales: Jack Norling
Concessions and Display Space: Donald Bark
Panels and Tents: Robert Guehler
Tractor and Truck Pull: Russell Stahl and Wiley Updike
Parking and Police: Scott Breunig and Stuart Phillips
Antique Farm Machinery: Andy Krafft
Antique Auto Show: Wiley Updike
Micro-Mini Tractor Pull: Dick Delp
Western Horse Show: Steve Hilleson and Paul Butler
Speed: C.H. Hough and James Meade
Craft Demonstrations: Marie Kinchner Rice, Ruth Haag,
and Eileen Weber
Caretaker: Herman Carlson
First Aid: Barbara "Boots" Hoffman, R.N. and local
EMT's
Farm Zoo: Matt Wilson 1983-1985; Gary Blankenship
1985

1986-1987
Ticket Sales: Jack Norling
Concessions and Display Space: Donald Bark
Panels and Tents: Robert Guehler
Tractor and Truck Pull: Wiley Updike
Parking and Police: Scott Breunig and Stuart Phillips
Antique Farm Machinery: Andy Krafft 1986; Michael
Krafft 1987
Antique Auto Show: Wiley Updike
Micro-Mini Tractor Pull: Dick Delp
Western Horse Show: Steve Hilleson and Paul Butler
Horseshoe Pitching: Kenneth Huff and Glenn Bower
Sheep Dog Trial: Dave Birch
Speed: C.H. Hough and James Meade
Craft Demonstrations: Marie Kinchner Rice, Ruth Haag,

and Eileen Weber
Caretaker: Herman Carlson
First Aid: Barbara "Boots" Hoffman, R.N. and local EMT's
Farm Zoo: Matt Wilson and Gary Blankenship

1988
Ticket Sales: John Hallaron and Nancy Lou Rex
Concessions and Display Space: Donald Bark
Panels and Tents: Robert Guehler
Tractor and Truck Pull: Wiley Updike
Parking and Police: Scott Breunig and William Haag
Antique Farm Machinery: Michael Krafft
Antique Auto Show: Wiley Updike
Micro-Mini Tractor Pull: Dick Delp
Western Horse Show: Steve Hilleson and Paul Butler
Horseshoe Pitching: Kenneth Huff and Glenn Bower
Sheep Dog Trial: Dave Birch
Speed: C.H. Hough and James Meade
Craft Demonstrations: Marie Kinchner Rice and
Eileen Weber
Caretaker: Andy Krafft
First Aid: Barbara "Boots" Hoffman, R.N. and local EMT's
Farm Zoo: Matt Wilson and Gary Blankenship

1989
Ticket Sales: John Hallaron and Nancy Lou Rex
Concessions and Display Space: Donald Bark
Panels and Tents: Robert Guehler
Tractor and Truck Pull: Wiley Updike
Parking and Police: Scott Breunig and William Haag
Antique Farm Machinery: Michael Krafft
Antique Auto Show: Wiley Updike
Micro-Mini Tractor Pull: Dick Delp
Western Horse Show: Steve Hilleson and Paul Butler
Electrician: Charles Bark
Caretaker: Andy Krafft
Livestock Maintenance: Duane Lackey
Horseshoe Pitching: Kenneth Huff and Glenn Bower
Sheep Dog Trial: Dave Birch
Data Management: Audrey Hoffman
Speed: James Meade
Craft Demonstrations: Marie Kinchner Rice and
Eileen Weber
First Aid: Barbara "Boots" Hoffman, R.N. and local EMT's
Farm Zoo: Matt Wilson and Gary Blankenship

1990-1991
Ticket Sales: John Hallaron and Nancy Lou Rex
Concessions and Display Space: Donald Bark
Panels and Tents: Robert Guehler
Tractor Truck Pull: Wiley Updike
Parking and Police: Scott Breunig and William Haag
Antique Farm Machinery: Michael Krafft
Antique Auto Show: Wiley Updike
Micro-Mini Tractor Pull: Dick Delp
Western Horse Show: Steve Hilleson and Paul Butler
Electrician: Charles Bark 1990; Harold Dannewitz 1991
Caretaker: Andy Krafft
Livestock Maintenance: Duane Lackey
Horseshoe Pitching: Kenneth Huff and Charles Hilliard
1990; Kenneth Huff and Paul Johnson 1991
Grandstand Entertainment: Don Augustine and
Donald Breunig
Craft Demonstrations: Marie Kinchner Rice and
Eileen Weber
Data Management: Audrey Hoffman
Sheep Dog Trial: Dave Birch
Speed: James Meade
First Aid: Barbara "Boots" Hoffman, R.N. and local EMT's
Farm Zoo: Matt Wilson and Gary Blankenship

1992
Ticket Sales: John Hallaron and Nancy Lou Rex
Concessions and Display Space: Donald Bark
Panels and Tents: Robert Guehler

Tractor and Truck Pull: Wiley Updike
Parking and Police: Scott Breunig and William Haag
Antique Farm Machinery: Michael Krafft
Antique Auto Show: Wiley Updike
Micro-Mini Tractor Pull: Dick Delp
Western Horse Show: Steve Hilleson and Adrian Butler
Electrician: Harold Dannewitz
Caretaker: Andy Krafft
Horseshoe Pitching: Kenneth Huff and Paul Johnson
Grandstand Entertainment: Don Augustine and
Donald Breunig
Craft Demonstrations: Marie Kinchner Rice and
Eileen Weber
Data Management: Audrey Hoffman
Sheep Dog Trial: Dave Birch
Speed: James Meade
First Aid: Barbara "Boots" Hoffman, R.N. and local
EMT's
Farm Zoo: Matt Wilson and Gary Blankenship

1993
Ticket Sales: John Hallaron and Nancy Lou Rex
Concessions and Display Space: Donald Bark
Panels and Tents: Robert Guehler
Tractor and Truck Pull: Wiley Updike and Gene Frieders
Parking and Police: Scott Breunig and William Haag
Antique Farm Machinery: Michael Krafft
Antique Auto Show: Wiley Updike and Warren
Greenwood
Micro-Mini Tractor Pull: Dick Delp
Western Horse Show: Steve Hilleson and Adrian Butler
Electrician: Harold Dannewitz and John Spoor
Caretaker: Andy Krafft
Horseshoe Pitching: Kenneth Huff and Paul Johnson
Sheep Dog Trial: Dave Birch
Grandstand Entertainment: Don Augustine and
Larry Dannewitz
Craft Demonstrations: Marie Kinchner Rice and
Eileen Weber
Data Management: Audrey Hoffman
Gazebo Information: Karen Breunig and
Cheryl Augustine
Speed: James Meade
First Aid: Barbara "Boots" Hoffman, R.N. and local
EMT's
Farm Zoo: Matt Wilson, Gary Blankenship, and
Joe Steffen
Ag Land Stage: Scott Breunig

1994
Ticket Sales: John Hallaron and Nancy Lou Rex
Concessions and Display Space: Donald Bark
Panels and Tents: Robert Guehler
Tractor and Truck Pull: Wiley Updike and Gene Frieders
Parking and Police: Scott Breunig and William Haag
Antique Farm Machinery: Michael Krafft
Antique Auto Show: Wiley Updike and
Warren Greenwood
Micro-Mini Tractor Pull: Dick Delp
Western Horse Show: Steve Hilleson and Adrian Butler
Electrician: Harold Dannewitz, Reed Johnson, and
John Spoor
Caretaker: Andy Krafft
Horseshoe Pitching: Kenneth Huff and Paul Johnson
Grandstand Entertainment: Don Augustine and
Larry Dannewitz
Craft Demonstrations: Eileen Weber and
Marie Kinchner Rice
Data Management: Audrey Hoffman
Gazebo Information: Karen Breunig and
Cheryl Augustine
Sheep Dog Trial: Dave Birch
Speed: James Meade
First Aid: Barbara "Boots" Hoffman, R.N. and local
EMT's

A blue ribbon bushel basket display at the 1963 Fair was judged for quality, edibility, assortment, uniformity, arrangement, and attractiveness.

Farm Zoo: Matt Wilson, Gary Blankenship, and
Joe Steffen
Ag Land Stage: Scott Breunig and Don Lawyer

1995
Ticket Sales: John Hallaron and Nancy Lou Rex
Concessions and Display Space: Donald Bark
Tractor and Truck Pull: Wiley Updike and Gene Frieders
Parking and Police: Scott Breunig and William Haag
Antique Farm Machinery: Michael Krafft
Antique Auto Show: Wiley Updike and
Warren Greenwood
Micro-Mini Tractor Pull: Dick Delp
Western Horse Show: Steve and Carole Hilleson
Electrician: Harold Dannewitz and Reed Johnson
Caretaker: Andy Krafft
Horseshoe Pitching: Kenneth Huff and Paul Johnson
Grandstand Entertainment: Don Augustine and
Larry Dannewitz
Fiddle Contest: Larry Robinson
Craft Demonstrations: Eileen Weber
Data Management: Audrey Hoffman
Gazebo Information: Karen Breunig and
Cheryl Augustine
Speed: James Meade
First Aid: Barbara "Boots" Hoffman, R.N. and local EMT's
Farm Zoo: Matt Wilson, Gary Blankenship, and
Joe Steffen

Ag Land Stage: Scott Breunig and Don Lawyer
Draft Horse Pull: Joe Steffen and Scott Breunig

1996
Ticket Sales: John Hallaron and Nancy Lou Rex
Concessions and Display Space: Donald Bark
Tractor and Truck Pull: Wiley Updike and Gene Frieders
Parking and Police: Scott Breunig and William Haag
Antique Farm Machinery: Michael Krafft
Antique Auto Show: Wiley Updike and Ula Greenwood
Micro-Mini Tractor Pull: Dick Delp
Western Horse Show: Steve and Carole Hilleson
Electrician: Harold Dannewitz and Reed Johnson
Caretakers: Andy Krafft and Jim Webber
Horseshoe Pitching: Kenneth Huff and Paul Johnson
Grandstand Entertainment: Don Augustine and
Larry Dannewitz
Fiddle Contest: Larry Robinson
Craft Demonstrations: Eileen Weber
Data Management: Audrey Hoffman
Gazebo Information: Karen Breunig and
Cheryl Augustine
Sheep Dog Trial: Dave Birch
Tents and Panels: Kenneth Tyrrell
Speed: James Meade
First Aid: Barbara "Boots" Hoffman, R.N. and local EMT's
Farm Zoo: Matt Wilson, Gary Blankenship, and
Joe Steffen

Ag Land Stage: Scott Breunig and Don Lawyer
Draft Horse Pull: Joe Steffen and Scott Breunig

1997
Ticket Sales: Nancy Lou Rex, John Hallaron and Roy Wahlgren
Concessions and Display Space: Donald Bark
Tractor and Truck Pull: Wiley Updike and Gene Frieders
Parking and Police: Scott Breunig and William Haag
Antique Farm Machinery: Michael Krafft
Antique Auto Show: Wiley Updike and Ula Greenwood
Micro-Mini Tractor Pull: Dick Delp
Western Horse Show: Steve and Carole Hilleson
Electricians: Harold Dannewitz and Reed Johnson
Caretakers: Andy Krafft and Jim Webber
Horseshoe Pitching: Kenneth Huff and Paul Johnson
Grandstand Entertainment: Don Augustine and Larry Dannewitz
Fiddle Contest: Larry Robinson
Craft Demonstrations: Eileen Weber
Data Management: Ginger Dannewitz, Office Manager
Gazebo Information: Karen Breunig and Cheryl Augustine
Sheep Dog Trial: Dave Birch
Tents and Panels: Kenneth Tyrrell
Speed: James Meade
First Aid: Barbara "Boots" Hoffman, R.N. and local EMT's
Farm Zoo: Matt Wilson, Gary Blankenship, and Joe Steffen
Ag Land Stage: Scott Breunig and Don Lawyer
Draft Horse Pull: Joe Steffen and Scott Breunig
Education: Nancy Lou Rex

1998
Ticket Sales: Nancy Lou Rex, John Hallaron and Roy Wahlgren
Concessions and Display Space: Donald Bark and Dan Bark
Tractor and Truck Pull: Wiley Updike and Gene Frieders
Parking and Police: Scott Breunig and William Haag
Antique Farm Machinery: Michael Krafft
Sandwich Auto Show: Doug and Nancy Carter
Micro-Mini Tractor Pull: Dick Delp
Western Horse Show: Steve and Carole Hilleson
Electricians: Harold Dannewitz and Reed Johnson
Caretakers: Andy Krafft and Jim Webber
Horseshoe Pitching: Kenneth Huff and Fred Morel
Grandstand Entertainment: Don Augustine and Larry Dannewitz
Fiddle Contest: Larry Robinson
Craft Demonstrations: Eileen Weber
Data Management: Ginger Dannewitz, Office Manager
Gazebo Information: Karen Breunig and Cheryl Augustine
Speed: James Meade
First Aid: Barbara "Boots" Hoffman, R.N. and local EMT's
Farm Zoo: Matt Wilson, Gary Blankenship, and Joe Steffen
Ag Land Stage: Scott Breunig and Don Lawyer
Draft Horse Pull: Joe Steffen and Scott Breunig
Education: Nancy Lou Rex

1999
Ticket Sales: Nancy Lou Rex, John Hallaron and Roy Wahlgren
Concessions and Display Space: Donald Bark and Dan Bark
Tractor and Truck Pull: Wiley Updike and Gene Frieders
Parking and Police: Scott Breunig and William Haag
Antique Farm Machinery: Michael Krafft
Sandwich Auto Show: Doug and Nancy Carter
Micro-Mini Tractor Pull: Dick Delp
Western Horse Show: Steve and Carole Hilleson

Electricians: Harold Dannewitz and Reed Johnson
Caretaker: Jim Webber
Horseshoe Pitching: Kenneth Huff and Fred Morel
Grandstand Entertainment: Don Augustine and Larry Dannewitz
Fiddle Contest: Larry Robinson
Craft Demonstrations: Eileen Weber
Data Management: Ginger Dannewitz, Office Manager
Gazebo Information: Karen Breunig and Cheryl Augustine
Speed: James Meade
First Aid: Barbara "Boots" Hoffman, R.N. and local EMT's
Farm Zoo: Matt Wilson, Gary Blankenship, and Joe Steffen
Ag Land Stage: Scott Breunig and Don Lawyer
Draft Horse Pull: Joe Steffen and Scott Breunig
Education: Nancy Lou Rex

2000
Ticket Sales: Nancy Lou Rex, John Hallaron and Roy Wahlgren
Concessions and Display Space: Donald Bark and Dan Bark

Tractor and Truck Pull: Wiley Updike and Gene Frieders
Parking and Police: Scott Breunig and William Haag
Antique Farm Machinery: Michael Krafft
Sandwich Auto Show: Doug and Nancy Carter
Micro-Mini Tractor Pull: Dick Delp
Western Horse Show: Steve and Carole Hilleson
Electricians: Harold Dannewitz and Reed Johnson
Caretaker: Jim Webber
Horseshoe Pitching: Kenneth Huff and Fred Morel
Grandstand Entertainment: Don Augustine and Larry Dannewitz
Fiddle Contest: Larry Robinson
Craft Demonstrations: Eileen Weber
Data Management: Ginger Dannewitz, Office Manager
Gazebo Information: Karen Breunig and Cheryl Augustine
Speed: James Meade
First Aid: Barbara "Boots" Hoffman, R.N. and local EMT's
Farm Zoo: Matt Wilson, Gary Blankenship, and Joe Steffen
Ag Land Stage: Scott Breunig and Don Lawyer
Draft Horse Pull: Joe Steffen and Scott Breunig
Education: Nancy Lou Rex

Photo by L.H.

The History Book Committee chose the design of the familiar triangle on the Home Arts building as an identifying symbol for *The Sandwich Fair Since 1888.*

311

SUPERINTENDENTS OF EXHIBIT BUILDINGS

Industrial and Horticulture Hall
1946-1947   Charles Howison
1948-1954   H.W. Bark
1955-1974   Louis Wagner
1975-1983   Louis Wagner, John Wagner
1984-present John Wagner

Grain, Grass, Seeds, Vegetables, etc.
1888   David Harmon
1889-1892   No records available
1893   Dan Knight
1894   No records available
1895   Dan Knight
1896-1897   Thomas Mercer
1898-1899   No records available

Heading changed in 1900 to Grain, Seeds, Vegetables, Etc.
1900-1904   D.K. Crofoot
1905-1917   George McDonald
1918-1947   Charles Howison
1947   Louis Wagner, became General
             Supt. of Horticulture

Fruits
1888   Jacob Budd
1889-1892   No records available
1893   George Kleinsmid
1894   No records available
1895   George Kleinsmid
1896   C.M. Yearley
1897   Thomas Mercer
1898-1899   No records available
1900-1904   D.K. Crofoot
1905-1917   George McDonald
1918-1947   Charles Howison

Headings changed in 1947 to Grains, Seeds, Forages, Vegetables, Fruits and Corn Show
1947-1984   Louis Wagner
1985-1986   John Wagner
1987-present John and Kathy Wagner

Agricultural Implements and Manufactures
Later known as Farm Implements and Vehicles
1888   Evan Lewis
1889-1892   No records available
1893   Orlando Slater
1894   No records available
1895-1896   P.F. Slater
1897   No one listed
1898-1899   No records available
1901-1903   No one listed

This department was not listed in the Premium book after 1903
Kitchen Dairy and Pantry
1888   Mrs. E. Coleman
1889-1892   No records available
1894   No records available
1893-1896   Mrs. James Howison
1897   No one listed
1898-1899   No records available
1900-1904   D.K. Crofoot
1905-1917   George McDonald
1918-1945   Charles Howison
1946-1947   Lila Belden

This department title was changed in 1948 to Dairy, Apiary, Culinary
1948-1951   Lila Belden
1952-1954   Nan Jean Beck

1955-1995   Renee (Doderlein) Monkemeyer

This department title was changed in 1987 to Open Show Foods
1995-1999   Renee Monkemeyer;
             Pam and Penny Monkemeyer
2000-present Renee Monkemeyer;
             Pam, Penny, Karen Monkemeyer
Flowers, Flowering Shrubs and Cut Flowers
1888   Lottie Logan

This department title was changed after 1888 to Plants and Flowers
1889-1892   No records available
1893   Miss Minnie Kennedy
1895-1896   Mrs. James Castle
1897   No one listed
1898-1899   No records available
1900-1904   D.K. Crofoot
1905-1917   George McDonald
1918-1947   Charles Howison
1948-1981   Frances Toombs
1982-1987   Ramona Butler
1988-1997   Susan Cromwell
1998-present John and Kathy Wagner

Needle Work, Household Fabrics and Manufacturers
1888   Mrs. G. Walter; Mrs. E.G. Coe, ass't.
1889-1892   No records available
1893   Mrs. Edwin Wright
1894   No records available
1895-1896   Mrs. M. Nathan
1897   D.K. Crofoot
1898-1899   No records available
1900-1904   D.K. Crofoot
1905-1917   George McDonald
1918-1947   Charles Howison

By 1936 this department was known as Needlework
1948-1959   Pauline Newton
1960-1988   Millie Carter
1989-1991   Millie Carter, Bonnie Young, and Pam
             Barrett
1992-1994   Millie Carter, Donna Leonard, and Bonnie Young
1995   Millie Carter, Donna Leonard, Pat Redden
1996-present Donna Leonard, Pat Redden

Painting and Photographing (Photographs)
1888   Mrs. Frank Barnes; Mrs. Cora West,
             ass't.
1889-1892   No records available
1893   Miss Lizzie Abbott
1894   No records available
1895   Mrs. Kate Smith
1896   Mrs. R C. Cook
1897   D.K. Crofoot
1898-1899   No records available
1900-1904   D.K. Crofoot
1905-1917   George McDonald

As of 1936 there was no department listed that included photographs, only paintings

1918-1946   Charles Howison

In 1947-1948 the department title was changed to Painting and Photography
1947   Charles Howison
1948   Pauline Newton

In 1949 the department title was changed to Art and Photography

Art
1949-1959   Pauline Newton
1960-1971   Millie Carter
Photography
1949-1956   Virginia (Mrs. H.W.) Bark
1957-1958   Helen Slauf
1959   Mrs. Otis Ivie
1960-1961   Harlan Walley
1962-1971   Renee Monkemeyer
1972-1985   Marilyn Popp
1986-1990   Karen Monkemeyer
1991   Karen Monkemeyer; Becky Morphey and
             Jodi Brummel, ass't.
1992-present Becky Morphey, Jodi Brummel, ass't.

Industrial Arts
1950-1965   David Graf
1966-1971   Louis Wagner
As of 1972 this department became part of Arts and Crafts

Woodworking and Handicrafts
1967-1971   Louis Wagner
As of 1972 this department became part of Arts and Crafts

Art
1972-1987   Ruth Nelson
1988-1992   Ruth Nelson and Cheryl Hearn
1993   Ruth Nelson, Cheryl Hearn, Pat Wolsfelt
1994   Ruth Nelson, Cheryl Hearn
1995   Ruth Nelson
1996-present Ruth Nelson, Pam Nelson, ass't.

Crafts
1972-1991   Ruth Nelson
1992-1995   Ruth Nelson, Julia Baker, ass't.
1996   Ruth Nelson; Julia Baker and
             Pam Nelson, ass't.
1997-1999   Ruth Nelson; Pam Nelson, ass't.
2000-present Ruth Nelson; Pam Nelson, Margie Butler,
             and Jan Miernicki, ass't.

Collections and Ceramics
1972   Ruth Nelson
1973-1976   Alberta Barker
1977   Ruth Nelson
1978-1985   Rachel Schmidt
1986-1995   Rachel Schmidt and
             Juanita Anderson, ass't.
1996   Jane Jacobson and
             Juanita Anderson, ass't.

Collections
1997-1998   Jane Jacobson; Bess Moss and
             Mary Lou Moris, ass't.
1999-present John Wagner; Bess Moss and
             Mary Lou Moris, ass't.

Ceramics
1997   Becky Morphey
1998-1999   Becky Morphey; Chris Wahlgren,
             consultant
2000-present Becky Morphey

Assistant Building Supt. to Ruth Nelson 1994-present:
Becky Morphey

Educational, Natural History, and Musical Instruments
1888   Henry Hess
1889-1892   No records available
1893   Prof. W.W. Wirt
1895   Prof. Hubbard
1896   Prof. Cross
1897   No one listed

Courtesy of D.R.S.

These boys show off their award-winning sheep.

1898-1899	No records available		1927-1930	No one listed
1901-1906	No one listed		1931	No records available
As of 1903 this department title was changed to			1932-1933	No one listed
Educational, Natural History			As of 1931 this department title was changed to	
1907	No records available		Educational	
1908-1912	No one listed		1934-1935	No records available
1913-1915	No records available		1936	No one listed
1916-1918	No one listed		1937-1939	No records available
1919-1921	No records available		1940-1943	No one listed
1921	No one listed		1944	No records available
1922-1926	No records available		1945	No one listed

As of 1946 this department title was changed to Education

1946-1947	L.G. Haskin
1948-1949	No reference in premium book
1950-1964	Agnes Stahl
1965	James C. Goddie

No education department existed between 1965 and 1994. As of 1994 the description of this department changed.
1994-present Nancy Lou Rex

LIVESTOCK SUPERINTENDENTS

1888
Cattle: W.H. Toombs
Horses: A.G. Greenman and R.O. Lincoln
Swine: Edwin Fraser
Sheep: Philo Slater
Poultry: George Keene

1889-1892
No records available

1893
Cattle: Charles Patten, William Rumney, M. Knight, Louis Rohrer, W.H. Toombs, Edwin Wright, Charles Dewey, Frank Seeley
Horses: J.H. Latham, I.M. Hay, Leonard Thorpe, F.A. Pratt, Seymour Toombs, T.H. Robinson, Robert Rumney, Louis Scheidecker, W.M. Foster
Swine: A. Lange
Sheep: J.P. Washburn
Poultry: William Fraser (Started in 1889)
Jacks and Mules: A. Ryther

1894
No records available

1895
Cattle: T.H. Robinson, Charles Dewey, I.M. Hay, W.H. Toombs, Louis Rohrer, Charles Patten, Frank Seeley, M. Knight
Swine: A. Lange
Sheep: Charles Scoggin
Poultry: William Fraser
Horses: George Amerman, George McDonald, Henry Scheidecker, Robert Rumney, Todd Benjamin, George McDonald, William Coultrip

1896
Cattle: I.M. Hay, Frank Seeley, Louis Rohrer, W.H. Toombs, Fred Stephen, M. Knight, Pernett Potter
Sheep: Walter Finnie
Swine: A. Lange
Poultry: William Fraser
Horses: George McDonald, Seymour Toombs, David Evans, Todd Benjamin, George Morahn, Harry Robinson, Joseph Cain

1897
Cattle and Sheep: J.H. Latham
Poultry: William Fraser
Horse Stalls: C.W. LaSuer
Forage: F.A. Pratt
Swine: No one listed

1898-1899
No records available

1900
Cattle/Sheep/Swine: L. Hubbard
Poultry: William Fraser

Photo by J.M.

This 1972 photograph shows the concrete dance floor on the south side of the Home Arts building enclosed by a decorative fence.

Horse Stalls: J.H. Latham

1901-1905
Cattle/Sheep/Swine: P.H. Potter, J.H. Latham (assisted in 1903 only)
Poultry: William Fraser
Horse Stalls: C.W. LaSuer

1906
Cattle/Sheep/Swine: P.H. Potter and J.H. Latham
Poultry: William Fraser
Horse Stalls: Thomas Mercer

1907
No records available

1908-1911
Cattle/Sheep/Swine: P.H. Potter
Poultry: William Fraser
Horse Stalls: Thomas Mercer and J.H. Latham

1912
Cattle/Sheep/Swine: P.H. Potter
Poultry: William Fraser
Horse Stalls: Thomas Mercer

1913-1915
No records available

1916-1919
Cattle/Sheep/Swine: J.H. Potter and S.D. Newton
Poultry: William Fraser
Horse Stalls: S.D. Newton

1920
No records available

1921
Cattle/Sheep/Swine: J.H. Potter and S.D. Newton
Poultry/Hares: William Fraser
Horse Stalls: S.D. Newton

1922-1924
No records available

1925
Cattle/Sheep/Swine: S.D. Newton
Poultry/Hares: William Fraser
Horse Stalls: S.D. Newton

1926
No records available
1927-1932
Cattle/Sheep/Swine: Henry White
Poultry/Hares: William Fraser
Horse Stalls: C.S. Bark

1933
Cattle/Sheep/Swine: Henry White and C.S. Bark

Poultry/Hares: William Fraser
No Horses Listed
Horse Pull: Ben Eade

1934-1935
Horse Pull: Ben Eade

1936
Cattle/Sheep/Swine/Horses: Henry White, C.S. Bark, Ben Eade, A.C. Baie
Poultry/Rabbits: William Fraser
Horse Pull: Ben Eade

1937
Cattle/Sheep: C.S. Bark
Poultry/Rabbits: William Fraser
Swine: Henry White
Horses: A.C. Baie and Ben Eade
Horse Pull: Ben Eade
1938-1940
Cattle/Sheep: C.S. Bark
Poultry/Rabbits: William Fraser
Swine: Henry White
Horses: A.C. Baie and Ben Eade

1939
No records available

1941-1943
Cattle/Sheep: C.S. Bark and Ben Eade

Poultry/Rabbits: Frank Skinner
Swine: Henry White
Horses: A.C. Bale

1944
Draft Horses: A.C. Baie
Sheep: C. Sherm Bark
Cattle: Ben Eade
Light Horses and Ponies: James Wiley

1945
Beef Cattle: Ben Eade
Dairy Cattle: No one Listed
Sheep: C.S. Bark
Swine: Henry White
Poultry/Rabbits: Frank Skinner
Horses: James Wiley

1946-1947
Beef Cattle: Ben Eade
Dairy Cattle: Ben Eade
Sheep: C.S. Bark
Swine: Henry White 1946 and Elmer Henderson 1947
Poultry: No Poultry in 1946 or 1947 because of disease
Rabbits: Frank Skinner
Horse Show: Latham Castle and Walt Nelson

1948
Beef Cattle: Ben Eade
Dairy Cattle: Doug Knights
Sheep: Elmer Henderson
Swine: Henry White and LeRoy Suppes
Poultry/Rabbits: Frank Skinner
Horse Show: Latham Castle and Walt Nelson

1949-1950
Beef Cattle: Ben Eade
Dairy Cattle: Doug Knights
Sheep: Elmer Henderson
Swine: LeRoy Suppes 1949, Henry White and
LeRoy Suppes 1950
Poultry/Rabbits: James Duvick, No Poultry in 1950
Horse Show: Walter Nelson and Latham Castle

1951
Beef Cattle: Ben Eade
Dairy Cattle: Doug Knights
Sheep: Elmer Henderson
Swine: Henry White and LeRoy Suppes
Poultry: No Poultry in 1951
Horse Show: Walter Nelson and Latham Castle

1952
Beef Cattle: Ben Eade and Donald Stahl
Dairy Cattle: Doug Knights
Sheep: Elmer Henderson
Swine: Henry White and LeRoy Suppes
Poultry: No Poultry in 1952

1953-1957
Beef Cattle: Don Stahl, Don Ogilvie 1956, Don Ogilvie
and LeRoy Suppes 1957
Dairy Cattle: Doug Knights
Sheep: Elmer Henderson and Wilbur Dienst
Swine: Henry White and Leroy Suppes 1953-1954;
LeRoy Suppes and Dutch Johnson 1955-1957

1958-1961
Beef Cattle: LeRoy Suppes
Dairy Cattle: Doug Knights
Sheep: Wilbur Dienst
Swine: Henry White and Orland McAllister 1958;
Henry White and Ed Duvick 1959-1961

History must have a beginning point. I have been involved with the fair for four years, being an exhibitor three of those years. I enjoy the Fair so much that I am already planning what to enter for next year. The Fair is well organized and a great event to meet old friends and make new friends. The exhibits and events are excellent quality. Thanks to the work of many dedicated people, the Fair lives up to its reputation of being the best county fair!

Judy Giese
Plano, Illinois

The collections building— it's just fantastic! The memories are worth so much to all of us "remember-when" people. Thank you!

Pat Newton
Somonauk, Illinois

It's Americana, good clean fun, a great family experience!

Mary Carlson
Sandwich, Illinois

Been coming for 55-60 years; enjoy cattle and hog judging. Worked at the Harrison Implement dealer at the Fair.

Floyd Derby
Aurora, Illinois

I remember riding the double-decker Ferris wheel as a child.

Laraine Ruberry
Oak Forest, Illinois

It's tradition! I'm handing it down to my children—the food, rides, and the people! Nothing beats our own Fair! I'm 36 and never missed.

Patty Hanson
Sandwich, Illinois

I love the Fair because I get cotton candy and I love the rides. I like going on the train; it's fun.

Laurel Skorup, student
Sandwich, Illinois

It gives us a chance to display our collections, meet friends, and enjoy the helpfulness and friendliness of all the workers in the Antique and Collectible section.

Lenny and Betty Venturo
Joliet, Illinois

I love the Sandwich Fair because I can come and relax with family and friends. I can look at all the great ideas and hard work of others! It inspires me to greatness!

Amber Stevenson
Schaumburg, Illinois

The prices are very reasonable. My daughter loves the steam train. My father grew up on a farm in Yates City, Illinois and some must have rubbed off on me. The animals are nice to see and it's good to expose my children to farm life.

Dahnelle Swanson
Streamwood, Illinois

You get to see old friends and meet new ones! I see people here that I only see once every year.

Nancy Glover
Plano, Illinois

I came here when I was a child. Now I can share the same fun with my own child.

Ann Marie Grooms
Romeoville, Illinois

I love the sights, the smells, the "down home" feel, but mostly all the people and the "visiting" that gets done.

Cindy Olson
Chicago Heights, Illinois

My boyfriend and I have always (since 1972) ended our summer and started our fall by taking a day off to come to the Sandwich Fair. We love this Fair— from eating Fay's cooking to harness racing!

Sue Gribble
Ottawa, Illinois

I love to see all of the talents of many people on display, as well as meeting friends and acquaintances that you haven't seen in awhile.

Ed Young
North Aurora, Illinois

I've been coming for 75 years.

Sidney Mander
Millbrook, Illinois

It's the best place to be a "country guy" for a day.

Tony Madeja
Chicago Ridge, Illinois

It's been our favorite fair for the past 20 years.

Mr. and Mrs. Kuhn
Park Ridge, Illinois

I love the Sandwich Fair because I get to help a friend in her booth and enjoy seeing the people. Since I can't walk enough to cover the whole thing, it is a good way to still be part of it.

Lorraine Crane
Sandwich, Illinois

The best people watching in the state!

Phil Kielas
Anawan, Illinois

We love the Sandwich Fair because it's a fun place to bring our family. We have been coming for the past 15 years, we wouldn't miss it for the world.

Jackie & Jim Walker & kids
Sugar Grove, Illinois

It's the Best!

M.A.Shaw
Somonauk, Illinois

Because it's a fun place to hang out.

Suzanne Nang
Batavia, Illinois

My mom and her friends work there. She makes me proud.

Samantha Grumieaux
Serena, Illinois

We enjoy this fair because it has a little of everything displayed in an interesting and entertaining way. Our favorite fair. We don't have to walk miles to see everything.

Sharon Lippold
Rutland, Illinois

I loved the round-robin baseball tournaments on the grounds—the town team competition around 1946-1947

.

N.B. Galloway
Morris, Illinois

It's small enough to enjoy in one day.

Sarah Cifant
Evanston, Illinois

I used to come to the Fair with the elementary school here in Sandwich with Miss Hall. Now I love to bring my kids and always look forward to corn dogs, lemonade, and a ride on the train.

Michelle Geihm
Aurora, Illinois

My husband and I had our first date at the Fair five years ago! We wouldn't miss it now!

Stacy Christian
Yorkville, Illinois

I love the train, the petting zoo, the horses, the demo derby, clean restrooms, big trees, and the looks on my kids' faces and those on my parents watching them.

Lynette Swedberg
Sycamore, Illinois

It's big, but it's still small town. Best fair in the state, including the state fair. No drunks.

Lee Haldorson
Joliet, Illinois

I can't remember ever missing a Sandwich Fair. We used to get a day off school. We'd take a picnic dinner and go to the Fair all day. We used to play Bingo down on the midway. I have worked at the Fair for 37 consecutive years selling "Butter Fudge." The first two years we were in a tent and then we moved to the steel building where we are now. I like to work with the people; the third generation is working with us now.

Charlotte Miller
Hinckley, Illinois

I've been coming to the Sandwich Fair for over 35 years. I always loved to come when I was young, but now I'm older and don't have to rely on others to get here. I love it so much I take a week of vacation from work and come every day.

Debra Jones
Aurora, Illinois

1962
Beef Cattle: Spencer Gord
Dairy Cattle: Doug Knights
Sheep: Norm Wesson
Swine: Ed Duvick

1963-1965
Beef Cattle: Spencer Gord
Dairy Cattle: Doug Knights
Sheep: Don Miller
Swine: Ed Duvick

1966
General Livestock Supt.: Donald Stahl
Beef Cattle: Spencer Gord
Dairy Cattle: Frank Mall
Sheep: Don Miller
Swine: Bob Guehler
Pork Carcass Show: Robert Guehler

Last year for livestock parade

1967-1969
General Livestock Supt.: Donald Stahl
Beef Cattle: Spencer Gord
Dairy Cattle: Frank Mall and G.W. Grandgeorge
Sheep: Wiley Updike
Swine: Bob Guehler
Poultry/Rabbits: Lyle Troeger and Charles Mall
Carcass Show: Robert Guehler

1970-1976
General Livestock Supt.: Donald Stahl
Beef: Spencer Gord 1970-1972; Charles Waechter 1973; Charles Waechter and Doug Stahl 1974-1976
Dairy: Franklin Mall and G.W. Grandgeorge
Sheep: Wiley Updike
Swine: Robert Guehler and LaVerne Mattson
Carcass Show: Robert Guehler
Poultry/Rabbits: Lyle Troeger and Charles Mall

1977-1979
General Livestock Supt.: Donald Stahl
Beef Cattle: Charles Waechter and Doug Stahl
Dairy Cattle: Frank Mall and G.W. Grandgeorge
Sheep: Wiley Updike
Swine: Robert Guehler
Carcass Show: Robert Guehler and Dick Delp 1978-1979
Poultry/Rabbits: Lyle Troeger and Charles Mall

1980-1982
General Livestock Supt.: Donald Stahl
Beef Cattle: Charles Waechter and Doug Stahl
Dairy Cattle: G.W. Grandgeorge and William Coultrip
Sheep: Wiley Updike
Swine: Richard Delp and Robert Guehler
Poultry: Lyle Troeger and Charles Mall
Dairy Goats: LaVerne Mattson
Carcass Show: Robert Guehler (No Carcass Show in 1981-1982)

1983
General Livestock Supt.: Donald Stahl
Beef Cattle: Charles Waechter and Doug Stahl
Dairy Cattle: G.W. Grandgeorge and William Coultrip
Sheep: Wiley Updike
Swine: Richard Delp and Robert Guehler
Poultry: Lyle Troeger and Charles Mall
Dairy Goats: LaVerne Mattson

1984
General Livestock Supt.: Donald Stahl
Beef Cattle: Charles Waechter and Doug Stahl
Dairy Cattle: G.W. Grandgeorge and William Coultrip
Sheep: Wiley Updike

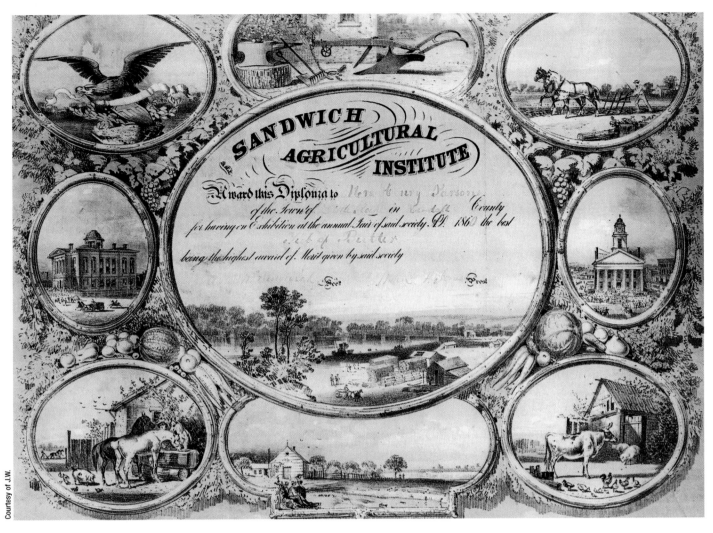

Courtesy of J.W.

The Sandwich Agricultural Institute, predecessor to the Sandwich Fair, issued exhibition certificates to participants who earned the "Highest Award of Merit" for specific entries. This one is for a tub of butter.

Swine: Richard Delp and Robert Guehler
Poultry: Lyle Troeger and Michael Crayton
Dairy Goats: LaVerne Mattson

1985-1986
General Livestock Supt.: Donald Stahl
Beef Cattle: Charles Waechter and Doug Stahl
Dairy Cattle: G.W. Grandgeorge and William Coultrip
Sheep: Wiley Updike
Swine: Richard Delp and Robert Guehler
Poultry: Michael Crayton and Lyle Troeger
Dairy Goats: LaVerne Mattson
Sheep Dog Trial: David Birch 1986

1987-1988
General Livestock Supt.: Donald Stahl
Beef Cattle: Charles Waechter and Doug Stahl
Dairy Cattle: G.W. Grandgeorge and William Coultrip
Sheep: Kenneth Tyrrell
Swine: Richard Delp and Robert Guehler
Poultry: Michael Crayton and Bob Carothers
Dairy Goats: LaVerne Mattson
Llamas: Donna Ricci
Miniature Horses: Joye Gommel
Sheep Dog Trial: David Birch

1989
General Livestock Supt.: Donald Stahl

Beef Cattle: Doug Stahl and Bob Pennington
Dairy Cattle: G.W. Grandgeorge and William Coultrip
Sheep: Kenneth Tyrrell
Swine: Robert Guehler and Richard Delp
Poultry: Michael Crayton and Bob Carothers
Dairy Goats: LaVerne Mattson
Llamas: Donna Ricci
Miniature Horses: Joye Gommel
Livestock Maintenance: Duane Lackey
Sheep Dog Trial: David Birch

1990
General Livestock Supt.: Donald Stahl
Beef Cattle: Doug Stahl and Bob Pennington
Dairy Cattle: G.W. Grandgeorge and William Coultrip
Sheep: Kenneth Tyrrell
Swine: Robert Guehler and Richard Delp
Poultry: Michael Crayton and Janie Allen
Dairy Goats: LaVerne Mattson
Llamas: Donna Ricci

1991
General Livestock Supt.: Donald Stahl
Beef Cattle: Doug Stahl and Bob Pennington
Dairy Cattle: William Coultrip
Sheep: Kenneth Tyrrell
Swine: Robert Guehler and Richard Delp
Poultry: Michael Crayton and Janie Allen

Dairy Goats: LaVerne Mattson
Llamas: Donna Ricci

1992
General Livestock Supt.: Donald Stahl
Beef Cattle: Doug Stahl and Bob Pennington
Dairy Cattle: William Coultrip
Sheep: Kenneth Tyrrell
Swine: Robert Guehler and Richard Delp
Poultry: Michael Crayton and Janie Allen
Dairy Goats: LaVerne Mattson
Llamas: Donna Ricci

1993
General Livestock Supt.: Donald Stahl
Beef Cattle: Doug Stahl and Bob Pennington
Dairy Cattle: William Coultrip and Mark Tuttle
Sheep: Kenneth Tyrrell
Swine: Robert Guehler and Richard Delp
Poultry: Michael Crayton and Janie Allen
Dairy Goats: LaVerne Mattson
Llamas: Donna Ricci and Leslie Friedrich
Draft Horses: Howard Koch D.V.M. and Cindy Davidson

1994
General Livestock Supt.: Donald Stahl
Beef Cattle: Doug Stahl and Bob Pennington
Dairy Cattle: William Coultrip and Mark Tuttle

Sheep: Kenneth Tyrrell
Swine: Robert Guehler and Richard Delp
Poultry: Michael Crayton and Janie Allen
Dairy Goats: LaVerne Mattson
Llamas: Donna Ricci and Leslie Friedrich
Draft Horses: Howard Koch D.V.M. and Cindy Davidson

1995-1997
General Livestock Supt.: Donald Stahl
Beef Cattle: Doug Stahl and Bob Pennington
Dairy Cattle: William Coultrip and Mark Tuttle
Sheep: Kenneth Tyrrell
Swine: Richard Delp
Poultry: Michael Crayton and Janie Allen
Rabbits: Brenda Craddock
Llamas: Donna Ricci and Leslie Friedrich
Draft Horses: Phil Nielsen and Cindy Davidson
Dairy Goats: LaVerne Mattson

1998
General Livestock Supt.: Donald Stahl
Beef Cattle: Doug Stahl and Bob Pennington
Dairy Cattle: William Coultrip and Mark Tuttle
Sheep: Kenneth Tyrrell
Swine: Richard Delp
Poultry: Michael Crayton and Jane Banka
Rabbits: Brenda Craddock
Llamas: Jeff and Mary Hoyt
Draft Horses: Phil Nielsen and Cindy Davidson
Dairy Goats: LaVerne Mattson

1999
General Livestock Supt.: Donald Stahl
Beef Cattle: Doug Stahl and Bob Pennington
Dairy Cattle: William Coultrip and Mark Tuttle
Sheep: Kenneth Tyrrell and Brad Temple
Swine: Richard Delp
Poultry: Michael Crayton and Jane Banka
Rabbits: Brenda Craddock
Llamas: Jeff and Mary Hoyt
Draft Horses: Phil Nielsen and Cindy Davidson
Dairy Goats: LaVerne Mattson

2000
General Livestock Supt.: Donald Stahl
Beef Cattle: Doug Stahl and Bob Pennington
Dairy Cattle: William Coultrip and Mark Tuttle
Sheep: Kenneth Tyrrell and Brad Temple
Swine: Richard Delp
Poultry: Michael Crayton and Jerry Hartel
Rabbits: Brenda Craddock
Llamas: Jeff and Mary Hoyt
Draft Horses: Phil and Rita Nielsen
Dairy Goats: LaVerne Mattson

4-H CLUB SUPERINTENDENT

1927-1937
No one listed

1938-1948
Ben Eade

JUNIOR FAIR SUPERINTENDENTS

1949
Livestock: Ben Eade and Elmer Henderson
Grains, Seeds, and Vegetables: Louis Wagner
Plants and Flowers: Frances Toombs
Home Economics: Helen Ogilvie

1950
Livestock: Ben Eade and Elmer Henderson
Grains, Seeds, and Vegetables: Louis Wagner
Home Economics: Helen Ogilvie
Plants and Flowers: Frances Toombs
Art and Photography: Pauline Newton and Virginia Bark
Industrial Arts: David Graf

1951
Livestock: Ben Eade and Donald Stahl
Grains, Seeds, and Vegetables: Louis Wagner
Home Economics: No one listed
Plants and Flowers: Frances Toombs
Art and Photography: Pauline Newton and Virginia Bark
Industrial Arts: David Graf

1952
Livestock: Ben Eade and Donald Stahl
Grains, Seeds, and Vegetables: Louis Wagner
Home Economics: Ruth Gerlick
Plants and Flowers: Frances Toombs
Art and Photography: Pauline Newton and Virginia Bark
Industrial Arts: David Graf

1953
Livestock: Donald Stahl
Grains, Seeds, and Vegetables: Louis Wagner
Home Economics: Ruth Gerlick
Plants and Flowers: Frances Toombs
Art and Photography: Pauline Newton and Virginia Bark
Industrial Arts: David Graf

1954
Livestock: LaVerne Johnson and Donald Stahl
Grains, Seeds, and Vegetables: Louis Wagner
Home Economics: Ruth Gerlick
Plants and Flowers: Frances Toombs
Art and Photography: Pauline Newton and Virginia Bark
Industrial Arts: David Graf

1955
Livestock: LaVerne Johnson and Donald Stahl
Grains, Seeds, and Vegetables: Louis Wagner
Home Economics: Ruth Gerlick, Clothing; Renee
Doderlein, Food
Plants and Flowers: Frances Toombs
Art and Photography: Pauline Newton and Virginia Bark
Industrial Arts: David Graf

1956-1957
Livestock: LaVerne Johnson and Elmer Henderson
    Beef: Donald Ogilvie, No one listed in 1957
    Dairy: James Herrman, Al Linden
    Sheep: Elmer Henderson, Wilbur Dienst
    Hogs: Robert Howey, T.W. Anderson
Grains, Seeds, and Vegetables: Louis Wagner
Home Economics: Renee Doderlein
Plants and Flowers: Frances Toombs
Photography and Hobbies: Virginia Bark 1956,
Helen Slauf 1957
Industrial Arts: David Graf

1958-1959
Livestock: Elmer Henderson
    Beef: James Herrman
    Dairy: Al Linden
    Sheep: Wilbur Dienst
    Hogs: Robert Howey, T.W. Anderson
Grains, Seeds, and Vegetables: Louis Wagner
Home Economics: Renee (Doderlein) Monkemeyer
Plants and Flowers: Frances Toombs
Photography and Hobbies: Helen Slauf 1958,
No one listed 1959
Industrial Arts: David Graf

1960
Livestock: Elmer Henderson
    Beef: James Herrman
    Dairy: Al Linden
    Sheep: Wilbur Dienst
    Hogs: Robert Howey, T.W. Anderson, and Ed Duvick
Grains, Seeds, and Vegetables: Louis Wagner
Home Economics: Renee Monkemeyer
Plants and Flowers: Frances Toombs
Photography and Hobbies: Harlan Walley
Industrial Arts: David Graf

1961
Livestock: Ed Duvick
    Beef: Warner White, Don Ogilvie, and Dale Rogers
    Dairy: Al Linden
    Sheep: Wilbur Dienst
    Hogs: Ed Duvick and Andy Krafft
Grains, Seeds, and Vegetables: Louis Wagner
Home Economics: Renee Monkemeyer
Plants and Flowers: Frances Toombs
Photography and Hobbies: Harlan Walley
Arts and Crafts: Millie Carter
Industrial Arts: David Graf

1962
Livestock: Ed Duvick
    Beef: Milford Clausen
    Dairy: Bob Anderson
    Sheep: Norman Wesson
    Hogs: Ed Duvick and Andy Krafft
Grains, Seeds, and Vegetables: Louis Wagner
Home Economics: Renee Monkemeyer
Plants and Flowers: Frances Toombs
Photography and Hobbies: No class listed
Arts and Crafts: Millie Carter
Industrial Arts: David Graf

A fairgoer at the 1987 Fair enjoys an ear of sweet corn.

1963
Livestock: Milford Clausen
    Beef: Clarion Clausen
    Dairy: Bob Anderson and Ron Anderson
    Sheep: Jack Smith and Al McCowen
    Hogs: Jack Suddeth
Grains, Seeds, and Vegetables: Louis Wagner
Home Economics: Renee Monkemeyer
Plants and Flowers: Frances Toombs
Photography and Hobbies: No class listed
Arts and Crafts: Millie Carter
Industrial Arts: David Graf

1964
Livestock: Milford Clausen
    Beef: Clarion Clausen
    Dairy: Bob Anderson and Ron Anderson
    Sheep: Al McCowen
    Hogs: Jack Suddeth
Grains, Seeds, and Vegetables: Louis Wagner
Home Economics: Renee Monkemeyer
Plants and Flowers: Frances Toombs
Photography: Renee Monkemeyer
Arts and Crafts: Millie Carter
Industrial Arts: David Graf

1965
Livestock: Milford Clausen
    Beef: Clarion Clausen
    Dairy: Bob Anderson and Ron Anderson
    Sheep: David and Nancy Birch
    Hogs: Jack Suddeth
Grains, Seeds, and Vegetables: Louis Wagner
Home Economics: Renee Monkemeyer
Plants and Flowers: Frances Toombs
Photography: Renee Monkemeyer
Arts and Crafts: Millie Carter
Industrial Arts: David Graf

1966
Livestock: Milford Clausen
    Beef: Clarion Clausen
    Dairy: Bob Anderson and Ron Anderson
    Sheep: David and Nancy Birch
    Hogs: Jack Suddeth
Grains, Seeds, and Vegetables: Louis Wagner
Home Economics: Renee Monkemeyer
Plants and Flowers: Frances Toombs
Photography: Renee Monkemeyer
Arts and Crafts: Millie Carter
Industrial Arts and Handicrafts: No one listed

1967-1970
Livestock and Farm Zoo: Milford Clausen
    Beef: Clarion Clausen
    Dairy: Bob Anderson and Ron Anderson
    Sheep: David and Nancy Birch
    Hogs: Jack Suddeth
Grains, Seeds, and Vegetables: John Wagner
Home Economics: Renee Monkemeyer
Plants and Flowers: Frances Toombs
Photography: Renee Monkemeyer
Arts and Crafts: Millie Carter
Industrial Arts and Handicrafts: No class listed

1971
Livestock and Farm Zoo: Milford Clausen
    Beef: Milford Clausen
    Dairy: Bob Anderson and Ron Anderson
    Sheep: David and Nancy Birch
    Hogs: Jack Suddeth
Jr. Livestock Sale: Gene Darfler and Buck Nesson
Grains, Seeds, and Vegetables: John Wagner
Home Economics: Renee Monkemeyer
Plants and Flowers: Frances Toombs

The many paved roads at the fairgrounds make it easier for visitors in wheelchairs to enjoy the Fair.

Photography: Renee Monkemeyer
Arts and Crafts: Millie Carter
Industrial Arts and Handicrafts: No class listed

1972
Livestock and Farm Zoo: Milford Clausen
    Beef: Milford Clausen
    Dairy: Bob Anderson and Ron Anderson
    Sheep: David and Nancy Birch
    Hogs: Jack Suddeth
Jr. Livestock Sale: Gene Darfler
Grains, Seeds, and Vegetables: John Wagner
Home Economics: Renee Monkemeyer
Plants and Flowers: Frances Toombs
Photography: Marilyn Popp
Arts and Crafts: Ruth Nelson

1973
Livestock: Milford Clausen
    Beef: Larry Hoffman
    Dairy: Bob Anderson and Ron Anderson
    Sheep: David and Nancy Birch
    Hogs: Jack Suddeth
Jr. Livestock Sale: Gene Darfler and Jerry Davis
Grains, Seeds, and Vegetables: John Wagner
Home Economics: Renee Monkemeyer
Plants and Flowers: Frances Toombs
Photography: Marilyn Popp
Arts and Crafts: Ruth Nelson

1974
Beef: Larry Hoffman
Dairy: Bob Anderson and Ron Anderson
Sheep: David and Nancy Birch
Hogs: Jack Suddeth
Jr. Livestock Sale: Gene Darfler and Jerry Davis
Grains, Seeds, and Vegetables: John Wagner
Home Economics: Renee Monkemeyer
Plants and Flowers: Frances Toombs
Photography: Marilyn Popp
Arts and Crafts: Ruth Nelson

1975-1976
Beef: Larry Hoffman

Dairy: Bob Anderson and Ron Anderson
Sheep: David and Nancy Birch
Swine: Kenneth Tyrrell
Jr. Livestock Sale: Gene Darfler and Jerry Davis
Grains, Seeds, Forages, Vegetables, Fruits: John Wagner
Home Economics: Renee Monkemeyer
Plants and Flowers: Frances Toombs
Photography: Marilyn Popp
Art: Alberta Barker
Crafts: Ruth Nelson

1977
Beef: Larry Hoffman
Dairy: Bob Anderson and Ron Anderson
Sheep: David and Nancy Birch
Swine: Kenneth Tyrrell
Jr. Livestock Sale: Jerry Davis
Grains, Seeds, Forages, Vegetables, Fruits: John Wagner
Home Economics: Renee Monkemeyer
Plants and Flowers: Frances Toombs
Photography: Marilyn Popp
Arts and Crafts: Ruth Nelson

1978-1979
Beef: Larry Hoffman
Dairy: Bob Anderson and Ron Anderson
Sheep: David and Nancy Birch
Swine: Kenneth Tyrrell
Jr. Livestock Sale: Jerry Davis
Grains, Seeds, Forages, Vegetables, Fruits: John Wagner
Home Economics: Renee Monkemeyer
Plants and Flowers: Frances Toombs
Photography: Marilyn Popp
Art: Rachel Schmidt
Crafts: Ruth Nelson

1980
Beef: Larry Hoffman
Dairy: Bob Anderson and Ron Anderson
Sheep: Don Stahl
Swine: Kenneth Tyrrell
Goats: Steve Miller
Jr. Livestock Sale: Jerry Davis
Grains, Seeds, Forages, Vegetables, Fruits: John Wagner
Home Economics: Renee Monkemeyer
Plants and Flowers: Frances Toombs
Photography: Marilyn Popp
Art: Rachel Schmidt
Crafts: Ruth Nelson

1981
Beef: Larry Hoffman
Dairy: Bob Anderson and Ron Anderson
Sheep: John and Ruth Ann Guehler
Swine: Kenneth Tyrrell
Goats: Steve Miller
Jr. Livestock Sale: Jerry Davis
Grains, Seeds, Forages, Vegetables,
Fruits: John Wagner
Home Economics: Renee Monkemeyer
Plants and Flowers: Frances Toombs
Photography: Marilyn Popp
Art: Rachel Schmidt
Crafts: Ruth Nelson

1982
Beef: Larry Hoffman
Dairy: Bob Anderson and Ron Anderson
Sheep: John and Ruth Ann Guehler
Swine: Kenneth Tyrrell
Goats: Steve Miller
Jr. Livestock Sale: Jerry Davis
Grains, Seeds, Forages, Vegetables,
Fruits: John Wagner
Home Economics: Renee Monkemeyer

Beacon News

Eighteen-month-old Brad Whitten of Sandwich was fascinated by the 70-pound pumpkin in 1967.

Plants and Flowers: Joan Curnutte
Photography: Marilyn Popp
Art: Rachel Schmidt
Crafts: Ruth Nelson

1983
Beef: Larry Hoffman
Dairy: Bob Anderson and Ron Anderson
Sheep: John Guehler
Swine: Kenneth Tyrrell
Goats: Steve Miller
Jr. Livestock Sale: Joye Gommel
Grains, Seeds, Forages, Vegetables,
Fruits: John Wagner
Home Economics: Renee Monkemeyer
Plants and Flowers: Joan Curnutte
Photography: Marilyn Popp

Art: Rachel Schmidt
Crafts: Ruth Nelson

1984
Beef: Larry Hoffman
Dairy: Bob Anderson and Ron Anderson
Sheep: John Guehler and Jean Fabrizius
Swine: Kenneth Tyrrell
Goats: Steve Miller
Jr. Livestock Sale: Joye Gommel
Grains, Seeds, Forages, Vegetables,
Fruits: Byron Curnutte
Home Economics: Renee Monkemeyer
Plants and Flowers: Joan Curnutte
Photography: Marilyn Popp
Art: Rachel Schmidt
Crafts: Ruth Nelson

1985
Beef: Larry Hoffman
Dairy: Bob Anderson and Ron Anderson
Sheep: John Guehler and Jean Fabrizius
Swine: Kenneth Tyrrell
Goats: LaVerne Mattson
Jr. Livestock Sale: Joye Gommel
Grains, Seeds, Forages, Vegetables, Fruits: Byron
Curnutte
Home Economics: Renee Monkemeyer
Plants and Flowers: Joan Curnutte
Photography: Marilyn Popp
Art: Rachel Schmidt
Crafts: Ruth Nelson

1986
Beef: Larry Hoffman
Dairy: Bob Anderson and Ron Anderson
Sheep: John Guehler and Jean Fabrizius
Swine: Kenneth Tyrrell
Goats: LaVerne Mattson
Grains, Seeds, Forages, Vegetables,
Fruits: Byron Curnutte
Home Economics: Renee Monkemeyer
Plants and Flowers: Joan Curnutte
Photography: Karen Monkemeyer
Art: Rachel Schmidt
Crafts: Ruth Nelson; Mary Ellen Huss, ass't.

1987-1990
Beef: Larry Hoffman
Dairy: Bob Anderson and Ron Anderson
Sheep: John Guehler and Jean Fabrizius
Swine: J.M. "Mick" Cronin
Goats: LaVerne Mattson
Grains, Seeds, Forages, Vegetables, Fruits: Byron
Curnutte and Kathy Wagner
Home Economics: Renee Monkemeyer
Plants and Flowers: Joan Curnutte and Cathy Meyer
Photography: Karen Monkemeyer
Art: Rachel Schmidt
Crafts: Ruth Nelson; Mary Ellen Huss, ass't.

1991
Beef: Larry Hoffman
Dairy: Bob Anderson and Ron Anderson
Sheep: Al Dietz
Swine: J.M. "Mick" Cronin
Goats: LaVerne Mattson
Grains, Seeds, Forages, Vegetables, Fruits: Byron
Curnutte and Kathy Wagner
Home Economics: Renee Monkemeyer
Plants and Flowers: Joan Curnutte and Cathy Meyer
Photography: Karen Monkemeyer; Becky Morphey and
Jodi Brummel, ass't
Art: Rachel Schmidt
Crafts: Ruth Nelson; Mary Ellen Huss, ass't.

1992-1993
Beef: Larry Hoffman
Dairy: Ron Anderson 1992, 1993 and
Pat McCormick 1993
Sheep: Al Dietz
Swine: J.M. "Mick" Cronin
Goats: LaVerne Mattson
Grains, Seeds, Forages, Vegetables, Fruits: Byron
Curnutte and Jeff Wilson
Home Economics: Renee Monkemeyer
Plants and Flowers: Joan Curnutte and Cathy Meyer
Photography: Becky Morphey; Jodi Brummel, ass't.
Art: Rachel Schmidt and Joanne Johnson
Crafts: Ruth Nelson; Mary Ellen Huss, ass't.

1994
Beef: Larry Hoffman
Dairy: Ron Anderson and Pat McCormick
Sheep: Al Dietz
Swine: J.M. "Mick" Cronin
Goats: LaVerne Mattson
Grains, Seeds, Forages, Vegetables, Fruits:
Byron Curnutte and Jeff Wilson
Home Economics: Renee, Pam, and Penny Monkemeyer
Plants and Flowers: Joan Curnutte and Cathy Meyer
Photography: Becky Morphey; Jodi Brummel, ass't.
Art: Rachel Schmidt and Joanne Johnson
Crafts: Ruth Nelson; Mary Ellen Huss, ass't.

1995
Beef: Larry Hoffman
Dairy: Ron Anderson and Pat McCormick
Sheep: Al Dietz
Swine: J.M. "Mick" Cronin
Goats: LaVerne Mattson
Grains, Seeds, Forages, Vegetables, Fruits:
Byron Curnutte and Jeff Wilson
Home Economics: Renee, Pam, and Penny Monkemeyer
Plants and Flowers: Joan Curnutte and Cathy Meyer
Photography: Becky Morphey; Jodi Brummel, ass't.
Art: Jane Jacobson and Joanne Johnson
Crafts: Ruth Nelson; Mary Ellen Huss, ass't.

1996
Beef: Larry Hoffman
Dairy: Ron Anderson and Pat McCormick
Sheep: Al Dietz
Swine: J.M. "Mick" Cronin
Goats: LaVerne Mattson
Grains, Seeds, Forages, Vegetables, Fruits:
Byron Curnutte and Jeff Wilson
Home Economics: Renee, Pam, and Penny Monkemeyer
Plants and Flowers: Joan Curnutte and Cathy Meyer
Photography: Becky Morphey; Jodi Brummel, ass't.
Art: Jane Jacobson and Joanne Johnson
Crafts: Ruth Nelson; Mary Ellen Huss and
Mildred Meyer, ass'ts.

1997
Beef: Larry Hoffman
Dairy: Ron Anderson and Pat McCormick
Sheep: Al Dietz
Swine: J.M. "Mick" Cronin
Goats: LaVerne Mattson
Grains, Seeds, Forages, Vegetables, Fruits:
Byron Curnutte and Jeff Wilson
Home Economics: Renee, Pam, and Penny Monkemeyer
Plants and Flowers: Joan Curnutte and Cathy Meyer
Photography: Becky Morphey; Jodi Brummel, ass't.
Art: Jane Jacobson and Joanne Johnson
Crafts: Ruth Nelson; Mary Ellen Huss and
Mildred Meyer, ass'ts.

1998
Beef: Larry Hoffman
Dairy: Ron Anderson and Pat McCormick
Sheep: Al Dietz
Swine: J.M. "Mick" Cronin
Goats: LaVerne Mattson
Grains, Seeds, Forages, Vegetables, Fruits:
Byron Curnutte and Jeff Wilson
Home Economics: Renee, Pam, and Penny Monkemeyer
Plants and Flowers: Joan Curnutte and Cathy Meyer
Photography: Becky Morphey; Jodi Brummel, ass't.
Art/Ceramics: Becky Morphey; Joanne Johnson, ass't.
Crafts: Ruth Nelson; Mary Ellen Huss and
Mildred Meyer, ass'ts.

1999
Beef: Larry Hoffman

This patriotic flag graphic appeared in an 1898 advertisement for the Fair that proclaimed "No pain will be spared to make this the best Fair in Northern Illinois."

Dairy: Ron Anderson and Pat McCormick
Sheep: Al Dietz
Swine: J.M. "Mick" Cronin
Goats: LaVerne Mattson
Grains, Seeds Forages, Vegetables, Fruits:
Byron Curnutte and Jeff Wilson
Home Economics: Renee, Pam, and Penny Monkemeyer
Plants and Flowers: Joan Curnutte and Cathy Meyer
Photography: Becky Morphey; Jodi Brummel, ass't.
Art and Ceramics: Becky Morphey; Joanne Johnson, ass't.
Crafts: Ruth Nelson; Mary Ellen Huss and Diane Stahl, ass'ts.

2000
Beef: Larry Hoffman
Dairy: Ron Anderson and Pat McCormick
Sheep: Al Dietz
Swine: J.M. "Mick" Cronin
Goats: LaVerne Mattson
Grains, Seeds, Forages, Vegetables, Fruits: Jeff Wilson
Home Economics: Renee, Pam, Penny, and
Karen Monkemeyer
Plants and Flowers: Cathy Meyer and Lisa Meyer
Photography: Becky Morphey; Jodi Brummel, ass't.
Art and Ceramics: Becky Morphey; Joanne Johnson, ass't.
Crafts: Mary Ellen Huss; Diane Stahl and Ruth Nelson, ass'ts.

GRANDSTAND ENTERTAINMENT

1888	Harness Races
1889	Balloon Ascension
1890	Crescent Band Concert
1891	Fireman Hose Races
1892	Harness Races
1893	Harness Races
1894	Harness Races
1895	Balloon Ascension, Parachute Drop
1896	Political Speeches
1897	Harness Races
1898	Balloon Ascension, Parachute Leap
1899	Baseball, Balloon Ascension
1900	Jubilee Singers, Dancers

1901	Baseball, Harness Races
1902	Baseball
1903	Harness Races
1904	Sandwich Union Band
1905	William's Dixie Jubilee Singers
1906	Harness Races, Baseball
1907	Gleason Horse Tamer
1908	Sandwich Fire Dept. Running Team
1909	Sandwich Union Band
1910	Rounds' Ladies Orchestra, Sandwich Union Band
1911	Baldwin Flying Machine
1912	Mills Brothers Flying Machine
1913	Murray and Ward Fun Makers, Mills Aviators
1914	Dunvette Troupe Aerialists
1915	Human Frogs, Toki Japs Jugglers
1916	Wilber's [or Wilder's] Society Circus, Three Toki Japs
1917	Dare Devil Mills, Six Hawaiian Serenaders
1918	Hill's Society Circus, Flying Machines
1919	Hill's Circus Deluxe
1920	Auto Polo, Daily Aeroplane Flights and Acrobatics
1921	Sports of the Plains Horses, Airdevil Dick Seal
1922	Flying LePearles, Musical Palmer Trio
1923	Six Big Vaudeville Acts
1924	Ferris Wheel Girls, Aerobat Joe Kiljoy
1925	Ponzinis' Monkeys, Vaudeville
1926	The Spirit of 1776 Theatre
1927	Dixon -Riggs Trio, Brown's Saxophone Six
1928	Gold Dust Twins; Gymnastic, Skating, Equilibrium Acts
1929	Baseball, Harness Races
1930	Baseball, Harness Races
1931	Vaudeville Acts
1932	Educated Horses and Mules
1933	Baseball, Horse Pulling Contest
1934	Horse Pulling Contest, WLS Stars - Mac & Bob & Tex Acheson
1935	Pat Buttram, Winnie, Lou & Sally
1936	Harness Racing, Soft Ball
1937	Pat Buttram, Winnie, Lou & Sally, Arkansas Woodchopper
1938	Georgie Goebel, Prairie Ramblers, Eakle Drum & Bugle Corps
1939	Charlie Agnew, Sparkling Girl Revue

1940	Sun's Glorified Revue, Dick Rogers All American Motor Maniacs
1941	Whitey Ford the Duke of Paducah, Lewis Bros. 3-Ring Circus, Midget Car Races
1942	Gay Nineties Revue, Bernie Cummins and His Band, Circus
1943	The Grahams of WLS, Hooray America Revue
1944	Summer Follies, 3-Ring Circus
1945	McKinley-Selby Rodeo, Summer Time Follies
1946	Summer Follies, Wonder Brothers Circus and Rodeo
1947	Siamese Twins, Summer Follies
1948	Western Ranch Round-Up, Jimmie Lynch Death Dodgers
1949	Roy Acuff, Joie Chitwood
1950	Roxyettes, Jack Gwyne Illusion Show
1951	Wonder Brothers Circus, Swenson's Thrillcade
1952	Golddust Twins, White Horse Troupe, Foster's Roxyettes
1953	Homer & Jethro, Ranch Rodeo, South of the Border Fiesta
1954	Captain Stubby, Aut Swenson's Thrillcade, Holter's Racing Ostriches
1955	Whitey Ford, Wonder Brothers Circus, Organist Ken Griffin
1956	Stars Over Ice, Tiny Hill Band, Auto and Cytrix Thrill Show
1957	Minnie Pearl, Salute to Rodgers and Hammerstein, Stars Over Ice
1958	Showboat Minstrels, Leo "Pancho" Carrillo
1959	Frosty Follies, Rhapsody in Blue Show
1960	Monte Carlo Revue, Rivers Golden Horse Show, Pearls of the Pacific Dancers
1961	Harmonicats, Venita Rich Talent Show, The Four Tunes
1962	Roy Rogers Liberty Horses, Johnny Rivers Diving Mules
1963	Myron Floren of Lawrence Welk Show
1964	Music Man Show, King's Thrill Circus
1965	Poncie Ponce of Hawaiian Eye, The Jyro Jets Tumblers
1966	The Harmonicats, Patsy Montana
1967	Homer & Jethro, Women Driver Auto Thrill Show
1968	Illinois Sesquicentennial Play, Demolition Derby
1969	Jim "Ed" Brown, Donald "Red" Blanchard
1970	Connie Smith, Big Band Show
1971	Wilma Burgess, Cristy Lane
1972	Diana Trask, Gene Holter Ostrich Race
1973	Roy Acuff, Jr., Motor Maniacs
1974	Sharon Stone, Clay Hart, Donald "Red" Blanchard
1975	Billy Thundercloud and the Chieftones, Bill Bailey's Banjo
1976	Gail Farrell of Lawrence Welk Show, Billy Walker and the Tennessee Walkers
1977	Stonewall Jackson and the Minutemen, Tom Netherton
1978	Mariah Singing Group, Welk's Bobby & Cissy
1979	Danny Davis and the Nashville Brass, John Conlee Country & Western Show
1980	Danny Davis and the Nashville Brass, Frankie Masters Orchestra
1981	Donna Fargo, The Hit Paraders
1982	Porter Wagoner, Clay and Sally Hart Show, NIU Show Band
1983	Brenda Lee
1984	Dottie West, McBarker Boys
1985	Reba McEntire, George King and the Fellowship
1986	Shelly West, The Arbors

1987	Marie Osmond, Britt Small and Festival
1988	The New Odessy, Louise Mandrell
1989	Cissie Lynn, Ricky Skaggs
1990	Mickey Gilley
1991	Tammy Wynette
1992	Lee Greenwood
1993	Eddie Rabbitt
1994	The Festival, Patty Loveless
1995	Kathy Mattea
1996	Shenandoah
1997	Neal McCoy
1998	Tracy Byrd
1999	Sammy Kershaw, David Lee Murphy & Ricochet
2000	Pam Tillis, Charlie Daniels Band

AG LAND STAGE ENTERTAINMENT

1993
Whoa Nellie Band
C.C. Cash Band
Western dance demonstration

1994
Rainy Day Singers
Sunny River Bank
Cherokee
Western Union
Clear Creek

1995
Cumberland Mountain Band
Sunny River Band
Cherokee
Western Union
American Legion Band

Photo by V.G.

Sheriff Roger Scott gets in the act as he appears to apprehend two suspicious "nurses," who are really Indian Valley Theatre actors George Scoughton (l.) and Don Austin (r.) promoting the Melodrama shows.

1996
JP & Cats
Cumberland Mountain Band
George James and Mood Express
Sunny River Band
Western Union

1997
Gene Ferrari
Buck Fever
5 Year Jacket
JP & Cats
Charley Stuart and Comet Country
Kent Brothers
Patty Jo Timmons

1998
Crossroads Band
Lindsay Sharer and Blackjack
Daniel Grove Band
The Silhouettes
Southern Storm

1999
Go Figure Band
Pattie Jo Timmons and Band
Picture This Band
Sunny River Band

2000
Lindsay Sharer and Blackjack
Patti Jo Timmons Band
Sunny River Band

INDIAN VALLEY THEATER—MELODRAMA SHOWS AND DIRECTORS

1983	"Ten Nights in a Bar Room"—Bernie and Glenn Harrison
	"The Banker's Dilemma"—Jaye Morrison
1984	"Run to the Roundhouse, Nellie"—Michele Wade
	"Alias Smedley Pewtree"-Ellen Werner
1985	"The Shagwood Secret"—Kathie Hart and Mark DePaoli
	"The Diligent Daughter"—Chris Williams
1986	"Never Fear, Strongheart's Here"—Gil Morrison
	"The Miner's Daughter"—Steve Keegan
1987	"Beautiful Beulah Belle"—Jaye Morrison
	"The Old Cookie Shoppe"—Rich Bryan
1988	"Her Heart Belongs to Heartburn"—Kathryn Hothan
	"The Widow's Might"—Cheri Loy
1989	"Plantation Malady"—Michele Wade
	"Girl of the Frozen North"—Dan Foss
1990	"The Peril's of Priscilla"—Dan Foss
	"Weeded to Villain"— Jay Gerlick
1991	"Belle of Bisbee"—Wayne Coyle
	"The Shagwood Secret"—Linda Johnson
1992	"The Villain Wore a Dirty Shirt"—Matthew Coyle
	"The Old Cookie Shoppe"—Cheri Loy and Beth VanMarter
1993	"Babes in Gangland"—Shelia Thompson
	"The Ratcatcher's Daughter"—Gil Morrison
1994	"The Scheme of the Driftless Shifter"—Dan Foss
	"Unhand Me, You Villain"—Chris Williams
1995	"A Legacy for Lucy"—Sharon Pagoria
	"Song of the Mounties"—Diane Hayes
1996	"The Ballad of Gopher Gap"—Rich Bryan
	"Diligent Daughter"—Tatia Beckwith
1997	"Blazing Guns at Roaring Gulch"—Terry Dobbs
	"Bad to the Last Drop"—Tim Leuken
1998	"Malled"—Tim Leuken
	"Girl of the Frozen North"—Linda Johnson

1999 "Shoot in at Graverock"—Tim Leuken
       "Villain of Glitter Gulch"—Jeff Metzger
2000 "Tillie the Teller"—Ken Poris
       "Mischief in the Magnolias"—Rich Bryan

PHOTOGRAPH CREDITS

FRONT MATTER:
Page vi Dedication (l. to r.):
Photo by K.L.B., Becky Morphey and Jodi Brummel
Photo by V.C.W., Nancy and Wiley Updike
Photo by J.E.H., unknown fairgoers
Photo by M.W., Joe Steffen
Photo by J.E.H., unknown fairgoer
Photo by K.B., unknown fairgoers
Photo by J.A.D., Mary Keeton, Beth Swanson, and
Gene Olson
Photo by V.G., School Children watching show circa
1992
Photo by K.M., Jackie Dannewitz, Joan Hardekopf,
Buttons, Vivian Wright, and Karen Breunig
Courtesy of SFA, Junior Exhibitors with leader and
trophy

Page vii Dedication, cont.:
Photo by J.E.H., unknown fairgoer resting on foot
massage machine
Courtesy of FF, Ruth and George Fritsch
Photo by J.A.D., Rich Augustine and Audrey Meyer
Photo by M.M., Doug Hardekopf
Photo by V.C.W., Dick Moore
Photo by V.G., Nancy Brady
Photo by V.G., Ed Dannewitz and Herman Carlson
Photo by J.A.D., John Wagner and grandson Ryan Rettig
Photo by V.C.W., Jim "Biff" Webber
Photo by V.G., Eleni Filippi and Heath Wright

CHAPTER 2:
Page 28 Past Presidents: (l. to r.)
Sandwich Free Press
Sandwich Free Press
Courtesy of DF
Courtesy of A.L.
Sandwich Free Press

Page 29 Past Presidents: (l. to r.)
Sandwich Free Press
Courtesy of SFA
Photo by V.G.
Courtesy of SFA
Photo by V.C.W.

CHAPTER 4:
Page 114 Ready, Set, Show top collage: (l. to r.)
Photo by V.C.W.
Courtesy of SFA
Photo by J.H.
Beacon News
Photo by V.G.
Courtesy of SFA

Page 114 bottom collage:
All photos Courtesy of D.R.S.

Page 129 Judges: (l. to r.)
Sandwich Record
Courtesy of N.U.
Sandwich Record
Sandwich Record
Photo by B.T.D.
Photo by G.S.
Photo by S.E.H.
Photo by S.E.H.

CHAPTER 6:
Page 201 Fairgoers eating: (l. to r.)
Photo by J.E.H.
Photo by V.C.W.
Photo by V.C.W.
Photo by V.G.
Photo by M.M.
Photo by M.M.

Page 209 Food vendors: (l. to r.)
Photo by J.L.
Photo by V.C.W.
Photo by J.A.D.
Photo by V.G.
Photo by K.L.B.
Photo by V.C.W.
Photo by V.C.W.
Photo by J.E.H.
Photo by K.L.B.
Photo by V.C.W.
Photo by P.G.
Photo by J.E.H.
Photo by V.C.W.
Photo by V.C.W.
Photo by J.E.H.
Courtesy of SFA
Photo by D.S.
Photo by V.C.W.
Photo by K.L.B.
Photo by V.C.W.
Photo by V.B.
Courtesy of SFA
Photo by V.C.W.
Photo by V.C.W.
Photo by V.C.W.

CHAPTER 7:
Page 221 Farm-related vendors: (l. to r.)
Courtesy of SFA
Courtesy of SFA
Courtesy of SFA
Courtesy of SFA
Photo by V.B.
Courtesy of SFA
Courtesy of SFA
Photo by V.B.

Page 227 Commercial vendors: (l. to r.)
Photo by S.C.
Photo by J.E.H.
Courtesy of SFA
Photo by K.L.B.
Courtesy of E.B.
Photo by J.E.H.
Courtesy of SFA
Photo by V.C.W.

CHAPTER 8:
Page 233 Family outings: (l. to r.)
Courtesy of SFA, John Abens family
Photo by E.S., Jackie and Lauren Dannewitz, Roberta
Larson
Courtesy of SFA, Unknown fairgoers
Courtesy of SFA, Doug Knights family in 1952
Courtesy of SFA, Alice Larson with Mary Lynn and Gary,
Hazel Hilliard with Linda
Courtesy of SFA, Unknown fairgoers
Courtesy of TF, Beverly Tuttle, Mary Duvick Tuttle,
Norman and Marilyn Tuttle Dienst, Nick and Wanda
Tuttle Scull and baby Jeff
Courtesy of SFA, Unknown fairgoers

Courtesy of SFA

1913 Sandwich Fair advertising poster

Page 241 Children: (l. to r.)
Courtesy of SFA
Photo by J.E.H.
Courtesy of SFA
Photo by M.M.
Courtesy of SFA
Photo by D.P.
Courtesy of SFA
Photo by D.P.
Courtesy of SFA
Courtesy of SFA
Photo by D.S.

Page 259 Fairgoers resting: (l. to r.)
Courtesy of FF, Russ and Carol Fritsch circa 1980's
Courtesy of FF, Fritsch Oasis 1939
Beacon News
Photo by T.G.
Photo by L.R., Pearl and Lyle Troeger in 1987
Photo by J.A.D., Jack E. Stahl in 2000

previous pages: Photo by B.V.
pages 322-323: An overveiw of the
midway in 1994.

112TH YEAR

SANDWICH FAIR SINCE 1888

Photo by M.M.